THE ISLAMIC MOVEMENT IN SOMALIA

A Study of the Islah Movement, 1950-2000

Adonis & Abbey Publishers Ltd
St James House
13 Kensington Square,
London, W8 5HD
United Kingdom

Website: http://www.adonis-abbey.com
E-mail Address: editor@adonis-abbey.com

Nigeria:
Suites C4 & C5 J-Plus Plaza
Asokoro, Abuja, Nigeria
Tel: +234 (0) 7058078841/08052035034

Copyright © Abdurahman M. Abdullahi (Baadiyow)

British Library Cataloguing-in-Publication Data
A catalogue record for this book is available from the British Library

ISBN: 978-1-909112-51-3 (paperback)
        978-1-909112-52-0 (hardcover)

The moral right of the author has been asserted

All rights reserved. No part of this book may be reproduced, stored in a retrieval system or transmitted at any time or by any means without the prior permission of the publisher

THE ISLAMIC MOVEMENT IN SOMALIA

A Study of the Islah Movement, 1950-2000

Abdurahman M. Abdullahi (Baadiyow)

TABLE OF CONTENTS

TABLE OF CONTENTS IV
ACKNOWLEDGEMENTS VII
A NOTE OF TRANSLITERATION X
LIST OF ABEREVIATION XI
POLITICAL MAP OF SOMALI REPUBLIC: XIII

Introduction and Overview 15

CHAPTER ONE 29
    Historical Background 29
    The Revival of Islam in the Nineteenth Century 32
    The Revival of Sufi Brotherhoods 38
    Militancy and Moderation in the Sufi Brotherhoods 66
    Colonialism and Somali Encounter 75
    Conclusion 86

CHAPTER TWO 89
    The Rise of Islamic Consciousness (1950-1967) 89
    Strengthening Factors of the Islamic Consciousness 93
    Stimulating Factors of Islamic Consciousness 120
    The Emergence of Islamist Elites 153
    Islam and the State in Somalia (1960-1969) 158
    Conclusion 161

CHAPTER THREE 164
    The Upsurge of the Islamic Awakening 164
    Institutions of the Islamic Awakening: The Proto-Muslim
    Brotherhood 171
    The Military Regime and the Islamic Awakening 203

The Islamic Awakening and the Regime: A Case Study of the Family Law 215
Conclusion 232

CHAPTER FOUR 234
The Emergence of the Islah Movement in Somalia: 234
The Formative Period (1978–1990) 234
Introducing the Muslim Brotherhood in Somalia (1953–1978)
.... 235
The Establishment of Islah Islamic Society in 1978 247
The Formative Period of Islah (1978–1990) 269
Conclusion 304

CHAPTER FIVE 308
The Islah Movement in the War-Torn Somalia (1991–2000): 308
Islah in the early years of the State Collapse (1991-1992) 310
The Political Strategy and Programs (1992–2000) 337
The Social Strategy and Programs (1992-2000) 358
Conclusion 372

CHAPTER SIX 375
Conclusion and the Aftermath of 9/11 375
Conclusion of the Research 375
Somalia in the Aftermath of 9/11 Terrorist Attack 389

Bibliography 396

Index 424

LIST OF TABLES AND FIGURES

TABLES

Table 1. Islamic persuasions in Somalia 22
Table 2. The Sufi Brotherhoods in Somalia................................66
Table 3. The Christian Missions in Somalia........................131
Table 4. The Islamist Organizations in Somalia (1950–1990)....281
Table 5. The Chronicle of Muslim Brotherhood in
Somalia (1953–1990)..304
Table 6. The chairmen of Islah and their qualifications...........388

FIGURES:

Figure 1. The Rural Qur'anic school....................................34
Figure 2. The historical centers of the Islamic Learning...........42
Figure 3. The Diagram of development of the
elites in Somalia...157
Figure 4. The symbol of the Military Coup of 1969................205
Figure 5. The emblem of Somali Socialist
Revolutionary Party..230
Figure 6. The logo of Islah Movement..248
Figure 7. The organizational structure of Islah......................262
Figure 8. The Model of Political Participation
(1994-2000)...342

ACKNOWLEDGEMENTS

This dissertation is a culmination of long years of learning process that started in 1959. I express my indebtedness to my parents Macallin Cabdullahi and Saynab Afrax Shadoor and pay homage to all my teachers during these long years. Special gratitude goes to my sweetheart, my wife Muxubo Xaaji Imaan, who has been there for me all through the ups and downs of life. She nurtured and raised our seven children because my job kept me away from home often. Without her support, encouragement, and patience, this work could not have seen the light of day. I also express my appreciation to my daughter Muna and sons Axmad, Cumar, Xasan, Cali, Khaalid, and Yaasir, who were deprived of attention, time and resources during long years of my humanitarian engagement in Somalia.

I am also indebted to Professor *Khālid Mustafa Medani*, my adviser who guided and advised me throughout the research period. He was very gentle and respected my research orientations and suggestions. Special thanks go to Professor *Rula Abisaab*, the director of the graduate program, and Professor *Malek Abisaab*, who were always encouraging. In all my academic achievements at McGill University, I pay homage to Professor Uner Turgay, the former director of the Islamic Institute and my supervisor during my MA thesis and after. I also express my gratitude to the director of the Islamic institute, F. Jamil Ragep, the library staff, and the administrators of the Islamic Institute, in especially, Adina Sigartau.

My gratitude goes to Professor Cali Sheikh Axmad, the President of Mogadishu University, for his continuous encouragement and support. A heartfelt thank goes to the key resource person for this research, Sheikh Maxamad Axmad

Garyare, the former vice-president of Nahdah and former chairman of Islah, who is an encyclopaedia in the field of the modern development of Islam in Somalia. I also wish to thank Xasan Xaaji Maxamuud, an expert in the Islamic movements in Somalia who provided numerous literatures from his library and shared his rich experiences with me. My appreciation also goes to Cabdiraxman Koosaar and Sheikh Cabdiraxman Xaashi who provided unpublished documents of Waxdah. Furthermore, I express my gratitude to Sheikh Cabdiraxman Xuseen Samatar, the former treasurer of Nahdah, who granted me a rare copy of the Constitution of Nahdah. Other important resource persons include Dr. Cali Baasha Cumar, Dr. Maxamad Yuusuf, Sheikh Axmad Rashiid Xanafi, Dr. Ibrahim al-Dasuuqi, Dr. Axmad Xasan al-Qudubi, Sheikh Ismaciil Cabdi Hurre, Sheikh Almis Xaaji Yahye, Sheikh Cusmaan Sheikh Cumar "Xidig," Mustafa Cabdullahi, Xasan Xaaji Maxamad Joqof, Sheikh Ciise Sheikh Axmad, and Axmad Cali Axmad all these individuals deserve my thanks and appreciation. I thank many scholars and researchers who contributed greatly to setting the stage of Somali studies. In particular, I thank pioneers such as Lee Cassanelli, Saciid Samatar, Maxamad Mukhtaar, Axmad Ismaciil Samatar, I.M. Lewis, Xuseen Aadam, and *Ḥassan Makki*. My thanks also go to other scholars such as Maxamuud Siyaad Togane, Ken Menkhaus, Andre Le Sage, Stig Hansen, Ibraahim Faarax, Maxamad Shariif Maxamuud, Maxamad Cusman Cumar, Scott Reese, Roland Marchal, Axmad Jumcaale, Yuusuf Axmad Nuur, Valeria Saggiomo and many others.

Finally, I am indebted to Professor Cabdi Ismaciil Samatar, who was very encouraging and wrote the recommendation letter submitted to the Institute of Islamic Studies, McGill University, as part of the application requirement for this program. I also express my gratitude to all my colleagues at the humanitarian agency, Mercy-USA for Aid and Development (1993-2007), especially its Executive Director, *"Omar al-Qādi"* and East African Program Director Fatxuddiin Cali Maxamad. They have contributed greatly to the completion of this work in many ways. My utmost gratitude goes to Dr. Markus Virgil Hohne for painstakingly taking his time to read through and make comments on this manuscript. Lastly, I offer my regards and blessings to all of those who supported me in any respect during the completion of the project.

A NOTE OF TRANSLITERATION

The system of transliteration of the Arabic words in this dissertation follows the system adopted by the Islamic Institute, McGill University, which are Unicode diacritic characters. Besides Arabic transliteration, Somali names and words are written according to Somali language orthography. Below is the sample of the Latinized Somali alphabet where long vowels are written by doubling the vowel. There are no diacritics or other special characters, although it includes three consonants diagraphs: DH, KH, and SH.

'	B b	T t	J j	X x	Kh kh	D d	R r	S s	Sh sh	Dh dh
[ʔ]	[b]	[t]	[dʒ]	[ħ]	[x]	[d]	[r]	[s]	[ʃ]	[ɖ]
C c	G g	F f	Q q	K k	L l	M m	N n	W w	H h	Y y
[ʕ]	[g]	[f]	[q]	[k]	[l]	[m]	[n]	[w]	[h]	[j]
A a	E e	I i	O o	U u	Aa aa	Ee ee	Ii ii	Oo oo	Uu uu	
[a]	[e]	[i]	[o]	[u]	[aː]	[eː]	[iː]	[oː]	[uː]	

To differentiate between Arabic and Somali names, Arabic locations and common names are *italicized*. Using Arabic, Somali and English language sources may create some confusion in the transliteration of the authors' names. Thus, the name of the author will follow the language of the work cited. This may result in different transliteration of names for example, Ali Ahmed as an author of Arabic sources is written as 'Ali Aḥmed' while, it is written as Cali Axmad in the Somali source.

LIST OF ABEREVIATION

ASWJ	Ahl al-Sunna wa al-Jamaaca (Sufi brotherhood organization)
AFIS	Amministrazione Fiduciaria Italiana in Somalia (Italian UN Trust administration for Somalia)
AMISOM	African Union Mission for Somalia
BER	Bottom-up Educational Revolution
BMA	British Military Administration
CC	Consultative Council
EB	Executive Bureau
EPLF	Eritrean People's Liberation front
FPENS	Formal Primary Education Networks
GSL	Great Somali League party
GSP	Great Somali Party
HDMS	Hisbiya Dastur Mutaqil Somalia
ICG	International Crisis Group
IGAD	Intergovernmental Authority on Development
MB	Muslim Brotherhood
NBC	Native Betterment Committee
MM	Mennonite Mission
NFD	Northern Frontier District
NIPE	National Institution for Private Education
NUF	National United Front
OLF	Oromo Liberation Front
PLGS	Liberal Somali Youth Party
RCC	Roman Catholic Church
SAFE	Schools' Association for Formal Education
SDM	Somali Democratic Movement
SIM	Sudan Interior Mission
SNF	Somali National Front

SNL	Somali National League
SNM	Somali National Movement
SNU	Somali National Union
SOBA	Somali Old Boys Association
SODAF	Somali Democratic Action Front
SPM	Somali Patriotic Movement
SSDF	Somali Salvation Democratic Front
SSF	Somali Salvation Front
SYC	Somali Youth Club
SYL	Somali Youth League
TFG	Transitional Federal Government
TNG	Transitional National Government
TPLF	Tigray People's Liberation front
UIC	Union of Islamic Courts
UNOSOM	United Nations Operation in Somalia
USC	United Somali Congress
USP	United Somali Party
USC/SNA	United Somali Congress/Somali National Alliance
USC/SSA	United Somali Congress/Somali Salvation Alliance
WSLF	Western Somali Liberation Front

Political Map of Somali Republic:

Introduction and Overview

The collapse of the Somali State in 1991 is puzzling given the fact that in previous decades it represented one of the most unified states and early democracies in Africa. Somalia's peoples share the same language, the Islamic faith, and belong mainly to one ethnic group. They are citizens of four countries in the Horn of Africa: Somali Republic, Djibouti, Ethiopia, and Kenya. Moreover, because of their massive migration since the collapse of the state, Somalis are now citizens of many states in all continents. However, Somalia faces three main challenges: the geo-political challenge; the mismatch between the state and the nation and strangeness between the state and society. The geo-political challenges stems from its strategic location that connects Asia, Europe, and Africa. This strategic crossroads attracted competition to dominate Somalia by various colonial powers.Also, being part of the Suez Canal and oil-rich Gulf region geopolitics, the Horn of Africa was incorporated into the Cold War Theater of operations by the 1950s. What is more, Somalia was drawn into regional conflicts because of geo-political tensions between Egypt and Ethiopia involving the Nile River politics.[1] Additionally, due to geographical implications, Somalia became a place where the double identity of "Arabness" and "Africaness" compete and conflict with each other.[2] It is where the Christian-Muslim borders are drawn, and

---

1. Osman Abdullahi, "The Role of Egypt, Ethiopia the Blue Nile in the Failure of the Somali Conflict Resolutions: A Zero-Sum Game" (paper presented at the annual meeting of the International Studies Association, Hilton Hawaiian Village, Honolulu, Hawaii, March, 2005).
2. See Ibrahim Farah, "Foreign Policy and Conflict in Somalia, 1960-1990" (PhD diss., University of Nairobi, 2009), 187.

Somalia championing the Muslim cause in the Horn of Africa, conflicted with Ethiopia and Kenya, where Christianity is dominant.³

The second challenge is the mismatch between the state and nation divided among four colonial powers: France, Britain, Italy and Ethiopia. As a result, nationalist sentiment has been aroused, aspiring to create a "Greater Somalia" in the Horn of Africa. This venture, however, positioned Somalia on the collision course with international conventions on the colonially inherited borders.⁴ It also situated Somalia in continuous conflict with its neighbours.

The third challenge is the strangeness between the state and society. Hence, the Somali traditional society based on clan system and Islam and the modern nation-state founded on secular ideology and European model of statehood strained many of the state-society relations.⁵ The pervasive state penetration in the society ineptly collided with the clans and Islam and instigated the emergence of three competing ideologies – clanism, Islamism, and nationalism - even though

---

3. Ibid, 190.
4. Somalia did not endorse the declaration of the Organization of African Unity on the sanctity of the borders in Cairo, 1964. See Saadia Touval, "The organization of African Unity and Borders," *International Organization* 21, no. 1 (1967): 102-127. Also, see the Organization of African Unity, "Resolutions adopted by the first ordinary session of the assembly of the heads of the state and government," Cairo, UAR, from 17 to 21 July, 1964.
5. The state-society relations can be described in six possible scenarios ranging from extreme cooperation to extreme conflict: 1) mutual collaboration; 2) mutual engagement; 3) conflictual engagement; 4) mutual disengagement; 5) enforced disengagement; and finally 6) resistance-revolutionary disengagement. See Tracy Kup erus, *Frameworks of State Society Relations,* available from http://www.acdis.uiuc.edu/Re search/S&Ps/1994Su/S&P_VIII4/state_society_relations.html (accessed on February 14, 2011)

these ideologies are dynamic, crosscurrent, and often overlap each other.⁶

All perspectives on the history of Somalia share paucity of references to and analyses of Islam as an important agent of historical change. This trend is evident from the major historical works that situate Islam in the peripheral role in their researches and analyses limiting it merely as part of the traditional structure and culture.⁷ However, new literature on the rising Islamist movements sprang up as part of the security studies literature that grew rapidly after 9/11.⁸ Comparatively, nonviolent Islamic works that majority of the Islamic scholars in Somalia were engaged received less Western academic interest except in a few anthropological works.⁹ Therefore, as a general trend and a common denominator among all these scholarship,

---

6. This division is purely theoretical and ideal. The possible six scenarios are Islamist/nationalist or nationalist/Islamist, clanist/nationalist or nationalist/clanist, and clanist/Islamist or Islamist/clanist. The first and the second categories are Islamists and secularists, although within each category, the emphases are different. The third category represents non-state actors that are not aiming at a national state at all. For details on conflicting loyalties in Somalia, see Abdurahman Abdullahi, "Tribalism, Nationalism and Islam: Crisis of the Political Loyalties in Somalia" (MA thesis, Islamic Institute, McGill University, 1992).
7. These studies include Ali Hersi, "The Arab Factor in Somali Society: the Origins and Development of Arab Enterprise and Cultural Influence in the Somali Peninsula" (PhD Thesis, University of California, Los Angeles, 1977); Mohamed Nuh Ali, "History in the Horn of Africa, 1000 BC to 1500 AD" (PhD Thesis, University of California, Los Angeles, 1985); Lee Cassanelli, *The Shaping of Somali Society: Reconstructing the History of a Pastoral People, 1600-1900* (University of Pennsylvania Press, 1982); Ahmed Samatar,*Socialist Somalia: Rhetoric and Reality*. London: Zed Press, 1988; Saadia Touval, *Somali Nationalism*; and David Laitin and Said Samatar, *Somalia: Nation in Search of a State* (Boulder: Westview Press, 1987.
8. See Karim-Aly Kassam, "The clash of Civilization: The selling of Fear", available from https://dspace.ucalgary.ca/bitstream/1880/44170/1/Islam.pdf (accessed on February 14, 2011).
9. I.M. Lewis, *Saints and Somalis: Popular Islam in a Clan-based Society* (Lawrenceville, N.J.: Red Sea Press, 1998).

the history of Islam and its role are marginalized, unless recognized as posing a security threat to the Western powers.

There is very little scholarship on the history of Islamist movements in Somalia that takes seriously both historical forces as well as the very ideas and internal organization of these movements. Indeed, reading the now voluminous literature on Islamist militancy in media and policy analysis of the proliferation of Islamist groups in Somalia, it often appears as if "Islam" was only recently discovered in Somalia. In reality, the rise of Islamism in Somalia, while sharing a great deal of similarities with other movements in the Muslim world, has roots in Somali history and the very particular local context of Somalia and its peoples. Moreover, while the nascent scholarship on Islamist politics in Somalia has tackled the important role of politics and regional factors in the rise of an Islamist organizations in the country, this book departs from this analysis by providing a detailed and empirically rich narrative of the Islah Movement which has influenced and made an impact on other Islamist organizations in recent decades.

This work tackles this neglected issue of the role of Islam and politics in Somalia within a historical context that is rare in recent scholarship. Moreover, while most scholarship on the subject of Islamist politics in Somalia has focused on structural and political factors to explain the attraction and rise of Islamism in the political trajectory of Somalia, this study focuses closely on the interplay of both Islamic and clan identification to discern both the political and ideational factors that have gained ascendancy in the context of Somalia in recent decades. Such an ambitious undertaking requires parsimony, and so this study focuses on the Islah Movement -- the official part of the Muslim Brotherhood (MB) global network in Somalia -- in order to tackle some key questions having to do with the different factors that have underpinned the political salience of Islamist movements in general. Thus, the primary argument is that in order tofully understand the trajectory of Islamist politics in Somalia, one must examine the evolving nature of state-society relations within a historical context that is specific to the Somali case. Moreover, this research maintains that the factors underpinning changes in state-society dynamics in Somalia are rooted in how the interplay between Islamism and clan has impacted local political dynamics prior to the collapse of the Somali state. In addition, it goes further by detailing how the prior history of the Islamist movement has resulted in both the development and diversification of Islamist politics. Using Islah as a unit of analysis, this study demonstrates how Somalia's Islamist movements have evolved into a contested terrain represented by the emergence of MB, Salafism, and militancy.

The evolution of the relationship between Islam, clan and politics in Somalia cannot be fully understood without an appreciation of the historical tension between political authority of the modern elites and the traditional authority. In addition to the divisive legacy of multiple colonial administrations in the pre-independence era, Somalia has long been challenged by the mismatch between the state and the nation and strangeness between the state and society. The constant tension between the state and the society characterized as extreme conflict caused the collapse of the state after 30 years of its inception in 1960. After the collapse of the Somali state in 1991 and the weakening of nationalism, clan-based armed factions and various Islamist movements, which had operated underground since the 1970s, came out the fore. In fact, the cosmology of the Somali society is centered on clan particularism and Islamic universalism, which are marked with microscopic and telescopic perceptions, respectively. This means that clan particularism often pushes communities to bigotry and narrow-mindedness, while Islam, unless it is given an extremist interpretation, calls for peace, brotherhood, and broad-mindedness.[10]

Traditional Islam in Somalia follows three main genealogies: the Ash'ariyah theology, Shafi'i jurisprudence, and Sufism. The Ash'ariyah theology was founded by Abu al-Hassan Al-Ash'ari (873-935AC) in reaction to the extreme rationalism espoused by the school of Mu'tazilah.[11] The Shāfi'īyah School of jurisprudence is also one of the major four Sunni schools of jurisprudence and it is rooted in the methodology and teachings of Abū 'Abdallāh al-Shāfi'ī (767–820). Somalia also adheres to the Shafi'i school introduced through its connection with Yemen.[12] Sufi Islam in Somalia belongs to the moderate form rooted in al-Ghazāli's way, and it had a significant missionary impact throughout Somalia.[13] Its tremendous influence is exercised through its two main brotherhoods: Qaadiriyah and Axmadiyah. Islamism challenges both the post-colonial secular

---

10. Such interpretation is used by extreme Salafism. Currently, it is the ideology of al-Qā'ida replicated by the Shabab in Somalia; both organizations use Islamic slogans to justify their violent actions.
11. *Mu'atazilah* is theological school founded by Wāsil ibn 'Atā (d. 748). The main assumption of this school is that reason is more reliable than tradition. See Majid Fakhry, *A History of Islamic Philosophy* (New York: Colombia University Press, 1983), 44-65.
12. The four main jurisprudence schools of the Sunni Muslims are *Mālikiyah, Ḥanafiyah, Shāfi'iyah,* and *Ḥanbaliyah.*
13. Abū Ḥāmed al- Ghazālī (1058–1111) is considered the scholar who best succeeded in combining Sufism and Islamic jurisprudence in his works, where he argued that Sufism originated from the Qur'an and was compatible with Islamic thought.

state by advocating its Islamization and the traditional society through reforms and revivalism. The two main conceptions of Islamism concerned with reform are Salafism and Muslim Brotherhood.[14]

Salafism had spread globally in as part of the rising influence of Saudi Arabia in global politics in 1960s. In Somalia, due to its being part of the Saudi geopolitical sphere, the influence of Salafism was noticeably augmented through students educated in the Saudi Islamic universities and through Somali migrant labour during the economic boom of the 1970s. Adherents of Salafia persuasion introduced to Somalia some aspects of Hanbali jurisprudence, mixing it with other jurisprudences under the pretext of not following a specific school of jurisprudence. Furthermore, they consider their principal duty to spread al-'Aqīdah al-Saḥīḥah (the right theology) according to their interpretation of Islamic theology, which eventually puts them on the collision course with the traditional Islamic belief system and practices of the society. The mother organization of Salafism was Al-Itixaad Al-Islami (The Islamic Union) founded in 1982, renamed as Al-Ictisam at the end of 1990s after fragmenting into various groups.

The Muslim Brotherhood was founded in 1928 by Ḥasan al-Bannā in Egypt and reached Somalia in the 1953 through Egyptian teachers and then via Somali students in Arab universities. It has inspired many Islamist organizations and individuals in Somalia; however, Islah Movement is the

---

14. The difference between traditional Salafia school and neo-Salafia could be summarized in a number of points: (1) Traditional Salafia supports the ruling establishment, while neo-Salafia are an oppositional movement. (2) Traditional Salafia belongs to a school and is not organized, while neo-Salafia constitutes an Islamic movement with a political program. (3) Neo-Salafia expresses itself differently, being closer to Jihadist groups and Da'wa persuasions.

organization that represents its international network. Followers of the MB methodology avoid divisive Islamic discourses on doctrinal matters and legal aspects within its society. Being open to the diversity of Islamic theology and practices, they are tolerant to the different theological views on Islam and despise rigid obsession with nuances of the religious doctrine. They believe that Sufism and other traditional practices should be accommodated and that the focus in Islamic activism should be directed toward social and political issues, rather than theological quibbling that divides Muslim communities. The following table indicates the dynamics of the three main persuasions in Somalia.

Islamic persuasions	Theology	Jurisprudence	Sufism	Remarks
Traditional Islam	Ash'ariyah theology	Shafi'iyah school of jurisprudence	Qaadiriyah and Axmadiyah	Confrontational with Salafism
Salafism	Salafia theology (al-aqidah al-Salafia)	Non-affiliation (they claim to follow directly the Qur'ān and the Sunna of the Prophet)	Intolerant, consider them innovation (Bid'a)/apostasy (shirk)	Confrontational with traditional Islam
Muslim Brotherhood	Tolerant of Ash'ariyah and Salafia theologies	Tolerant to all schools of jurisprudence	Selective acceptance/ tolerant	Tolerant to Salafism and Sufism

Table 1. Islamic persuasions in Somalia and their relations

History is a subjective process of recreating past occurrences and also a matter of perspective. In the past, Somali history was approached from the perspectives of the modernization and dependency theories. Both theories agree in essentializing the demise of tradition, which means Islam and clan in the Somali case. Islam was addressed from the margins of history, through Orientalist and secularist discourses and security perspectives. It was seen as having only social values and functions, whereas in the political arena, it was considered apolitical. However, that conception has been changing because of the public emergence of Islamism since the collapse of the state in 1991. Subsequently, the public emergence of Islamism sparked a new interest within intelligence and security studies, and early journalistic articles and rudimentary studies on this issue were produced.[15] That interest has grown substantively after 9/11 when Somalia was identified as a possible haven for terrorism, and the Islamic movements were treated as part of the threat to the Western civilization.[16]

In that context, the perceived threat resulted in the actors not volunteering to provide information to researchers, and local detractors were offering hearsay and inaccurate politically motivated information. In security studies, hearsay evidence is not discarded but is used to dig more information. Given these constraints, a few studies were produced but lacked in-depth historical background and accurate information, despite their obvious merits. These early sources are credited with discovering a few important facts such as that the Islamist movements in Somalia are not monolithic and that they ranged

---

15. Examples of such studies include Roland Marchal. "Islamic Political Dynamics in the Somali Civil War: Before and After September 11." In *Islamism and its Enemies in the Horn of Africa*, edited by Alex De Waal. Place: Indiana University Press, 2006, 114-146; Also, Michael Shank. "Understanding Political Islam in Somalia" in*Contemporary Islam, Dynamics of Muslim Life* Journal No. 11562, March 2007.
16. Former NATO secretary general William Casey issues a statement considering "Islamic fundamentalism" the major threat to the western civilization. See Bassam Tibi, *The Challenge of Fundamentalism: Political Islam and the New World Disorder* (University of California Press, 2002), 3.

from peaceful evolutionaries to militant revolutionaries.[17] Moreover, it became clear through these studies that these movements had doctrinal and methodological differences. Despite the studies of these movements and their historical evolution, the roots of their ideologies and methodologies remain puzzling. It remains a dark hole in the history of Somalia in general and in the development of the modern Islam in particular. Deciphering this puzzle would provide a better conceptualization of the Islamist movements within the historical context of Somalia.

Islamist movements were given a variety of taxonomies by different scholars. Proponents of the Islamist movements use friendly terminologies such as *Islamic revival, Islamic renaissance, Islamic awakening*, and *Islamic renewal*. On the other hand, most Western scholars use such terminologies such as *radical Islam, militant Islam, extremist Islam, Islamic terrorism, revolutionary Islam*, and *fundamentalist Islam*. Other soft definitions include *Islamism, Islamic movement, Islamist movement* and *Islamic resurgence*. This book uses Islamism or Islamist movement to signify a popular movement advocating the reordering of Muslim states and societies in accordance with the Islamic Shari'a. Thus, Islamist is an activist in realizing the objectives of the Islamic movement. Conversely, non-Islamists include majority of the Muslims who are neither secular nor Islamic activists. On the other hand, the terminology of Islamic movement had broad definition and encompasses all activities related to spreading Islam. Its comprehensive definition is given

---

17. Andre Le Sage's work was the first substantive field study of the Islamic movements. Even though this work contains some flaws, it was an important milestone in understanding Islamism in Somalia. See Andre Le Sage, *Somalia and the War on Terrorism*.

by the International Crisis Group, that is, "the active assertion and promotion of beliefs, prescriptions, laws, or policies that are held to be Islamic in character".[18]

This book aims to explore the historical evolution of moderate Islamism since the return of Italy, as a country administering UN trusteeship to Somalia from 1950 until the formation of the first national government after the outbreak of the civil war at Arta Conference in Djibouti in 2000. It covers 50 years of turbulent Somali history, in which civilian governments, military dictatorships, armed opposition factions, and Islamist movements were interacting and shaping the Somali history. Understanding the historical evolution of Islamism provides a better conception of its present implications in Somalia. With respect to the Islamist movement, it should be noted that it was underground and dealing with unfavorable environments. As a result, most of these organizations' activities and plans were not recorded, and their documents were either destroyed or kept in secrecy. However, this study is fortunate to be able to discover valuable primary sources of the Islamist organizations.[19]

---

18. See the International Crisis Group Report, "Understanding Islamism," Middle East/North Africa Report no. 37-2 (March, 2005), 1.
19. Sheikh Cabdiraxman Xaashi, one of the founders of Waxdah, is credited for preserving some of these documents. Also, Sheikh Cabdiraxman Koosaar, one of the early members of Waxdah, provided the by-law of Waxdah, which was identical with the one kept by the Cabdiraxman Xaashi. Also, the only two persons who are alive are Sheikh Maxamad Axmad Nuur (Garyare) and Sheikh Cabdiraxman Xuseen Samatar. The author succeeded in interviewing both of them at length.

Organization of the Book

This work consists of six chapters. The first chapter provides a historical background of Islam in Somalia until 1950. It navigates through the early impulse of Islam in the Horn of Africa and its spread in Somalia through massive migration from Arabia. This chapter in particular explicates the revival of Islam in the nineteenth century and the use of the Islamic scholars' inventive systems and effective techniques to educate the population through Qur'anic schools, Islamic education circles and Sufi orders' settlements. The two main Sufi orders – Qaadiriyah and Axmadiyah – are examined. In addition, the way these Sufi orders countered colonialism and their early militancy and moderation are analyzed. The modern anti-colonial institutions that emerged after the Second World War are also discussed.

Chapter Two examines the rise of Islamic consciousness after Italy's return to Somalia in 1950 as a UN trusteeship administrator. In this period, cultural foundations for the emergence of the Islamic awakening were laid. This chapter explores the role of Islam and its revival in the period from 1950 to 1967 in the context of changing political and cultural conditions in Somalia. This includes the formative period of the Somali state and the early years of independence (1960-1967). Specifically, this chapter delves into the underlying factors for the emergence of Islamic consciousness. These factors include the strengthened capacity of the Islamist elites and provocations of Christian missionaries and the debates on the selection of the Somali language script. In this context, cultural competition between Egyptian Arabic schools and Western education through local schools and scholarships is demonstrated. This chapter concludes by depicting the process of elite formation and the beginning of their ideological divide that gradually marginalized Islamist elites.

Chapter Three examines the Islamic awakening and its early institutions from 1967 to 1978. It reconstructs the history of three pioneering organizations, namely, (the Organization for Islamic Renaissance) or "Nahdah," *Ahl al-Islām* (the People of Islam)or "Ahal," and *Wahdat al-Shabāb al-Islāmī* (the Union of Islamic Youth) or "Waxdah." Moreover, the conflict between the Islamic awakening and the military regime is examined, and the case study of the Family Law and its role in fragmenting and radicalizing the Islamic awakening is presented.

Chapter Four contains a case study of the Islah Movement. It explores this movement's historical development from 1978 to 1990 in three stages. The first stage is the early period of the introduction of the MB ideology to Somalia and Somali students' contacts with the MB in Egypt, Sudan, and Saudi Arabia. The second stage explores the establishment of the Islah Islamic Society, its nature, objectives, structure, and recruitment strategies. The third stage examines the programs of Islah and its activities from 1978 to 1990 in the light of the Somali sociopolitical realities during the dictatorial regime. This chapter depicts challenges, limitations, achievements, and major activities of the movement before the collapse of the state.

Chapter Five explores the history of the Islah Movement in Somalia during the civil war (1991-2000), dividing this period into three sections. The first section sets the stage and provides a brief background on Somalia after the collapse of the state (1991-2000). It also explores the Islah Movement during 1991-1992, its survival strategy, policies, and interactions. Moreover, it explores the conference of Islah leadership in 1992 in Djibouti and strategy developed for the stateless Somalia. The second section examines the political strategy, theoretical challenges, and reconciliation programs of the Islah Movement. The third section investigates the social development strategy of Islah with a special focus on education. The concept of developing a popular educational revolution and its implications are explained.

Chapter Six offers the final summary and conclusions in the form of general themes of historical construction and analysis since the 1950s. It looks into the implications of the 9/11 U.S. Global War on Terrorism for the resurgence of extremism in the name of Islam that challenged Islamic moderation and complicated the political conditions of Somalia.

CHAPTER ONE

Historical Background

Somalia is connected to the Arabian Peninsula since ancient times, and its relations grew with the advent of Islam in Arabia in 610 AD. Because of the religio-political turmoil and ecological calamities in Arabia, successive waves of immigrants scrambled to the Horn of Africa for safety, economic opportunities and propagating Islam. Detailed historical records of the Islamic influx and its expansion into the Somali coast remain controversial; nevertheless, historians agree that Islam reached Somalia peacefully through trade and migration in the first century of the Muslim Calendar (700-800 AD).[1] The process of Islamization was intensified by continual migration, interactions, and preaching; and with its urbanization, and changes in the modes of production that was taking place in the Somali coast.[2] Interactions between the new immigrants and local Somalis have continued through intermarriage and common bonds of faith. As a result, many coastal cities of Banaadir, including Mogadishu, Marka, Baraawe, and Warsheik, were established and flourished. Manifestly, mass conversion of Somalis to Islam occurred between the eleventh and thirteenth centuries AD.[3]

---

1. 'Ali Sheikh Aḥmed Abubakar, *Al-Da'wa al-Islāmiyah al-Mu'āsira fi Al-Qarni al-Ifriqī* (Riyadh, Saudi Arabia: Umayya Publishing House, 1985), 9. Also, David D Laitin, and Said Samatar, *Somalia: Nation in Search of a State* (Boulder: Westview Press, 1987), 8.
2. I.M. Lewis, Lewis, *A Modern History of Somalia: Nation and State in the Horn of Africa* (London: Longman, 1980), 20.
3. In the Islamic Calender it is between fifth to seventh centuries.

With Islamization, some successful city-states emerged in different parts of the Horn of Africa. In the northern regions, the cities of Zaylac and Berbera were connected with the Ethiopian plateau and the historical Islamic city of Harrar. Zaylac is famous for being the capital city of the Sultanate of Ifat, which was inherited after its collapse in 1415 by the Adal Sultanate, a multi-ethnic Muslim state inhabited by Somalis, Oromo, Afar, and Harrars. This Muslim state was in conflict with Abyssinia during the reign of Ethiopian Emperor Negus Yeshaq (1414-1429).[4] This state is remembered for its legendary leader Imaam Axmad Ibrahim (Gurey), who captured most of the Ethiopian highland saved only by the Portuguese military intervention.[5] On the other hand, the southern part of Somalia interacted with early Arab and Persian migrants and later with the Omanites' sultanate linking them with the Swahili hybrid civilization in East Africa. In the late fifteenth to mid-seventeenth centuries, the first centralized state of Somali ethnic origin was established in today's southern Somalia by the Ajuran clan-family, termed by Professor Cassanelli as a "pastoral power."[6] After the disintegration of this dynasty, southern Somalia remained under a variety of local powers until the arrival of Oman dynasty in the seventeenth century.

Although Somalia was connected with the Islamic world culturally and commercially, it remained politically peripheral until the seventeenth century. The expansion of the Ottoman

---

4. On the Christian-Muslim push-pull wars refer to J. Spencer Trimingham, *Islam in Ethiopia* (London: Oxford University Press, 1952).
5. Portuguese forces arrived Ethiopia on February 10, 1541 with the request of the emperor Gelawdewos under the command of Cristovao da Gama and both Da Gama and Imam Ahmed we killed during the war. See Trimingham, *Islam in Ethiopia*, 173.
6. Lee Cassanelli, *the Shaping of Somali Society, Reconstructing the History of a Pastoral People, 1600-1900* (Philadelphia: University of Philadelphia Press, 1982), 84, 98.

Empire into Egypt in 1517, and its subsequent seizure of the ports of Aden (1538) and Sawakin (1557) on the Red Sea was the beginning of Somali political integration with the world of Islam. From these ports, the Ottomans were able to extend their influence into the Indian Ocean and the Horn of Africa. However, when the Ottoman power declined and Suez Canal was opened in 1869, Egypt showed interest in the Somali coast. As a result, it established its presence in the northern Somali ports of Berbera and Zaylac and the religious center of Harrar in 1875.[7] The emergence of the *Mahdiyah* movement in Sudan in 1884 resulted in a hasty Egyptian withdrawal in 1885. In the southern part of Somalia, in the seventeenth century, Mogadishu declined economically because of the long-lasting Portuguese sea blockade and nomadic encroachments from the interior. It was ruled by the Omanis until 1871. In 1889, Italy established its presence there and finally purchased Mogadishu from the Omanis in 1905.[8] After this brief historical sketch, we now turn to the revival of Islam in the Somali peninsula, the advent of colonial powers and Somali reactions.

---

7. Harrar was the capital city of the Islamic emirates where Muslim leader Ahmed Ibrahim Gurey launched a war of conquest in the sixteenth century to the Ethiopian highlands. Harrar is the holiest city of Islam in the Horn of Africa.
8. "On January 13, 1905, Italy purchased the BanaadirPort for 3.6 billion lire and acquired the right to maintain commercial installations at [Kismayo] in the British Jubaland". See Daniel William Puzo, *Mogadishu, Somalia: Geographic Aspects of its Evolution, Population, Functions and its Morpholog* (PhD Thesis submitted to the University of Los Angles, 1972), 60. See also, Edward Alpers, "Mogadishu in Nineteenth Century: A Regional Perspective," *Journal of African History*. Vol. 24, No. 4, 1983, 441-459.

The Revival of Islam in the Nineteenth Century

In the nineteenth century, the Muslim world was experiencing reform and revival of Islam associated with the emergence of the new revivalist movements and reorientation, and renaissance of the Sufi orders. Somalia as part of this reform and revival, its Islamic scholars initiated inventive and sustainable system of education, using effective techniques to educate the population. These techniques deserve an in-depth academic research that we will not be able to include in this brief description. We can argue, however, that prior to the modern school system that came with colonialism, traditional education in Somalia was "community-centered and locally administered."[9] It was also an Islamic-centered system that was based on partial or full memorization of the Qur'an in early childhood. This basic school, termed Dugsi or Malcaamat, was usually established collectively by the community. The Somali way of learning the Arabic alphabet, so as to easily memorize the Qur'an, was invented by the Somali scholar Sheikh Yuusuf al-Kawnayn, who introduced around the 13th century the notation system for Arabic alphabets in the Somali language known as "Higaadda".[10] In general, children begin to learn at the age of five and graduate at the age of ten or eleven, with the second revision of memorization called "Nakhtiin".[11] Every

---

9. Abdinoor Abdullahi, *Constructing Education in the Stateless Society: The Case of Somalia* (PhD thesis submitted to the University of Ohio, 2007), 25.
10. Sheikh Yusuf al-Kawnayn (Aw-Barkhadle) is one of the oldest known Islamic scholars who propagated Islam in Somalia. Little is known about his biography; however, I. M. Lewis reconstructed some insights from oral traditions and findings of Cerulli in Harrar. His tomb is located at Dagor, about 20 km from Hargeysa. See I.M. Lewis, *Saints and Somalis*, 89-98.
11. Qur'an is normally memorized in two processes. The first process is a bottom-up process until all the Qur'an is memorized, on average within 3-4 years. The second

school is independently run by a highly respected teacher in the community called Macallin. These teachers are paid fairly for their service in a variety of ways by individual members who send their children into their custody.[12] These schools are spread throughout Somalia, even in the pastoral areas, providing basic Islamic education and subsequently contributing to the elimination of illiteracy. They adjust to the different conditions of the nomadic style of life by repositioning themselves with the roving pastoral nomads in their seasonal settlements. The Qur'anic school sites are very simple and environmentally friendly. Generally, students gather beneath a shady tree or in a shelter constructed from local wood and grass and sit on the ground or on woven-grass mats. They use local materials such as wooden slates and ink made of milk mixed with powdered charcoal as educational materials. The wooden slates are made from special wood that is washable and reusable for many years. Every student must have at least four such wooden slates, using one slate each day to write certain verses of the Qur'an to be memorized during that day. The other three slates are reserved with the previous three days' lessons to be revised every day. In addition to that there is a continuous process of affirming memorization through collective recitation techniques of the Qur'an called "Subac".[13]

---

phase is to repeat memorization using a top-down methodology. During this time, some students become "kabir", which means "Qur'anic teacher under training," and while helping the teacher, also reaffirm their memorization. This author experienced this process, being raised in a family famous for teaching the Qur'an.

12. Among the pastoral nomads, teachers are paid in kind such as goats, cows, and camels and in the agricultural areas with different crops. In the cities, teachers are paid cash. Orphans and vulnerable students are provided with scholarships.
13. "Subac" is from the Arabic Sab'a that means seven, designating the seven chapters of the Qur'an recited in the seven days of the week. It is one of the many ways of reciting the Qur'an in Somalia. Memorizers of the Qur'an sit in a circle and everybody recites

Figure1. Rural Qur'anic school in Somalia where students are sitting on the ground and holding wooden slates used as environmentally-friendly educational material

These schools provide an opportunity for mass education that is accessible and affordable for the general population. This community-supported system remained sustainable for centuries and functions well until today. Almost all Somali children in villages, towns, and cities go through some form of Qur'anic schooling. As a result, Arabic is the first alphabet taught to every Somali child so that they are at least able to recite the basics of the Qur'an. Consequently, it could be speculated that the number of the Qur'anic schools are an

---

one verse in a loud voice and passes to the next person to recite the next verse, continuing in that way like a relay race. From time to time, they all join in at the end of a verse in a loud chorus. This form of reciting is also used a demonstration by the teachers of the Qur'an to the parents of the students that their children memorized Qur'an.

indication of the Islamic penetration in a particular community and in the society at large.

The second level of Islamic education is assigned to the mosques and small prayer sites called "Mawlac". Some dedicated graduates from the Qur'anic schools proceed to the higher level of Islamic learning, which aims to produce Islamic scholars of different calibers. Since opportunities for higher education are confined mostly to specific locations in urban centers, it was not affordable to all students. Thus, a self-supporting system of scholarships to promote Islamic education was established by the communities. This scholarship package encompasses free education offered by the learned scholars and free accommodation provided by the community members. This system, called "Jilidda Xer-cilmiga" (feeding seekers of knowledge), in which dwellers of cities provided food for the rural students of the Islamic studies. This system was the most prominent factor in the success of early education and Islamization in Somalia. These students, upon their return to their original home territories, established Islamic education centers and provided Islamic services to their communities. Its integrative societal impact is immeasurable; it is beyond our limited scope to elaborate on it here. Moreover, some of these students remain in the urban centers, establish new villages, and initiate the process of settlement and urbanization of the pastoral population. The curriculum of "mosque schools" constitutes the Arabic grammar, studies of Shafi'i jurisprudence, interpretation of the Qur'an "Tafsiir", and learning of the prophetic tradition "Xadiith".[14] This form of

---

14. Prophetic tradition implies the narration of a saying, or of an act, or of an approval (*Taswib*) of the Prophet (sws), irrespective of whether the matter is authenticated or

education is a life-long learning without age constraint. Usually, it has no hierarchy of subjects and at any stage of learning, students often have only one teacher and one subject while duration of the courses are flexible.[15]

This type of education has produced different levels of Islamic scholars, with a few becoming outstanding scholars all over Somali territories. Some of these scholars focus on the studies of jurisprudence and became judges and teachers while may belong to one of the Sufi orders. Others combine their studies with Sufism at an early stage and focus on spreading Sufi orders. Students join and leave courses at will and few of them qualify to be Islamic scholar to obtain official permission from their teachers "Ijaaza" (a permission to exercise the authority of being a sheikh or Sufi master). Graduates who are more committed to the Islamic knowledge are sent as emissaries of their Sheikh to their home territories in order to propagate Islam, as recommended by the Qur'an.[16]

The third level of the Islamic education is Sufism, dispensed by the masters of the Sufi orders. Sufi orders, called "*turuq*" (pl.) in Arabic, which mean, way, path, and method in Islam, focus on spiritual purification under the guidance of a spiritual master. Followers of Sufism seek a closer personal relationship with Allah through special disciplines and spiritual exercises.

---

still disputed. It is often has the same meaning as *Hadith* or *Sunna* of the Prophet of Islam.

15. See Ibrahim Mohamud Abyan and Ahmed Gure Ali. "Non-formal Education in Somalia" (A document produced for the United Nations Education and Cultural Organization at a meeting of experts on alternative approaches to school education at the primary level, held in Addis Ababa, 6-10 October, 1975).
16. See the verse from the Qur'an (9:122), "and it is not proper for the believers to go out to fight (Jihad), all together. Of every troop of them, a party only should go forth, that they may get instructions in Islamic religion, and that they may warn their people when they return to them, so that they may beware (of evil)."

Generally, a Sufi order takes the name of its founder, such as Qaadiriyah for the Sufi order founded by Sheikh Cabdulqaadir al-Jeylaani. Although it is beyond our topic to delve into its details, it should be understood that Sufism in Somalia is an extension of the similar phenomenon in the Muslim world with the added Somali specificity. Islamic learning focusing on the Qur'an and the basics of jurisprudence had a limited impact on the clannish non-Arabic-speaking and pastoral societies. Nonetheless, Sufi orders, with their symbolical activities and closeness to people's culture, contributed greatly to the revival of Islam among the masses, using innovative mobilization techniques. The most popular techniques are called "Dikri" in which religious poems "Qasaaid" are created and chanted in a chorus and in an artistic manner, blessing people, reciting the Qur'an for the sick and diseased, annual remembrance of deceased parents (close and distant), the commemoration of the birth of the Prophet "Mawliid", visiting the blessed sheikh's tombs "Siyaaro", etc. These techniques create collectiveness, a sense of belonging and mutual support for the adherents of the Sufi orders. They also create a web of trans-clan networks in society, diluting clan polarization and segmentation. Moreover, these networks enable their members to create business contracts and marry each other's daughters to bolster their relations.[17]

---

17. On the Somali Sufi orders and their teachings refer to I. M. Lewis, Saints *and Somalis*.

The Revival of Sufi Brotherhoods

Although Sufism existed and was practiced since the early Islamic history, most of the organized brotherhoods emerged in the eleventh, twelfth and thirteenth centuries AD. For instance, Qaadiriyah was founded by Sheikh Abdulqadir al-Jeylani (1077-1166); Axmadiyah was founded by Ahmad Ibn Idris al-Fasi (1760-1837); and Shaadaliyah was founded by Abu-Xasan al-Shaadali (1196-1258). In the Somali peninsula, the advent of Sufism has been recorded since early fifteen century with the arrival of 44 Islamic scholars under the leadership of Sheikh Ibrahim Abu-Zarbai in 1430. It was also reported that Sheikh Jamaal al-Addiin bin Yuusuf al-Zaylici (d. 1389), the author of the book Nasbu al-Rāya li Ahādith al-Hidāyah, possibly was one of the Sufi Sheikhs in the Horn of African region. However, this remains a speculation, since there are no more accounts of him.[18] Nevertheless, its renewal and reform as an organized movement was noted from the last quarter of the nineteenth century to the middle of the twentieth century. Indeed, Said Samatar wrote, "These years between 1880 and 1920 can be described as the era of the Sheikhs in Somali history."[19] Revival is an important dimension of the historical experience of Muslims; Sufi reformation entailed shifting from individual Islamic activities to institutionalized orders.[20] Traditionally, Sufi order masters belong to all three categories of Islamic scholars

---

18. See Moḥamed Aḥmed Jum'āle, *Dawr 'ulamā Junub al-Somāl fi al-Da'wa al-Islāmiyah (1889-1941)* (PhD thesis submitted to the University of Omdurman, Khartoum, 2007), 84.
19. Said Samatar,*Oral Poetry and Somali Nationalism: The Case of Sayid Mohamed Abdulle Hassan* (Cambridge: Cambridge University Press, 1982), 97.
20. Scott Steven Rees, *Patricians of the Banadir: Islamic Learning, Commerce and Somali Urban Identity in the Nineteenth Century* (PhD thesis submitted to the University of Pennsylvania, 1996), 306.

in Somalia, the Culumo or Wadaado. In their communities, they are easily identified by the titles attached to their names: Sheikh (Islamic jurist and teacher), Macallin (Qur'anic teacher), and Aw (a person with an elementary Islamic education). After joining a Sufi order by taking the oath of allegiance called *Bay'a* and receiving a banner, a chain, and the litanies "Awraad" of the order, some of them retain their original titles, while others may change to the title Khaliif, the marker of the Sufi masters.[21] The stimulus for their revival, as described by Trimigham, was the emergence of charismatic spiritual preachers with a talent for mass mobilization during this period.[22] However, this *raison d'être* is not enough to explain the phenomenon. It seems that this revival is not an isolated occurrence in Somalia but could be related to similar revivalist movements in the Muslim world that could be linked with the increased awareness of external threats and the decline of morality in Muslim societies.

Traditional Sufi orders have taken mainly peaceful approaches to socio-religious reform through Islamic propagation and spiritual revitalization.[23] As such, they dominated religious life, reaching out to populations in the

---

21. Since there is no certification system in traditional education, the minimum requirement to bear the name of "Sheikh" is the capacity to contract marriages and administer the law of inheritance. On the other hand, the title of "Macallin" is carried by those who have dedicated their life to the teaching the Qur'an, and "Aw" is a less significant title demonstrating simply that a person went through some kind of elementary Islamic education. See Abdurahman Abdullahi, "Tribalism and Islam: The Basics of Somaliness" in *Variations on the Theme of Somaliness*, edited by Muddle Suzanne Liluis (Turku, Finland: Centre of Continuing Education, AboUniversity, 2001), 233.
22. See Trimigham, *Islam in Ethiopia*, 1952. Also, Rees, *Patricians of the Banadir*, 302-303.
23. The nature of peacefulness of Sufi Orders may be interrupted because of external provocations, such as colonialism in the case of many scholars, exemplified by Sayid Maxamad Cabdulle Xasan, and internal doctrinal conflicts, such as the conflict between Bardheere Jamaaca and Geledi Sultanates and current fighting between Al-Shabaab and Sufi Order of Ahl al-Sunnawa al-Jamaaca.

urban and rural areas alike, most of whom had identified with one of the Sufi orders by the nineteenth century. Sufi sheikhs, besides their complementary role in running community affairs, established Islamic commonwealth centers Jamaacooyin (somalized Arabic word of *Jama 'a* in plural form) whose dwellers gave their allegiance only to their Sufi masters/sheikhs.[24] Moreover, in contradiction to conventional historiography that considers Sufi orders to be mainly apolitical, many leaders of the Sufi orders and their disciples became the supreme leaders of their communities. In this way, clan allegiances and loyalties were diluted and at times transformed into ideological loyalties. Occasionally, both religious and secular authorities are combined in one leader creating a strong Sufi master or sheikh. Moreover, most of the Islamic education centers were located in settlements in agricultural areas and around water wells and many of these were later transformed into villages, towns, and cities. In this way, the Sufi orders transformed pastoral society into settled communities engaged in agriculture and/or trade.[25]

These Sufi orders remain active across Somalia with popular support, despite the fact that modern elites who do not belong to any Sufi order have emerged with the development of modern education and modern Islamic movements eschewing

---

24. Certainly, all *Jama'a* communities in Somalia, estimated by I.M. Lewis in the 1950s to account for more than 80 communities, are under the leadership of a master/sheikh, and the clan factor has no much space. Of these, over half were Axmadiyah, and the remaining was distributed almost equally between Qaadiriyah and Saalixiyah (note here Lewis is not including Saalixiyah in Axmadiyah which is incorrect). See Lewis, *Saints*, 35. Moreover, Professor Mukhtar produces 92 Jamaaca in 1920s in the Italian colony, where 50 Jamaaca were located in the upper Juba, 30 in Banaadir, 4 in Lower Juba, and 8 in Hiiraan. See Mohamed Mukhtar, *Historical Dictionary of Somalia*. African Historical Dictionary Series, 87 (Lanham, MD: Scarecrow Press, 2003), 127.
25. Laitin and Samatar, *Somalia: Nation*, 45.

Sufism. Briefly, the main characteristics of Sufi orders in Somalia are as follows. They are affiliated with the wider networks of Sufi brotherhoods in the Muslim world. Their leadership is absolute and authoritative, and succession is not necessarily based on heredity; however, the Khaliif (Sufi master) designates his successor in his lifetime. Often, most of the Sufi masters nominate their sons, believing that their blessing (Baraka) is dormant in them, and members of the order will pay great respect to the son derived from respect for his father. Every Sufi master has an official Sufi genealogy connecting him to the founder of his order. Membership is acquired by new aspirants through direct formal initiation (allegiance). Every member has to comply with the policies and procedures of the orders that include regular recitation of litanies. Finally, members take the common name of Ikhwaan (brethren) that connotes their relation to pan-Islamic brotherhood.[26]

There are two main Sufi orders in Somalia: Qaadiriyah and Axmadiyah. Each Sufi order has its local offshoots.[27] Qaadiriyah has two main branches, Zayli'iyah and Uweysiyah. Zayli'iyah was founded by Sheikh Cabdiraxman al-Zaylici (1815-1882), who was based in Qulunqul near Dhagaxbuur in the Somali territory in Ethiopia. Uweysiyah was founded by the spiritual master Sheikh Uweys ibn Axmad al-Baraawe (1846-1907), and its seat was located in Balad al-Amiin near Afgooye, about 40 km south-west of Mogadishu. Axmadiyah has three offshoots in

---

26. Spencer Trimigham, *Islam in Ethiopia*, 236-237.
27. Most scholars fail to distinguish between the original Sufi order and their later derivatives. Sometimes these Sufi orders are said to be three, making Saalixiyah a separate order from Axmadiyah and also neglecting the existence of the Rufaaciyah order. See Laitin and Samatar,*Somalia: Nation*, 45.

Somalia: Raxmaaniyah, Saalixiyah, and Dandaraawiyah. Raxmaaniyah was founded by Maulana Cabduraxman ibn Maxamuud (d. 1874). Saalixiyah was founded by Sheikh Maxamad Saalax around 1890s. It has two branches: southern branch introduced by Sheikh Maxamad Guuleed al-Rashiidi (d.1918) and northern branch by Sayid Maxamad Cabdulle Xasan (1856-1920). Dandaraawiyah was introduced by Sayid Aadan Axmad and has a limited following in northern Somalia.[28]

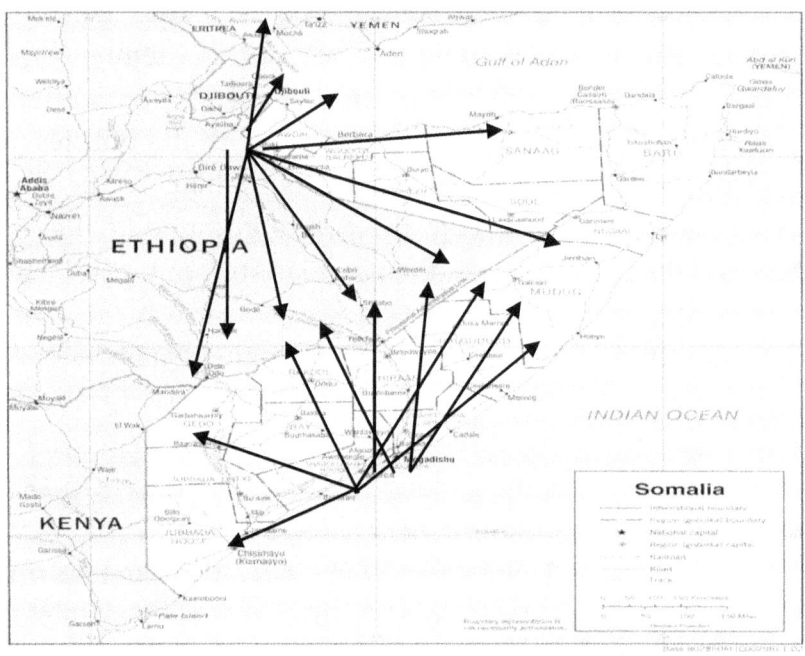

Figure 2. Historical Islamic learning centers: Banaadir region (Mogadishu, Marka &Barava) and Harrar&Jigjiga region. Direction of the arrows shows directions of the emissaries and scholars graduated from the Islamic centers.

---

28. Cabdirisaq Caqli, *Sheikh Madar*: *Asaasaha Hargeysa* (biographical work on Sheikh Madar written in Somali Language, no date or publishing house).

In gathering together the pieces of the early history of the Sufi orders, it is important to note that there were two regional centers of Islamic learning in pre-colonial Somali territories. These centers were connected with Yemen, Zanzibar, Oman, Saudi Arabia, and Egypt. One of these centers was in the Banaadir region, where the cities of Mogadishu, Baraawe, Marka, and Warsheik are located. In these centers, famous Islamic scholars and prominent Sufi sheikhs have been spreading Islam to the clans of the interior. They also established pan-clan networks through common affiliation to one of the Sufi orders. Students traveled to Banaadir via trade routes connecting this area with the southern and middle regions of Somali territories.[29] The other Islamic education centers were located in the historical cities in western Somali territories (currently, Somali state of Ethiopia) such as Harrar, Jigjiga, and surrounding areas. In particular, Qulunqul is renowned as the Qaadiriyah Sufi center and had its special importance as the site of the founder of Zaylciyah branch of Qaadiriyah, Sheikh Cabdiraxman al-Zaylici. Islamic scholars and students of Islamic studies were traveling between Harrar, Jigjiga, and surrounding areas and the northern and north eastern Somali regions that include the current Somaliland and Puntland adminstrations. Other Sufi orders were marginal late-comers. The two main Sufi orders, Qaadiriyah and Axmadiyah, and their offshoots were spreading their messages along with Islamic education centers.

---

29. See trade routes in early Somalia in Laitin and Samatar, *Somalia: Nation*, 9-10.

Qaadiriyah Brotherhood

The oldest Sufi order in Islam was founded in Baghdad by Abdulqadir al-Jeylani (d. 1166) and was brought to western and northern Somali territories in the early sixteenth century by *Abubakar b. 'Abdallah al-'Aidarūsi* (d. 1502) from Hadramout in Yemen.[30] Followers of Qaadiriyah in Somalia are roughly estimated by Professor Said Samatar to be as many as 75% of the population, and this order is unmatched in terms of popularity and dispersion in every region.[31] It grew first in the historic city of Harrar, the metropolis of Islam in the Horn of Africa, and spread through Arab immigrants from Yemen to Mogadishu and surrounding cities. It remains obscure, however, when and how the Brotherhood spread from there to other parts of Somali territories until nineteenth century. The city of Harrar, being the center of Islamic learning for the entire region, was clearly the place where many Somalis resided and educated. Moreover, historical records show that after Egypt withdrew precipitately because of military pressure from the Sudanese *Mahdiyah* movement, Ethiopia conquered Harrar in 1887.[32] The Ethiopians massacred the population and the city's Islamic scholars, closed learning centers, and desecrated Islamic shrines.[33] In this juncture, Menelik, the Ethiopian Emperor,

---

30. See Moḥamed 'Abdallah Al-Naqīra, *Intishār al-Islam fi sharq Ifrīqiyah wa munāhadat al-Garbi Lahu* (Riyadh: Dar al-Marīkh, 1982), 160.
31. There is no exact statistical data on Sufi affiliations, but this high percentage reflects that the majority of the Somalis belong to the Qaadiriyahorder. See Said Samatar (ed.), *In the Shadows of Conquest: Islam in Colonial Northeast Africa*(Trenton, NJ: The Red Sea Press, 1992), 8.
32. See E. Sylvia Pankhurst, *Ex-Italian Somaliland* (Read books design, 2010).
33. For more details on the implications of the Ethiopian conquest of Harrar see Abubakar, *Al-Da'wa*, 25-26. A notable example is that the historic Mosque in Harrar was converted to Church and remains as such until today.

boasted: "I hoisted my flag in [Amir Abdullaahi's] capital and my troops occupied his city. Gragne (Garan) died. Amir Abdullaahi in our day was his successor. This is not a Muslim country, as everyone knows".[34] As a consequence of this conquest, some surviving Islamic scholars moved to locations distant from Harrar. Thus, from the Somali perspective, the town of Jigjiga replaced Harrar and became a new thriving center of Islamic learning in the area.[35] The two most prominent scholars, Sheikh Cabdiraxman al-Zaylici and Xaaji Jaamac made their residence in Jigjiga and Qulunqul respectively. Sheikh Zaylici focused on spreading the Qaadiriyah order, while Xaaji Jaamac established an Islamic learning center in Jigjiga. From these two centers and their satellite sub-centers, Islamic education and the Qaadiriyah order spread hand in hand in the surrounding regions in the late 19th century and early 20th century. Moreover, even before the time of Sheikh Cabdiraxman al-Zaylici, Islamic communes Jamaacooyin were established in many parts of western and northern Somalia. The most famous was Jamaaca Weyn founded by Sheikh Madar Axmad Shirwac (1825-1918), the founder of Hargeysa city, along with other centers in Gebiley and Borama. In the following discussion, we will trace the development and revival of the Qaadiriyah order in western/northern and southern Somalia separately. There were also independent Islamic education centers in Gal-Cusbo in Hiiraan region, Roox in Nugaal region, and Xaafun in Bari region that do not belong to Sufi brotherhoods. Although it is

---

34. This quotation is recorded in Laitin and Samatar,*Somalia: Nation*, 53.
35. The renowned Qaadiriyah Islamic scholars in Jigjiga were Sheikh Cabdiraxman Axmad Gole (Af-Guriye), Sheikh Cumar al-Azhari, Sheikh Cabdullahi Al-Qutubi, Sheikh Cabdisalam Xaaji Jaamac, Sheikh Maxamuud Macallin Cumar, and many others. Sheikh Cabdullahi Sheikh Cali Jawhar interviewed on July 29, 2009, Borama, Somaliland.

outside the scope of this panoramic overview, it is crucial to note that these centers produced famous scholars. For instance, Gal-Cusbo produced Sheikh Cabdalla Qoriyow and Sheikh Cabdalla Migaag, who were judges for the Darawiish Movement led by Sayid Maxamad Cabdulle Xasan (1900-1921).[36] In addition, Roox, located 50 km north of Gaalkacyo, was the center of Xaaji Yuusuf Maxamad Fiqhi Idris, the teacher of Sheikh Cali Majeerteen and other prominent scholars.[37] Moreover, Xaafun education center was well connected to the Arabian Peninsula and from there Sheikh Nuur Cali Colow, the modern founder of Salafia School (Wahaabiyah) in Somalia was educated.[38]

Qaadiriyah in the Northern Somali Territory

In northern Somali territory, the Qaadiriyah order was directly linked to Harrar and later to Jigjiga and Qulunqul. Sheikh Cabdiraxman al-Zaylici (1820-1882) was born in Kidle, near Mubarak, a town in the Bakool region, about 160 Km northwest of Mogadishu.[39] After finishing his basic education in his home district, he pursued further Islamic education in Mogadishu. He frequented the famous Islamic education center of Sheikh

---

36. Ḥassan Ḥaji Moḥamūd, *Al-Somāl: al-Hawiyah wa al-Intim*ā (unpublished work).
37. Aw Jāma''Umar 'issa, *Safaḥāt min tārīkh al-'allāma al-Ḥāji 'Ali 'Abduraḥman Faqīh (1797-1852)* (Sana: Markaz Ibadi li dabat wa nashri, 2009), 13.
38. In 1928, Sheikh Nuur Cali Colow had moved to the town of Xaafuun, which used to be a center of Islamic learning, to further his Islamic education. During this period, the town was a thriving trade center that exported salt. It was a center of Islamic learning with three mosques populated with the students of Islamic knowledge. The most prominent Islamic scholar was Sheikh Maxamad Aw-Suufi who, according to accounts, studied in Sudan, Egypt and Saudi Arabia. This short biography was abtained from interview with Cabdulqaadir Sheikh Nuur Cali Colow and Cabdirisaaq Sheikh Nuur Cali Colow, the two sons of Sheikh Nuur, on May 8-10, 2009, Toronto, Canada.
39. Reese, *Patricians of Banadir*, 309.

Abiikar Muxdaar and received Sufi training from his Qaadiriyah master Sheikh Ismaciil al-Maqdishi.[40] Later, he traveled for pilgrimage and met with the Qaadiriyah Sufi master, Sheikh Fadal al-Qādiriyah, who offered him Ijaaza and pointed him to return to Somali territories. Upon his return via Berbera, he taught Islam in Harrar for many years and then traveled to Mogadishu in 1850. The purpose of his Mogadishu trip was to receive the permission of his Sufi master Sheikh Ismaciil al-Maqdishi to establish a Qaadiriyah center in Qulunqul, near Dhagaxbuur. Sheikh Cabdiraxman became the unchallenged master of Qaadiriyah in Somalia, and his disciples include prominent scholars such as Sheikh Maxamad Ismaciil Timacade, Sheikh Aadan Mustafa al-Hobyi, Sheikh Axmad Gole (Af-Guriye), Sheikh Cabdisalam Xaaji Jaamac, Sheikh Yuusuf Dubad, and many others.[41] Here we produce short biography of Sheikh Madar Axmad Shirwac, who is one of the first known reformers in northern Somali territory.He exemplifies the role that the traditional Islamic scholars in pre-colonial and early colonial periods played in reforming society and renewing Islam.

Sheikh Madar Axmad Shirwac (1825-1918) was a Sufi guide, social reformer and jurist. He was born in Hadayta near Berbera into a nomadic family. In his early childhood, he memorized the Qur'an and learned the Arabic language in a pastoral Qur'anic school, a mobile school moving with the pastoral seasonal movements. Berbera was the commercial port connected with

---

40. See Yāsin 'Abdirisāq al-Qarḍhāwi, *Dhukhāir al-Nukhba min Tarājim 'Ulamā Sharq Ifrīqiyah* (no publishing house, 2005), 29.
41. The successor of Sheikh Cabdiraxman al-Saylici was designated to Sheikh Abubakar bin Yusuf al-Qutubi. See al-Qarḍhāwi, *Dhukhāir al-Nukhba*, 31. On the biography of Sheikh Cabdiraxman Al-Saylici, see Martin, B.G. "Sheikh Zayla'i and the Nineteenth-century Somali Qadiriya," edited by Said Samatar,*In the Shadows of Conquest*,11-32.

the historic Islamic city of Harrar and Islamic scholars, students, and business people were frequently traveling between these two cities. Other cities did not develop in this area during this period. While Berbera was the regional trade hub, Harrar was the regional seat of Islamic learning. After Britain's takeover of Aden in 1839, Berbera was supplying livestock to the British garrison in Aden. Consequently, pastoralists in the area, benefiting from the lucrative business opportunity, became more affluent, and trade between Berbera and Harrar was also thriving. As a result, many Somalis lived in Harrar for business, work, and as students of Islam. By 1855, as related by Richard Burton, the British intelligence officer, about 2,500 Somalis lived in Harrar, one third of the total population of the city.[42] Two of the three most prominent scholars were ethnic Somalis, namely, Xaaji Jaamac and Kabiir Khaliil. Kabiir Khaliil most likely originated from the Berbera area and, after residing in Harrar, had a resounding influence on the people from his home area.

In contrast to the community-supported education system in other parts of Somalia, students in Harrar had to be able to support themselves and be capable of buying expensive Islamic text books. Therefore, poor students had a very slim chance for higher education in Harrar. The father of Sheikh Madar was among those affluent pastoralists who benefited from the lucrative business in Berbera and was capable of supporting his son's education in Harrar. Sheikh Madar studied in Harrar for 20 years, becoming an authoritative Islamic scholar and Qaadiriyah Sufi master. He was assigned by his Sufi master Kabiir Khaliil to return to his home area and preach Islam,

---

42. Richard F. Burton, *First Footsteps in East Africa* (BiblioBazaar, 2009), 139. Also, Caqli, *Sheikh Madar*, 26.

Qaadiriyah order and to resolve conflicts between clans disturbing trade routes between Berbera and Harrar.[43] Sheikh Madar had founded Jamaaca Weyn (the big commune) as the seat of Islamic learning in the 1860s (the founding of the city Hargeysa). He also mobilized other sheikhs in the area, built homes for his commune, and constructed his Grand Mosque in 1883. From there, Islamic education began to boom, the Shari'a was applied in the community, and reconciliations between feuding clans were initiated. Sheikh Madar was assisted by other fellow sheikhs who returned with him from Harrar, e.g., Sheikh Haaruun Sheikh Cali and Xaaji Faarax Ismaaciil, whom he sent to the cities of Berbera and Bulaxaar to teach Islam.[44]

Sheikh Madar, benefiting from his experiences gained in Harrar, introduced three reforms in the way of life of the pastoral communities, according to Cabdirisaq Caqli. First, he introduced permanent settlement, reforming nomadic life based on following after the rains and pastures. Second, he brought together members from various clans in affiliation of brotherhood, changing the culture based on clan loyalties. Third, he promoted and directed his followers toward agriculture, changing the culture of nomadic pastoralism.[45] In the era of Sheikh Madar, the Turkish rule was extended to northern Somali territory, and Sheikh Madar had good rapport with the Turkish rulers and, subsequently, Egyptians who took over Somali coastal ports and conquered Harrar by 1875. Egypt's sudden withdrawal from Harrar and the Somali coast created a strategic vacuum that was filled by the Ethiopians

---

43. See Caqli, *Sheikh Madar*, 48-49.
44. Sheikh Madar sent Sheikh Axmad Boon to Berbera and Sheikh Kabiir Cumar to Bulaxaar. See Ibid.
45. See Caqli, *Sheikh Madar*, 184.

who captured Harrar in 1887. The Ethiopians threatened the divided and unprotected Somali clans, and Sheikh Madar repeatedly appealed for British authorities to help counter the Ethiopians. However, the British had good relations with the rising Ethiopian Empire and responded with a cold shoulder. The choice for Somalis appeared very limited, being conflicting clans without a common authority and facing threats of Ethiopian expansion from the West and the British colonialism from the east. Lacking domestic political leadership, Somalis preferred the British rule to that of their Ethiopian neighbors. The reason for this hard choices are numerous, however, one of the most important for the pastoral Somalis was that Ethiopians frequently looted their livestock to feed their soldiers while Britain was engaged in livestock business with them through the city of Berbera.[46]

Qaadiriyah in Southern Somali Territory

In southern Somali territory, historical records show that in 1819, Sheikh Ibrahim Hasan Yabarow, reported by some historical records as belonging to the Qaadiriyahorder, established the first Islamic center in the Juba valley.[47] However, the Sufi affiliation of Sheikh Ibrahim Yabarow is highly controversial. As the founder of the town of Baardheere where Baardheere Jamaaca was spreading its Islamic reformist propaganda, he belonged, according to some scholars, to the Axmadiyah order. Others even think that he belonged to Salafia

---

46. See Ibid. 156-162.
47. Historical literature uses the Italian misspelling "Gebero" instead of Yabarow. See Salah Mohamed Ali, *Hudur and History of Southern Somalia* (Cairo: Nahda Book Publisher, 2009), 29. See Cassanelli, *Shaping*, 35-36.

school (Wahaabiyah) that was prevalent in Saudi Arabia.[48] Besides, oral collections show that Sheikh Abiikar Muxdaar is considered an early known scholar of the Qaadiriyah order in Banaadir. Titled *Sheikh al-Shuyūkh* (the teacher of the teachers), he was the teacher/mentor of many famous sheikhs in the Somali territories, such as Sheikh Cabdiraxman Suufi, Sheikh Axmad Xaaji Mahdi, and Sheikh Cabdiraxman al-Zaylici.[49] The history of Sheikh Abiikar Muxdaar is not well recorded; however, he is buried in Warsheik, where he migrated (made Hijra) from Mogadishu, shunning immoral dancing rituals known as Manyaas that were rampant in Mogadishu.[50]

Another prominent scholar is Sheikh Cabdiraxman bin Cabdullah Suufi (1829-1904), who graduated from the Islamic education center of Sheikh Abiikar Muxdaar in Warsheik and joined both the Axmadiyah and Qaadiriyah orders.[51] Sheikh Cabdiraxman Sufi succeeded Sheikh Abiikar Muxdaar after the death of the latter and became the most prominent Islamic scholar in Mogadishu. He heralded a new era of improved quality of Islamic education in Banaadir, since he did not travel to the outside world to complete his education as was the

---

48. See Jum'āle, *"Dawr 'Ulamā Junub al-Somāl"*, 40-41.
49. See Cassanelli, *Shaping*, 215-216. Also, see Al-'Eli, Sheikh 'Abdiraḥman ibn Sheikh 'Umar. *Al-Jawhar al-Nafis fi Khawās al-Sheikh Aweys* (Mombassa, Kenya: Sidik Mubarak & Sons, no date). Also, Xassan Xaaji Maxamad interviewed by the author on June 30, 2009, Nairobi, Kenya.
50. Sheikh Abiikar Muxdaar migrated first to Nimow (a village near Mogadishu) nine times and then finally moved to Warsheik. See Al-'Eli, *Jawhar al-Nafis*, 120. Also, see Cassanelli, *Shaping*, 216. The immoral dancing rituals were one of the problems of Mogadishu, and Islamic scholars tried to stop it but failed until Sheikh Aweys arrived and ended these rituals. See also, Mohamed Qassim. "Aspects of Banadir Cultural History: The Case of the Baravan Ulama" in *The Invention of Somalia*, edited by Jumale Ahmed (Lawrenceville: The Red Sea Press, 1995), 29-42.
51. Sheikh Suufi gave his allegiance to Sheikh Uweys al-Baraawi after he solved the problem of immoral dancing in Mogadishu.

custom of the sheikhs before him. Another prominent scholar in Banaadir was Sheikh Axmad Xaaji Mahdi (d.1900), also a disciple of Sheikh Abiikar Muxdaar. He was an ardent critic of the Italian colonialism and was intolerant to living in Mogadishu under the rule of the Italians and to decadent dance rituals; he migrated to Nimow, 20 km south of Mogadishu. There, he established his Islamic learning center called *Dār al-Hijra*.[52] However, after the Lafoole incident in 1896, when an expeditionary force of 13 Italians were massacred by Somali warriors, angry Italians shelled his village, and he subsequently moved to Day Suufi in the deeper interior areas, influencing different clans to resist the Italians.[53] He was also stationed for many years in Baarmaale near Rage-Ceele, about 100 km north of Mogadishu, and established his teaching center there.[54] Later, Sheikh Axmad established his learning center at Waraabaale, between Mogadishu and Afgooye.[55] One of his disciples was Sheikh Ibrahim Cali Gacal (1887-1965), known for his strong Islamic propagation programs.[56]

---

52. Jum'āle, *Dawr 'Ulamā*, 193.
53. Lafoole is located between Mogadishu and Afgoye, about 20 km from Mogadishu. It was the first site of armed confrontation between the Italians and Somalis. This event is commemorated by establishing University College of Education at Lafoole. For more information on this event, see Robert Hees, *Italian Colonialism in Somalia* (University of Chicago Press, 1966), 63.
54. Baarmaal was a famous center of Qur'anic studies among the Maxamad Muuse sub-clan of Abgaal (Hawiye), where the famous Sheikh Walaal established his school, and many students from the region memorized the Qur'an there. As late as 1907, the acting Italian governor considered Sheikh Axmad Mahdi the most listened-to propagandist in this area of Shabeelle region.
55. At Warabaale, Sheikh Axmad Mahdi received Sheikh Uweys al-Baraawi upon his return as Qaadiriyah Sufi Master in 1882. Al-'Eli, *Jawhar al*-Nafis, 122.
56. Sheikh Ibrahim was a servant of Sheikh Axmad Mahdi, responsible for washing his clothes and bringing fish from Mogadishu. He later established his center of education at Garasbaaley near Mogadishu for about 50 years. Xasan Xaaji Maxamad (Hasanley) interviewed on June 30, 2009, Nairobi, Kenya. Xasan Xaaji was one the close disciples of Sheikh Ibrahim and married to one of his daughters.

In southern Somali territory, the name of the Qaadiriyah order is associated with the legendary Sufi Master, Sheikh Uweys al-Baraawi (1847-1909), the founder of the Qaadiriyah branch of Uweysiyah. He was born in Baraawe, and his most notable teachers and mentors were Sheikh Maxamad Tayni and Sheikh Maxamad Jenai al-Bahluul, who recommended him to travel to the Qaadiriyah order headquarter in Baghdad.[57] As Sheikh Uweys went on pilgrimage, he proceeded to Baghdad where he obtained the Ijaaza and the Qaadiriyah mantle from Sheikh Mustafa bin Salman, the head of the order.Subsequently, Sheikh Mustafa offered Sheikh Uweys the responsibility of spreading Qaadiriyah in the Horn of Africa.

Upon his return in 1882, Sheikh Uweys introduced himself to Sheikh Cabdiraxman al-Zaylici and visited his center at Qulunqul on his way to Mogadishu. His best known hagiographer, Sheikh Cabdiraxman Celi, relates that the disciples of Sheikh Uweys numbered 500 and records the names of 150 of them.[58] Qaadiriyah/Uweysiyah is not confined to Somalia but extends to East African countries, such as Kenya, Tanzania, Uganda, Mozambique, and Malawi. His prominent disciples in Somalia include Sheikh Faraj (d.1925), known as Sufi Baraki, the first successor of Sheikh Uweys; Sheikh Qaasim al-Baraawi (1887-1921), a famous scholar in Baraawe and the author of the famous Qaadiriyah collection of biographic accounts of Sheikh Uweys and Sheikh Cabdiraxman al-Zaylici;[59] Sheikh Cabdullahi al-Qudubi (1879-1952), an erudite scholar of theology and philosophy who authored many works though

---

57. Al-'Eli, *Jawhar al-Nafis*, 8.
58. Ibid., 17-25. Also, See Reese, *Patricians*, 216.
59. Sheikh Qassim authored numerous Sufi poems. See Qasim, *Aspects of the Banadir*, 33-34.

most of them remain unpublished;⁶⁰ and Sheikh Cabdiraxman Celi (1895-1962), a prolific poet and reciter of Qaadiriyah poems called "Qasaaid", who authored the famous hagiographical book of *Jawhar al-Nafīs*.⁶¹ The historic visit of Sheikh Cabdiraxman Celi in 1960 (1380 H) to the tombs of many Islamic scholars indicates the extent to which Qaadiriyah was rooted in the Banaadir region. During this visit, he and his companions visited more than 40 important tombs of famous Qaadiriyah Islamic scholars in Banaadir, Baay, and Bakool regions.⁶² Finally, in Mogadishu, the traditional family of Reer Fiqhihadbeen producing Islamic jurists and scholars for centuries. During the colonial era, Sheikh Maxamad, Sheikh Muxyidiin and his brother Sheikh Abiikar Sheikh Muxiyidiin were teachers of Islamic jurisprudence and many students graduated from their education center.

---

60. Sheikh Cabdullahi al-Qudubi was born on the night of the death of Sheikh Cabdiraxman al-Zaylici in Qulunqul. Among his famous Qaadiriyah disciples were Sheikh Cabdiraxman Celi and Sheikh Maxamuud Abgaalow. See Mohamed Mukhtar, *Historical dictionary*, 201. Also, see al-Qarḍhāwi, 40, and Al-'Eli, *Jawhar al-Nafīs*, 236.
61. Sheikh Cabdiraxman Celi was born near the Islamic center of learning of Warsheik in 1895, studied the basic Islamic principles with Sheikh Maxamad bin Faqi Yuusuf, Sheikh Aadan Maxamuud, Sheikh Maxamad Sheikh Xuseen. He also took Ijaazah from his Sufi masters, Sheikh Cabdullahi al-Qudubi, Sheikh Axmad Macallin Cusman al-Gandarshiyi, Shariif Xasan Cusman. See Mohamed Mukhtar, *Historical dictionary*, 200.
62. The towns visited were Warsheik, Mogadishu, Balad al-Amiin, Baidoa, Buura Hakaba, Biyooley, Gandarshe,Marka, Jaziira, Jowhar,Gololey, Afgooye, and Warabaale (near Afgooye). For the route of the journey and locations visited, refer to Al-'Eli, *Jawhar al*-Nafīs, 155-185. In these 40 tombs, the only woman mentioned was the mother of Sheikh Aweys, Faduma bintu Baharow.

Axmadiyah Brotherhood

The Axmadiyah Brotherhood was founded by Ahmad Ibn Idris al-Faasi (1760-1837). Its derivatives in Somalia are Raxmaaniyah, Saalixiyah, and Dandaraawiyah. In general, Axmadiyah and its branches combine Sufism with reformism putting greater emphasis on intimate knowledge of the Qur'an and Shari'a.[63] They have also shown more militancy in Somalia compared with the Qaadiriyah order.

Axmadiyah/Raxmaaniyah

Most of the written literature mistakenly states that Axmadiyah was brought to Somalia by Sheikh Cali Maye Durogba of Marka after he returned from Mecca in 1870.[64] Yet, oral narrations and some unpublished work unanimously inform differently. These oral accounts confirm that Axmadiyah was brought to southern Somali territory by Mawlaana Cabdiraxman bin Maxamuud (d. 1874) who is the founder of Raxmaaniyah branch of Axmadiyah.[65] He was born in the village of Araa-moog near Afgooye.[66] After acquiring a basic Islamic education, he traveled for further studies to *Zabaid* in Yemen where he remained many years. During his pilgrimage to Mecca, he met with Sayid Axmad Bin Idriis who, after intensive spiritual training, appointed him the representative of Axmadiyah in Somali territory. Upon his arrival, Mawlaana Cabdiraxman appointed five disciples, known in the Axmadiyah circles as "the five

---

63. Trimigham, *Islam in Ethiopia*, 242.
64. See Trimigham, *Islam in Ethiopia*, 242. Also, see Cassanelli, *Shaping*, 195.
65. See Sheikh Cusman Xidig, *Tarjumatu Sayidii Aḥmed* (unpublished manuscript). Also, see Jum'āle, *Dawr 'Ulama*, 85.
66. Sheikh Cusman Xidig, *Tarjumatu*, 113.

stars," and sent them to various locations and clans.⁶⁷ These emissaries included Sheikh Xasan Macallin, the acknowledged head of Axmadiyah in Somalia who settled in a village between Afgoye and Balcad. The other four emissaries were Sheikh Maxamuud Waceys, Sheikh Yahye Cadow (known as Xaaji Weheliye),⁶⁸ Sheikh Maxamad Yuusuf, and Sheikh Xasan Barrow. Sheikh Cali Maye (d. 1917) was a disciple of Sheikh Xasan Macallin and became a prolific scholar. He spread the Axmadiyah order from his Islamic center in Marka through teaching and sending emissaries to many regions in the Somali territory. He was later erroneously assumed to be the founder of Axmadiyah because of his immense popularity. Sheikh Cali Maye received all his Islamic teaching in Marka and represented the new home-grown generation of Islamic scholars demonstrating the improved quality of the Somali educational institutions. He also demonstrated the capacity of local Somali scholars, as epitomized by his distinguished teachers Sheikh Abu-Ishaq al-Shirāzi, Sheikh Moḥamed Bin 'Ali Al-Budasiye, Sheikh 'Abdurahmān Hāji al-Dāroodi, and Sheikh Nur Samow al-Ḥamadāniyi.⁶⁹

To implement the outreach program to distant clans, Sheikh Cali Maye sent 44 emissaries to various regions and sub-clans. Their task was to propagate Islam and the Axmadiyah teaching among their clans, and they gained great success "especially from the tribes of Middle Shabelle region."⁷⁰ For instance, the

---

67. Sheikh Cusman Xidig interviewed by the author on July, 30, 2009, Hargeysa.
68. As related, Haaji Weheliye recommended to the father of Sheikh Uweys, Sheikh Mohamed bin Mahad, that he name his son Uweys and foretold him that the boy would have an important role in spreading the Qaadiriyah order. See Al-'Eli, *Jawhar al*-Nafīs, 114-115.
69. Jum'āle, *Dawr 'Ulamā*, 85, 222. Also, Trimigham, *Islam in Ethiopia*, 242.
70. Sheikh Cusman Xidig interviewed by the author on July, 30, 2009, Hargeysa.

most prominent among these scholars were Sheikh Axmad Abiikar "Gabyow" (1844-1933), a gifted poet-sheikh known for his religious poetry, Sheikh Muuse Cigalle, the grandfather of the Somali president (2009-2012) Sheikh Shariif Sheikh Axmad, and Sheikh Daauud Culusow, the founder of the historical coastal town of Mareeg in the district of Ceeldheer. More than 12 emissaries were sent to Middle Shabelle and Galguduud area.[71] Most of these emissaries established Islamic education centers, became supreme leaders of their sub-clans, and formed small emirates where they ruled according to the Islamic Shari'a law. Through the establishment of new education centers in many places, new generation of scholars were also produced, and the process of Islamization and reorganization of the society took on further strides. Many of these centers have been working for generations and are still functioning.[72]

One of the brilliant disciples of Sheikh Cali Maye was Sheikh Daauud Culusow who founded the town of Mareegat the coast of Indian Ocean in 1891. Young Daauud left his native area in

---

71. Some of the emissaries were Sheikh Daauud Culusow and Sheiklh Ibrahim Maxamuud who were sent to Waceysle sub-clan of Abgaal. Moreover, Xaaji Aadan and Xaaji Yusuf were sent to Habargidir sub-clans of Cayr and Suleyman, respectively. Furthermore, Sheikh Muuse Cigale and Sheikh Axmad Gabyow were sent to Harti sub-clan of Abgaal. Also, Sheikh Cali Sheikh Muuse and Sheikh Cali Mataan were sent to Wacbudhan sub-clan of Abgaal. From the southern clans, Sheikh Saalax Daahir was sent to Bagadi sub-clan and Sheikh Xasan Duubweyne was sent to Irdho/wanleweyn area. Sheikh Cusman Xidiginterviewed by the author on July, 30, 2009, Hargeysa. Also, Sheikh Axmad Kadare interviewed on April 16, 2009, Nairobi, Kenya.
72. One example of these centers is Ceeldheer Islamic Education Center administered by Sheikh Cusman Xidig. Sheikh Cusman Xidig was born in 1942, and his Sufi genealogy from top-down is as follows: (1) *Sayid Aḥmed bin Idris*, (2) Maulana Sheikh Cabdiraxman Maxamuud, (3) Sheikh Xassan Macallin, (4) Sheikh Cali Maye, (5) Sheikh Maxamad Sheikh Cali Maye, (6) Sheikh Axmad Sheikh Daauud, (7) Sheikh Cusman Sheikh Cumar "Xidig". Sheikh Osmaan Xidig interviewed by the author on July, 30, 2009, Hargeysa.

the district of Ceeldheer about 300 km north of Mogadishu and traveled to Banaadir, seeking Islamic knowledge. He memorized the Qur'an in Baarmaale, which is about 100 km north of Mogadishu, and then studied for a while in Cagaaran, a village near Marka. Cagaaran was the seat of Islamic learning established by the famous Sheikh Cali Majeerteen who migrated from Mudug region. Daauud finally joined the school of Sheikh Cali Maye in Marka, from which he later successfully graduated. Sheikh Cali Maye sent him to his clan, Waceysle, with two other disciples from the area, namely, Xaaji Cumar Muudey and Macallin Cusmaan Kulmiye. During his farewell remarks, Sheikh Cali Maye clarified roles and responsibilities of his emissaries by stating: "I made my son Daauud the neck and you are the two hands".[73] Sheikh Cumar Muudey became the judge of the Mareeg town while Macallin Cusman initiated the Qur'anic school. Sheikh Daauud founded a mosque, opened an Islamic court and invited his people to a new era of Islamic rule. In the first organized congregation of the clan members held at Mareeg, he ordered them to bathe in the Indian Ocean, as related in the famous story known as "Maalinta Bad-galka" (the day of entering the sea). This event was intended to clean the bodies and clothes of people before a collective prayer was conducted.[74] Since that day, Sheikh Daauud opened Qur'anic schools, declared the supremacy of Islamic Shari'a, resolved clan conflicts, restructured clan authorities, and founded a standing army. The principality founded by Sheikh Daauud in

---

73. Sheikh Cusmaan Xidig interviewed by the author on July, 30, 2009, Hargeysa.
74. Ibid.

his constituency was facing two local military threats. One threat was emanating from the neighboring Suldaan Cali Yuusuf of Hoobya, and the other from the Darawiish headquarter in Beletweyne, the capital city of Hiiraan region, where Daraawiish operated from 1913 to 1915.[75] Both of these principalities were attempting to extend their frontier to the constituency of Sheikh Daauud. To thwart these threats, Sheikh Daauud mobilized his people and eventually eliminated these threats after many bloody confrontations.[76] Besides his numerous sons who became prominent Islamic scholars and numerous disciples who took his mantle after his death, such as Sheikh Axmad Sheikh Daauud, other prominent scholars educated in Marka came to the scene. A young Islamic scholar, Sheikh Ibrahim Maxamuud, who graduated from Marka School, established his headquarter in the town of Messegaway, 25 km from the district of Ceeldheer to the south. He continued the reform program initiated by Sheikh Daauud and later became famous for his modernizing approach, in which he established modern school and hospital in Messagaway and lobbied that children should be sent to receive modern education.[77] As a result, most of his children and grand children are comparatively highly educated.[78]

---

75. Daraawiish forces took over Beledweyne under the leadership of Xaaji Maxamuud Macalin "Cagadhiig" in 1913 and attempted to extend its influence to the coastal area of the Indian Ocean under the rule of Sheikh Daauud, the habitat of Waceysle sub-clan of Abgaal.
76. Cusman Xidig interviewed by the author on July, 30, 2009, Hargeysa.
77. Sheikh Ibrahim, nicknamed "Yare," was a true reformist scholar of his age. In 1959, before the Somali independence, he constructed in his home town an elementary school, dispensary, and court with the funds he collected from his sub-clan Cali-Gaaf. Then, he demanded that the government send teachers and health personnel. Moreover, he mobilized Qur'anic teachers to allow their Qur'anic students to attend modern school. As a result of his vision and actions, people of Messagaway are more

Axmadiyah/Saalixiyah

Saalixiyahwas founded by Sudanese Sheikh Moḥamed Sālaḥ who was the disciple of Sheikh Ibrahim al-Rashid, the founder of the Rashidiyah branch of Axmadiyah. Other branches of Axmadiyah, such as Sanuusiyah (1787-1859) and Marganiyah (1793-1852), dissented and founded their own branches. In Somalia, Saalixiyah was first introduced by Sheikh Maxamad Guleed al-Rashidi (d. 1918), appointed by Sheikh Moḥamed Sālah as his representative. Sheikh Maxamad Guleed al-Rashidi settled in the agricultural area of Misra Weyn located about 90 km north of Mogadishu. It is the settelement of the Shiidle people (originally bantu) and established there the first agricultural community. However, within a short period of time, more than 15 other affiliated Jamaaca were established along the banks of the Shabelle River.[79] The Saalixiyah Jamaaca applied strict Islamic rules such as compulsory attendance of the congregational prayers and participation in the recitals of litanies. Also, women were required to wear modest Islamic dress. The other important rules were that all members should participate in social solidarity programs and charities and comply with Islamic values and norms. Every Jamaaca has a mosque, Qur'anic school and community leader who besides providing Islamic education, engage in conflict resolutions and

---

educated compared with those in its surroundings. Yahye Sheikh Amir interviewed by the author on June 23, 2010, Nairobi, Kenya.
78. Among them Professor Yahye Sheikh Caamir, the Dean of the faculty of Management and Economic of Mogadishu University and the famous medical doctor Dr. Ilyaas Sheikh Ibrahim and so on.
79. The most prominent of Saalixiyah Jamaaca are: Macruuf, Mubaarak, Shiin, Sabya, Raxaale, Buqda, Nisra Weyn, Mirsa Yarey, Sheikh Bashiir, Jilyaale, Basra/Aw-Mubaarak, Bald-Amin, and Jama'at Nuur. Axmed Rashid Xanafi interviewed by the author on July 30, 2009, Hargeysa.

reconciliations. In the far south, near Bardheere town, Sheikh Ali Nairobi (d. 1920) was active in spreading the mission of Saalixiyah.

To illustrate the southern Saalixiyah, we will explore Sheikh Bashiir's Saalixiyah commune in the Region of Middle Shabelle. This Jamaaca is one of the 15 Jamaaca settlements along the banks of Shabelle River. It was founded in 1919 by Sheikh Bashiir Xaaji Shuceyb who moved from Jamaaca Macruuf, located near Bulo-Burte district of Hiiraan region, after a devastating epidemic in 1917 and 1918.[80] After the death of Sheikh Bashiir, Sheikh Xanafi (d. 2002) succeeded as the sheikh of the Jamaaca and after his death; Sheikh Maxamad Amiin took the mantle of the Sheikh of the Jamaaca. Traditionally, there are four consultative members called shuruud who assist the sheikh/leader of the Jamaaca in administrative matters. The Jamaaca constitutes a small principality in which all members are required to comply with a set of rules and a value system. For instance, all members should regularly frequent congregation prayer and Friday prayer in the Jamaaca Mosque, and those who fail to do so should leave the Jamaaca.[81] The Jamaaca Sheikh undertakes functions such as conflict resolution, provision of legal services, conducting marriage contracts, as well as performing occasional functions such as festivities for the birthday of the Prophet (Mawliid), Ciid celebrations, annual commemoration of deceased dignitaries (siyaaro), etc. Members of the local community are known as *al-Ansār*, while those who arrive from other regions are called

---

80. Axmad Rashid Xanafi interviewed through email on November, 18, 2009, Mogadishu.
81. Conditions for membership are: (1) accepting the Saalixiyah order, (2) recommendations from other three members, (3) allegiance to comply with the value system and regulations of the Jamaaca.

migrants (*al-Muhājirūn*) emulating the era of the Prophet Maxamad. In contrast to the Jamaaca in northern Somalia which converted nomads into settled communities and pastoralists into agricultural cultivators, the Jamaaca in southern Somalia are established within settled agricultural communities. However, they share with all other Jamaaca communities the duty of creating a new across-clan community whose allegiance is only to their Islamic leader.[82]

Other prominent Saalixiyah Sheikhs in the southern resistance against Italian colonialism were Sheikh Cabdi Abiikar "Gaafle" (1852-1922) and Sheikh Xasan Barsane (1853-1928). Sheikh Gaafle, after finishing his basic education in his home village of Carmadobe, advanced his Islamic education in Ceel-Gaal, near Marka. After the Lafoole incident in 1896, he became a prominent leader and a warrior against the Italians. He forged alliance with Sayid Maxamad Cabdulle Xasan to create a common front against the infidels and received some firearms from him. He continued to fight until a disastrous end of his resistance in 1908.[83] The other leader, Sheikh Xasan Barsane opposed the Italian expansion policy in 1924 and refused to accept their domination. The Italian fascist governor, Mario de Vecchi, estimated that Somalis possessed "more than 16,000 rifles or six times as many as those assigned to the local defense forces".[84] This situation was unacceptable to the Italian military ruler. Therefore, de Vecchi ordered the surrender of these rifles. However, when most of the clans complied with the order, Sheikh Xasan Barsane decided to confront the governor. Italian

---

82. Jeylani Hanafi interviewed by the author on December 21, 2009, Hargeysa.
83. Italian forces took full control of Middle Shabelle area and Biyamaal resistance were broken. See Robert Hess, *Italian colonialism*, 91.
84. Ibid., 151.

authority depicted Sheikh Xasan Barsane simply challenging their authority and refusing to their anti-slavery policies. Nevertheless, he bluntly argues in his letter sent to the Italian authority, his total rejection of the Italian laws and his abidance to the Islamic Shari' a.[85] After many bloody encounters, Sheikh Xasan was captured on April, 1924 and later died in the Mogadishu prison. Sheikh Xasan Barsane is remembered for his last attempt of armed resistance against Italian colonialism in the Banaadir region of Somalia. It is noteworthy that colonial resistance in Banaadir lacked unifying leaders and were mainly conducted through segmented pockets of resistance organized by various clans and local Sheikhs.

In a parallel development, Sayid Maxamad Cabdulle Xasan (1856-1920) introduced Saalixiyah into north of the Somali peninsula in 1895. He was born in northern Somalia and in his early childhood studied Islam in Harrar and Mogadishu, returning home in 1891. Three years later, he traveled to Mecca for pilgrimage and returned to Somalia a completely changed man after he came under the charismatic influence of Sheikh Maxamad saalax (1853-1917), the founder of the Saalixiyah order. Sayid Maxamad considered himself as legitimate Saalixiyah representative in the Somali peninsula. He initiated work to criticize the Qaadiriyah order, British colonialism, Ethiopian invasion, and Christian missionary activities. Having emigrated from Berbera after the conflict with the Islamic scholars of Qaadiriyah order and the British authority, he established his own center in Qoryaweyne in the Dulbahante (sub-clan of Hart-Darood) country. He recruited fresh followers,

---

85. See the letter written By Sheikh Hasan Barsane to the Italians in Hees, *Italian colonialism*, 151.

mobilized a strong army, resolved clan conflicts, and in 1899 began to wage relentless wars against the British, Italians and Ethiopians for more than 20 years. On the other hand, he also fought against his own people who repudiated to accept his authority and to follow his Saalixiyah order or ignored his call for Jihad or sided with the British authority. Having developed an authoritarian behavior, he was engaged in relentless diatribe and conflict with many segments of the society. However, as a symbol of Somali nationalism and for his unchallenged poetical polemic and pioneering the anti-colonial movement, his Darawiish movement has been the focus of many academic studies. Many works have been published on this subject, and so this short background will not go further into his biography.[86]

Axmadiyah/ Dandaraawiyah

Dandaraawiyah was founded by Sayid Maxamad al-Dandaraadawi, another disciple of Sayid Ibrahim al-Rashid. This Sufi brotherhood is less popular in Somalia and is confined to certain towns in northern Somali territory. After the death of Ibrahim al-Rashid, the order's succession was disputed between the followers of Sheikh Maxamad Saalax and disciples of al-Dandaraadawi. Sayid Aadan Axmad followed Dandaraawiyah

---

86. Abdisalam Issa-Salwe, *The Failure of the Daraawiish State: The Clash between Somali Clanship and State System* (paper presented at the 5th International Congress of Somali Studies, December 1993). Abdi Sheik Abdi, *Divine Madness: Mohammed Abdulle Hassan (1856-1920)* (Zed Books Ltd., London, 1993). Douglas L Jardine, *The Mad Mullah of Somalia* (London: Jenkins, 1923 and New York: Negro Universities Press, 1969). Said Samatar, *Oral Poetry and Somali Nationalism: The Case of Sayyid Mahammad Abdille Hasan* (Cambridge: Cambridge University Press, 1982).

and introduced it in north of the Somali peninsula.[87] Sayid Aadan embarked at Bulaxaar port located in the south east of Berbera at the Indian Ocean coast and then established his first Jamaacacenter in Xaaxi near the town of Oodweyne. One of the founders of this Jamaaca was Sheikh Muuse Cabdi, the father of the erudite Islamic scholar Sayid Axmad Sheikh Muuse.[88] After many years, Sayid Aadan moved to the town of Sheikh where he established the second center. The town of Sheikh became the headquarter of the order, and Sayid Aadan and many of his disciples were spreading Islam from there to neighboring communities and were connected with similar orders in Egypt, Zanzibar, and Syria. The Jamaaca was renowned for its modernist ideology and its good rapport with the British authorities. For instance, it allowed the opening of one of the first modern schools in the town, while most Somaliland territories were opposing such schools. As a result, the famous Sheikh College School, the first of its kind in British Somaliland was opened in 1943.[89] The impact of this school on Dandaraawiyah was tremendous in the way that the strength of the order was weakened and children of its early disciples became modern elites in Somaliland politics. For instance, the first Somali civil engineer in Somaliland, Cali Sheikh Jirde, is the son of the Dandarawiyah leader Sheikh Maxamad Xuseen.

---

87. See Caqli, *Sheikh Madar*, 192, 185. No detailed studies have been done about this order. Caqli's book on Sheikh Madar provides an unpublished reference work of Ibrahim Xaaji Cabdullahi, *"Gamgam"*, *the Ahmadiyah Dariiqa of Sheikh*. Also, see, Sayid Maxamad Yuusuf, *Somaliland: Sooyaalka Somaliland ka hor 26 Juun 1960* (Dariiqo Publisher, 2001), 25-27.
88. Sheikh Muuse studied in Mecca and returned to his home area in Oodweyne district (near Burco town). Axmad Ibrahim Xasan interviewed by the author on December 21, 2009, Hargeysa.
89. Suldaan Maxamuud Axmad Sheikh Ciise interviewed by the author on December, 16, 2009, Hargeysa.

Other prominent Dandaraawiyah members included Axmad Sheikh Maxamad Cabsiiye who was the Speaker of the Somali Parliament in (1964-66).[90]

Name of the Order	Founder of the Order in Somalia	Center of the Order
Qaadiriyah Zayliciyah Uweysiyah	Sheikh Cabdiraxman al-Zaylici (d.1882) Sheikh Uweys al-Baraawi (d.1909)	Qulunqul (Dhagaxbuur) Beled al-Amiin (Agooye)
Axmadiyah Raxmaaniyah	Mawlaana Cabdiraxman Maxamuud (d. 1874).	Basra (Afgooye)
Saalixiyah (south)	Sayid Maxamad Guuleed Al-Rashid (d. 1918)	Misra weyn (Jowhar)
Saalixiyah (north)	Sayid Maxamad Cabdulle Xasan (d.1920)	Qoryaweyne (Laas-Caanood)
Dandraawiyah	Sayid Adan Axmad (the second half of 19th century)	Xaaxi, Sheikh town

Table 2. The Sufi Brotherhoods in Somalia

Militancy and Moderation in the Sufi Brotherhoods

Militancy means here the use of violent approaches to achieve doctrinal objectives and to impose leadership within Sufi brotherhoods, while moderation simply signifies tolerance and the avoidance of all forms of violent behavior to achieve political and doctrinal objectives. In general, Sufi brotherhoods are moderate and use peaceful means of propagating Islam that offer due consideration to the norms and customs of the people. Sometimes they use innovative means to assimilate and absorb

---

90. The former speaker of the parliament is the father of Suldaan Maxamuud, whom the author has interviewed on December, 16, 2009 in Hargeysa.

pastoral communities and illiterate masses and mobilize them into common action. With blood-shedding being in principle the most heinous crime in Islam, Somali scholars usually abstain from clan fighting in the harsh pastoral environment. Their role is limited to conflict resolution, community education, and conduction of religious functions. However, there were four historical events when militancy emerged, and Islamic scholars led internal fighting to gain politico-religious hegemony. These events constitute historical precedents for current militancy and extremism in Somalia and offer lessons that doctrinal differences may develop into violent confrontation between Islamists.

The first incident occurred in the town of Bardheere as a confrontation between the Baardheere Jamaaca and the Geledi Sultanate at Afgooye.[91] The Baardheere Jamaaca was founded in 1819 by Sheikh Ibrahim Yabarow, introducing some reforms such as outlawing tobacco and popular dancing, and prohibiting ivory trade.[92] The Jamaaca began to implement some elements of Islamic Shari'a such as the wearing of decent Islamic dress for women. In the mid-1830s, after receiving strong adherents among new pastoral immigrants, the Jamaaca

---

91. The narration of this event was misnamed as *"Baardheere Jihad"* by most historians and, in particular, professor Cassanelli. In fact, internal wars between Muslims should not be called *Jihad*. It is a misnomer that militant Baardheere Jamaaca used to justify their war with the other Muslims. Note that Suldaan of Geledi did not call it *Jihad*. See details of this event in Cassanelli, *Shaping*, 136-139.

92. Baardheere was founded in 1819 by Sheikh Ibrahim Xasan Yabarow, a native of Daafeed, a town between Afgooye and Buur-Hakaba, who was refused to establish a reformist religious community in his home district. Daafeed sources claim that Sheikh Ibrahim was affiliated with the Axmadiyahorder. See, Cassanelli, *Shaping*, 136. However, the nature of Jamaaca is highly disputed as a Qaadiriyah settlement, as Trimigham argued. See Trimigham, *Islam in Ethiopia*, 240-41. Moreover, it was also labelled as being Wahaabiyah by many European explorers. See, Cassanelli, *Shaping*, 136.

Historical Background

decided to expand its sphere of influence to other regions during the era of Shariif Cabdiraxman and Shariif Ibrahim, who originated from the Ashraaf Sarmaan residing in Bakool region.[93] By 1840, the Jamaaca warriors reached Baidoa area and Luuq and finally sacked Baraawe, the historic seat of the Qaadiriyah order where both Suldaan Yuusuf Maxamad of Geledi and Sheikh Maadow of Hintire had studied.[94] Baraawe accepted the capitulation conditions that included prohibiting tobacco and popular dancing, andadopting Islamic dress code. They also agreed to pay an annual tax of 500 Pessa.[95] This action provoked a concerted response from the clans of the inter-river areas under the charismatic leadership of the Geledi Suldaan Yuusuf Maxamad. The Geledi sultanate mobilized an expedition force of 40,000 from all clans in the reverine areas, stormed Baardheere, and burned it to the ground. Cassanelli characterized this conflict as one between the rising power of Islamic reformists and the established traditional power of the Geledi. Moreover, he adds the economic factor of curbing the lucrative ivory trade as well as a clan aspect, which stemmed from the armed immigrant nomads, the followers of the Jamaaca, being perceived as a threat to the local population.[96] The external actors' role in this conflict was not well researched; however, it is said that Sayid Bargash, the Suldaan of Zanzibar, was on good terms with the Geledi Sultanate in the confrontation to the threat perceived as a Wahaabiyah

---

93. Cassanelli, *Shaping*, 137.
94. Suldaan Yusuf Maxamad and Sheikh Maadow were the most powerful leaders who together reacted to the Baardheere militant expansionists.
95. Aw-Jāma Omar Isse, *Safaḥāt min Tārikh al-'allāma al-Ḥāji 'Ali 'Abdiraḥman Faqigh (1797-1852)*.Sana: Markaz Ibādi li dabāt wa nashri, 2009, 124.
96. Cassanelli, *Shaping*, 140-14. Also see, Virginia Luling, *Somali Sultanate: The Geledi City-State over 150 Years* (London: Haan Publications, 2002), 23.

penetration which was considered antigonistic to the traditional Islam in the southern Somalia.[97]

The second incident is connected with the arrival of Sheikh Cali Cabdiraxman (Majeerteen) (1787-1852) in Marka in 1846 and his confrontation with the dominant Geledi sultanate. Sheikh Cali Majeerteen was born in Nugaal region between Garoowe and Laascaanood in the current Puntland State of Somalia. He traveled to Mecca and Baghdad for further studies where he met and studied "with the disciples of Muḥammad 'Abdulwahhāb" and came back to his home area.[98] He established an Islamic education center at Xaalin wells near Taleex in Nugaal Valley. However, he emigrated from his home after getting into conflict with his clan and moved to the eastern region under the tutelage of Majeerteen Suldaan Nuur Cusmaan. Here also, Sheikh Cali found it unacceptable to live with the overt violation of Islamic Shari'a by the Suldaan Nuur of Majeerteen and formed an alliance with Xaaji Faarah Xirsi, a rebel suldaan of Majeerteen. Xaaji Faarah attempted to establish a new sultanate or to overthrow his cousin. Under the arrangement between Sheikh Cali and Xaaji Faarax, Xaaji Faarax would take political responsibility and Sheikh Cali would administer religious affairs.[99] To achieve this goal, Sheikh Cali sent a letter to the ruler of Sharja Sheikh Saqar al-Qāsimi offering his allegiance and requesting his support.[100] However, Sheikh Saqar could not respond promptly and, dismayed,

---

97. Jum'āle, *Dawr 'ulamā*, 41.
98. Aw-Jāma, *Safahāt*, 12.
99. This form of alliance is similar to the alliance of King Saud and Sheikh Mohamed Abdul-Wahhab in creating SaudiKingdom.
100. See the letter in Aw-Jāma, *Safahāt*, 110-117. The writer of this letter is controversial and other report informs that it was written by one of the Idagale Sultanate of Isaaq sub-clan.

Sheikh Cali traveled to India and then Zanzibar and remained there for 15 months under the custody of Suldaan Said al-Bu-Saīdi (the father of Sayid Barkash). Having in mind to establish an Islamic Emirate, Sheikh Cali arrived in Marka in 1847, four years after the defeat of Baardheere Jamaaca by the dominance of Geledi Sultanate that ruled over the vast territories of the southern Somali regions. However, the Biyamaal clan, the major clan of Marka, was rebelling against the Geledi Sultanate. Sheikh Cali Majeerteen arrived at Marka in alliance with the Biyamaal clan.[101] He settled in the area near Marka with the consent of the Biyamaal clan and began his activities and education programs. According to Virginia Luling (1939-2013), it is believed that "he himself had had plans to form a colony at the port of Mungiya (the point where the Shabelle River was closest to the Indian Ocean coast), and has obtained a permission to do so from Sayid Sa'id of Zanzibar."[102] However, initially, he attempted to play the role of a peacemaker between Suldaan Yuusuf of Geledi and the Biyamaal clan and sent a letter to Suldaan Yuusuf requesting him that he accepts his reconciliation proposal. However, when Suldaan Yuusuf refused his offer, he arbitrarily declared war against him and seemingly "have raided some of Yuusuf's dependent villages near the river" like Golweyn.[103] The reaction of Geledi Sultanate was rapid and Sheikh Cali's followers were defeated in confronting the Geledi Suldaan's forces in 1847. Sheikh Cali's expectation of receiving assistance from the Suldaan of

---

101. Sheikh arrived Marka with five boats, 150 followers, and substantial quantities of firearms and ammunitions estimated to be 40 rifles and 4 cannons. See Luling, *Somali Sultanate*, 24.
102. Ibid.
103. Ibid.

Zanzibar was dashed; instead, it is thought that the Suldaan of Zanzibar helped the Suldaan of Geledi to confront what was perceived as the threat of the Wahaabiyah. The doctrinal inclination of Sheikh Cali Majeerteen is evident in the letter he sent to the clans of Baraawe, showing that he considered the Geledi Sultanate as a polity adhering to deviated sect (*firqa al-Ḍālah*). Commenting on the outcome of the war, Sheikh Cali stated that "in reality ours [deaths] are in the paradise and theirs are in the hell" and "if you are among the deviated sect which Suldaan Yuusuf leads, there is no relation between us, and your blood will not be saved from us."[104] The intolerance of Sheikh Cali to the propagation of Islam among his people, his mobilization of armed followers, and his siding with the Biyamaal clan against the Geledi Sultanate all indicates that he belonged to a militant ideology akin to that of Bardheere Jamaaca, a new militant tendencies that was emerging during this period in many Muslim countries.

The third significant event was the arrival in Berbera in 1895 of Sayid Maxamad Cabdulle Xasan. This was not only the beginning of armed encounters with the colonial powers but also the initiation of an internal conflict among Somali Sufi orders. Upon his arrival in Berbera, Sayid Maxamad challenged the authority and credentials of the Qaadiriyah establishment, setting up the competing Saalixiyah order and building his own mosque, the Saalixiyah propagation center. Sayid Maxamad began to publicly criticize some practices of Qaadiriyah Sheikhs and introduced fatwa on some controversial issues. These issues included prohibition of chewing Qaad and tobacco, the practice

---

104. Aw-Jāma, *Safahāt*, 152.

tolerated by Qaadiriyah scholars.¹⁰⁵ However, Qaadiriyah scholars succeeded in overcoming Sayid Maxamad'schallenges through religious public debate. Scholars such as Aw Gaas and Xaaji Ibrahim Xirsi invited Sheikh Madar from Hargeysa, head of the Qaadiriyah order in the region, and Sheikh Cabdullahi Caruusi, the teacher of Sayid Maxamad Cabdulle Xasan, to participate in a meeting held in Berbera in 1897 aiming to discuss the issues of what is lawful and what is prohibited in Islam. However, after heated discussions on the issues, followers of Qaadiriyah in Berbera repudiated Sayid Maxamad, and the British authorities intervened to maintain public order and the religious status quo of the city. As a result, Sayid Maxamad was compelled to emigrate from Berbera, carrying with him doctrinal enmity against Qaadiriyah. This deep-rooted conflict between Qaadiriyah and northern Saalixiyah had two dimensions, one political and one doctrinal. First, Sayid Maxamad was aiming to establish an Islamic Emirate under his leadership without consulting other prominent scholars. His unilateral, authoritarian, and controversial approach annoyed many scholars and clan leaders. Second, Saalixiyah questioned the doctrinal credentials of the rival Qaadiriyah order, condemning them as heretical and claiming that only Saalixiyah was authentic and original. This theological controversy escalated into a polemic exchange and then developed into bitter propaganda against each other.[106] For instance, Sheikh

---

105. Khat (Catha edulis Forks.), known in Somalia as Qaad or Jaad, is a plant whose leaves and stem tips are chewed for their stimulating effect. Its lawfulness and prohibition in Islamic the jurisprudence is highly disputed. On June 24, 2014, the sale of khat was also prohibited in Britain.

106. See Sheikh Uweys's poems in Samatar, Said S., 1992. *Sheikh Uways Muhammad of Baraawe, 1847-1909. Mystic and Reformer in East Africa*, in: Said S. Samatar (ed.), *In the*

Uweys wrote poems vilifying the Saalixiyah order. Here are some selected excerpts from the poem, translated by B.G. Martin.[107]

> The person guided by Mohamed's law,
> Will not follow the faction of Satan [Saalihiyah]
> Who deem it lawful to spill the blood of the learned?
> Who take cash and women too: they are anarchist
> Do not follow those men with big shocks of hair,
> A coiffure like the Wahabiyah!
> Publicly, they sell paradise for cash, in our land; they are a sect of dogs
>
> They have gone astray and make others deviate on earth,
> By land and sea among the Somalis
> Have they no reason or understanding? Be not deceived by them
> But flee as from a disaster, from their infamy and unbelief.

This verbal polemic was countered by a similar diatribe of poems by Sayid Maxamad, which concluded: "A word to the backsliding apostates, who have gone astray, from the Prophet's way, the straight path? Why is the truth, so plain, hidden from you?"[108] This verbal polemic developed into physical attacks on the leaders of Qaadiriyah, and on April 14, 1909, followers of Saalixiyah attacked and murdered Sheikh Uweys al-Baraawi at Biyooley village in southern Somalia. When Sayid Maxamad heard of the death of Sheikh Uweys he recited a victory hymn saying, "Behold, at last, when we slew

---

Shadows of Conquest. Islam in Colonial Northeast Africa. Trenton, NJ: The Red Sea Press, 48-74.
107. See complete translation in Ibid, 55-56.
108. Martin, Bradford G., 1993.*Shaykh Uways bin Muhammad al-Barawi, a Traditional Somali Sufi,* in: G. M. Smith and Carl Ernst (eds.), *Manifestations of Sainthood in Islam.* Istanbul: ISIS, 225-37. Also, Samatar,*Shadows of Conquest,* 59.

the old wizard, the rains began to come!"[109] The implications of this conflict in Somalia were tremendous, affecting anti-colonial resistance and tarnishing the image of the Saalixiyah order among the southern Somali population.

The fourth incident occurred among Saalixiyah and Dandaraawiyah in northern Somali territory. Before the arrival of Sayid Maxamad in northern Somali territory, there was the Dandaraawiyah order, an offshoot of Axmadiyah, in the towns of Sheikh and Xaaxi. Sayid Maxamad demanded from the Dandaraawiyah order to follow him claiming absolute authority over the order. After refusing the Sayid's initiative, the conflict between the Dandaraawiyah and Sayid Maxamad escalated. Sayid Maxamad dispatched to the town of Sheikh, the seat of the Dandaraawiyah, about 80 cavalry troops with the message that they should participate in the Jihad against the British infidels. Sending an armed mission without consultation was perceived as a threat by the Dandaraawiyah. They captured most of the soldiers and surrendered them to the British forces stationed in Laylis between Sheikh and Berbera.[110] In reaction, Sayid Maxamad dispatched a strong military expedition and razed Sheikh to the ground.[111] Later, the Sayid Maxamad's bright points were romanticized by Somali nationalists in their efforts to nurture national consciousness by narrating a glorious past and reconstructing symbols, heroes,

---

109. The Somali version is "Candhagodoble goortaan dilaa roobki noo da'aye." See Samatar, *Shadows of Conquest*, 61.
110. Sultan Maxamuud Axmad Sheikh Ciise interviewed by the author on December 16, 2009, Hargeysa.
111. The leadership genealogy of the Dandarawiyah in Somalia is as follows from top-down; (1) Sheikh Aadan, (2) Sheikh Nuur, (3) Sheikh Maxamad Xuseen (d. 1964), (4) Engineer Cali Sheikh MaxamadXuseen (d. 2009), (5) Suldaan Maxamuud Axmad (collective leadership). This information was reported by Suldaan Maxamuud Axmad Ciise on December, 16, 2009, Hargeysa.

and myths. In this approach, self-inflicted wounds, civil wars, massacres, and human atrocities are downplayed and belittled.[112] However, in tracing the background of the current extremism in the name of Islam, it is necessary to bring up other episodes of Sayid Maxamad that suggest the historical roots of the current extremism in Somalia.[113] The roots that are similar to the early militancy between the Sufi orders and modern Islamists – points to the influence of the Wahaabiyah ideology based on "exclusivity and absolutism", and the use of violent means to impose their Islamic interpretation on other Muslims.[114]

Colonialism and Somali Encounter

In the late nineteenth century, as part of the colonial scramble for Africa, Somali peninsula was colonized by four countries: Italy, Great Britain, France, and Ethiopia. Colonial historiography stresses that colonial interest in Somalia was a stepping stone to other vital interests in various other countries. Britain claimed, for example, that its interest in the territories was simply to supply fresh meat to its garrison in Aden after their occupation

---

112. Adeed Dawisha, *Arab Nationalism in the Twentieth Century: From Triumph to Despair* (Princeton Press, 2003), 63.
113. There are resemblances between Sayid Maxamad's activities and slogans and current extremist organizations like Al-Shabaab and Xizbul-Islaam. These are (1) personal rule; (2) exclusion of other Islamic organizations and monopoly of religious legitimacy; (3) excessive use of violence against other Muslims; and (4) selective and haphazard application of Shari'a. All these actions are disguised under the slogan of *Jihad* against the enemies of the Islam and infidels.
114. Abdurahman Abdullahi, "Recovering the SomaliState: the Islamic Factor." In *Somalia: Diaspora and State Reconstitution in the Horn of Africa*, edited by A. Osman Farah, Mammo Mushie, and Joakim Gundel (London: Adonis & Abby Publishers Ltd, 2007), 196-221, 211.

in 1839.[115] However, historical records show earlier British strategic interests in the region, imposing commercial treaty on the people of Berbera in 1827 and signing a similar treaty with the governor of Zaylac in 1840.[116] Similarly, France claims that it just needed the Somali coast to establish coaling facilities for its ships on their way to French colonies in Indo-China and Madagascar; the two countries were admittedly vying for global supremacy by capturing more foreign lands and communication routes. Therefore, both these countries took over areas that were later termed British Somaliland in 1885 and French Somaliland in 1887, demarcating their colonial borders in 1888. Furthermore, Britain possessed another Somali-populated tract of land, called the Northern Frontier District (N.F.D), adjacent to its colony in Kenya. The Italian interest was clearer in aiming to boost its image as one of the great European powers in the scramble for Africa. It also aspired to extend its sphere of influence in Eritrea to the Ethiopian highlands. However, after its defeat at Adwa in 1896, it acknowledged that the occupation of Somalia was in support of their strategic plan in Ethiopia.[117] Italy's colonial venture was supported by Britain so as to thwart the French colonial plans. It started with a commercial treaty in 1885 and taking over the total administration of Banaadir, leased from the Zanzibar dynasty in 1892. Italy gradually expanded its possessions through direct administration until the creation of a fully-fledged Italian colony by 1927.[118] Finally,

---

115. Samatar, *Socialist Somalia*, 16.
116. Mohamed Osman Omar, *The scramble in the Horn of Africa: History of Somalia (1827-1977)* (Mogadishu: Somali Publications, 2001), 28.
117. Robert Hees, *Italian Colonialism*, 172.
118. The creation of the fully fledged Italian colony occurred during fascist rule after capturing the last independent Somali sultanate, and the submission of Boqor

Ethiopia was an emerging African empire in the nineteenth century and, being recognized as an independent African state on good terms with the major Western powers, it pushed its claim for part of Somali territory. It also impressed other powers that it was a local power to be reckoned with in grappling and sharing the Somali booty. Consequently, the Somali people who are culturally quite homogeneous, but politically not united enteredthe twentieth century divided into five parts among four powers. The colonial domination and division of the Somalis has inflicted an enormous psychological distress and touched their nerve and heart, provoking uncoordinated spontaneous resistance.

The Somali encounters with colonialism may be divided into two stages. The first stage (1889-1927) concluded with the Italian defeat of the Majeerteen Sultanate at Baargaal (in current Puntland State of Somalia) in 1927. Leaders during this period were traditional leaders and, in particular, Islamic scholars. During the second stage (1943-1960), the Somalis were led by the new nationalist elites. The difference between the two periods is that the first encounter was a complete rejection of the Christian invaders of Muslim lands, and people were mobilized under the banner of Islam. The second struggle was founded on gaining the status of a legitimate independent state, in line with the established world order of nation-states. The 15-year gap between 1927 and 1943 is regarded as the years of disorientation, a transitional time from the dominance of the traditional elites to the emergence of nationalist elites. During these years, the Somali people went through harsh experiences

---

Cusman Maxamuud, the ruler of Majeerteen in November, 6, 1927. See Robert Hess, *Italian colonialism*, 156.

such as participating in the Italian-Ethiopian war (1935-1941) and the Second World War (1941-1945) as colonial soldiers of the warring sides. For instance, historical records show that "Somali colonial troops eagerly fought against Ethiopians, their traditional enemy" and more than 6000 participated in the war.[119] Likewise, in the Second World War in the Horn of African theatre, Somali colonial soldiers fought on both sides, for Britain and for Italy. First, we will examine the role of the *Ulama* in the first encounter and explore their diminishing role in the second period though planned marginalization and exclusion.

The initial Somali reaction to the rule of the colonial powers was led primarily by the religious leaders. Sufism is known to have formed an obstacle against colonial administration and westernized system of education.[120] The assumption that the Saalixiyah order was anti-colonial while the Qaadiriyah order remained acquiescent and even collaborated with the colonizers has no historical basis. The well-known historical fact is that "Sheikh Aweys promoted resistance to the European colonizers in German-occupied Tanganyika, and even Uganda and eastern Congo."[121] The evidence of this encounter with colonialism is circumstantial, and any singular approach or prioritization of militancy is simply not borne out. These approaches should be seen as complementing each other, depending on the situational analysis and evaluation of the available options. For instance, Sayid Maxamad Cabdulle Xasan led a Daraawiish Movement for roughly 21 years (1899-1920), against British, Italian, and

---

119. Robert Hees, *Italian Colonialism*, 174.
120. Qaadiriyah in the north strongly opposed attempts by the British administration to open secular schools. Lewis, *A History*, 37. Also, Lewis, *Saints*, 9.
121. Lewis, *Saints*, 36.

Ethiopian forces. Many other active anti-colonial movements had been witnessed in many parts of Somalia. Examples are the Lafole massacre (1896), where disciples of Sheikh Axmad Mahdi, who belong to the Qaadiriyah order, were accused of anti-colonial activities and the Italians retaliated. The Biyamaal revolt (1896-1908) led by Macalimiin (Islamic teachers) continued resisting colonization for 12 years and ultimately networked its resistance with the northern Daraawiish Movement, demonstrating the unity of purpose and Islamic consciousness. Moreover, revolts against Italians in Banadir region led by Sheikh Xasan Barsane (d.1926) and Sheikh Bashiir (d.1945) in the Buroa region against British colonialism demonstrate their uncompromising attitude toward colonial programs. Unfortunately, most of these movements had been suppressed by 1924, and their leaders were either eliminated or contained. Finally, the independent Majeerteen Sultanate was brutally suppressed in 1927, finalizing the Italian occupation of Somalia. Since then, the era of independent leadership in the Somali society was over. It took 100 years to conquer the Somali territories completely, since the British agreement with the Somali clans in Berbera in 1827 to the Italian conquer of the Majeerteen Sultanate in 1927. Traditional elders were contained and integrated by a variety of means, including persuasion and intimidation, while Islamic scholars were oppressed, marginalized and excluded. Somali Islamic scholars confronted colonial incursion by different means, including both violent and non-violent means. Those who opted for violent means have been recorded widely in the Somali history, while the peaceful activists were neglected and marginalized. It seems that Somali nationalists, who appropriated all forms of armed encounters as part of the history of Somali nationalism, were tilted toward militarism in the struggle against hegemonic Ethiopia. Perhaps, for that reason, Islamic scholars who engaged in cultural activities and reform programs, invigorating internal resilience to the colonial cultural hegemony as a whole, have not been given enough attention in the Somali historiography.[122]

How did the colonial states deal with the traditional leaders? Traditional leaders, comprising clan elders and Islamic scholars, were the supreme leaders of their communities before the colonial states reshaped the societal equation and changed the praxis of power. The colonial regimes dealt with these leaders through "bureaucratic integration" of the clan elders. At the outset, clan elders signed agreements with the colonial powers and were recognized as local partners. What facilitated their commonality was that the "man-made" secular laws of the colonial states were by their nature closer to the "man-made" Somali customary law known as Xeer, administered by the clan elders. Putting into practice a policy guideline, colonial states employed clan elders, provided them with salaries, and used them as official representatives of their communities. In the late 1950s, there were 950 salaried clan elders in the Italian Somaliland and 361 in the British Somaliland.[123] On the other hand, Islamic scholars, through the policy of containment, were oppressed and marginalized, although some of them were later incorporated. For instance, Sorrentino, who was the Italian commissioner in Mogadishu in 1896, distributed 296 Thalers to

---

122. Exceptions are the interest of Professor Mukhtar in this issue in the *Historical Dictionary of Somalia* and the work edited by Said Samatar, who questions conventional historiography in re-examining the Qaadiriyah and Saalixiyah and emphasizes the need for more research.
123. Abdurahman Abdullahi, *Tribalism and Islam*, 229.

the notables and Islamic scholars "to gather friends for Italy."[124] Islam was perceived by the colonial power as a menace to the colonizers' so-called "civilizing mission" and cultural hegemony, and therefore, had to be sidelined. Most of these scholars were either actively resisting colonial incursion through violent means or sought to persuade the masses against collaborating with the infidels "Gaalada". However, after the failure of an armed resistance and the triumph of colonialism, a new approach was gradually developed. Colonial powers also adopted more sensitive methods to satisfy the religious sentiments of the population and initiated a policy of "winning people's hearts and minds". This approach led colonial governments; in particular the Italian fascists, to construct mosques, respect Islamic scholars, accept Islamic laws in their most sensitive aspects such as in the family affairs, and establish Islamic courts employing Islamic scholars as magistrates and judges.[125]

The second stage began with the long process of creating an elite with a new vision for the society and the state. The colonial powers endeavored to employ more Somalis in the lower echelons of the colonial civil and military labor force and opened selective schools, in which children of the traditional elite were given priority and privilege.[126] In line with this strategy, the Somali territories were gradually incorporated and absorbed into the colonial economic and political system. However, the anti-colonial sentiment of the early years did not die out entirely but was transformed into a modern and

---

124. Robert Hess, *Italian Colonialism*, 33.
125. Itlain built mosques remain functing in Baidoa, Beledweyne and Dhagaxbuur.
126. Pankhurst, Sylvia. *Ex-Italian Somaliland*, 212, 214.

peaceful political struggle for independence.[127] In practice, the modern state formation in Somalia had begun with the establishment of social organizations that were different in form and functions from the traditional institutions such as the religious establishments of mainly Sufi orders and clan leadership. These organizations initially began in the British Somaliland and later in the southern Somalia, under the rule of the British Military Administration (BMA) in 1941. Indeed, the Italian fascist rule prohibited all forms of organization in Somalia.[128] These new social organizations began with the formation of the Somali Islamic Association 1925 in Aden by the exiled Xaaji Faarax Oomaar to support his political activism and advocacy for the improved conditions of the Somalis.[129] Gradually, other organizations appeared, such as Khayriyah in 1930, which promoted welfare and education, the Officials' Union, founded in 1935 to lobby for equal rights with expatriates for Somali employees, and the offshoot of the latter, the Somali Old Boys Association (SOBA). The earlier social organizations in southern Somalia were *Jamiyat al-Kheyriyah al-Wadaniyah* (Patriotic Beneficiary Union), founded in 1942,[130] Native Betterment Committee (NBC), founded in 1942,[131] and the Somali Youth Club (SYC), founded in 1943. The modern political development of Somalia began in the early years of the

---

127. On the development of Somali nationalism see Saadia Touval. *Somali Nationalism: International Politics and the Drive for Unity in the Horn of Africa* (Cambridge: Cambridge University Press, 1963).
128. Lewis, *A History*, 121.
129. See Touval, *Somali Nationalism*, 65.
130. Mohamed Mukhtar, *Historical dictionary*, 106. Also, Salah Mohamed Ali, *Hudur and the History of Southern Somalia* (Cairo: Mahda Bookshop Publisher, 2005), 340.
131. Abdurahman Abdullahi, "Non-state Actors in the Failed State of Somalia: Survey of the Civil Society Organizations during the Civil War (1990-2002)." *Darasat Ifriqiyah*, 31 (2004): 57-87. See Salah Mohamed Ali, *Hudur*, 361.

Second World War, after the 1941 defeat of Italian Fascism in the Horn of Africa and the establishment of the BMA in most parts of the Somali territories. The BMA, although it had completely destroyed existing small economic projects and infrastructures, brought an improved political environment by abolishing the "restrictions of the Italian regime on local political associations and clubs."[132] The destroyed or removed projects by the BMA include the railway line connecting Mogadishu, Afgooye, and Villagio Della Abruzi; Afgooye Bridge; salt production machinery in Xaafuun; and Majayaan and Qandala mines.[133] This new policy encouraged advances in the political consciousness of the Somalis after many of them had participated in the two wars: the Italian–Ethiopian War of 1935 and the Second World War (1941-45). As a result, the Somali Youth Club (SYC), a pan-Somali youth organization, was formed on 15 May 1943 in Mogadishu with the encouragement of the BMA.[134] From its founding membership of 13 men, this club developed into political party in 1947 and was renamed the Somali Youth League (SYL).[135]

Comparable rise in political consciousness was appearing in the British Somali Protectorate, and this led to the establishment

---

132. I. M. Lewis, *A Modern History,* 121.
133. See Poalo Tripodi, *The Colonial Legacy in Somalia: Rome and Mogadishu: from Colonial Administration to Operation Restore Hope* (London: Macmillan Press, 1999), 45.
134. On the relations between SYC and BMA, refer to Cederic Barnes, "The Somali Youth League, Ethiopian Somalis and the Greater Somali Idea c1946-1948". Journal of East African Studies, v.1, no.2, 2007, 277-291.
135. The founding fathers of modern Somali Nationalism are: Haji Maxamad Xussein, Maxamad Xirsi Nuur (Sayidi), Cabdulqaadir Sakhaa-Uddin, Cali Xasan Maxamad (verduro), Dheere Xaaji Dheere, Maxamad Cali Nuur, Daahir Xaaji Cusman, Maxamad Cabdullahi Faarax (Xayesi), Khaliif Hudow Maxamad, Maxamuud Faarah Hilowle (Farnaajo), Yaasin Xaaji Cusman, Maxamad Cusman Baarbe, and Cusman Geedi Raage. See, Abdulaziz Ali Ibrahim "Xildhiban", *Taxanaha Taariikhda Somaaliya* (London: Xildhiban Publications, 2006), 13.

of the party known as the Somali National League (SNL) in 1951. These two major parties, the SYL and the SNL, adopted corresponding nationalist platforms by the 1950s. At the same time, other particularistic parties were shifting toward a similar nationalist course. In 1950, the former Italian colony was returned to Italy under the UN trusteeship after a five-year debate on the future of the Italian colonies defeated in the Second World War. According to the UN mandate, Italy had to manage the colony and bring it to full independence in 1960. This episode concludes one chapter of southern Somalia's experience in changing administrations from early attempts of creating Italian colony (1889-1923), Italian fascist rule (1923-1941) and British Military Administration (1941-1950) to a post-war Italy (1950-1960).[136] Italy took responsibility to prepare southern Somalia for independence in a very short time, with a significant shortage of financial resources.[137] During this formative period, some prominent Islamic figures were incorporated into the process for the trusteeship to gain popular support and legitimacy. However, most Islamic scholars were focusing on socio-cultural activities, watching suspiciously for the rise of the new elites and colonial domination. Northwestern Somalia remained in the British protectorate since 1888 until the Somali independence 1960 except for 8 moths under Italian occupation (August 1940- March 1941) in

---

136. Sally Healy argues that perhaps because of "frequently shifting colonial administrations", Somali nationalists envisioned the possibility of new territorial arrangement. See Sally Healy, "Reflections on the Somali state: What Went Wrong and why it Might not Matter." In *Milk and Peace, Drought and War: Somali Culture, Society and Politics* edited by Markus Hoehne and Virginia Luling (London: Hurst&Company, 2010), 271.
137. In 1951, the budget of the Italian administration was cut by a quarter. See Tripodi, *The Colonial Legacy*, 60-61.

the Second World War.

Finally, the new era of nationalistic fervor had begun in Somalia as part of a changing world after the end of the Second World War, and there ensued the rise of national liberation movements in the colonized territories. As Saadia Touval examined, four main factors were the cornerstones of such national consciousness in Somalia.[138] These are the religious contradiction between Somali Muslims and Christian colonizers, state borders that divided the Somali territory, intervening natural posture of Somali nomads, and the fact that colonial powers were subverting each other, which sometimes worked for the benefit of the Somalis, invigorating the consciousness of their unity. Somali Islamic scholars were not only reviving Islam but also have laid the foundation of the national identity. They infused Islamic and national identities into their binary distinction of "Muslims versus Christians" in their confrontation with neighboring Ethiopia and their encounters with the European colonial powers.[139] They had also maintained or invented genealogies linking many Somali clans to Arab ancestry. However, in the era of nationalism, the monopoly of Islamic scholars as the only educated group in society was over and a new generation that was educated in the colonial schools was taking the lead. These new elites, encouraged by the colonial states and establishing their own systems of laws and different cultural values, were mimicking the Europeans. As a result, rising nationalism, secularism, and westernization were spreading rapidly to the annoyance of Islamic scholars, who were marginalized in the process. This

---

138. Touval, *Somali nationalism*, 61-84.
139. Ibid., 62.

background is aimed to provide the historical dimension to the account of the modern Islamic movement and its dislocation within the modern state and society.

Conclusion

Although there is no precise date for the advent of Islam in Somalia, historians generally agree that Islam reached Somalia peacefully through trade and migration in the first century of the Muslim Calendar (700-800 AD). It was a safe refuge for the oppressed groups from the continuous conflicts in Arabian Peninsula and beyond. These groups, upon their arrival, established coastal towns and introduced new technologies and ideas. The Islamization of the Somali peninsula was gradual through assimilation and cultural infusion, and provided the Somali people with a worldly outlook, vibrancy, and partial changes in their modes of production in the religious settlements and urban trading centers. As a result, a new form of governance emerged among the Muslim population in the Horn of Africa, particularly in the Adal emirates that were headquartered in Saylac and Harrar. In the sixteenth century, the two superpowers of the world, the Ottoman Empire and Portugal, were at loggerheads in the Indian Ocean, and both Somali Sultanates and Ethiopian Empire were drawn into the superpower rivalry, played out in religious sentiments. The strongest of these Muslim principalities was the Ajuran dynasty that thrived for more than 300 years between 15th to 17th centuries. However, this dynasty had declined with Portugal's blockades of the Indian Ocean coast, nomadic incursions from the interior, and due to its dictatorial political culture. From around 1800 onward, Somali territories began to slightly integrate into the Islamic world. The Ottoman Empire, Egypt, and Oman were Muslim countries that attempted to incorporate parts of Somali territories into their sphere of influence.

Islam was taking strong strides among Somalis since 19th century with improved systems of Islamic education, increased settlement and urbanization, and revitalization of the Sufi orders. The process of Islamic education begins with the memorization of the Qur'an, followed by a community-supported system of higher Islamic studies and Sufi order attachments. Two major centers of Islamic learning have developed: the Banaadir coastal cities and Harrar and Jigjiga areas in the western parts of Somalia. From these centers, Islamic education and Sufi orders were being revived, reorganized, and spread throughout Somalia. These orders were linked with Mecca, Yemen, and Baghdad. The impact of the Sufi orders in Somalia is enormous; their emergence diluted the rigid clan divisions and proved the irrelevance of clan affiliations in the Sufi leadership. Sufi orders were generally interconnected and focused on their economic viability through establishing agricultural colonies and converting roving nomads into settled communities. Overwhelming majority of the Islamic scholars was anti-colonial but acted differently. Islamic scholars and Sufi orders were in agreement that Islam begins with education and therefore, focused on spreading Islamic education. The result of their concerted efforts and legacy is that Somalia remains an orthodox Sunni territory with unified Shafi'i jurisprudence.

Islamic scholars have left a lasting imprint on the history of Islam in Somalia, and their disciples, scattered in different locations and clans, are continuing to convey the message of Islam and the Sufi rituals. In the colonial encounter, both militancy and moderation were used as they suited the conditions in the northern and southern parts. Nevertheless, Somali people were completely incorporated into the colonial system by 1927 when the last local dynasty was conquered and native leaders were totally integrated into the colonial system of governance. After 15 years of disorientation from 1927 to 1943, a new social and political organization emerged led by the new political elites. The traditional system was gradually declining, and a new era of incorporation of Somalia into the secular world system appeared. Within this system, a new form of Islamic movement emerged in a chain of successive stages in reaction to and relation with modern statehood. The next chapter will deal with the initial stage.

CHAPTER TWO

The Rise of Islamic Consciousness (1950-1967)

Islam and Somaliness were harmonious terms used to signify pan-clan anti-colonial ideologies, resisting both Christian colonialism and growing westernization.[1] As was discussed in the second chapter, Islamic scholars were alienated from leadership positions in the 1930s and the new elites were steadily taking over national leadership. During this period, the role of Islam as a common faith and belief system was plainly understood by the general public, regardless of their level of Islamic commitment, personal piety, and Sufi order affiliation.[2] However, consciousness of the political aspect of Islam that aimed to create a state and society based on definitive references to Islam had not yet developed. The common vision and strategic priority of the Somali people before independence was centered on the liberation of the country from the colonial yoke, while after independence, this vision involved bringing together the divided Somali nation colonized by different colonial states. Indeed, general Islamic consciousness was always at a high level because of its role in championing the Muslim cause in the Horn of Africa and due to Somalia's

---

1. Historically, Somalis and other Muslims in the Horn of Africa were fighting Ethiopia and European colonialists, considered to be Christian. This conflict is rooted to the 15th century push-pull wars between Muslims and Ethiopian Empire in the Horn of Africa. Similarly, in the 19th century, Somali responce to the European colonialism was manifested in religious terms.
2. In Somalia, Islam is a common identity; therefore, Somaliness became synonymous with Muslimness.

geographical location at the Christian-Muslim converging lines.³ Moreover, as a strategic region connecting the oil-rich Arabian Peninsula with the Suez Canal and the Indian Ocean, it had attracted European colonialism and Cold War superpower rivalry, further niggling and provoking both Islamic and nationalistic consciousnesses.

Thus, both national and Islamic identity and consciousness were intertwined in the historical development of Somalia, offering supra-clan identity to the traditional society for which primordiality is a key factor. What these two ideologies have in common is the inculcation in people a rejection of foreign domination and a call to resist it. Because of this commonality, both Islamic and nationalistic slogans were used indiscriminately to mobilize the masses for anti-colonial campaigns. These dual ideologies and forms of struggle gave rise to a successive chain of methods (armed or peaceful) for liberating the nation from the colonial yoke in diverse conditions and contexts. At the same time, the nationalist elites, besides eliminating colonialism, aimed to create a national ideology and national symbols that would conform to the accepted norms of established world order that led to an independent Somali nation-state. Consequently, Somali nationalists, although were not openly advocating secularism, were aware of global trends and were very selective in their ways of employing Islam within nationalist aspirations. Thus, they established around 1960 and 1970 Islamic leaders, such as

---

3. Somalia was in conflict with Ethiopia and Kenya because of the colonial legacy that attached parts of Somali territories to Kenya and Ethiopia. In both these countries, Christianity is dominant. For more details on the Somali conflict with its neighbours, see Saadia Touval, *Somali Nationalism: International Politics and the Drive for Unity in the Horn of Africa* (Cambridge: Cambridge University Press, 1963).

Imam Aḥmad Ibrāhīm (Gurey) and Sayid Maxamad Cabdulle Xasan, as national heroes and symbols.[4] Both of them played a crucial role in leading historical wars with Ethiopian and European powers.[5] Other elements that prompted the development of the national and Islamic consciousness were religious antagonism between the "Christian infidels" and Somali Muslims, given that it is "exceedingly difficult and humiliating for a Muslim society to accept non-Muslim rule."[6] Christian missionary activities had been resented in earlier times by the Somalis; as such activities were considered a threat to the Islamic faith. The earliest missionaries were French Catholics who began activities in British Somaliland in 1891, as well as the Roman Catholic Church in Mogadishu and the Swedish Overseas Lutheran Church in Kismaayo, established in 1896. Furthermore, the Mennonite Mission and the Sudan Interior Mission joined the Christian venture in the 1950s, with the return of Italy as the UN trusteeship administrator. Details

---

4. To eternalize their historical memory as great leaders of the Muslim nation, both these two Islamic scholars were recognized as national heroes. Manifesting their role, their statues had been erected in the capital city of Mogadishu in 1971. During the civil war, both sculptures were destroyed in claiming that Islam prohibits statues that are complete and solid figures. On the Islamic viewpoint, see Al-Qardawi, *al-halal wa al-Haram fi al-Islam* (International Islamic Federation of Student Organizations, 1989), 97-104. However, there were also economic reasons as well as deliberate destruction of all artefacts in Somalia.
5. Imam Ahmed fought against Ethiopian and Portuguese intervention forces, representing Christian superpowers of that time, from 1531 until he was killed in 1543. Ahmad's war with Ethiopia is described in detail in the *Futuh al-habaša* ("The Conquest of Ethiopia"), written in Arabic by Ahmad's follower *Shihāb al-Addin Aḥmad ibn 'Abdulqādir*. Sayid Maxamad fought against Ethiopia and Britain in 1900-1921. References on Sayid Mohamed are many; however, two academic works stand out: Abdi Sheik Abdi, *Divine Madness: Mohammed Abdulle Hassan (1856-1920)* (Zed Books Ltd., London, 1993), and Said S. Samatar,*Oral Poetry and Somali Nationalism: The Case of Sayyid Mahammad Abdille Hasan* (Cambridge: Cambridge University Press, 1982).
6. Touval, *Somali Nationalism*, 62.

of the Somali responses to the Christian venture will be elaborated in later sections.

Besides the commonalities between Islam and nationalism stated above, the rising Islamic consciousness was specifically linked with the development of Arabic education and connections with the Arab/Islamic world. The Arabic language is the language of the Qur'an, the language of the Prophet Muhammad in which his traditions are recorded, and the language of Islamic jurisprudence and business transactions in pre-colonial Somalia. Somali nationalists, however, were divided on the importance of the Arabic language and relations with the Arab world. Their polarization into pro-Western and pro-Arabic/Islamic factions was gradually developing in the 1950s, along with the development of modern education. Moreover, because of Somalia's strategic location during the Cold War era, this country witnessed strong competition between the Eastern block, represented by the Soviet Union and China, and the Western block, represented by the former colonial masters and the USA. Within these local, regional, and international dynamics, Islamic consciousness began to emerge and grow.

The development of Islamic consciousness in general should be seen as a historical evolution and as a response to the challenges of various tensions. The early Islamic revival, pioneered by the emerging Sufi orders, had played on the preservation of Islamic faith and its advancement to new frontiers and countered early colonial incursions militarily and culturally. When the first confrontation failed to fend off European challenges, modern Islamic consciousness emerged for a new round of encounters. This chapter will examine the cultural and political foundations of the emergence of this

Islamic consciousness. It examines the role of Islam and its revival in the period from 1950 to 1967 in the context of changing political and cultural conditions in Somalia. This takes place in the formative period of the Somali state and the early years of independence (1960-1967). Specifically, this chapter will explore factors underlying the emergence of Islamic consciousness in the 1950s and 1960s. These factors will be classified into two categories: Factors strengthening capacity of the Islamic consciousness and factors provoking Islamic consciousness.

Strengthening Factors of the Islamic Consciousness

Somalia's proximity to the Arabian Peninsula resulted in a strong linguistic and cultural influence, carrying with it the Islamic faith. The impact of this influence reached a pinnacle when Somalia joined the Arab League in 1974, although its Arab nationalism and identity remained weak.[7] Most Somali clans boast Arab descent and developed genealogies that connect them to Arab ancestry albeit strong scholarly arguments posit that Somali origin is from the Lake Turkanaareain northern Kenya.[8]

---

7. Arab nationalism did not develop in Somalia, although most of the Somali clans attach their genealogy to Arab ancestry. One of the reasons may be internal division of the Somalis and their entanglement in attempts to unite the Somali territories through Somali nationalism. Joining the Arab League was primarily motivated by economic reasons and was the accumulative impact of Arab education since the 1950s. The Arab League is a regional organization of Arab states formed in Cairo on March 22, 1945; it currently has 22 members. See official website available from http://www.arableagueonline.org/las/index.jsp (accessed on June 16, 2009).
8. Herbert S. Lewis, "The Origins of the Galla and SomaliAuthor".*The Journal of African History*,Vol. 7, No. 1 (1966), 27-46.

Five Arab countries in particular have had direct historical links with Somalia: Egypt, Saudi Arabia, Oman, Yemen, and Sudan. The cultural influence of these countries was swinging from time to time, proportional to their socio-economic development and strategic goals. For instance, the influence of Oman was limited to its nominal rule over parts of Somalia in the nineteenth century, which ended in selling its "property" to the Italians in 1905.[9] On the other hand, Yemen had the strongest connection with the Somalis in terms of reciprocal settlements of the populations and commercial linkages.[10] In 1956, the Yemeni community in Mogadishu was so numerous that they were offered four seats in the legislative assembly consisting of 70 seats.[11] Conversely, according to the statistics of 1955, 10,600 Somalis lived in Aden among 103,900 Yemenis which means 10% of its population.[12] Moreover, *Zabīd*, the famous Islamic learning center in Yemen, was where many Somali Islamic scholars were educated. Somali students frequented this place during the annual Hajj "pilgrimage" and brought back affiliations to Sufi orders and Islamic knowledge.[13] Indeed, the Shaaficiyah jurisprudence and the Qaadiriyah order were introduced to Somalia through Yemeni scholars who

---

9. On January 13, 1905, Italy purchased the Banaadir Ports [Mogadishu and its environs] for 144,000 pounds or 3,600,000 Lire and began to administer over Somalia directly in place of the earlier Banaadir commercial company. See Robert Hess, *Italian colonialism in Somalia* (Chicago: University of Chicago Press, 1966), 86.
10. Edward Alpers, *The Somali community at Eden in the Nineteenth Century* (North-eastern Studies Volume 8, No. 2-3, 1986), 143-168.
11. I. M. Lewis, *A Modern History of Somalia: Nation and State in the Horn of Africa* (London: Longman, 1980), 145.
12. Najmi Abdul-Majid, *Eden (1839-1967)* (Markaz Ubadi li darsat wa Nashr, 2007), 259.
13. Zabid is a town on Yemen's western coastal plain and is one of the oldest towns in Yemen. It was the capital of Yemen from the 13th to the 15th century and a center of the Arab and Muslim world due, in large part, to its being a center of Islamic education.

propagated them in Harrar and Mogadishu. Yemen, through its historical migrations and settlements in Somalia, injected a major cultural influence and provided Islamic education for generations.[14] Somalis of Yemeni origin in Mogadishu were custodians of the Arabic language and Islamic culture pioneering its role in education and society. However, their political and cultural influence in the period 1950-1967 was comparably low. With respect to the influence of Sudan, it is important to note that Sudan does not share a border with Somalia, and initially its influence was rather indirect. The Sufi masters Ibrahim al-Rashid and Sayid Mohamed Salah of Sudanese origins living in Mecca introduced Axmadiyah and its Saalixiyahoffshoots through Somali disciples. In addition, both countries promoted anti-colonial Islamic Jihad with the same ideological background as the *Mahdiyah* movement in Sudan and the Darawiish Movement in Somalia.[15] In the modern era, however, relations between the two countries were bolstered through shared British colonial experience and working within British colonial establishment. Moreover, modern education in British Somaliland was rooted in the British-established Gordon College and *Bakht al-Riḍāh* Institute of Educationin Sudan, so that modern elites from British Somaliland were educated primarily in Khartoum and co-educated with their Sudanese colleagues. These elites who pioneered modern education in

---

14. Early Islamic scholars in Banaadir originated from Yemen and Hadramout in particular. Sheikh Abiikar Muxdaar, known as "Sheikh al-Shuyuukh" (the teacher of teachers), and other prominent Islamic scholars originally arrived from Yemen.
15. The *Mahdiyah* Movement was founded by Muḥammad Aḥmad Al Mahdi (1844-1885) who proclaimed himself the Mahdi (the prophesied redeemer of Islam who will appear at the end of times) in 1881 and declared a *Jihad* against Anglo-Egyptian authority in Sudan. He raised an army and led a successful religious war to topple the Anglo-Egyptian rule of Sudan.

Somaliland are exemplified by the father of modern education in British Somaliland, Maxamuud Axmad Cali, and many of his colleagues who were educated in Sudan. Maxamuud Axmad Cali was the first Somali student to join the school which *Salāḥ al-Addīn* Club founded in Berbera in 1932 by Moḥamed 'Ali Luqmān al-Muḥāmi, a Yemeni scholar who worked for a business company called Antonan headquartered in Aden. As al-Muḥāmirelates in his letter:

> In Berbera, I have opened a school and a club of *Salāḥ al-Addīn* with the contribution of the Arab and Indian Muslim businessmen. Then, I organized [a] football team. I made a speech in the mosque about the backwardness of the Somalis and Arabs in the country. Many youth surrounded me and among them was Maxamuud Axmad Cali whom I convinced to leave his village and to accept a scholarship to Sudan.[16]

In addition to that, it was reported that the first modern school in British Somaliland was opened in the 1930s by the Sudanese teacher Kheyr al-Allah, an employee inthe British protectorate. This teacher, as reported by Hasan Makki, worked in the school opened by Moḥamed 'Ali Luqmān in Berbera.[17] The Sudanese government's role was marginal in the period under investigation, despite the fact that its role increased after the 1970s with the emergence of the modern Islamic movement in Sudan.[18] As for the Saudi Arabian influence, that country was

---

16. Translation from Arabic by the author. See Moḥamed Ali Luqmān Al-Muḥāmi. *Rijālun wa Shu' ūnun wa Diktiyāt* (Yemen: 2009), 177. Also, collected works of Al-Muḥāmi, Moḥamed Ali Luqmān (Nov. 6, 1898-March 22, 1966).*Rāid al-Nahdah al-fikriyah wa al-adabiyah al-hadīthah fi al-Yaman* (collected works, Yemen, 2005), 483.
17. Makki, *Al-Siyasāt*, 87.
18. The Muslim Brotherhood was introduced to Sudan in 1949; however, its effective organizational establishment took place in 1954. It took over power through military coup on 30 June, 1989.

lagging behind economically and educationally during the 1950s and 1960s. Therefore, beyond being the abode of the holy shrines of Mecca and Medina, where Somali Muslims traveled frequently for pilgrimage, with some of them remaining there, Saudi Arabia did not have much influence to offer. A few prominent Islamic scholars who were educated there introduced Salafiyah/Wahabiyah school of Sheikh Moḥamed Bin 'Abdiwahhāb in Somalia. However, the strong Saudi influence on Somalia began in the 1970s after the opening of the first Saudi-sponsored Institute of Islamic Solidarity in Mogadishu and subsequent confrontation with the Soviets and their influence in Somalia.[19] Moreover, the oil economic boom attracted thousands of Somali laborers and students who were admitted to the Saudi universities to challenge the socialist military regime in Somalia.[20] In the period 1950-1967, Egypt exercised the strongest influence on Somalia among all Arab states, and it left a lasting imprint on this country. On these grounds, focus will be directed to the role of Egypt in the development of Somali nationalism and its cultural competition with Western countries. The Sudanese factor in modern education in the British Somaliland will also be explored.

Egyptian Cultural and Political Influence on Somalia

The Somali territories always constituted one of the Egyptian strategic areas of interest, its connection being historically

---

19. The Institute of Islamic Solidarity was opened in 1968 by the Islamic League. See 'Abdi-shakūr 'Abdulqādir, "Lamḥatun 'an al-saḥwa al-Islamiyah fi Al-Somāl." Available from http://www.aljazeera-online.net/index.php?t=9&id=31 (accessed on 23 June, 2010).
20. Sheikh Maxamad Garyare interviewed by the author on June 17, 2009, Toronto, Canada.

based; Egypt even temporarily occupied parts of Somali peninsula and attempted to annex it in the nineteenth century.[21] Moreover, the centrality of Egypt in the Middle East and Africa was unquestionable. Egypt was taking the leading role in the Arab world in the 1950s and was also one of the founding countries of the Non-Aligned Movement of positive neutrality.[22] The prestige of the Egyptian Revolution and the charismatic image of the Egyptian President Jamāl 'Abdi al-Nāsser (1918-1970); as well as the ideology of Arab nationalism with its strong propaganda machine, was influencing every country in the Arab world. In addition, the Islamic activism of the Muslim Brotherhood (MB) and its ardent opposition to the popular regime, with the consequent repression of its members, also inspired and attracted some people. The clash between the Egyptian revolutionary regime and the MB in the 1950s represented a developing ideological conflict in the Arab world that was being replicated in other countries.

The modern Islamic Revival in the Arab Middle East evolved at the beginning of the 19th century when Jamāl al-Addīn al-Afghāni (1839-1897) and his disciple Moḥamed 'Abdou (1849-1905) called for the reform of Islamic thought.[23] Their movement was in response to foreign intervention in Egypt and offered a formula for Muslims to be selective in

---

21. Mohamed Osman Omar. *The Scramble in the Horn of Africa: History of Somalia (1827-1977)* (Mogadishu: Somali publications, 2001), 72-92.
22. The Non-Aligned Movementwas an international organization of the third world countries organized to safeguard their sovereignty in the polarized world during the Cold War. It was founded in April 1955, and the Egyptian President Jamāl 'Abdi Nāsser was one of the founders demonstrating leadership at the global stage.
23. Nikki R. Keddie, "*Sayyid Jamal al-Din "Al-Afghani*" in 'Alī Rāhnamā (ed.) *Pioneers of Islamic Revival* (Palgrave Macmillan, 1994), 11-29.*also*, Yvonne Haddad, "*Mohamed Abdu: Pioneer of Islamic Reform*" in 'Alī Rāhnamā (ed.) *Pioneers of Islamic Revival* (Palgrave Macmillan, 1994), 30-63.

adopting some elements of Western civilization while maintaining their faith and value system. Moreover, by 1928, the MB was founded by Hasan al-Banna (1906-1949) and provided the organizational setting and programs aiming at the application of Islam to politics and public life.[24] However, the Egyptian Revolution of 1952, which brought Jamāl 'Abdi al-Nāsser to power later sought to modernize Egypt through Arab nationalism and socialist transformation. Wishing to foster a closer alliance with the Soviet Union, 'Abdi-Nāsser perceived the MB as his regime's biggest ideological threat. Hence, this organization was banned and thousands of its members were imprisoned. As a result, MB members went underground and many of them migrated to other countries, vehemently spreading their ideology. Gradually, in connection with locally created similar institutions, the Egyptian Islamic phenomenon was transformed into a worldwide Islamic movement. This Egyptian cultural influence, through written literature and radio broadcasts, has introduced to Somalia, ideologies of Arab nationalism and MB, influencing Somali nationalists and Islamists respectively.

In general, the major Egyptian external policies during Nasser's era were shaped by considerations of thecountry's relationship to Western dominance, Egypt's homogenizing role in the Arab world, and its challenge of Israel. In addition to Islamic solidarity and historical links, relations between Somalia and Egypt had strategic dimensions and developed into reciprocal geopolitical and ideological imperatives in the 1950s,

---

24. On the academic history of Muslim brotherhood in English language see Richard Mitchell, *TheSocietyoftheMuslimBrothers* (London: Oxford University Press, 1969). Also, see Brynjar Lia, *The Society of the Muslim Brothers in Egypt: The Rise of an Islamic Mass Movement* (Reading, UK: Garnet, 1998).

applied at both state and non-state levels. At the state level, the underlying dynamic was that Egypt's interest in the Horn of Africa became contingent upon its strategic interests in the River Nile and the Suez Canal.[25] These two waterways constitute economic arteries through which the lifeblood flows that have long shaped Egyptian history and its relations with other nations. Somalia, being located at the southern outlet of the Red Sea into the Indian Ocean, stands as a strategic backdrop to the Suez Canal politics. Moreover, Somalia had a disputed border with Ethiopia, a country that is the major source of the Nile water and one with which Egypt has uneasy relations. This locates Somalia within the vital sphere of the Nile politics as well. On the other hand, the strategic imperative of Somalia's relations with Egypt has emanated mainly from its drive for pan-Somali irredentist politics of the "Greater Somalia" and its strategic relations with the Arab countries. Integral to this drive was the demand that the Somali-inhabited region of Ethiopia must be united with the Somali Republic. Consequently, the Somali foreign relations and domestic politics have been doggedly focused on seeking all possible avenues of support for its nationalistic aspirations.

Bearing in mind the strategic considerations stated above, Egypt became an active member in the discussions on the future of Italian colonies such as Eritrea, Libya, and Somalia that have been conducted by the four powers (USA, France, Britain and Soviet Union) and other interested countries since 1947.[26]

---

25. Abdullahi Osman, "The Role of Egypt, Ethiopia the Blue Nile in the Failure of the Somali Conflict Resolutions: A Zero-Sum Game" (paper presented at the annual meeting of the International Studies Association, Hilton Hawaiian Village, Honolulu, Hawaii, 2005).

26. On 19 September 1945, British Foreign Secretary Mr. Bevin had declared that Egypt substantially contributed to the allies' victory in Africa and that Egypt's interest on

Moreover, Egypt became an active member of the UN Advisory Council, consisting of Egypt, Columbia, and the Philippines, acting as a watchdog in Somalia under the UN trusteeship.[27] Consequently, the Egyptians used the opportunity of their direct presence in Somalia to take forward their connections with the Somalis and their emerging nationalist leaders. Egyptian special space among the Somali people was directed at arousing Islamic sentiment and nationalistic solidarity, linking Egyptian elites with nationalist elites as well as with Islamic preachers and scholars. In particular, Egyptian Ambassador Kamāl al-Addīn Salāḥ played an important role in networking Somali nationalist movements with Egyptian Arab nationalism. Kamāl al-Addīn opposed writing Somali language with the Latin alphabet and pushed the Somali Youth League (SYL) leaders toward Egypt through education and scholarships.[28] Because of Ambassador Kamal's impressive success in achieving many of these goals, adversaries to the Arab/Islamic trend assassinated him in April 1957.[29] By 1957, Egypt had been advancing its Somali engagement on two main fronts and had already shown some tangible progress. The first

---

the settlement on former Italian colonies was understandable. The Egyptian position was closer to the British position in a number of points (Salah Mohamed Ali, *Hudur and History of Southern Somalia*. Cairo: Nahda Book publisher, 2005), 294.

27. The first Egyptian representative in Somalia was Mr. *Moḥamed Rajab*, who was replaced by Ambassador *Kamāl al- Addin Sālah* in 1953.
28. One such example is the scholarship offered to Sakhaa-uddin, the prominent leader of the SYL.
29. *Kamāl al- Addin Sālaḥ*was assassinated in April 1957 by Maxamad Sheikh Cabdiraxman known as "Wiilow". The assassin was sentenced to a life term in jail. *Kamāl al- Addin* was given first-class honours; the Egyptian Cultural Club in Mogadishu bears his name. See, Mohamed Mukhtar, *Historical Dictionary of Somalia* (African Historical Dictionary Series, 87. Lanham, MD: Scarecrow Press, 2003), 130.Also, Makki, *Al-Siyāsāt*, 117.For a detailed description of the role of *Kamāl al-Addin* and his assassination, see Aḥmed Bahā al-Addīn, *Mu' āmaratūn fi Ifrīqiyah* (Qāhira: Dar Ihyā al-kutub al- 'Arabiyah, 1956).

front was coaching and nurturing like-minded pro-Egyptian politicians among the rising political and Islamic leaders. The secondcomplementary program was to make education the breeding ground for future leaders and a priority for the development of the country and its cultural linkages.[30]

Regarding coaching and nurturing political leaders, Egypt had good relations with the Somali Youth Leagues (SYL), being the only Arab country that was a member of the interested governments in the 1947 conference with the big four powers on the issue of Somalia's future.[31] It also responded positively to the demands of the SYL to provide early educational assistance. The SYL opposed the return of Italy to Somalia and its relations with Italy were marred by tensions after the UN mandated Italy to administer Somalia. Revolutionary Egypt under Nasser with its anti-imperialistic propaganda was regarded as a role model whose footsteps should be followed. The powerful "Voice of Arabs" Radio (Sawt al-'Arab) in Cairo, established a Somali section and hosted many fervent Somali nationalist leaders, such as Xaaji Maxamad Xuseen, Maxamuud Xarbi and Sheikh Axmad Sheikh Muuse.[32] The speeches of these leaders were

---

30. The Egyptian member of the Advisory Council, Moḥamed Ḥasan Al-Zayāt, articulated in the beginning of the mandate the necessity to "fight illiteracy, adopt good educational plans, and create schools, more schools with better teachers." See Poalo Tripodi, *The Colonial Legacy in Somalia: Rome and Mogadishu: From Colonial Administration to Operation Restore Hope* (London: Macmillan Press, 1999), 51.
31. These countries included Australia, Belgium, Brazil, Canada, Czechoslovakia, China, Ethiopia, Greece, India, Netherlands, Poland, South Africa, Yugoslavia, Egypt, Italy and Pakistan. See Salah Mohamed Ali, *Hudur and History of Southern Somalia* (Cairo: Nahda Book Publisher, 2005), 365.
32. Maxamuud Xarbi was an ardent Somali nationalist and campaigned throughout his political career for Djibouti to unite with Somalia. After a controversial referendum in Djibouti in 1958, he had a conflict with the French authorities and left the country to live in Cairo. He later moved to Mogadishu. However, in September 1960, he and several of his associates died in a plane crash on a return trip from China to Somalia. See Touval, *Somali Nationalism*, 127. Moreover, Sheikh Axmad Sheikh Muuse is the

heard in the Somali territories, and during their time in Cairo, they made acquaintance with similar liberation movements in the Arab World. To counter the Egyptian anti-colonial propaganda of the "Voice of Arabs", Somali-language program, the British Broadcasting Corporation (BBC) Somali program was established in 1957. However, when the SYL gradually drifted toward Italy and was contained through a variety of means of persuasion, its enthusiastic nationalist orientation began to moderate; indicating the effect of what Johannes called "Political domestication" and Maxamad Shariif Maxamuud called the "wisdom and insightfulness of some leaders of SYL."[33] This trend did not please some factions in the party such as Xaaji Maxamad Xuseen who was elected as the party chairman in 1957. Xaaji Maxamad represented the Nasserite model of a non-aligned movement of positive neutrality and, as such, was considered by Italy and USA to be anti-Western and pro-Communist. The categorization of party leaders into moderates as pro-Western and radicals as anti-Western had begun within the Cold War atmosphere and political vocabulary of the time. Xaaji Maxamad's strong articulation of the "Greater Somalia" issue, using his exceptional

---

founder of *Hizbu Allah* in Burco and one of the first Somali Islamic scholars who graduated from al-AzharUniversity.

33. USA and Italy orchestrated a policy of keeping Somalia aligned with the West. Their approach was to cultivate pro-Western orientation in the dominant SYL party. Reciprocally, this had warranted the SYL the support of the West to overshadow other parties in 1956. See, OkbazghiYohannes, *The United States and the Horn of Africa: An Analytical Study of Pattern and Process* (Westview Press, 1997), 204-212. Moreover, the moderate SYL leadership, in particular Aadan Cabdulle Cusman, convinced the majority of the party central committee to follow a peaceful path and to cooperate with Italy to smoothly gain the independence within the mandated date. On this matter, see Mohamed Sharif Mohamud, "*al-Ra'is Ādan Abdulle Osman Awal Raīs li al Ja mhūriyah alSomāliyah,*" 2009, available from See http://arabic.alshahid.net/columnists/1 458 (accessed on June 6, 2010).

communication skills and mastery of the Arabic language spiced with Somali poetry and Qur'anic verses had captured the imagination of the masses and religious circles. In particular, Xaaji Maxamad received the support of many Islamic scholars for his strong Islamic tendency and support for the Arabic language and culture. However, in an orchestrated conspiracy with the participation of the USA and Italy, he was expelled from the SYL party in May 1958.[34] Xaaji Maxamad and other prominent politicians represented unwarranted competing ideologies in Somalia and established the Great Somali Party (GSP) characterized by the West as "extremist and anti-Italian position of the SYL", "an old-time nationalist rabble-rouser," and the advocate of the "pro-Egyptian policy."[35] Indeed, as later events reveal and contrary to conventional rhetoric, Western powers prevented the emergence of a democratic political culture in Somalia under the pretext of confronting communism.[36] However, the Egyptian influence on Somali politics was not weakened. Egypt kept good relations with Somalia against all challenges and after its independence signed agreements on economic, culture, and military cooperation.[37]

---

34. Poalo Tripodi, The *Colonial Legacy*, 87.
35. Tripodi characterises Xaaji Maxamad Xuseen policies as "extremist," while Touval considers him as merely pro-Egyptian. See Touval, *Somali Nationalism*, 91; and Tripodi, *Colonial Legacy*, 87. Also, the *Time Magazine* branded Xaaji Maxamad as "an old-time nationalist rabble-rouser," quoted from Elby Omar, *Fifty Years, and Fifty Stories: the Mennonite Mission in Somalia, 1953-2003* (Herald Press, 2003), 31.
36. See Yohannes, *The United States and the Horn of Africa*, 211.
37. See Touval, *Somali Nationalism*, 178.

Introduction of Arabic Schools into Somalia

The second wave of the Egyptian intervention in Somalia was in the field of education, which was experiencing exponential growth. The first direct Egyptian involvement in the education sector started in response to a request from the SYL party in 1950 for the Egyptian assistance in the field of education. This request was prompted by the fear that the Italian return to Somalia might result in the closure of the SYL schools that offered basic education.[38] The party was not on good terms with Italy and, with the encouragement of the BMA (1941-1950), was running successful schools that were in breach of the educational monopoly of the Roman Catholic Mission. The Egyptian response to the party's request was swift and affirmative, and the offer of the first 25 scholarships to the graduants of the SYL Arabic schools subsequently increased annually.[39] Moreover, Egypt dispatched two Islamic scholars from the al-Azhar Islamic establishment, Sheikh 'Abdalla al-Mashhad and Sheikh Moḥamūd Khalīfa, to propagate Islam and to explore possibilities of further Egyptian engagement in Somalia. With their report, supported by the Egyptian UN Advisory Council member, Egypt signed an agreement with the Italian UN trusteeship authority to establish al-Azhar Mission schools in Somalia. Subsequently, a team of al-Azhar scholars, initially consisting of six teachers and preachers, was dispatched to Somalia in 1953.[40] These scholars were well

---

38. Makki, *Al-Siyasāt*, 142.
39. Moḥamed Sharif Moḥamud,"Tarjumat li Sharif Moḥamud 'Abdiraḥman, Ra'is al-Rābidat al Islāmiyah," 2009. Available from http://arabic.alshahid.net/columnists/650 (accessed on April 21, 2010).
40. These scholars are: *Sheikh Abubakar Zakariya (the chairman), Sheikh Ismāīl Ḥamdi, Sheikh Yūsuf 'Abdul-mūnim Ibrahim, Sheikh Mohamed Qa'ida Aḥmad, and Sheikh Maḥamad al-Mahdi Maḥmud.* See Makki, *Al-Siyāsāt*, 142.

received by the SYL party that issued the following statement: "The Arabic language is the official language of the SYL party and all the Somali people and Arabic language is the endowment from Allah to the people of Somalia who are part of Islamic world".[41] For many SYL members and Islamic scholars in Somalia, the arrival of the prestigious al-Azhar scholars was a major encouragement toward a better Islamic future.

The first task of the al-Azhar Mission was to set up the Institute of the Islamic Studies in 1953 called in the Italian language, *Scoula Disciplina Islamica*.[42] The objective of the institute was to train Islamic judges and teachers of the Arabic language and Islamic studies. These qualifications were in short supply and badly needed for the Italian trusteeship administration to expand educational programs in which Arabic language and Islam had to be taught beside the Italian language. Also, parts of the court system were applying the Islamic law, which required judges qualified in Islamic jurisprudence. The Egyptian drive in the field of education was also bolstered in terms of secular education. The second Egyptian educational mission under the Egyptian Ministry of Education arrived in Somalia in 1954. This mission promoted the Arabic language and sought to provide modern education up to the secondary level using Egyptian curriculum, in line with Egyptian state schools. Within this framework, schools were opened in collaboration with the Somali Islamic League, a non-state organization founded by Islamic scholars. By 1958, with the assistance and encouragement from the Islamic League, 15 schools were built and opened in successive years in

---

41. Makki, *Al-Siyāsāt*, 142.
42. Abdurahman Abdullahi, *Tribalism, Nationalism and Islam: Crisis of the Political Loyalties in Somalia* (MA thesis, Islamic Institute, McGill University, 1992), 105.

many regions of Somalia.⁴³ It was reported that the number of students enrolled in these schools in 1958 was about 1,200.⁴⁴ Furthermore, some of the graduants of these schools were granted scholarships to Egyptian universities. In the period 1952-1959, according to Axmad Maax, Egypt provided more than 86 scholarships in different fields; however, Daily Telegraph, quoting from one Italian Member of Parliament putsit at the exaggerated number of 300 scholarships.⁴⁵ Most likely, these scholarships were about 200, as reported by Aḥmad Bahā al-Addīn.⁴⁶ The growth of these schools and their impact on the infusion of Arab/Islamic culture were remarkable. Moreover, the SYL published a weekly newspaper in the name of *al-Waxdah* in Arabic in 1957-1969.⁴⁷

In British Somaliland, development of education in general was slow due to people's suspicions of the possibility that Christianity, disguised in education, would be introduced. Islamic scholars blocked all British attempts to introduce modern education. However, when the British authority reviewed its policy and with the emergence of the new Somali elites educated in Sudan in Arabic based Islamic curriculum, modern education was launched smoothly. In contrast to Italian Somaliland, modern education in British Somaliland was directly connected to Sudan, which was also under the British

---

43. These schools were opened in Gaalkacyo, Beletweyne, Bosaaso, Kismaayo, and Baidoa. Moreover, other schools were opened in Eil, Baraave, and Marka.
44. See Moḥamed Abdul-Mumin Yūnus, *Al-Somāl Wadanan wa sha'ban* (Al-Qāhira: Dar al-Nahdah al-'Arabiyah, 1962), 67.
45. See Aḥmed Barkhat Mah, *Wathāiq 'an al-Somāl wa al-Ḥabasha wa Eriteriya* (Al-Qāhira: Shikat al-dhawbagi li Daba'āt wa Nashr, 1985), 308. Also, see Bahau Addin, *Mu'āmaratūn*, 150.
46. Bahāu al-addīn, *Mu'āmaratūn*, 102.
47. SYL weekly newspaper *Al-Waḥdah* was edited by *Moḥamed Sabri*, Cabdiraxman Faarah (Kabaweyne) and Cabdiraxman Xasan. See Makki, *Al-Siyasāt*, 150.

rule. In this way, modern education in the Arabic language was introduced by the returnees from Sudanese scholarships in 1942.[48] The first two elementary schools in the Arabic language were opened in Berbera and Burco by Maxamad Shire Maxamad "Gaab" and Yusuf Ismaciil Samatar "Gaandi," respectively, both of whom were educated in Sudan. These schools used Sudanese curriculum and textbooks.[49] Schools in other regions followed suit. In addition, more students were successively sent to Sudan and later to al-Azhar. By 1944, the British authority had re-engaged in modern education and adopted Arabic for elementary education. By 1949, it had assisted more than 29 Qur'anic schools with an enrollment of 1,250 students. This policy contrasted with the Italian system that never supported traditional Islamic education. Therefore, though education was very limited, the Arabic language flourished in northern Somalia. Moreover, there were political party schools, such as those of the SYL and Somali National League(SNL) promoting Arabic/Islamic education. Furthermore, specialized schools of Islamic studies began in 1959 with the establishment of the Burco Islamic Institute, which later became

---

48. The first Somali returnees from the *Bakht al-Riḍa* institute were Yuusuf Ismaciil Samatar, Maxamad Shire Maxamad, and Cabdisalam Xasan Mursal. See Makki, *Al-Siyasāt*, 154. Details on the history of education in the British Somaliland see Fawzia Yuusuf Xaaji Aadan, Geedi *Nololeedkii Yusuf Xaaji Aadan (1914-2005): Taariikhdiisii Halgan ee Waxbarashada, Siyaasadda, Dhaqanka, iyo Suugaanta* (London: African Publishing, 2007).
49. Sudanese textbooks and Egyptian books were also used in some schools in the Italian Somaliland. Salah Mohamed relates that HudurSchool built in 1954 used textbooks imported from Sudan. The school also used textbooks borrowed from the Egyptian elementary curriculum, imported probably by the SYL party for its schools. See Salah Mohamed Ali, *Hudur*, 255.

part of the chain of the al-Azhar schools in Somalia.⁵⁰ Another important factor for raising national and Islamic awareness in British Somaliland was the opening of Radio Hargeysa in 1943, which broadcasted in the Arabic and Somali languages. Moreover, the first modern newspaper in Arabic language appeared in 1948 under the name *Jarīdat al-Somāl*, meaning Somali Journal, published by Maxamad Jaamac Uurdoox and printed in Aden.⁵¹ By 1958, other newspapers in Arabic language had a strong presence. The most important was the weekly journal *Qarn-Ifrīqiyah* (Horn of Africa) edited by Cumar Maxamad Cabdiraxman (Cumar-dheere), which continued until 1960. This journal was famous for its strong nationalist rhetoric and advocacy for the "Greater Somalia."⁵² Another celebrated weekly newspaper in Arabic language was *al-Lewā*, edited by Axmad Yusuf Ducaale and Axmad Jimcaale. All the above points demonstrate that Arabic culture was, comparatively to the Italian Somaliland, more rooted in British Somaliland. The reasons were, besides the already mentioned contact with British Sudan, the region's proximity and direct commercial connection to Yemen.

After the independence and the unification of the former Italian Somalia and British Somaliland in July 1960, state schools became unified under a common curriculum. However, the non-state education system continued and remained free. In northern Somalia, Egyptian Arabic schools similar to those of the south were not available. Only a few Egyptian al-Azhar

---

50. The Burco Islamic Institute was one of the two al-Azhar secondary schools in Somalia. See 'Abdiraḥman al-Najjār, *al-Islāmu fi Al-Somāl* (Al-Qāhira: Madba'at Al-Ahrām Al-Tijāriyah, 1973), 45.
51. Makki, *Al-Siyāsāt*, 151.
52. Ibid, 152.

teachers were teaching at the two Islamic institutes in Hargeysa and Burco. Some of these teachers were also teaching Arabic and Islam at the state's high schools. There were also three non-governmental elementary/intermediate schools with Arabic curriculum: Sheikhada School (*al-Ḥuda li al-Banāt*), a*l-Falāḥ al-Wadaniyah* school, and a*l-Barawe* school. These schools were pioneers of the Arabic/Islamic education in Somaliland beyond elementary level. Moreover, the Egyptian library in Hargeysa played an important role in spreading Arabic/Islamic culture and became the center of Islamic awareness in northern Somalia. The library, besides providing extracurricular reading material for students of the Arabic schools, was also engaged in specific cultural activities. For instance, it imported Egyptian newspapers *al-Ahrām* and *Akhbār al-Youm* and occasionally organized Islamic lectures and screened Egyptian films. Similar cultural programs were conducted in the Mogadishu Egyptian Cultural Center. The library, with its rich supply of Arabic books and Egyptian newspapers, occasional film shows, Arabic concerts, and seasonal series of lectures, was an established part of Egyptian cultural manifestations in Somalia.

Integrating Traditional and Modern Education

Arabic-curriculum schools succeeded in solving the problem of parallel modern and traditional education. As the previous chapters described, the traditional Islamic education in the Somali territories begins with the memorization of the Qur'an in early childhood. In urban areas, while children were still in the Qur'anic schools, they also joined modern schools at the age of six, and parallel education continued for a while. Colonial governments and successive Somali regimes have failed to unify these education systems. On the other hand, in the pastoral areas where there were no schools, or where children were from poor families that cannot afford to send them to modern schools, the option was either to drop education or continue in the traditional line of education. The first social stratification begins at this early stage, and many children dropped out of education or never had an opportunity for it. Aside from many children who dropped out of the modern education for various reasons and joined the unqualified work force later, those who continued education pursued two clearly demarcated divergent routes. The first route was modern education, taught in Italian, Arabic, or English, at three levels: elementary, intermediate, and secondary. This route mostly leads either to government jobs or to the pursuit of higher education. The second route is the traditional higher Islamic education in mosque circles, which didnot provide certificates and was not recognized by the state education system, thereby rendering scholars educated in the traditional system unqualified for government jobs. The latter route was taken by the majority of students in rural areas or by those who were not happy with modern education. The question worth addressing was: What will be the future of these traditionally educated Somalis? Their education was not recognized, and their fate was marginalization. Obviously, since these students were older than 15, when they reached a certain level in the traditional education and they did not speak Italian or English, they had no hope in modern schools. The only avenue for them was the limited adult education aimed at the elimination of illiteracy.

This challenge has been dealt with in the Arabic language school system. Because of the mastery of the traditionally educated students of the Arabic language and Islamic jurisprudence, they could be considered for entry into Arabic schools. A way of dealing with this educational parallelism was introduced by Sheikh 'Abdiraḥmān al-Najjār, the head of the al-Azhar mission to Somalia in 1957-1963. To integrate the two systems without eliminating each other, he introduced a special institute for the traditional Islamic students called the Mogadishu Islamic Institute. The institute gave an opportunity for these students to be admitted after qualifying tests in Arabic and Islamic subjects. Students were admitted at either intermediate or secondary level, depending on the evaluation process. They were offered a one-year intensive program, and those who qualifiedwere admitted to either intermediate or secondary al-Azhar schools. The integrative program was very successful, and all Arabic schools established such programs in which students who qualified were admitted to the general Arabic high schools. This integration also encouraged the traditional education and offered hope for many students from rural areas or from poor families. In this way, the traditional education and modern education were networked only through Arabic-curriculum schools. Other schools with an Italian or English curriculum could not accommodate these students because they represented a complete break from tradition. In conclusion, Arabic language education was growing and by 1971 in Mogadishu alone, there were nine elementary schools, two intermediate schools, and two high schools. The famous Jamāl 'Abdi al-Nāsser high school alone had a total enrolment of 925 students.[53] There were also eight al-Azhar Islamic institutes (six intermediate- and two secondary-level schools) in

---

53. Al-Najjār, *al-Islām fi al-Somāl*, 47.

the eight regions of Somalia.⁵⁴ In total, in 1971 there were 35 Egyptian-administered schools across Somalia and about 655 teachers working in these schools and government schools with an annual budget of 1.5 million Egyptian pounds.⁵⁵ Finally, Egyptian teachers and Arabic textbooks of the Arabic language and Islamic studies were provided to the government schools, so the Egyptian influence in the Somali education was tremendous, although it still fell short in competing with the major languages of Italian and English used as the languages of administration in the country.

The Emergence of Early Islamic Organizations

Although Islamic parties did not succeed much in the political arena, they exerted major cultural influences. The Somali Islamic League and *Hizbu Allah* parties represented southern and northern versions which carried similar views on creating a closer link with the Arab/Muslim world and promoting Arabic language and Islam. The Somali Islamic League, established in 1950 in Mogadishu, was the first effective organization in Somalia after the Second World War. "Its program could be summarized as follows: (1) to work towards realizing the independence and unity of Somalia, (2) offering priority to the educational development and preservation of the cultural and Islamic identity of the country and (3) strengthening relations and cooperation with the brotherly Arabic countries."⁵⁶ The most prominent leaders of the Islamic League were Shariif

---

54. Ibid., 45.
55. 'Ali Sheikh Aḥmed Abūbakar, *Al-Da'wa al-Islāmiyah al-Mu'āsira fi Al-Qarni al-Ifrīqi* (Riyadh, Saudi Arabia: Umayya Publishing House, 1985), 68.
56. Mohamed Sharīf Moḥamūd, "Tarjumat li Sharif Moḥamūd" (the biography of Sharif Mohamud).

Maxamuud Cabdiraxman "Mara-Cadde" and Shariif al-Caydaruusi.[57] To understand the role played by Shariif Maxamuud in the Islamic movement, this study will produce here his short biography.

Short Biography of Shariif Maxamuud Cabdiraxman (1904-1994)

In his early childhood, Shariif Maxamuud lived in Luuq where he memorized the Qur'an. Then he traveled to Egypt to further his education during the Urabi Revolt and the Egyptian independence in 1923.[58] He was greatly influenced with the Egyptian politics and ideologies of Arab nationalism and MB during these years. He returned to Somalia in the 1930s during the Italian Fascism rule where he protested against fascist policies and humiliating practices against the Somalis. As a result, he was exiled to Bander Qaasin (now Bosaaso). Moreover, during the Italian–Ethiopian war where many Somalis were soldiered in the colonial army, Shariif Maxamuud refused to issue the *fatwa* allowing fighting soldiers to break fasting of the Ramadan. His rationale was that the war was between two Christian countries, and Muslims had nothing to do with it. His refusal enraged Italian colonists who were trying to propagandize the war as a legitimate war. Furthermore, when the MBA tried to impose the Kiswahili language in Somalia, he mobilized Islamic scholars and aborted the attempt, insisting on preserving the role of the Arabic language. He was

---

57. Sheikh Cabdiraxman Hussein Samatar interviewed by the author on October 30, 2009, Nairobi, Kenya. Also, see Mukhtar, *Historical Dictionary*, 199.
58. This short biography is based on writing of the son of Shariif Maxamuud in his brief biography, Mohamed Sharīf Moḥamūd, "Tarjumat li Sharif Moḥamūd".

again exiled to the town of Baraawe in an attempt to contain his continuous agitation against colonial policies. In the early years of SYL, Shariif Maxamuud was one of their leading members and its spokesperson during the visit of the four-power commission in 1948. His oratory and articulations were prominent in putting forth national issues and explaining the wishes of the Somali people. However, he resigned from the SYL in the late 1940s for unknown reason and founded the Somali Islamic League (SIL) in 1950. The main focus of this organization was the preservation of Islamic /Arabic heritage against westernization, secularization, and Christianization.

The conviction of Shariif Maxamuud that Somalia belongs to the Arab world was unparalleled. For instance, during the Great Palestinian Revolution led by Sheikh Amīn al-Ḥuseini in 1936-38, he mobilized Somali masses for support and assistance. His sermons and speeches in the mosques have been raising the awareness of the Somali masses for the plight of thePalestinian people. Moreover, he established an intimate relation with Arab countries and in particular Egypt. He devotedly supported Egypt in the tripartite invasion in 1957 of Israel, France and Britain and collected donations from the Somali people which were delivered to the Egyptian authorities. In addition, he met the President of Egypt Jamāl Abdi al-Nāsser and Anwar al-Sādāt who was during this time chairman of the Islamic Solidarity. Shariif Maxamuud's connections and relations with the Arab countries annoyed Italy, and hewas accused of lobbying to make Somalia a member of the Arab League, a dream that was realized in 1974. In that same direction, he also lobbied to block Israel from establishing relations with the new state of Somalia by agitating the public to refuse the arrival of the Israeli delegation that was invited to participate in the celebration of the Somali independence in 1960, the objective that was realized successfully.[59]

On the role of Islam in the Somali state, Shariif Maxamuud also worked with many of his colleagues to oppose any secular views in the constitution of Somalia of 1960. The constitution included clauses that made Islam the basic source of the legislation.[60] After the independence, Shariif Maxamuud focused on education and promotion of the Arabic language seeking the assistance and support of the Arab League in establishing a university in Somalia. This request was approved finally in 1971 and the news was welcomed by the President Siyaad Barre. However, the project was aborted by Italy's friends in the government. Upon hearing the news, they contacted Italy and proposed an alternative project, according to which the university would be funded by European Common Market (later European Union) through Italy and the Italian language would be the language of instruction.[61] During the military rule, the Islamic League and other Islamic organizations were prohibited. Nevertheless, Shariif Maxamuud's struggle produced Islamic elites who pioneered the Islamic awakening in Somalia and confronted all efforts of secularization, Christianization, westernization, and socialism. During the civil war, Shariif Maxamuud moved to the town of Baraawe and then to Mombassa in Kenya. From there, he traveled to Cairo where he died in 1994.

---

59. Ibid.
60. Sheikh Garyare interviewed by the author on July 24, 2010, Hargeysa, Somaliland
61. Dr. Maxamad Aadan Sheikh, former minister during Military regime credited for initiating the Somali National University claims that only Italy was ready to provide higher education assistance to Somalia. Other countries that Somali government requested assistance were not forthcoming. Dr. Maxamad Aadan Sheikh interviewed by the author on August 5, 2010, Helsinki, Finland.

The role played by the Islamic League was tremendous in preparing the cultural ground upon which the modern Islamic awakening was founded and flourished. Along with many other scholars and politicians, the League's leaders undertook the task of protecting Islamic heritage against the challenges of Christianization and westernization. They continued the ideals of earlier attempts to establish in the British Somaliland similar organizations to the one founded by Xaaji Faarax Omaar in Aden in 1925.[62] The leaders also inherited the anti-colonial position of early Islamic scholars, utilizing new means and strategies. Moreover, they were promoting in the early yearsof the nationalist SYL party to make Arabic language the official language of the state.[63] The SYL wrote to the Egyptian Prime Minister Mustafa Nohās, requesting educational assistance for Somalia. The initial objectives of these early leaders of the Islamic consciousness in the 1950s were to promote Arabic education in order to compete with the growing Italian language schools after Somalia's return to that Western country's administration under the UN trusteeship. The Somalis were always suspicious of the colonial education, fearing Christianization of their children. Moreover, Islamic scholars were also encountering increased activities of Christian missionaries engaged in spreading their religion through educational institutions. Furthermore, one of the major tasks was to oppose the writing of the Somali language in the Latin script, or in the locally invented Cusmaaniya, perceived to be

---

62. The "Somali Islamic Organization" is considered to be the first of its kind, and its founder, Faarah Oomaar, was exiled by the British authorities to Aden and later to Ethiopia, charged with anti-colonial campaigning and agitation. See, I. M. Lewis, *A Modern History*, 114.
63. See Sayid Omar Abdullahi, *Somali-Egyptian Relations* (MA Thesis, submitted to the Institute of Islamic and Arabic Studies in Cairo, 2006).

the beginning of secularizing Somali society.⁶⁴ To implement their objectives, the Islamic League took two steps. Firstly, it advocated making Arabic the official language of the country. To pursue this step, the League submitted a signed petition to the Italian authorities and the UN Advisory Council in November 1950, seeking to affirm that the official language of Somalia is the Arabic language. Below are key excerpts of this petition, signed on behalf of Somali leaders and scholars by Shariif Maxamuud Cabduraxman, the chairman of the Islamic League.⁶⁵

> We, the Somali Islamic scholars, clan leaders and elders, prominent personalities and leaders of the political parties, submit to the administrative authority of Italy what we have agreed ultimately with respect to the popular official language of the country. We have selected Arabic language as the official language for the following reasons.
>
> 1. The Arabic language is the language of religion and the Qur'an.
> 2. The Arabic language is the language of Islamic courts in all regions of the country and remains as such until today.
> 3. The Arabic language is the language of trade and correspondence since the spread of Islam and until today.
> 4. The Arabic language is the language spoken by the majority of the population.
> 5. The Arabic language has been chosen by the people in consensus to be their official language.

---

64. The Somali language was not committed in writing until 1973 when the military regime unilaterally issued a decree to use the Latin alphabet without any opportunity for public dialogue.
65. See the original Arabic version of the petition in al-Najjār, al-Islām fi al-Somāl, 99. It is translated by the author.

Secondly, the Islamic League lobbied Egypt and the Arab League to open competitive schools with instruction in the Arabic language and to provide scholarships to the Somali students in their universities.[66] To realize this objective, the Islamic League needed a competent partner with common interests and aspirations. That partner was the revolutionary Egypt under the charismatic leader Jamāl 'Abdi al-Nāsser and the Egyptian member in the UN Advisory Council for Somalia. With the cooperation of SIL and the great desire of the Somali Islamic leaders and nationalist political parties, these schools were established and flourished, as will be seen in the next section.

In northern Somalia, comparable efforts were made by Sayid Axmad Sheikh Muse (d. 1980), a graduate from the al-Azhar University in the 1950s. As related by Sheikh Cabdiraxman Xaashi, Sayid Axmad had some initial contact with the Egyptian MB and was also influenced by the Nasserite ideology.[67] As a partner of Xaaji Maxamad Xuseen during their study in Cairo and working on the Somali "Voice of Arabs" radio program, he lobbied for the Arabic language, which resulted in the establishment of the first Islamic institute in Burco.[68] In 1956, he established an Islamic political party called *"Hizbu Allāh"* (Party of God), which carried the ideology of MB, based on applying the Islamic Shari'a to all aspects of the life of the Muslims

---

66. The earlier fruits were that Saudi Arabia provided 10 scholarships in 1954 to the Somali students. Sheikh Cabdiraxman Huseen Samatar, a former secretary of Nahdah who worked in the World Muslim League in Somalia since 1981 was among these students benefited from the Saudi scholarships. Sheikh Cabdiraxman Xuseen Samatar interviewed by the author on November 1, 2009, Nairobi, Kenya.
67. Sheikh Cabdiraxman Xaashi interviewed by the author on November 14, 2009, Djibouti.
68. Cabdirisaaq Caqli interviewed by the author on November 22, 2009, Hargeysa.

including political aspects. To spread his ideology, Sayid Axmad authored a book titled *Hizbu Allāh wa Hizbu al-Shaydān*, which means "the party of God and the party of the Satan." Besides his cultural connections, Sayid Axmad was a businessman who exported Somali livestock, particularly camels, to Egypt and was organically connected to Egypt through marriage to his Egyptian wife.[69] Later, *Hizbu Allāh* and the Khayriyah Charity constituted the foundations of the Somali National League (SNL). Moreover, among the earlier graduates of the Al-Azhar University who closely worked with Sayid Axmad were Sheikh Cusmaan Dubad from the town of Borama in northern Somalia, who later became director of the Islamic Institute in Burco, and Sheikh Cali Ismaciil Yaquub, who became a prominent member of the Parliament in the 1960s. Although there is no conclusive proof of their membership in the Egyptian MB, there is little doubt that they were influenced by its ideology, at least to a certain extent.

Stimulating Factors of Islamic Consciousness

The factors stimulating Islamic consciousness across Somali territories included increased activities of Christian missionaries, the spread of Italian-language schools, and disputes over the selection of orthography of the Somali language between the camps of the Arabic language and the Latinized alphabet. Moreover, increasing westernization of the urban elite and the growth of un-Islamic value systems and norms were causing concerns.

---

69. Axmad Ibrahim Xasan interviewed by the author on November 22, 2009, Hargeysa.

The Growth of Christian Missionary Activities

One of the major factors that provoked Islamic consciousness in the 1950s was the growing activities of the Christian missionaries after the return of Italy. Fierce competition was growing apace between the Egyptian Islamic Missions and the Christian Missions. The founding of the first al-Azhar Mission in 1953 coincided with the arrival of the Mennonite Mission (MM) in the same year, while the introduction of the Egyptian modern school system was matched by the arrival of the Sudan Interior Mission (SIM) in 1954. As part of this competition, the Roman Catholic Church (RCC) increased its educational programs. Italy licensed Christian missionaries under the pretext of the UN charter granting religious freedom. Looking back over history, comparable activities had instigated earlier encounters with British colonialism, which remained in the collective memory of the people who opposed the introduction of modern education. The introduction of Christianity in Somalia was done by the French Catholic Mission, which opened an orphanage at Daymoole in 1891, a few kilometers from Berbera. The presence of this mission was one of the factors that provoked Sayid Maxamad Cabdulle Xasan's Jihad against Britain and Ethiopia. It is related that Sayid Maxamad Cabdulle Xasan, infuriated with his squabble with the Qaadiriyah order and with British authorities' siding with them in 1897, passed Daymoole on his way out of Berbera. Out of curiosity, he stopped to question one of the 69 children in the Mission's orphanage boarding school with three priests and three sisters.[70] Sayid Maxamad asked the boy, "What is your

---

70. Said Samatar, *Oral Poetry*, 107.

name?" and the boy replied, "John Abdillahi." Then he asked, "What clan are you from?" and the boy answered, "I belong to the clan of the father."[71] The name of the boy and his clan affiliation demonstrated a total change in the culture and religion of these boys. Subsequently, as Sayid's historiography explains, his antipathy toward colonialism and the tolerant Qaadiriyah order grew out of proportion. Professor Lewis explains the reaction of Sayid as follows: "This fired his patriotism and he intensified his efforts to win support for the Saalixiyah, preaching in the mosques and streets that his country was in danger and urging his compatriots to remove the English 'infidels' and their missionaries."[72] However, in reaction to the Sayid's propaganda expressed in poetic literary form, all Christian missionary activities were banned in 1910 in the British Somaliland and strict rules were enforced afterwards.[73]

In southern Somalia, the Swedish Overseas Lutheran Church established its first station in Kismaayo in 1896 and expanded its activities to Juba Valley villages such as Jamaame, Mugaambo and Jilib. The Mission also set up health clinics and elementary schools as well as local churches in these areas. It preached the Gospel mainly to plantation workers of what was originally the "Bantu population of the Juba Valley" and

---

71. There are many versions of this conversation, though all convey same meaning. See another version in, Abdisalam Issa-Selwe, *The failure of Daraawiish state: The clash between Somali clanship and state system*
   (paper presented at the 5th International Congress of Somali Studies, December 1993), 3. Also, see http://www.somalimission.org/index.php?option=com_content&view=article&id=9:the-persecuted-christian-church-in-somalia&catid=3:articles&Itemid=3
72. Lewis, *A History*, 67.
73. Lewis, *A History*, 103. The SwedishChurch wanted to return to Somalia after the Second World War but was refused entry by British Military Administration. See, Omar Elby, *Fifty Years*, 13.

attracted some adherents.⁷⁴ During this period, Jubaland was under British administration and the Mission enjoyed unlimited freedom of work under state protection. However, after Italy annexed Jubaland in 1925, the church was expelled from Somalia in 1935 forever leaving behind its properties accumulated over more than 30 years and its small Somali Christian congregations. The eviction of the protestant church was triggered by the Swedish government's position toward Italian designs for the Horn of Africa and went well with the rival RCC. It was a policy intended to win the hearts and minds of the Muslim Somalis during the Italian campaign against Ethiopia.⁷⁵ As for the RCC, it worked under a less hostile environment during the Italian colonial period and was mostly confined to the Italian community, orphans, and freed slaves. "It drew no designs for traditional Christian missionary work among the Muslim Somalis. Her [the RCC] most direct attempt at proselytizing was to get orphans off the streets into boarding schools and instruct them in the Catholic faith."⁷⁶ During Italian Fascist rule, the church was able to build in 1928 a large cathedral that became the symbol of the Muslim city of Mogadishu under Italian administration. Besides providing religious services to the Italians in Somalia, the RCC by 1939 was running with government subsidies, 12 elementary schools, in which 1,776 pupils were enrolled.⁷⁷ Italy granted considerable freedom to the RCC while at the same time demonstrating its support and promotion of Islam in constructing mosques,

---

74. RobertHess, *Italian Colonialism in Somalia* (Chicago: Chicago University Press, 1966), 170.
75. Omar Elby, *Fifty Years*, 8.
76. Omar Eby, *A Whisper in a Dry Land: A Biography of Merlin Grove, Martyr for Muslims in Somalia* (Herald Press, 1968), 7.
77. Touval, *Somali Nationalism*, 73.

shrines, and Hajj convoys for the dignitaries. During the BMA, the church maintained its activities and its orphanages received British support of 0.65 shilling per day per orphan.[78] It also boasted having 8,500 followers in 1950, almost all of whom were expatriate Italians.[79] According to the UN 1957 report, "Italian Catholic missionaries operated more than 20 institutions in Mogadishu alone during that time."[80] However, after the independence and departure of many Italian expatriates from Somalia, the Church started losing followers, claiming only 2,623 members in 1970.[81] It maintained its activities afterwards and administered churches, hospitals, schools, orphanages, and cultural centers.[82]

The most zealous missionary activities that triggered most of the resentment among the Somali population were the protestant denomination of the Mennonite Mission (MM) and Sudan Interior Mission (SIM) which joined the Christian venture in the 1950s. MM interest in Somalia had begun in 1950 when the secretary of Eastern MM and Charities Orie O. Miller visited Mogadishu. Wilbert Lind and his family were sent to Somalia in January 1953 to represent the Protestant presence since the Swedish Overseas Lutheran Church had been banned in 1935. Opening their headquarters in Mogadishu, the

---

78. Salah Mohamed, *Hudur*, 360.
79. After the evil war of 1991 and the destruction of the Diocese of Mogadishu, Catholocs estimates the number of their adherents in Somalia as about 100 persons. See this information available from http://en.wikipedia.org/wiki/Roman_Catholicism_in_Somalia (accessed on May 11, 2009).
80. Abdirahman Ahmed Noor, *Arabic Language and Script in Somalia: History, attitudes and prospects* (PhD diss., Georgetown University, 1999), 63.
81. See detailed statistics of the activities of the Diocese of Mogadishu available from http://www.catholic-hierarchy.org/diocese/dmgds.html (accessed on May 12, 2009).
82. The last Roman Catholic Bishop of Mogadishu, Salvadore Colombo was murdered in 1989 followed by successive demonstrations and conflict between growing Islamists and the government and bloody demonstrations occurred on July 14, 1989.

Mennonites were running programs in Mogadishu, Jowhar, Mahadaay, Jamaame, Bula-Burte, and Kismaayo by 1968. As recorded by Cabdiraxman Axmad Nuur, the MM was focusing on converting people in riverine areas. The "Church was enjoying a trend towards the Gospel among the people of riverine communities in the South. On occasions, hundreds of people would come together to hear the Gospel. Then, the government moves enforced the cessation of all church activities."[83] The mission expanded rapidly and, by 1969, its six locations had more than 30 missionaries. It administered several language and elementary/intermediate schools, a clinic and hospital, and a bookshop.[84] However, March 24, 1962 became the turning point in the mission's expansion when the Somali government ordered cessation of all their missionary activities such as schools and hospitals because of their rigorous proselytization activities.[85] This was in reaction to the assassination of Mr. Merlin Grove in July 1962 which occurred after the government allowed the reopening of the mission schools.[86] This event prompted the adoption of Article 29 of the Somali Constitution prohibiting the spreading of other religions in Somalia.[87] Moreover, three months later, the government

---

83. Abdirahman Ahmed Noor, *The Arabic Language*, 54.
84. Makki, *Al-Siyāsāt*, 143.
85. "Rumours swept the towns: Wesselhoeft had baptized 21 Somali School boys in the Shabelle River. The mission had ordained Somali priest in Jamama. New Somali believers distributed Arabic Gospel tracts in Mogadishu." See Omar Elby, *Fifty Years*, 32.
86. Mr. Merlin Grovewas assassinated by Yasiin Cabdi Axmad Ibrahim who was angry at the distribution of Christian literature written in the Arabic language at the Cabdulqaadir mosque in Mogadishu.
87. See Somali Constitution of 1960, article 29, which states, "Every person shall have the right to freedom of conscience and freely to profess his own religion; however, it shall not be permissible to spread or propagandize any religion other than the religion of Islam."

issued a directive requiring "teaching Islam in private schools as well as public." The MM complied, while the SIM closed its schools and left the country.[88] The military regime of 1969 nationalized all private schools and institutions in October 1972 including mission properties and mission personnel were expelled from Somalia in 1976. Nationalization of the private schools and expulsion of religious missions were not confined to Christian missionaries; these measures also included al-Azhar Mission and the Egyptian Educational Mission.[89] However, after the Somali-Ethiopian war in 1977-78 and following a massive refugee influx, the MM was allowed to return to provide relief assistance to the refugee camps.[90]

The second ardent mission was SIM operated by Canadian Missionaries who arrived in Somalia on September 15, 1954, although had requested to enter Somalia in 1948.[91] This mission is one of the international, interdenominational Christian mission organizations united under the name of Serving in Mission.[92] The goals of SIM include planting, strengthening and partnering with churches around the world. SIM established a number of schools when they arrived in Somalia in 1954 and claimed to have 30-40 Somali converts by 1963. Through its strong language school, it attracted more than 350 students by

---

88. See Omar Elby, *Fifty Years*, 37.
89. Ibid; 64-65.
90. See brief history of Mennonite Mission in Somalia available from http://www.gameo.org/encyclopedia/contents/S6586.html (accessed on May 12, 2009).
91. Helen Miller, *The Hardest Place: the biography of Warren and Dorothy Modricher* (Guardian Books, 1982), 166
92. Four major churches are united in the Serving in Mission organization. They are the Africa Evangelical Fellowship, Andes Evangelical Mission, International Christian Fellowship,
and Sudan Interior Mission, available from http://en.wikipedia.org/wiki/Serving_In_Mission (accessed on May 12, 2009).

1965.⁹³ The most important accomplishment of SIM was translating the New and Old Testaments into the Somali language using Latin alphabet in 1966. It is noteworthy that the Somali language was not committed to a written form until 1972, and the conflict over selecting an alphabet was one of the major conflicts between Islamic scholars and secular groups. The use of the Latin alphabet by SIM offered more weight to the secular agenda over the Islamic scholars' drive. Probably, SIM acquired experience in working with Muslim communities by avoiding establishing churches. Instead, it organized its Somali adherents into the Somali believers' fellowship orders and secretive congressional teams. Finally, besides all its stated activities, SIM was also running two hospitals and three clinics until 1969, after which it abandoned its open activities.

Protestant Christian missionaries were attracting Somalis by a variety of means. They were offering good English programs that were in high demand in Somalia and provided education that led to scholarships at prestigious universities in the USA.[94] As a result, most of the Somalis claiming to be Christians were in the category of "rice Christians" or "scholarship Christians," as celebrated Somali writer Nuruddin Faarax calls them.[95] In his literary article titled "The Skin of the Dog," Maxamuud Siyaad Togane, a Somali-Canadian poet and writer, characterizes the motivations of these Somalis was mostly seeking worldly lucre and quotes the Somali proverb *"dantaada maqaar Aybaa loogu*

---

93. Makki, *Al-Siyāsāt*, 144.
94. Many Somali students who claimed to be Christians were admitted in the Goshen College in Indiana, USA, supported by the Mennonite Mission scholarships.
95. "Rice Christians" are people who formally declared themselves Christian for material benefits. Nuruddin Faarax, a prominent Somali novelist called them "scholarship Christians". Mohamud Siyaad Togane interviewed by the author on November 3, 2009, Montreal, Canada.

seexdaa" meaning, "To achieve your goals, you may sleep in the skin of a dog."⁹⁶ The focus of Christian missionaries on education evolved from their perceptions of schools as important avenues for conversion.⁹⁷ According to Bishop Shanahan, one of the pioneers of the Catholic missionaries in Nigeria; "those who hold the school, hold the country, hold its religion, holds its future."⁹⁸ Some ambitious students in the mission schools founded the Somali Christian Association in 1963 to receive these privileges until they had achieved their career goals and then most of them reclaimed their Islamic faith.⁹⁹ One such example is Professor Said Samatar, who was from a family of well-known Islamic scholars and joined a mission school in the town of Qalaafo. Interviewed by Professor Axmed Samatar on how to negotiate being from religious family background and Christian missionary connection, he replied: "Well, basically I went from one *kitāb* (book) to another. [Laughter] And now I am returning to the original *kitāb*" [Qur'an]. Remembering his father's advice on this sensitive issue, he said: "I remember him [his father] saying that with the missionaries, I should practice the Shi'ite doctrine of *Taqiya*, meaning dissembling, the art of artful deception. That's what he encouraged me to do…. So that is basically what I practiced!"¹⁰⁰

---

96. See Mohamud Togane, *"The Skin of a Dog."* Zymurgy Literary Review 6, Volume III, Number 2, autumn 1989, 95-100.
97. Magnus O. Bassey, *Western Education and Political Domination in Africa: A Study in Critical and Dialogical Pedagogy* (Bergin & Garvey, 1999), 53.
98. Ibid.
99. Professor Said Samatar was the chairman of the Somali Christian organization and Mohamud Siyaad Togane was the vice-chairman. Two interviewees professed to be Christians reclaimed publicly their Islamic faith after graduating from the university. They requested anonymity. I have also interviewed Togane who confirmed this information on November 3, 2009, Montreal, Canada.
100. See Ahmed Ismael Samatar's interview with Professor Said Sheikh Samatar at the 2005 Annual Meeting of the African Studies Association, Washington, D.C. Bildhan:

Another example is Maxamuud Togane, who was closely associated with the MM but affirms that he remained Muslim and believes that majority of the so-called Somali Christians are in this category.[101]

The strongest Christian provocation of the Muslim faith that stirred emotions in Mogadishu was the event that led to the assassination of Merlin Grove of the MM. The incident exploded when Warren Modricker from SIM had made what could be considered a "spiritual assault" by arranging the distribution of scripture leaflets in Arabic at Cabdulqaadir Mosque after the Friday prayer.[102] The distributor was a Somali claiming to be Christian, who, when was caught, stated that he was sent by the Christian missionaries.[103] There were two missions located near each other in Mogadishu: the MM and SIM. In reaction, a Somali man decided to avenge his religion and assassinated the Mennonite Mission's head Merlin Grove on July 16, 1962.[104] The rage of the public upon hearing the news of distribution of Christian literature and subsequent murder of Merlin Grove was out of proportion, and the issue of converting Somalis to Christianity became top of the national agenda. The

---

*An International Journal of Somali Studies.*Volume 6, 2006, 1. Moreover, this quote is also in the footnote 52 of the unpublished poem of Mohamud Togane "In Memory of Wilbert Lind (1920-2007).

101. Mohamud Siyaad Togane interviewed by the author on November 3, 2009, Montreal, Canada.
102. Ibid.
103. The distribution of Christian literature to the Somali public was ascertained by the Mission. As Omar Elby writes, "Later they learned that only the last charge was true; zealous new [Somali] believers gave out Christian Literature in Mogadishu Markets." See Omar Elby, *Fifty Years*, 32.
104. See Eby, Omar, *A Whisper in a Dry Land* (Herald Press, 1968). Warren Modricker predicted such a response in 1958 when he wrote a letter to the director of SIM saying, "Islam will not sit idly and take it on the chin without a 'fight', but by the Grace of God through the victory of Calvary, let us as a mission go forward." Miller, Helen, *The Hardest Place*, 180.

first government action was swift, ordering missions to comply with a set of policies, such as ceasing any forms of spreading Christianity, including Islamic teaching and Arabic language in their curriculum, and building mosques in their boarding schools.[105] This event had also called for the enactment of Article 29 of the constitution prohibiting the propagation of other religions in Somalia.[106]

In the conclusion, Christian missionary activities in Somalia were linked to five countries; namely, France, Sweden, USA, Canada and Italy. It is notable that British missionaries never attempted to introduce itself in Somalia even though Britain ruled parts of Somalia for about 80 years. Moreover, it is worth mentioning that missionary activities were prohibited three times in Somalia: two of the events were undertaken by British and Italian fascist authorities mainly to win the hearts and minds of their Somali subjects. The closed down missions were the French Catholic Mission in 1910 and the Swedish Lutheran Overseas Church in 1935. On the other hand, the third action was carried out by the revolutionary Somalia in 1972 as part of general nationalization policy of the educational institutions in the country. As a result, all Christian institutions were closed and the Missions were expelled in 1976. The continuous disruption of the missionary activities minimized the presence of Christian minority in Somalia. Moreover, the collapse of the state in Somalia and the civil war that broke out afterwards caused the destruction of Christian properties and institutions along with many state institutions. Furthermore, some Christian

---

105. Togane interviewed in Montreal on November, 3, 2009.
106. See Somali Constitution, Article 29 which states, "Every person shall have the right to freedom of conscience and freely to profess his own religion; however, it shall not be permissible to spread or propagandize any religion other than the religion of Islam."

believers in Somalia were targeted by armed clan militia or armed extremists in the name of Islam and were persecuted and murdered. Following are the list of Christian missions operated in Somalia.

Name of the Christian Mission	Denomination	Home Country	Year of arrival in Somalia (current status)
French Catholic Mission	Catholic	France	1891 (expelled 1910)
Swedish Lutheran Overseas Church	Protestant	Sweden	1896 (expelled 1935)
Roman Catholic Church	Catholic	Italy	1904 (closed 1991)
Mennonite Mission	Protestant	Canada	1954 (expelled 1976)
Sudan Interior Mission	Protestant	USA	1954 (expelled 1976)

Table 3. Christian Missions in Somalia

Selecting Somali Language Orthography

The Somali language is spoken by the Somalis settled in the vast areas in the Horn of Africa and was not committed to writing until 1972. The question of language in terms of the official language and which orthography should be used was one of the provoking factors in the Islamic consciousness. It was one of the contested arenas between Islamic scholars and emerging modern elites. Captain Richard Burton, the British Intelligence officer who visited northern Somali territories and Harrar in 1854, was the first to use Latin script to write the Somali language. Other attempts were initiated in 1897 by Christian missionaries, as represented by de Laragasse and de Sampont who devised a Latinized alphabet for Somali and wrote the first Somali-English and English-Somali dictionaries.[107] These missionary activists claimed, "The great desire, not the will of

---

107. Evangeliste de Larajasse, *Somali-English and English-Somali dictionary* (London: Kegan Paul. Trench & Trubner, 1897).

the propaganda of Rome notwithstanding, the Roman characters should be used for all classical works which missionaries publish on the language of the people they are sent to. Therefore, we are for writing Somali phonetically, employing the Roman characters with their Latin pronunciation."[108] Moreover, a number of Western scholars and Orientalists also attempted to develop Somali grammar and a Latinized script. The most noted among them was Kirk, who in 1905 wrote a grammar book of the Somali language using the Latin script.[109] Andrzejewski also published a number of papers and books in the Latinized Somali language.[110] Abraham published Somali-English and English-Somali dictionaries in 1964 and 1967, respectively.[111] Moreover, Italian scholars Enrico Cerulli and Mario Moreno published books and articles in the Somali language with the Latin script.[112]

The first Somali reaction to the growing trend of marginalizing Arabic and replacing it with the Somali language written in the Latinized alphabet was noted in 1941. Shariif Maxamuud Cabdiraxman, the distinguished advocate of the Arabic language, who was one the first pioneers of modern

---

108. Abdurahman Ahmed Noor, *Arabic Language*, 139.
109. J.W.C. Kirk, a British infantry soldier and rifleman stationed in British Somaliland, published a grammar of Somali, Yibir, and Madhiban in 1905.
110. Andrzejewski (1922-1994) was a scholar of Somali linguistics and professor of Cushitic languages and literature at the School of Oriental and African Studies, University of London.
111. Roy C. Abraham is the author of a Somali-English dictionary (1964) and an English-Somali dictionary (1967).
112. Mario Martino Moreno is the author of *Il Somala della Somalia* (The Somali of Somalia) (Rome: Istituto Poligrafico dello stato, 1955). Enrico Cerulli was an Italian scholar of Somali and Ethiopian studies and a politician. From January 1939 to June 1940, he was Governor of East Shewa and later of Harrar, two provinces of Italian East Africa. He also headed the political office for East Africa in the Ministry of Foreign Affairs. He authored a voluminous body of works including *Somalia: scritti vari editi ed inediti*. 5 vols.

education in Somalia, confronted Mr. Colin Wood of the BMA in Mogadishu. Mr. Wood had been striving to commit the Somali language into a written form. However, Sharif Maxamuud met with Mr. Wood and argued that "Arabic was the language of the land and it is the duty for the British Government to make it official."[113] The issue of the language in Somalia loomed everywhere and was debated even at United Nations headquarters, since Somalia was under the UN trusteeship.[114] Most Somalis preferred Arabic to be their official language and believed that if the Somali language had to be committed into a written form, Arabic script should be used. On the other hand, colonial administrators, Christian activists, and Orientalists were poised to isolate Somalia from the Arabic/Islamic world and make Italian or English the official language of the country. Moreover, they sought to affirm the use of the Latin alphabet in cases where the Somali language was to be committed to writing. The language debate continued for years, deliberating on three proposals: the Latin alphabet, the Arabic, and Cusmaaniya, the latter being invented by the Somali scholar Yassin Cismaan Yuusuf Keenadiid.[115] The majority of the Somalis supported the Arabic alphabet because it is the first language they learn in early childhood to enable them to recite the Qur'an and understand Islam. Second, they considered themselves belonging to the Arab nation, having genealogies connecting them to Arab ancestors. At the same

---

113. Noor, *Arabic Language*, 119.
114. This debate occurred in session in the UN headquarters in 1955, with the representatives of Somali political parties, two ministers from Italy, and the representative from the UN Trusteeship Council participating in the deliberations. The decision was to develop the local Somali language instead of relying on other languages. See Noor, *Arabic Language*, 125.
115. Ibid.

time, they were fearful that the Latin alphabet would affect their Islamic education and culture.

Against the wishes of the people, the Italian UN trusteeship administration AFIS (Administrazione Fiduciaria Italiana in Somalia) advocated writing the Somali language in the Latin script, and in 1952, the daily newspaper of AFIS, *Corriere Della Somalia*, published a page in the Latinized Somali language. Also in the 1950s, the British government financed a project for developing a script for the Somali language and B.W. Andrzejewski, who worked on that project, proposed the Latin script. Furthermore, in 1955, AFIS with the collaboration of the British Protectorate authority and UNESCO held a conference on the Somali language in Mogadishu where the participants recommended the Latin script. In their strong drive to write the Somali language in the Latin script, its proponents argued that "Latin characters are economical, technically superior, less time-consuming and more international than merely Western. It is also compatible with the modern technology and communicating with the outside world."[116] In 1954, the SYL resolved to make Arabic the official language of the country. Pursuing that policy, Aadan Cabdulle Cusman, the first president of Somalia after independence in 1960, expressed to the Advisory Council that "the only language which the people of Somalia can use easily is the Arabic language – the language of the Qur'an which they learn in their early childhood in the Qur'anic schools".[117] The issue was not resolvedand after independence the conflict continued among the two mutually antagonistic proponents of the Latin and Arabic alphabets.

---

116. Noor, *Arabic Language*, 143.
117. Hamdi al-Sālim al-Sayid, *al-Somāl Qadīman wa Ḥadīthan* (Al-Qāhira: Dar al-qawmiyah li dabā'at wa Nashr, 1965), 380.

After independence the government formed another language committee, but conclusive decisions were not made because of religious sensitivity and the strong opposition by Islamic scholars. One example of the opposition was the demonstration organized from many mosques in Mogadishu after the Friday congregational prayer in 1966 against the three-member committee sponsored by UNESCO for the introduction of the language.[118] The visit of the committee and their proposal to use Latin alphabet coincided with the translation of the Gospel into Somali language by the Mennonite missionaries in the same year. Proponents of the Arabic alphabet had a great influence on the population since they appealed to their faith. In 1962, Shariif Maxamuud stated: "As Latin script, its relationship to Somalia is a relationship to colonialism. The colonial powers had brought it and imposed it on us. Today, we get rid of the political colonial ghost. So, we must also get rid of its traces and cultural legacy. The adoption of Latin script will always remind us the activities of the colonial power and the existence of their psychological domination over our lives."[119] Ibrahim Xaashi Maxamuud, another ardent advocate for the Arabic language, articulated the same points, saying, "Somalia came in contact with Latin script as a result of colonialism. We are compelled to learn it. Now that we are free, we must get rid of all colonial roots. And Latin will remind us of the dark deeds of colonialists."[120] Moreover, in 1967, in a public debate on written

---

118. Three European scholars namely, Andzrejewski, Strelcyn and Tubiano were hired by UNESCO to advise the Somali government on the appropriate script for Somali language. And, of course they recommended the Latin script.
119. Noor, *Arabic Language*, 149-150.
120. Ibrahim Xaashi was a graduate of the al-AzharUniversity in 1957 with Sheikh Cabdulqani Sheikh Axmad. He was also influenced by Nasserite ideology and founded the *Nasru Allah* organization, the liberation movement of western Somalia

Somali held in Mogadishu, Jeneral Maxamad Abshir Muuse, one of the devoted supporters of the Arabic script argued, "How can you differentiate the Muslim identity from the Somali identity? To me, being a Somali and being aMuslim is one and the same thing. The terms 'Somali' and 'Muslim' are synonymous in my mind. Islam provides our code of life. It is our state religion. Hence, the question of a script for our language puts our basic cultural and spiritual values at stake."[121] Maxamuud Axmad Cali, the Father of Education in northern Somalia, was also one of the ardent advocates for the Arabic script for Somalia.

Thus, proponents of the Arabic script regarded the Latin script as a means of Christian infiltration and continuance of the colonial legacy. The debate on the language script was temporarily halted when President Cabdirashiid Cali Sharmarke announced, "As long as I am in power, I shall never permit the adoption of Latin."[122] Thus, he maintained the status quo until it was broken by General Maxamad Siyaad Barre, who in 1972 issued a presidential decree to write Somali language in the Latin alphabet.[123] This controversial issue, debated for more than 30 years, was concluded with the triumph of the Latin script, an indication of the supremacy of secularism over the Islamic agenda. Yet, this debate had created awareness among Islamic scholars of the rise of secularism and the necessity for

---

which later was renamed Western Somali Liberation. Sheikh Cabdiraxman Xuseen Samatar interviewed by the author on December 1, 2009, Nairobi, Kenya. See also, Ibrahim Xaashi, *Al-Somal bi Luqat al-Qur'an* (Mogadishu, 1962).

121. See Hussein M Adam, *Historical Notes on Somali Islamism* (paper prepared for the International Somali Studies Association conference in Djibouti, December 2007).
122. Noor, *Arabic Language*, 151.
123. On politics and foriegn influences in adopting Somali script, see David Laitin, *Politics, Language and Thought: The Somali Exprience* (University of Chicago Press, 1977).

Islamic confrontation. The impact of this awareness would become evident in the future development of the Islamic Awakening.

Westernization and the Emergence of Modern Elites

The introduction of modern education in Somalia was the most important factor in the rise and spread of Somali nationalism and the emergence of modern elites. In the pre-colonial era, political and religious power was in the hands of the traditional elites that included clan elders and Islamic scholars. The traditional elites were systematically marginalized with the rise of modern education and its production of modern elites. However, modern education was comparatively recent in the Somali territories because the Christian missions that pioneered education in the colonial Africa were challenged and their educational activities were blocked by the Somali Islamic scholars.[124] Also, because of political unrest and volatile security and the lack of vested interests, colonial governments did not allocate enough resources to develop modern education. With such slow process, the elite formation was sluggish, deficient and divergent, mired within the Cold War atmosphere and Muslim-Christian tensions.

Indeed, educational systems in the Somali territories could be classified into traditional and modern, state and non-state

---

124. As late as 1942, they controlled 99 percent of the schools, and more than 97 percent of the students in [Africa] were enrolled in mission schools. By 1945, there were comparatively few literate [Africans] who had not received all or part of their education in mission schools. Magnus O. Bassey, *Western Education and Political Domination in Africa: A Study in Critical and Dialogical Pedagogy* (Bergin & Garvey, 1999), 27. In Somalia, Christian missionaries were either expelled or were very conservative, fearing the resentment of the Muslim population.

education. The traditional education was described in Chapter Two and remains essentially Islamic, with Qur'anic memorization and the studies of the Arabic language and jurisprudence as its core subjects. Most of the modern elites passedthrough Qur'an memorizationin their early childhood. Modern education was introduced during the colonial era and was taught in colonial languages, adopting colonial curricula that promoted Western world outlook. Thus, Italian and English became the official languages of education while Arabic language was kept as part of the curricula. Moreover, modern non-state education embodied a hodgepodge of different schools and curricula, such as Christian Mission schools, Egyptian Arabic schools, Italian schools, and others.[125] Some graduates from these schools were granted scholarships to study overseas.[126] In examining elite formation in Somalia and its impact in creating an ideologically conflicting society, our focus will turn to the state education system, since Arabic education and missionary activities have already been explored.

Modern elites are a product of modern education that began with the arrival of colonialism which was necessarily secular. It introduced and nurtured Western values and governance system based on the separation of religion and politics. The early involvement of Christian missionaries in education created the idea in the minds of the Somali population that modern education is correlated with Christianity and that it has to ensure permanent colonial domination through Christian conversion and cultural assimilation. As Abdirahman Ahmed

---

125. Some of these schools are: Russian Banaadir High School, Italian schools, and Saudi Islamic Solidarity School.
126. After 1960, many Somali students were sent to Russia, Eastern Europe, China, Italy, Egypt, USA, Syria, Iraq and many other countries.

Noor noted, "The amount of education offered by colonial government depended on (a) African people's level of religious conversion and cultural assimilation; (b) the nature of trained labor required by colonial administration, and (c) the degree of people's acceptance of, or resistance to that education."[127] Therefore, before the Second World War, minor education programs in the former Italian colony were bequeathed to the RCC with the objective limited to providing qualified workers for jobs unsuitable for the "superior race" of Italians.[128] Moreover, the Italian Fascist regime that took power in 1922 prohibited education in all Italian colonies.[129] A document discovered in 1939 after the defeat of Italy in the East African war states, "The goal of education was to train the pupil in the cultivation of soil or to become qualified workers in the jobs not admissible for the Italian race."[130] Moreover, this goal was discriminatory in that "cultural" schools were reserved only for the sons of "obedient" notables and these children were expected to succeed their fathers in serving colonial masters as interpreters, clerks, and office "boys".[131] In British Somaliland, the expulsion of the Christian Mission in 1910 and the subsequent atmosphere of suspicion, as well as the impact of the Jihad of Sayid Maxamad Cabdulle Xasan, delayed all attempts of introducing modern education until after the

---

127. Noor, *Arabic Language*, 48.
128. Italy was ruled by a fascist regime from 1922 to 1943, a far right ideology based on racism and authoritarianism.
129. Mohamed Sharif Mohamūd, "'Abdirizāq Hāji Hussein, Rais Wasāra al-Somāli (1964-1967), 2009", available fromhttp://arabic.alshahid.net/columnists/6110 (accessed on April 21, 2010).
130. Pankhurst, Sylvia. *Ex-Italian Somalila* (London: Watts & Co., 1951), 212.
131. Abdurahman Abdullahi, "Tribalism, Nationalism and Islam: The crisis of the political Loyalties in Somalia" (MA thesis, Islamic Institute, McGill University, 1992), 63.

Second World War.[132] Indeed, a combination of the Somali resistance to taxation, suspicions of mixing Christianity with modern education, and insufficiency of colonial financial allocations contributed to postponing the introduction of modern education in British Somaliland. However, a new trend transpired with the concerted efforts of small educated Somali elites in Sudan and tremendous Somali participation in the Second World War. As a result, in 1945, 400 students were attending seven elementary schools, besides numerous Qur'anic schools supported by the British authority. The Growth of modern education was very slow because of resource deficiency, and only in 1950, the first two intermediate schools were opened. However, modern education expanded gradually afterwards and, according to the records of the public office reproduced by Ahmed Samatar, the total number of students in Somaliland had increased from 623 in 1948 to 6,209 in 1959.[133]

In the former Italian Somali colony under the BMA, modern education began "without ceiling."[134] For a variety of reasons after the Second World War, the Somalis took great interest in modern education through local initiatives of social activists and political parties. Emerging political parties were competing with each other in attracting public support by investing in the field of education. A pioneering role in this race was taken by the SYL, which made the advancement of modern education

---

132. Touval, *Somali Nationalism*, 64.
133. Ahmed Samatar, *Socialist Somalia: Rhetoric and Reality* (London: Zed Press, 1988), 47.
134. This terminology used by Salah Mohamed means that freedom of establishing schools and even local organizations was granted. During the fascist rule, these activities were prohibited. See, Salah Mohamed, *Hudur*, 358.

one of its major objectives.¹³⁵ The party had opened many adult night classes with the generous contributions of its members and by 1948, 65% of its classes were taught in English compared with 35% in Arabic.¹³⁶ These schools proliferated in the major cities such as Mogadishu, Marka, Kismaayo, Baidoa, Bosaaso, and Hargeysa.¹³⁷ Other political parties were also following suit and conducting similar education programs, albeit smaller in scope and magnitude. In 1947, in the former Somali Italian colony under the BMA, besides various non-state schools, there were only 19 state-funded elementary schools that taught basically in Arabic with English as the second language. Their budget was £16,198 out of a total BMA expenditure of £1,376,752, or 1%.¹³⁸ During this period, Macallin Jaamac Bilaal became famous as director of one of the early schools in Mogadishu.¹³⁹ The trend was spreading horizontally and within three years, by 1950, there were 29 schools with an enrolment of 1,600 students and employing 45 teachers.¹⁴⁰ It is noteworthy that the first secondary school in the history of Somalia was founded by Shariif Baana Abba in the Xamar-Jajab district of Mogadishu in 1949 with the support of the Native Betterment

---

135. The Somali Youth League (SYL) was the first political party in Somalia. It was founded as youth organization in 1943 and transformed into a political party in 1947. Being the major nationalist party, it became the ruling party (1956 -1969).
136. Noor, *Arabic Language*, 63.
137. Makki, *Al-Siyasāt*, 141.
138. The policy of teaching the Arabic language in elementary schools had been in line with prevalent practice in British Somaliland. See, Salah Mohamed, *Hudur*, 358- 359. The first intermediate school was opened by the SYL in Mogadishu in 1949, and Mr. Ismaciill Cali Huseen was appointed the principal of this school. See Makki, *Al-Siyasāt*, 141.
139. Noor, *Arabic Language*, 52.
140. Lee Cassanelli and Farah Sheikh Abdulkadir, "*Somali Education in Transition*" (*Bildhan*, vol. 7, 2007), 91-125. There is a discrepancy with the statistical data of the numbers of student enrolment. This paper gives 1,600 while Tripodi gives 2,850. See Tripodi, *The Colonial Legacy*, 59.

Committee (NBC), a local charitable organization.[141] Shariif Baana was a benevolent Somali merchant and a chairman of NBC. NBC was selling sugar with the aim of using its profits to finance social developmental projects in education, orphanage development and humanitarian assistance.

When AFIS was mandated in 1950 to prepare Somalia for independence within 10 years, the objective of education was radically changed. As related by Tripodi, these objectives were: "To provide the majority of the Somalis with at least primary education; to offer the small intelligentsia already existing in the country higher education; and to promote the formation of new, well-educated elite."[142] Accordingly, a five-year development program was launched in 1952 in collaboration with UNESCO. Within this plan of action, modern schools, technical institutes, and teachers' training programs were established. As a result, according to Professor Lewis, "by 1957 some 31,000 children and adults of both sexes were enrolled in primary schools, 246 in junior secondary schools, 336 in technical institutes, and a few hundred more in higher educational institutions."[143] Indeed, this was a notable advance in the modern education compared with the conditions before the 1950s, when fewer than 2,000 students were receiving education. However, there were only eight intermediate public schools and seven of them used Italian language as the language of instruction.[144] Besides general trend of expanding public education, specialized schools such as School of Politics and Administration were

---

141. In 1948-49, the charity constructed a school with the capacity of 500 students and building for orphanages. See Salah Mohamed, *Hudur*, 361-62.
142. Tripodi, *The Colonial Legacy*, 59.
143. Lewis, *A History*, 140
144. Noor, *Arabic Language*, 59

established in Mogadishu in the 1950s. The main objective of this institute was to train Somali officials and political leaders and integrate them into the Italian system of governance. Many of the students admitted to the institute were either members of the SYL or members of other political parties. Some of the graduates of this institute were offered scholarships for further studies at Perugia University in Italy. Others were employed during the speedy Somalization program in the government administration after 1956. During this period, 4,380 Somalis were absorbed in the government employees which constituted (88%) of labor force. Indeed, this was a large number compared with that of the British Administration in Somaliland during the same years where only 300 were employed in the state administration with only 30 (10%) of them being Somalis.[145] Other institutes were also opened in 1954, the most important of which was the Higher Institute of Law and Economics, later to become Somalia's University College. It subsequently developed into the Somali National University in 1970s.[146] Moreover, scholarships, seminars, and official visits to Italy were provided to the Somali elites to familiarize them with the Italian language and culture. Gradually, through better modern education and improved employment privileges, new Somali elites with an Italian culture emerged. These elites became leaders of the political parties, senior administrators, district councilors and provincial governors. They were also employed in the security

---

145. Somalization of administration was a program giving Somalis responsibility in administering the country through training and coaching by Italian administrators. The great difference in administrative style and nurturing of the new elites is evident in the two colonies of the British and Italians under the UN trusteeship. See Tripodi, *The Colonial Legacy*, 75.
146. Lewis, *A History*, 141.

apparatus of the state.[147] The role of the new elites was growing even more rapidly as they emerged as the ruling elite by 1956, when they replaced Italians in all senior administrative positions to prepare Somalia for the independence in 1960. Nonetheless, in the higher echelons of education, there was not much development to boast. "According to UN report on Somalia, three years prior to independence, there was not a single Somali medical doctor, professional pharmacist, engineer, or high school teacher in Somalia."[148] However, there were 37 Somali students in the Italian universities in 1957-58, among whom 27 were expected to graduate in 1960.[149]

With the Somali independence in 1960 and unification of British and Italian Somaliland, the modern elites became the national leaders of the Somali state. This time, the issue of competing Arabic and Italian languages was expanded to include English language, the official language of elites from British Somaliland. Therefore, the language problem became even more complicated and the adopted education policy was

---

147. The first eight police officers were sent to Italy for training in 25 August, 1952. They were Maxamad Siyaad Barre, Xuseen Kulmiye Afrax, Maxamad Ibrahim Maxamuud (Liiq-liiqato), Maxamad Abshir Muuse, Cabdalla Cali Maxamad, Daauud Cabdulle Xirsi, Maxamad Caynaanshe Guuleed and Maxamad bin Khamiis. Also, first 13 civilian officers were sent in 1953. They were Xaaji Cumar Sheegow, Xaaji Bashiir Ismaaciil, Cabdirashiid Cali Sharmaarke, Daahir Xaaji Cusman, Cali Shido Cabdi, Cali Cumar Sheegow, Nuur Axmad Cabdulle (Castelli), Axmad Cadde Muunye, Cusman Cumar Sheegow, Xasan Maxamad Xassan (Waqooyi), Cabdi Sheikh Aadan, Maxamad Sheikh Gabyow and Aweys Sheikh Maxamad. See Maxamad Ibrahin Maxamad "Liiq-liiqato", *Taariikhda Somaaliya: Dalkii Filka Weynaa ee Punt* (Mogadishu: 2000), 127

148. Noor, *Arabic Language*, 52.

149. "In 1960, the year of independence, only 27 seven Somalis would receive university degrees in Italy; one in medicine, six in political science, one in social science, nine in economics and business administration, one in journalism, three in veterinary medicine, two in agronomy, one in natural science, one in pharmacy, and one in linguistics." See Mohamed Osman Omar, *The Road to Zero: Somalia's self destruction* (HAAN associates, 1992), 45.

based on a mixed system of three languages: English, Arabic, and Italian. Arabic became the language of elementary education and English took precedence in intermediate and secondary education. However, Italian was still the language of administration and it also maintained its role through specialized Italian schools and scholarships to Italy. Moreover, Italian language took over the university level in the 1970s. Moreover, after independence, Somalia's future political orientation was taking shape and stiff competition between the East and the West was tearing Somalia apart. This competition focused on three major intervention areas: education, military and economic development.

In the education sector, external actor's competition mainly focused on providing scholarships to shape the elites' socio-political orientations. For instance, theincomplete statistical data shows following trends: in the 1960s, about 500 civilian students were studying in the Soviet Union, 272 in Italy, 152 in Saudi Arabia, 86 in USA, 40 in Sudan, 34 in UK, 32 in France, and 29 in India.[150] This indicates that the total number of scholarships from the Western countries was less than that from the Soviet Union alone. However, these data are incomplete as Arab nationalist countries that provided generous scholarships, such as Egypt, Syria and Iraq are missing. Moreover, scholarships from China and other Eastern bloc countries such as Czechoslovakia, Poland, Romania, and East Germany are also unaccounted for. Obviously, Somalia was turning its face to the East and the new elites trained in the socialist countries and their allies in the Arab world would play a major role in the

---

150. Luigi Pastaloza, *The Somali Revolution* (Bari:Edition Afrique Asie Amerique Latine, 1973), 350.

future Somali politics. Looking into the military sector, this trend is even more evident. After the Somali dissatisfaction with the small size of Western assistance for military purposes, the Soviets agreed in 1962 to help the Somalis build a strong army, as part of a Cold War strategy to balance the USA presence in Ethiopia. According to Laitin and Samatar, "a joint western countries' proposal for the military assistance to Somalia was $10 million for an army of 5,000 persons. However, the Soviet offer was a loan of $52 million and an army of 14,000 persons. Thus, the Soviets succeeded in taking over the training of the Somali army".[151] As a result, Somali military officers trained in the Soviet Union alone were estimated at more than 500 by 1969. Thus, the majority of modern elites, though initially educated in Western education system, were in some way indoctrinated with the socialist ideology.[152] Elites trained in the socialist countries were adding a far left drift to the growing westernization; the ramifications of this phenomenon would be experienced during the military regime in 1969.

The Modern Elites and Political Clanism

The colonial policy of selecting sons of clan elders to be educated in cultural schools was aimed at establishing a line of genealogical continuity of the ruling elites. The traditional elites now had the opportunity of dwelling in the cities, towns, and the villages because most of them were salaried and were connected with the colonial administrations. Moreover, many traditional Islamic scholars were also settled in urban areas or

---

151. See Laitin and Samatar, *Somalia: Nation*, 78.
152. Ahmed Samatar, *Socialist Somalia*, 78.

even founded their own settlements and villages.[153] Dwelling in the cities and towns offered children of these traditional elites the opportunity to be educated in modern schools and get an early employment at the state institutions. Of course, another competitive line of urbanized Somalis were those who had early contact with the Italians and British or were former irregular warriors who participated in the Italian-Ethiopian war and Second World War and afterwards settled in the cities. Moreover, there were small merchant elites that, in combination with the original urbanized people of the Banaadir coast, constituted a majority in urban areas. Educated children of the traditional elites provided continuity through blood relationship between the traditional and modern elites. It seems that the marginalization of the traditional elites had been compensated by empowering their progenies within the modern state institutions. In this way, blood-related elites with clearly demarcated roles were created where fathers and cousins managed social affairs and their children dominated the modern political landscape.[154] It is also worth mentioning that the traditional elites had a long history of intermarriages for a variety of reasons including bringing about a harmonious society and, therefore, many clan elders and Islamic scholars had next of kin relations with one another. Furthermore, the early Somali elites were mainly new immigrants to the urban cities or soldiers recruited during the colonial era. Thus, the gap between the traditional and modern elites was very narrow, and

---

153. Towns in Somalia were established near water sources. These sources can be rivers, sea, and wells. Early traders were those literate people who received the traditional Islamic education. Moreover, in every settlement, a mosque, a Qur'anic school, and Islamic education circles were established.

154. On the formation of modern elites, see Abdullahi, *Tribalism*, 62-75.

some of them even represented traditional elites that were transformed into modern ones. This process took place after 1951 with the establishment of the Territorial Council where among its 35 members traditional elites were dominant. In the British Somaliland, this phenomenon was even stronger and the Advisory Council consisted of clan elders.[155]

The gap between traditional and modern elites was expanding along with the expansion of modern education and urbanization. When educated children of the traditional elites became urbanized, they acquired urban culture and norms. This is an area where change occurred gradually or sometimes even through a cultural breach. Modern education provided universal education for the entire population and the earlier privileges of the notables' sons were distributed to other social segments as well. In an urban setting, children tended to interact with their neighborhoods not with the members of their clans. They played differently, watched films and frequented cinemas. Some of them even went to night clubs, smoked, drank alcohol and had extramarital sexual relationships. They dressed in European dress, read European books and journals, and ate European food. This process of acculturation began to transform the urbanite Somali generation by inducing them to mimic the dominant white European cultural norms. With the influx of pastoral migrants to the cities after the independence in 1960, rapid social mobility and a hybrid urban culture were developing combining conservative pastoral Somali culture and the urbanized European culture. During those years, the nationalist elites were seemingly at a crossroads between their inherited outlook and the emerging elite values; between a

---

155. Lewis, *A History*, 144.

conservative religious education and liberal modern education, and between inter-clan dependency and self-reliance of urban life. This growing westernized culture that was affecting social life provoked resentment among conservative Islamic scholars.

In political activities, modern elites failed to overcome traditional cleavages and allegiances. Most of the political parties in the 1950s were based on clan divides, except the SYL, although they were articulating nationalist ideals and sentiments.[156] The main parties in the Italian Somaliland in the 1950s were the SYL, Xisbiya Dastuur Mutaqil Somaaliya (XDMS), the Somali National Union (SNU), the Great Somali League (GSL) and the Liberal Somali Youth Party (PLGS).[157] On the other hand, in the same period, the main political parties in British Somaliland were the Somali National League (SNL), the United Somali Party (USP) and the National United Front (NUF).[158] All these political parties were advocating against clanism and were campaigning to discredit it on every occasion. They were attempting to speak in the language of modernity, promoting a national ideology that disdains clanism and calls for its elimination. Nevertheless, during political elections,

---

156. The SYL was a nationalist party; however, most of its members were drawn from Darood (50%) and Hawiye (30%), failing to recruit other major clans, such as Digil and Mirifle, that had formed their own party, HDMS. See Lewis, *A History*, 146. However, these percentages seem highly speculative and only indicate that early years of SYL was dominated by these two clan families.

157. These five parties participated in the municipal and general elections of 1954, 1958, and 1959. In these elections, the SYL received an overwhelming majority, while HDMS was registered as the second opposition party. For details on the performance of these parties in these elections, see Touval, *Somali Nationalism*, 88.

158. The SNL was formed in 1951 with the same nationalist program as the SYL and with the development of the Haud question where Somali territory was given to Ethiopia. The NUF emerged as a convention and common platform for all parties and organizations; however, it developed later into a political party with a strong nationalist agenda. The USP appeared in 1960, attracting former members of the SYL in British Somaliland. See Touval, *Somali Nationalism*, 104-108.

political clanism usually brought out its ferocious clout without ignominy, since there was no way to hold political office in the parliament or in the government other than through first passing the knotty test of political clanism. Political clanism was the only place where everybody mobilized his/her clan to get elected by their home constituency. During the early years of the political experiences in the 1950s, the foundations of the Somali political culture were developed.[159] This culture was partially implanted within the political system and partially emanated from the traditional Somali culture. It could be mainly summarized in the following points: the imperativeness of clan affiliation and subsequent nepotistic behavior; the commoditization of politics for economic gain; falsification, fraud and violence as political means, ambivalence and dependence on foreign patronage. This ambivalent political culture that depends on clan attachment and personal interest breeds endless proclivity and personal voracity extinguished only through raiding national coffers and seeking external patronage.

As a result, the new urban phenomena of political clanism developed within the modern Somali elites during their early political participation in the 1950s. This phenomenon is distinct from the traditional clan system dictated by the ecological setting and mode of life based on subsistence and collectivism. It developed in the urban milieu as a continuation of extended family networks. It is a form of cooperation and socialization

---

159. Details on political clanism refer to Aweys Osman Haji and Abdiwahid Osman Haji, Clan, sub-clan and regional representation 1960-1990: Statistical Data and findings. WashingtonD.C.1998. Also, Maryan Arif Qasim, *Clan versus Nation* (Sharjah: UAE, 2002).

among clan members dwelling in the cities. These clan members cooperate and socialize in assisting new rural immigrants and vulnerable members of the community and in organizing marriage festivities and burial services. Clan members create informal organizational networks with recognized representatives in the urban setting. In this way, in an urban setting, sub-clans sustain their clan networks by reorganizing them and collaborating with the sub-clans based in their original home territory. However, this network gradually develops a particularistic political consciousness and results in comparing the political role of its sub-clan members with that of other clan members. The leaders of the sub-clan take stock of the employment, economic well-being, and political role of the clan members. This "book-keeping" is very important in collecting contributions called Qaaraan. Therefore, this web of networks functions effectively, each seeking privileges and developments of his particular community networks. These networked clan organizations were used by the political elites vying for elections in their home districts, and thus, clans were extremely politicized. The electoral system introduced by the Italians also promoted the emergence of political clanism and weakened nationalistic agenda. Mario d'Antonio, criticizing the electoral system in Somalia, as quoted by Tripodi, writes:

> Even in this circumstance, it was necessary to proceed carefully in introducing radical innovative measures. Two tendencies with different social structures, style of lives and mentality in Somalia had to be reconciled. On the one side, old Somalia, tribal, traditionalist, pastoral, strongly tied to the past and to its ethnicity and religion, and on the other side modern developing Somalia, with its working people of cities and small villages, which created elective municipalities, organized in several political parties, which quickly

adopted a modern style of life and tend to introduce the productive techniques of the West.[160]

Such reconciliation did not occur institutionally though traditional clan system and political parties were accommodating each other and beyond the nationalistic rhetoric, political clanism was sprouting its roots deep into the new elites.

Moreover, instead of exploring some form of reconciliation and accommodation, modern elites were pushing to confront what they considered the greatest threat to nationhood: the virulent effect of political clanism or "the cancer of the Somali state."[161] They attempted in vain to apply three methods. The first was the proportional representation of the clans in the government and rank and file of the public service to create a balanced society where all citizens would have a share based on clan differentiation. However, maintaining this balance was not easy in practice. Some clans that received better economic and educational opportunities and benefited from these privileges occupied important government positions. This situation created resentment of the other marginalized clans. The second method was the glorification of the Somali nation and denying and shaming clans and clanism. In so doing, nationalist elites entertained the notion that the less is said about clanism the easier it would be to eradicate it. Therefore, nationalism was praised and glorified in the public mass media and through songs and poetry, while clanism was depicted as the greatest

---

160. Tripodi, *The Colonial Legacy*, 77-78.
161. Abdalla Omar Mansur, "Contrary to a Nation: The Cancer of the Somali State," in Jumale (ed.), *The Invention of Somalia* (Lawrenceville: The Red Sea Press, 1995), 106-116.

national challenge and malady. The third method suggested that clanism should be dealt with through legislative powers and laws intended to curb the influence of clanism. These laws were intended to reduce the authority of the clan elders and to lessen clan solitary. In applying this legislation, the use of clan names was banned. The military regime of 1969 employed an even more radical approach by abolishing the *diya* system (blood compensation paid collectively by clan members), renaming clan elders and introducing a compulsory insurance system for vehicles to eliminate the collective Diya-paying system in urban settings. This means that in the case an accident occurred, the insurance paid damages instead of the clan.

Finally, during the military regime, modern elites buried the effigy of clanism publicly within socialist propaganda and elimination of insidious clanism became a priority program called *Dabar-goynta qabyaaladda* meaning "eliminating clanism." However, none of these approaches produced tangible results. According to another perspective advocated by the Islamic scholars, clan cleavage could be diluted, but not eliminated, and the Somali people could be united by reviving Islamic values of brotherhood and solidarity, an argument which found its historical practices in the Jamaacooyin of the Sufi orders. From that point of view, Islamist elites were putting forth a different agenda for Somalia.

The Emergence of Islamist Elites

Modern Islamist elites were developed through two processes. The first was formal education in Arabic/Islamic schools where some graduates of these schools had an opportunity to further their studies at Arab higher education institutions such as

Egypt, Syria, Iraq, and Saudi Arabia. This does not mean that these students were automatically subjected to an Islamic agenda since most Arab institutions of higher learning had also been secularized during the colonial period and in the subsequent Arab nationalist movements. Nevertheless, students of Arabic schools were imbued with Islamic/Arabic culture and some of them, either through direct contact or by reading published literature, became aware of the new Islamist trends in the Muslim world. The second process was through those who, after becoming traditional Islamic scholars in Somalia, traveled abroad and joined Islamic higher learning institutions. These scholars contacted Islamic scholars and students from many Muslim countries where modern Islamic revivalist movementswere active and were influenced by them. They could be called "transitional Islamic scholars"since they bridged the divide between the traditional and modern educationalsystem. Indeed, these scholars were the pioneers of the modern Islamic movements in Somalia. The most notable among them were: Sheikh Cali Suufi, Sayid Axmad Sheikh Muuse, Sheikh Cabdulqani Sheikh Axmad, Sheikh Nuur Cali Colow, Sheikh Maxamad Axmad Nuur (Garyare), Sheikh Maxamad Macallin Xasan, Cabdullahi Macallin and Sheikh Cabdiraxman Xuseen Samatar, Sheikh Cali Ismaaciil, Sheikh Ibrahim Xaashi, Shariif Maxamuud and others.

The marginalization of the Islamist elites began from the unequal job opportunities. For instance, graduates of Arabic high schools and universities could not compete for local jobs with graduates from the government schools or other secular non-state schools because of the language barriers. The language of the administration in Somalia remained either Italian or English until Somali language was committed into writing in 1972. Moreover, Arabic high schools were limited in scope and were offering a general high school diploma in arts and science while the al-Azhar schools focused on Islamic jurisprudence and Arabic language. In comparison, the two Italian high schools in Mogadishu were offering both a general high school scientific diploma and specialized technical education.[162] This technical education aimed at providing a trained workforce for the government civil service and private companies. Such schools offered specialization in the fields of accounting, administration and technical training in civil engineering. Consequently, Arabic education could not compete in the local market linguistically or qualitatively. Therefore, the only jobs available for the graduates of Arabic schools and universities were low-paying jobs of either teachers of Arabic and Islamic subjects in the schools and judges or could join the national army.

This structural inequality through diversified curricula and languages created a bifurcation of the elites. Discrimination against the elites educated in Arabic in otherwise equal-opportunity jobs for all citizens forced many of them to explore alternative ways and contemplate changing the system. The Islamic students saw that their colleagues who graduated from the Italian and English schools were given more opportunities, either to be sent to USA and Europe or to be given high-salaried jobs in government institutions. Those students educated in Arabic realized that the only equal opportunity for them was to join the national army or explore scholarships in the socialist countries such as the Soviet Union, East Germany, or China. In

---

162. These two schools were "liceo scientifico" and "Scuola Regineria and Geometero". Graduates had a high potential for finding local jobs. Axmad Cali Culusow interviewed by the Author on June 120, 2009, Nairobi, Kenya.

these countries, all Somalis were equal, since new languages had to be learned. Exceptions were a small number of civilian scholarships and cadet officers sent to Italy who had to be graduates from Italian schools, while at the same time, civilian scholarships and cadet officers sent to Egypt, Syria, and Iraq had to be conversant in Arabic.

The trend of sending young Somalis to Eastern and Western countries with either Socialist or capitalist ideologies eventually brought a cultural and ideological schism orchestrated through the Cold War fever. A significant number of professional Somalis graduated from many universities in the world could not get jobs in the government institutions upon their return. They were unemployed because of the corruption and nepotism in the government. In this situation, only those of them who had strong clan backing or knew an influential political leader were able to get a good job and even received easy promotion. Therefore, there were two main forms of marginalization: linguistic and clan marginalization. This ultimately created numerous strains that necessitated a change in the system. With respect to the Islamic scholars with their meager resources and capacity, they were simply advocating the revival of the Islamic culture and respect for the Arabic language.

The bifurcation of the elites and their development, as illustrated in the figure (3), demonstrates the four types of elites in Somalia. The traditional elites consist of clan elders and Islamic scholars, and modern elites consist of non-Islamist and Islamist elites.[163] The modern elites are super-structural which was created mainly through modern education. As the diagram

---

163. Non-Islamist elites are the majority of the Somali elites who are not actively advocating application of Shari' a, but are not against it. They do not consider themselves belonging to secular elites.

indicates the dynamics of Islam (traditional and modern), clan (represented by elders) and the state (represented by non-Islamist elites) is the most challenging issue in Somalia.

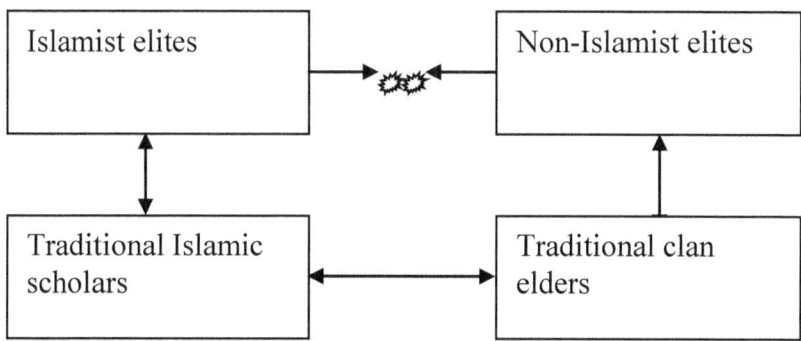

Figure 3. The diagram of development of the elites in Somalia

The relations between the traditional elites were cordial and collaborative in order to maintain community cohesion; however, non-Islamist elites and the Islamist elites were antagonistic because of their different position on the nature of the state. Non-Islamist elites resolutely covet to retain the nature of the inherited post-colonial state whereas Islamists advocate zealously for its Islamization.[164] The free choice of the citizens through democratic process, as peaceful resolution of the conflict, was blocked by the non-Islamist elites with the support of the western powers, the consequence of which was the breeding extremism in the name of Islam and curtailing moderate Islamism in general.

---

164. The diagram of the Somali elite formation and their relations was developed by the author. See Abdurahman Abdullahi, "Tribalism, Nationalism and Islam: The crisis of the political Loyalties in Somalia (MA thesis, Islamic Institute, McGill University, 1992), 92-101.

Islam and the State in Somalia (1960-1969)

One of the most prevailing provocations for the Islamic consciousness was the tension between the secular state legislation and the demand by Islamist elites for implementing the Islamic Shari'a. However, this issue was not evident in Somalia in the 1960s. On the one hand, people were not much aware of legal matters and the legal issues that touched their lives directly were in accordance with Islam. Moreover, the Islamist elites had not enough power to demand complete Islamization of the state and society. Indeed, Somalia had a long history of application of parts of Shari'a as interpreted by the Shafi'i school in conjunction with a variety of local customs and laws (Xeer). Successive colonial administrations avoided interfering in issues that were religiously sensitive. However, after the introduction of the modern idea of the nation-state and the development of the Somali national identity, secular ideas started to emerge. These secular laws were looked upon as being similar to the Somali customary law that sometimes contravened Islamic laws. In the Constitution of the Somali Republic adopted in 1960, Islam was declared "the religion of the state," and accordingly, Somalis were to be governed in compliance with "the general principles of Islamic Shari'a."[165] Moreover, other article affirms that "the doctrine of Islam shall be the main source of laws of the state"[166] and "laws and provisions having the force of law shall conform to the

---

165. See Article 1, Paragraph 3 of the Constitution of SomaliRepublic of 1960. See also Article 30, Paragraph 2 that states, "The personal status of Muslims is governed by the general principles of Islamic Shari'a."
166. Ibid, Article 50

Constitution and to the general principles of Islam."[167] According to these Articles, "a law might be declared null and void by the constitutional court not only if it contravenes a specific provision of the Constitution but also if it contravenes the general principles of Islam."[168] Moreover, family and property laws remained in the realm of the Shari'a and were subject to strict interpretation by selective Shafi'i jurists.[169] Also, the penal code had clear Islamic inclinations in prohibiting drinking and selling alcohol; banning gambling, prostitution and abortions.

Based on the above, it could be said there were no obvious legal issues that provoked the Islamic consciousness. The concept of the Islamic state was not at stake during those years. Moreover, political leaders had close relations and networks with the prominent Islamic scholars and conflicts in the name of Islam were avoided. A clear example is Dr. Cabdirashiid Cali Sharmaarke who was the prime minister and president and belonged to the Qaadiriyah order being a disciple of Sheikh Muxyiddiin Celi. Moreover, most of the leaders were in good terms with the Islamic scholars and at times frequented their education circles or invited them to their homes. Furthermore, Islamic credentials of Somali state and its relations with the Muslim World were good. Somalia was a member of the World Islamic League founded in 1962 and became a founding member of the Islamic Conference in 1969. Moreover, al-Azhar Islamic scholars were frequently offering Friday sermons in the

---

167. Ibid, Article 98, Paragraph 1.
168. Paolo Contini, *The SomaliRepublic: an Experiment in Legal Integration* (London: Frank Cass & Company, 1969), 59.
169. Ibid., 35. The main reference law book for the Kadis in Somalia is *Kitab Al-Minhaj Li-Al-Imam Al-Nawawi*.

major mosques in Mogadishu and other cities and Islamic propagation was given unrestricted freedom.

In the 1960s, the MB's Islamic activism was apparently extended to Somalia. Two events in 1967 were particularly provoking Islamic emotions and sentiments. The first was the persecution of Sayid Qutub, the preeminent ideologue and prolific theoretician of the modern Islamic revivalism in Egypt. The second was the disastrous defeat of the Arab countries in the war with Israel in 1967. The explanation given for the defeat was the curse of Allah befalling the secular states, and so Islam emerged in the forefront as the national collective identity capable of healing the emotional breakdown of the Muslim world. The impact of the defeat of the Arab army in 1967 was the establishment of new organizations and solidarity with the Islamic call for revival and reform. Moreover, with the growing role of Saudi Arabia as the main challenger of the nationalist and secular Arab states and its offer of refuge for the persecuted MB, it appeared to be the champion of Islam and custodian of the holiest shrines. In the 1960s, there was no clear differentiation between the ideology of the MB and Salafia teachings in the eyes of the general public. The issue was Islam against the secular oppressive military regimes claiming Arab nationalism and connected with Socialist countries in attempting to overthrow what they considered as conservative reactionary Arab states. Therefore, Saudi Arabia was endangered by the revolutionary Arab regimes, and in alliance with Western countries during the Cold War era, Islam was employed against socialist regimes. The employment of Islam in fending off the socialist ideology was manifested in the establishment of numerous Islamic higher education institutions and charities to promote Islam globally. These institutions included the Islamic University in Medina, the Muslim World League in Mecca, Dar al-Ifta and World Muslim Youth. These institutions built mosques and Islamic schools, sponsored Islamic scholars, provided scholarships and held Islamic conferences. Somalia received a good share from the services of these institutions.

Conclusion

The development of the Islamic consciousness should be seen as historical evolution and a range of responses to the challenges from specific tensions. It was concurrent with the growing nationalism in the second half of the twentieth century and both of these ideologies constitute the identities that shaped the modern history of Somalia. They provided a supra-clan identity in a traditional society and shared in being indistinguishable from anti-colonial resistance ideologies. However, with the introduction of a modern education system and competition between Western education in the Italian and English languages and modern education in Arabic in the 1950s, the trends of westernization and Arabism began to emerge. The culture of westernization, carrying with it secularization of the state and society, and Arabism, delivering the Islamic consciousness, nationalism, and anti-colonialism, were fiercely competing with one another. In the 1950s, the Egyptian regime and the MB were promoting Arab nationalism and Islamism, respectively. Somalia, besides its Islamic solidarity and historical link with Egypt, became the strategic and geopolitical backyard of the Egyptian Nile River and Suez Canal waterways politics that was also in harmony with the priority agenda of the Somali irredentism directed against Ethiopia. Consequently, Egyptian cultural influence on Somalia took an added momentum in the 1950s and 1960s within the Cold War politics and mutual strategic cooperation.

Specifically, two broad sets of factors had contributed to the growth of Islamic consciousness in the 1950s and 1960s. The first set contributed to the increased capacity of the society and its resilience in withstanding the torrent ideas of westernization and western modernization. These factors included the introduction of the Egyptian system of schools, the formation of early Islamic organizations, the provision of scholarships to Somali students in the civil and military higher institutions in Egypt and other Arab countries, and other cultural means. These developments had created a new Arabic-speaking Somali elite, political leaders, and Islamic scholars who advocated against westernization and secularization, and lobbied for Arabism and Islamism. Some of these scholars were influenced by the MB ideology and the Salafism of Saudi Arabia. The second set of factors was involved in provoking the Islamic consciousness. They included the activities of Christian missionaries, in particular, the Protestant MM and SIM, which arrived in Somalia in 1953 and 1954, respectively. Moreover, the choice of the Somali language orthography was a battleground for Islamists and westernized elites. The popular demand for the use of the Arabic alphabet to write the Somali language was supported by Islamist scholars while the Latinized script was advocated by the westernized elites and was supported by the Western institutions.

After the independence in 1960, within the local, regional, and global context of the Cold War, regional competition, and transformation of the Somali society, the Islamic consciousness was gradually growing along with the growing westernization of the elites. The manifestations of this growth were the appearance of modern Islamist scholars educated in Arab universities who were marginalized in the job market and the proliferation of Arabic schools, books, newspapers, and libraries. Nevertheless, in the first nine years of the independence, there were no tangible conflicts between Islamic scholars and the new elites. Their common priorities of the entire nation were focused on the consolidating the independence and pursuing the "Greater Somalia" project. Islamic scholars educated during these years later became pioneers of a new era of the Islamic awakening, in which Islamic activities took new dimensions.

Finally, Somali society in this period (1950-1967), tradition and modernity coexisted, the state was not in direct conflict with Islam, and tolerance and dialogue were exercised. The first faultiness became visible in the late 1960s with the growth of the Islamist elites and their rejection of marginalization. This led to the increased Islamic activities, establishment of early Islamic organizations and widening gap between the non-Islamist and Islamist elites. This widening gap and the conflict will be analyzed in the following chapter.

CHAPTER THREE

The Upsurge of the Islamic Awakening

The awakening of Islam started to take preliminary shape after Somalia's independence in 1960 and benefited from opportunities provided by the freedom and civil liberty during the first nine years of the independence. It also took advantage from the impact of the events that caused the rise of Islamic consciousness since 1950s. The new independent Somali state has been facing great challenges stemming from the low human resources, the politicization of clans, the low economic performance, and the pressure from the neighboring countries that were considered enemies. These challenges undermined societal cohesion and development even though some form of democracy was implemented in which two parliamentary and presidential elections were held. Besides that, various civic institutions and social organizations started to emerge.[1] However, the hasty introduction of the unfamiliar model of democracy to the Somali traditional society brought about clan divisions, rampant corruption, widespread turmoil and resentments.

Within this socio-political context, spurred on by the earlier rise of Islamic consciousness in the 1950s, the emergence of the broad-based Islamic awakening was ushered in at the end of the

---

1. Apart from political parties, during 1960-1969, there were several active civil society organizations. The most prominent of these were the General Confederation of Somali Labour, Somali Youth Council, Organization of Somali Women, and Somali Student Solidarity Organization. See Abdurahman Abdullahi, "Non-State Actors in the Failed State of Somalia: Survey of the Civil Society Organizations in Somalia during the Civil War," *Darasāt Ifrīqiyyah* 31 (1994): 57-87.

1960s. This trend was an outcome of the cultural divide promoted by multi-curriculum education programs, in Arabic, Italian, and English, and links with conflicting actors in the Cold War atmosphere. The split of the elites into non-Islamist and Islamist factions slowly began to emerge, challenging social cohesion and the unifying aspects based on ethnicity, religion, and national aspiration. The roots of this division can be found in the clash between the nature of the state and the nature of the society. The post-colonial nation-state was nationalistic, hierarchical, centralized, and quasi-secular, while the society was clannish, egalitarian, decentralized, and Islamic. Under these strained conditions, the society as a whole was torn apart by the elites who gravitated toward competing ideologies such as liberal Western democracy, Socialism, and Islam. Although they possessed a strong cultural foundation, the weakeste and least developed elites during this time were the Islamists.

Consequently, in 1967, the country was in search of a new ideology, having been embarrassed by malpractices within the liberal democratic system; thus, socialism and Islamism were luring. Socialism was promoted by the socialist countries, and thousands of the Somali students were offered scholarships and indoctrinated in those countries. These students became later the elites that challenged the workings of liberal democracy. On the other hand, the Islamists were not happy with the entire secular foundation of the nation-state and opposed the growing leftist ideology, as well as the liberalist malpractices. They were dissatisfied with the state policy on Islam that remained very similar to the inherited colonial approach based on the existence of two separate spaces: public and private. Islam which Islamists advocated as comprehensive and applicable to all aspects of life was relegated to the private realm. They were not satisfied with Islamic window dressing such as the establishment of a Ministry of Religious Affairs and occasional gestures of politicians during Islamic festivities.

In 1967, after the pitiful political and social harvests of the first years of independence, Dr. Cabdirashiid Cali Sharmarke was elected President of Somalia, and he appointed Mr. Maxamad Xaaji Ibrahim Cigaal as the Premier. The new regime undertook two new objectives. The first one aimed to bolster the influence of the ruling party of SYL and to weaken other competing parties. This direction was supported by Western countries and conservative Arab regimes, in particular Saudi Arabia which offered considerable financial assistance.[2] The goal of this new policy was to empower friendly SYL in order to curb the Soviet influence in Somalia and to reverse previous policies geared toward the Eastern blocks initiated by Dr. Cabdirashid Cali Sharmarke in 1963. Therefore, the regime initiated policies intended to encourage the fragmentation and clanization of other parties. Consequently, more than 60 clan-based parties competed for 123 seats in the parliament during the 1969 election.[3] As planned by the state, all Members of

---

2. Saudi Arabia offered a loan of $50 million to Somalia designated to cover the election expenses in support of the SYL regime as reported by Moḥamed Sharīf Moḥamūd. However, the amount of the loan during this period seems exaggerated. It may be $5 Million. See Moḥamed Sharīf Moḥamūd, "*Faslun fi al 'Alāqāt al Somāliayah al Sa'ūdiyah*", 2010 (Somali Saudi relations), available from http://arabic.alshahid.net/Columnists/85 98 (accessed on February 6, 2010).

3. The new parties included *Hizbu Allāh*, a political party founded, among others, by Sheikh Xasan Sheikh Cabdullahi (af-Guriye) and Sheikh Cumar Sheikh Cabdullahi Al-Qudubi in 1969. Besides these two traditional scholars who founded the party, two students from the traditional Islamic circles were included in the central committee of the party. These students were Maxamad Yuusuf Cabdiraxman and Cabdullahi Cali Axmad. In the 1969 elections, the party fielded Sheikh Axmad Shire, brother of the President Cabdirashiid Cali Sharmaarke, as candidate. However, the party did not gain any seats in the parliament and was disbanded after the military coup of 1969.

Parliament from the small, clan-based parties were absorbed within the SYL after the election.[4] In the process, the National Army was implicated in rigging the election to dent its nationalistic image and weaken its credibility. At the same time, the Somali masses became utterly dismayed with the government because of widespread corruption, economic stagnation, rampant unemployment, and clan fighting caused by the rigged election. This state of affairs was characterized by Cabdalla Mansuur as "democracy gone mad."[5]

The second objectiveundertaken by the regime was aimed at changing national policies on "Greater Somalia" that was the foundation of the Somali foreign policy. Since the independence, Somalia supported Somali liberation movements in the Northern Frontier District (NFD) in Kenya, Western Somalia in Ethiopia and French Somaliland (Djibouti) to foster their unification as missing three parts of "Greater Somalia".[6] The new policy aimed at improving relations with the Western countries and curbing Soviet influence in Somalia embodied in their technical support for the Somali army. Prime Minister Cigaal undertook the soft foreign policy approach of détente which was aimed at alleviating Somalia's political, military, and economic ailments. He established congenial neighborly relations with Kenya and Ethiopia and restored the relationship with Britain severed in 1962. Somalia had broken diplomatic

---

Maxamad Yuusuf Cabdiraxman interviewed by the author on February 19, 2010, Kuwait.

4. In 1969, all MPs joined the SYL except one person, the former Prime Minister Cabdirisaaq Xaaji Xuseen.
5. Cabdulla Mansur, "Contrary to a Nation: The Cancer of Somali State'" in Ali Jimale Ahmed (ed), *The Invention of Somalia* (Lawrenceville, NJ, Red Sea Press, 1995), 114
6. See Lewis Fitzgibbon, *The betrayal of the Somalis* (Rex Collings, 1982). Also, I. M. Lewis, *Nationalism & self determination in the Horn of Africa* (Ithaca Press, 1983).

relations with Britain "when the special British NFD Commission determined that, despite the fact the majority of the Somalis in the region wished to join the Somali Republic, Britain should grant Kenya independence and announced that Kenya will decide on the matter."[7] The new Somali foreign policy was welcomed by Western powers and Somalia's neighboring countries but was perceived as a sell-out for the cause of Somali nationalism by domestic political opponents such as leftists and Islamists.[8] Thus, the two policies of the regime were unpopular and their ramifications lead to the subsequent political uncertainties. The assassination of President Sharmarke on October 15, 1969 and Prime Minister Cigaal's overt clannish maneuvering in the parliament to elect a new president were the preludes to the military coup on October 21, 1969.

In retrospect, it can be argued that the year 1967 was the culmination of the Arabic cultural influence and the early stage of maturation of Islamist elites. In this year, the first organization for Arabic educated Islamist elites in Somalia was established under the name *Munadamat al-Nahdah al-Islāmiyah* (The Organization of the Islamic Renaissance). It became known as Nahdah and soon other Islamic organizations followed. The Somali Islamic awakening was not an isolated phenomenon; it was part of a worldwide Muslim upheaval after the defeat of the Arab forces during the war with Israel in 1967. This defeat set off a wave of soul-searching and the demand for a new ideology to replace the defeated secular Arab nationalism. The answer to the national cataclysm was to seek solace in Islamism

---

7. See Ibrahim Farah, "Foreign Policy and Conflict in Somalia, 1960-1990" (PhD diss., University of Nairobi, 2009), 107.
8. Ibid., 117.

which was until then suppressed by the Arabic nationalist/socialist regimes. Therefore, Islamist movements inspired by *Ḥassan al-Banna, Mawlāna al-Maudūdi*, and *Sayid Qutub* were gaining ground and amassing support. This awakening had been simmering since the suppression of the MB in Egypt in 1954 and the execution of the famous Egyptian Islamic scholar *Sayid Qutub* along with two other members of the MB in 1966.[9] This event greatly shocked and inspired Muslims all over the world. Many Somali Islamic scholars changed their positive views on the Egyptian regime that they had held because of its earlier provision of educational opportunities for Somalis and its ardent support for the Somali nationalistic cause.[10] As a result of this incident, the MB literature garnered immense interest and attracted a huge readership. In particular, two of Sayid Qutub's works became extremely popular: *Ma'ālim fi al- Ṭarīq* (Milestones) and *Fī Ḍilāl al-Qur'ān* (In the Shade of the Qur'an), the latter being a 30-volume commentary on the Qur'an with an innovative method of interpretation.

---

9. Sayid Qutub (1906-1966) was an Egyptian Islamist scholar and the leading intellectual of the Egyptian Muslim Brotherhood in the 1950s and 1960s. He was imprisoned (1954-64) and then hanged in 1966 by the Egyptian regime under President Nasser's rule. The other two members of MB were Muhammad Yusuf Awash and Abd al-Fattah Ismail. See Zafar Bangash, "Remembering Sayyid Qutb, an Islamic intellectual and leader of rare insight and integrity", available from http://web.youngmuslims.ca/online_library/books/milestones/remember.htm (accessed on January 28, 2010).

10. The Egyptian Embassy in Mogadishu attempted to explain to some traditional Islamic scholars that the execution of Sayid Qutub was in defence of Islam. Sheikh Maxamad Garyare related that during these days, he saw a group of Somalis in the mosque reading a pamphlet in Arabic. One of them was translating the following from Arabic to Somali: *Sayid Qutub huwa dālun mudilūn*, which means Sayid Qutub, had deviated from the true Islamic path and was leading people astray. Sheikh Maxamad Garyare interviewed by the author on August 5, 2008, Hargeysa.

The Islamic awakening in Somalia acquired a new momentum with the military coup in 1969 and the adoption of Socialism as the official national ideology in 1970. The military regime had adopted modernization policies in line with Socialism which went against the culture of the people and Islamic laws thereby widening the fissure and ideological polarization of the society. This chapter will examine the Islamic awakening since 1967 and, in particular, will focus on the first period of the military regime (1969-1977). It will explore the institutions created to foster the Islamic awakening which in this study will be called "the Proto-Muslim Brotherhood." These organizations are Nahdah (Renaissance), *Weḥdat al-Shabāb al-Islāmi* (the Union of Islamic Youth) known as "Waxdah", and *Ahl al-Islām* (the People of Islam) known as "Ahal." The impact of other Islamic organizations such as the Salafia organization, known as *Jam'iyat Ihyā al-Sunna* (Revivification of the Prophet's Tradition) was negligible during this period and will not be discussed here.[11] Likewise, Sufi organizations such as *Jam'iyat Ansār al-Addīn* (The Association of Helpers of Religion) in Hargeysa and *Jam'iyat Himāt al-Addīn* (The Association of Protectors of Religion) in Mogadishu are also not included here. Moreover, this chapter focuses on the military regime, its Socialist programs and its confrontation with the Islamic awakening. The watershed conflict between the Islamic awakening and the military regime concerned in the

---

11. *Jam'iyat Ihyā al-Sunna* was founded in 1967 by Sheikh Nur Ali Olow (1918-1995), a pioneer and prominent scholar who relentlessly preached the methodology of Salafism in Somalia for 60 years (1935-1995). This organization's activities included a school for adults and Islamic circles in the biggest mosques in Mogadishu. Also, it held specialized Islamic education circles for politicians and prominent personalities in the house of General Maxamad Abshir and Yaasin Nuur Xassan. Sheikh Maxamuud Axmad interviewed by the author, May 1, 2009, Toronto, Canada.

secularization of the Family Law in 1975 will be produced as a case study. Finally, the fragmentation and the emergence of the new tendency of extremism within Islamic awakening will be presented.

Institutions of the Islamic Awakening: The Proto-Muslim Brotherhood

Apart from traditional Sufi brotherhoods and institutions of Islamic consciousness that were established in the 1950s, the late 1960s ushered in three organizations that took the Islamic call to a new stage: Nahdah, Waxdah, and Ahal. Furthermore, the rift between Islamists and non-Islamists was correlated with internal divisions within each camp. In the non-Islamist camp, the conflict between leftists and liberal democrats wasraging. Equally, in the Islamist camp, doctrinal disagreements between the Sufi orders and Salafism, and difference in the comprehension and approaches to Islamic propagation between Salafism and the MB were growing. These conflicts exacerbated the traditional clan tensions in Somalia and spurred the emerging class conflict. This chapter focuses on tracing the dynamics in Islamic activism by reconstructing the history of these institutions in the modern history of Somalia.

Munadamat al-Nahdah al-Islāmiyah (Nahdah)

The first Islamic organization to bridge the Islamic consciousness and Islamic awakening was Nahdah. Its founders included what could be termed "transitional Islamic scholars," meaning those scholars who were initially educated in the traditional way and later graduated from universities in the

Arab/Islamic world.[12] These scholars were exposed to both traditional and modern systems of education and were well equipped to deal with both the traditional society and modern issues. The history of Nahdah is not well recorded and, therefore, in reconstructing it, three primary resources encountered during field research for this study will be used as a basis. The first significant source is the bye-laws of the organization written in the Arabic language, kept in the custody by one of the founding members.[13] The two other sources are oral narratives from two founding members: Sheikh Maxamad Garyare and Sheikh Cabdiraxman Xuseen Samatar. The bye-laws consist of 31 articles encompassing all aspects of the organization. Most notably, the bye-laws offer a detailed legal basis for acquiring and revoking membership, as well as for financial matters. For example, there are five articles that regulate membership: from eligibility and acquiring membership to conditions for its revoking, and disciplinary action taken against members and the discretion of the disciplinary committee.[14] Moreover, regulations on financial affairs are wide-ranging and include sources of income, financial management, disciplinary measures to be taken against members with outstanding membership fees, and the

---

12. The founders of Nahdah are: Sheikh Cabdulqani Sheikh Axmad (President), Sheikh Maxamad Axmad Nuur Garyare (Vice-President), Cabdiraxman Faarah Ismaciil "Kabaweyne" (Secretary-General), Sheikh Cabdullahi Macallin Cabdiraxman (Deputy Secretary-General), Cabdiraxman Xuseen Samatar (Treasurer), Shariif Calawi Cali Aadan (Deputy Treasurer), and Bashiir Macallin Cali Maxamuud, Maxamuud Cusman Jumcaale, and Maxamad Axmad Xuseen (members). These names were recorded in the Article 4 of the bylaws of Nahdah.
13. This copy of the bylaws was retained by Sheikh Cabdiraxman Xuseen Samatar, the Treasurer of Nahdah. Sheikh Cabduraxman Xuseen Samatar interviewed by the author on December 1, 2009, Nairobi, Kenya.
14. The Bylaw of Nahdah, articles 4, 5, 6, 7, and 30.

determination of the financial year. Furthermore, the bye-laws regulate the process of financial allocations and the discretion of the treasurer.[15] In the preamble, the rationale of Nahdah is clearly expressed as follows:

> In these difficult conditions in which Islamic society is facing a number of diverse adversaries and raids allied against its religion and its existence, in which it wrestles also with poverty and illiteracy and all other signs of backwardness, it is compulsory for its sincere sons to rush to work and rescue it from these obliterating threats. In order to fulfill this duty, *Munadamat al-Nahda al-Islamiyah* was launched with the grace and guidance of Allah in Mogadishu on 1387 H (1967).[16]

The main objectives of Nahdah were threefold: "(1) Making the Qur'an the constitution of the Muslims and applying Islamic Shari'a law in all aspects of their lives. (2) Struggling against all state of affairs and ideologies that do not comply with Islamic Shari'a law. (3) Strengthening brotherly relations between Muslims and reinstating their [lost] unity."[17] It is striking to note that these objectives were very general and that none of them targeted specific local issues. They also do not provide a strategy for realizing these broad objectives in their own environment. In fact, such strategy was not even mentioned in the bye-laws. Moreover, the influence of the MB was clear in the bye-laws, as evidenced by such slogans as *"al-Qur'ānu Dastūruna"* (Islam is our constitution) and the mentioning of the

---

15. Ibid, articles 8, 9, 10, 11, 16, and 27 of the bylaw.
16. All citations from Somali and Arabic to English are translated by the author. The exact date is not recorded in the bylaws.
17. See Article 3 of Nahdah bylaw.

strengthening brotherly relations among Muslims.[18] Nahdah's president, Sheikh Cabdulqani, the vice president, Sheikh Maxamad Garyare, and its Secretary General Sheikh Cabdiraxman Faarax (Kabaweyne) were all members of the MB.[19] There were also other founding members who sympathized with the MB.[20]

Membership in the organization was severely restricted and only people with specific qualities were targeted for the membership. These qualities included being a "conscious" Muslim with good manners and commitment to Islam. Although it is difficult to define and measure what being a "conscious" Muslim constituted, it probably referred to a Muslim who was aware of the glorious Muslim civilization and the deplorable state of affairs of Muslims in the contemporary

---

18. This is part of the famous motto of the Muslim Brotherhood: *Allāh Gāyatuna, al-Rasulu Za'īmunā, al-Qur'ānu Dustūrunā, al-Jihādu Sabīluna, al-Mawt fi Sabīl al-Allāh Asmā Amānīna* [translation: God is our goal, the Qur'an is our constitution, The Prophet is our leader, the struggle is our way, and death in the service of God is the loftiest of our wishes]. See Hassan alBanna. *The Message of Teaching*, available from http://web.yo ungmuslims.ca/online_library/books/tmott/index.htm(accessedon January 28, 2010).
19. Sheikh Cabdulqani (1935-2007) was born in the Bakool region of Somalia. After memorizing the Qur'an at an early age, he underwent a traditional Islamic education and was subsequently offered admission to the al-Azhar University inEgypt in 1951 from where he graduated in 1957. He returned to Somalia and worked as a lecturer at the Somali University Institute and also joined the Ministry of Justice and Religious Affairs. In 1967, he was one of the founders of the Nahdah Islamic organization. During the military regime he became Minister of Justice and Religious Affairs in 1970, but was imprisoned in 1973. In 1982 he traveled to Kuwait and worked in the Islamic encyclopedia project until his death in 2007. See his short biography "*Al-Sheikh 'Abdulqani Sheikh Aḥmed Adan: Mu'asas al Nahdah al Islāmiyah intaqala ilā Rahmat Allāh*" published on September 1, 2007, available from http://www.Islah.org/arabic/Sh%20Ab dulqani.htm (accessed on October 14, 2009).
20. Sheikh Maxamad Garyare interviewed by the author on May 10, 2009, Toronto, Canada; and Sheikh Cabdiraxman Xuseen Samatar interviewed by the author on December 13, 2009, Nairobi, Kenya. Sheikh Cabdiraxman Xuseen Samatar confirmed that the MB and Salafia had been vying for winning the graduates from Arabic universities and most of them sympathized with the MB including himself.

world. Such a person would have believed in the necessity of struggle to rectify and reverse this situation. Technically, to acquire membership, an aspirant would have to submit an official written application and pay 10 Somali shilling as admission fee with recommendations from three members.[21] The final decision about membership was taken by the Executive Bureau or the local executive branches.[22] Two important requirements for retaining the membership were paying monthly fees and remaining a devoted Muslim. The bye-laws did not require more than that from members. For example, they did not require from the members to participate in specific activities or programs. Expelling a member from the organization was somewhat more complicated and called for a long process of verification and, in the end, a majority vote of two-thirds of the Executive Bureau.[23]

The organizational structure of *Nahdah* comprised *Majlis al-Shūra* (Consultative Council "CC"), Maktab *al-Tanfidi* (Executive Bureau "EB"), chapters, and various other committees. The number of the members of the CC was not specified and could be determined for each term. Conversely, the number of the EB members was limited to nine executives.[24] These were the president, the vice-president, the secretary-general, the deputy secretary-general, the treasurer, the deputy treasurer, and three other members without portfolios. Although this structure seems very modern, the absence of a fixed number of the

---

21. The exchange rate of the Somali shilling to the US dollar from 1960-1971 was 7.14286: $1. Accordingly, the admission fee was equivalent to $1.40. See Maxamad Huseen Amin, *Taariikhda Bangiyada Somaaliyeed* (Sharjah: UAE, Amazon Printing Press, 2004), 65.
22. See Article 4 of Nahdah bylaws.
23. See Article 6 of Nahdah bylaws.
24. See Article 18 of Nahdah bylaws.

members for the CC and terms for them were the deficiencies in the bye-laws. Moreover, important portfolios for similar Islamic organizations such as external relations and Islamic activities were entirely missing. The bye-laws also demonstrate a certain lack of dynamism by not addressing issues such as membership drives and policies to expand membership. Finally, it is not clear from the bye-laws how many founding members there were. Only the names of the executive members were recorded. In relation to this, it is impossible to estimate Nahdah's membership. Sheikh Maxamad Garyare confirmed that the founding members were nine Executive Bureau members and the Consultative Council was not been formed, although the bye-laws contained such a provision.[25] Moreover, despite the increase in membership, neither Sheikh Maxamad Garyare nor Sheikh Cabdiraxman Samatar could reliably estimate how many members Nahdah had before it was abolished in 1969. However, both of them confirmed that Sheikh Maxamad Macallin and Sheikh Cali Xaaji Yuusuf joined Nahdah. After the organization was banned as part of the general policy of the military regime, informal networking continued between its members and activities were sustained in their personal capacities.

Nahdah had engaged in various Islamic activities, but here wewill depict only two programs that left a great imprint on the Islamic awakening. The first was the establishment of Islamic libraries and the bringing of the MB literature to Somalia. The second includes the activities presented at the *Da'wa* programs

---

25. Sheikh Maxamad Garyare interviewed by the author on January 7, 2009, Toronto, Canada.

in the mosques and the Islamic centers. Sheikh Maxamad Garyare said the following about the first program:

> After the formation of Nahdah, I wrote a letter to *Sheikh 'Abdallah Aqīl* telling him about our new organization and explaining to him the lack of Islamic literature in Somalia.[26] I requested his help on that matter and he replied promptly saying *"la taḥmil haman,"* meaning "don't worry". *Sheikh 'Abdallah 'Aqīl* was well aware of my membership in the MB in my early student years in Saudi Arabia. Within a month-and-a-half, he sent a complete library of selected modern Islamic books and reference works which included textbooks used in the special training and education programs of the MB. These Islamic books arrived in multiple shipments and were shelved in the library of the Ministry of Religious Affairs, the library of Nahdah, my home and the home of Sheikh Cali Xaaji Yuusuf.[27]

During these years, students in the Egyptian Arabic high schools and students of the Islamic Solidarity Institute, established by the World Muslim League in 1967, were frequenting these libraries.[28] Graduates from these schools played prominent roles in the Islamic awakening and Islamic movements.[29] Moreover, some dedicated students who

---

26. Sheikh Abdallah Aqil was a member of the MB and Director of Islamic Affairs in the Ministry of Religious Affairs, Kuwait.
27. Cali Xaaji Yuusuf is the son of Xaaji Yuusuf, the disciple of Sheikh Cali Maye who was sent to his sub-clan, Suleiman of Habargidir settled in the Galguduud region. Cali Xaaji worked extensively with the EgyptianCulturalCenter in Mogadishu and became a member of Nahdah. Cali Xaaji Yuusuf interview by Sayid Cumar Cabdullahi on December 27, 2009, Mogadishu, Somalia.
28. The Muslim World League (*Rābiḍah al-'Ālam al-Islāmi*) was founded in Mecca in 1962 as a non-governmental organization concerned with Islamic affairs. Its worldwide headquarters were in Jeddah, and the organization was sponsored and financially supported by Saudi Arabia.
29. The role of this institute is crucial in the development of the Islamic awakening. Many of its former students later became prominent scholars in the Islamic movements. For instance, Dr. Cali Sheikh Axmad, Dr. Maxamad Yuusuf, Sheikh Cabdulqaadir Faarah (Gacamey), Sheikh Cabdullahi Diiriye Abtidoon, Sheikh Cumar Faaruuq, Sheikh Yuusuf Aadan, and many more.

frequented general Islamic circles in mosques were encouraged to read specific books that were internally circulated. The effect of these books was great, and an entire generation of high school students was gradually converted to the ideology of the MB without acquiring actual membership. It was the era of recruiting people to the idea not to the organization, which was also the general case in Egypt during this period.

Besides direct Islamic summons, many Islamic circles were established in mosques, and weekly lectures were held in the Nahdah center, regularly attracting hundreds of students. The most popular Islamic circle was the Qur'anic commentary of Sheikh Maxamad Macallin Xasan. In the following, his short biography will be provided and comments of witnesses about the effect that his circle had in the Islamic awakening will be presented. Sheikh Maxamad was a distinguished Islamic scholar and exceptional Qur'anic commentator who succeeded in attracting people from all walks of life to his Islamic education circle, held in the famous Cabdulqaadir Mosque in Mogadishu in the 1970s. He was born near Buur-Hakaba in 1934 where he memorized the Qur'an in his early childhood.[30] In 1942, he traveled to an area near Jigjiga and Harrar, where he frequented Islamic education centers for about ten years.[31] In1952, he started teaching Islam in the city of Hargeysa at the

---

30. The date of his birth is an approximation as he was born in a rural area. According to the testimony of Sheikh Maxamad Macallin in an interview with the BBC, his passport indicated that he was born in 1936.
31. When Sheikh Maxamad Macallin arrived in the area of Jigjiga, he met Sheikh Maxamad Cabdullahi who became his first teacher. Later, Sheikh Maxamad Macallin became Qur'anic teacher. Then, he frequented the education circle of Sheikh Cali Jowhar and Sheikh Baraawe. See Maxamad Xaaji Cabdullahi "Ingiriis", *Taariikh Nololeedkii Sheikh Maxamad Macallin (the biography of Sheikh Mohamed Moallim)*, available from http://www.himilo.com/?pid=content&aid=4 (accessed on December 17, 2009).

Grand Jami'i Mosque. After five years, Sheikh Maxamad decided to travel to Egypt to further his Islamic studies and finally joined al-Azhar University in 1958. He obtained his Bachelor of Arts and Master's degrees in Islamic theology and philosophy and returned to Mogadishu in 1968.[32] The years of Sheikh Maxamad's education in Egypt were a difficult period of brutal suppression of the MB and although he was influenced by the teachings of the MB, he did not officially join the organization.[33] When Sheikh Maxamad Macallin returned to Mogadishu, he received a heartfelt welcome at the Nahdah Headquarters, where he later joined the organization. He became a pivotal figure in the *Da'wa* program, as enunciated by Sheikh Maxamad Garyare:

> We knew that he was a very talented Islamic scholar who combined traditional Islamic education with experience in teaching and a higher degree from al-Azhar University.[34] Finally, we decided that Sheikh Maxamad Macallin had to start Qur'anic commentary in Sheikh Cabdulqaadir Mosque. Sheikh Cabdullahi Dirir was the administrator of the mosque who belonged to the Qaadiriyah order.[35] Sheikh Cabdulqani, who was a close friend of Sheikh Cabdullahi, convinced him to allow Sheikh Maxamad Macallin to conduct Islamic education circle in the mosque. Sheikh Cabdullahi

---

32. One of his Sheikhs was Sheikh Abdul-Halim Mohamud, the famous Sheikh of al-Azhar in Egypt.
33. Sheikh Maxamad Macallin interviewed by Maxamuud Sheikh Dalmar of the BBC in 1994 published on August 21, 2009, available from http://www.bbc.co.uk/somali/news/story/2009/08/090821_falanqeynta21082009.shtml (accessed on December 17, 2009).
34. This discussion was held between Sheikh Cabdulqani, Sheikh Maxamad Garyare, and Cabdiraxman "Kabaweyne." Sheikh Maxamad Garyare interviewed by the author on July 5, 2009, Toronto, Canada.
35. Sheikh Cabdullahi Dirir worked in the Ministry of Education, Department of the Scholarships. He was the vicegerent of Sheikh Cabdullahi al-Qudubi, the famous Qaadiriyah scholar who founded the mosque. Sheikh Maxamad Garyare interviewed by the author on January 12, 2010, Toronto, Canada. Also, Maxamad Yuusuf Cabdiraxman interviewed by the author on February 29, 2010, Kuwait.

finally accepted on the condition that he should not teach "Wahabiyah" as Sheikh Nuur Cali Colow did. Sheikh Maxamad Macallin was educated by Qaadiriyah Sheikhs and was well aware of their concerns.[36] As a result, Sheikh Maxamad Macallin accepted the conditions and started the historical Islamic circle that took Islamic awakening to higher strides. We advised him to use the exegesis of "In the Shade of the Qur'an," the Qur'anic commentary by Sayid Qutub, as the main reference. Sheikh Maxamad Macallin superbly succeeded in attracting all types of Somalis, including prominent politicians and higher ranking officers from the former regime, employees of the notorious National Security Service, high government officials, traditional Sufi scholars and high school students.[37]

Sheikh Maxamad Macallin started his first education program in the last months of 1968 at the Sheikh Cabdulqaadir Mosque while being employed at the Ministry of Religious Affairs. After a few years, he became the deputy director working with Sheikh Maxamad Garyare, who was director of the Department of the Islamic Affairs. The popularity of the Qur'anic commentary of Sheikh Maxamad Macallin was unprecedented because he introduced a new methodology for Qur'anic commentary. This innovative method was based on reciting certain verses from the Qur'an and translating them directly from Arabic to Somali according to a system called laqbo (translating Islamic text from Arabic to Somali) in Somali traditional education. He also offered free commentary in the Somali language to emphasize the meaning of the concepts of

---

36. One of his teachers was Sheikh Cali Jowhar who was a disciple of Sheikh Cabdisalam Xaaji Jaamac, a renowned family of Islamic scholars belonging to the Qaadiriyah order in Jigjiga.
37. Sheikh Maxamad Garyare interviewed by the author on July 5, 2009, Toronto, Canada.

Islam.[38] The instruction was held between the afternoon prayer and Isha prayer, a convenient time for most people. However, his popularity annoyed the military regime and, as Sheikh Maxamad Macallin mentioned in the BBC interview in 1994, the regime attempted to persuade him to stop the program by promoting him to the position of director of the Islamic affairs in 1973. In order to make him leave the country, the regime also tried offering him an ambassadorial position.[39] However, with the growth of the leftist influence and after the Family Law of 1975, Sheikh Maxamad and 60 other high-ranking government officials were dismissed from their positions. Subsequently, he was sentenced to seven years (1976-1982) of solitary confinement in the notorious maximum security prison of Labaatan Jirow, and again four years (1984-1988) in the main prison of Mogadishu.[40] As evident from this short biography, Sheikh Maxamad was imprisoned at the end of the Islamic awakening period and remained in prison at the beginning of the formation of the Islamic movement in 1978. Sheikh Maxamad Macallin is held until today in high esteem for his contribution to the Islamic education during early years of the Islamic awakening. Although his disciples later had various disagreements when they came into contact with different Islamic ideologies, they were always respectful of him and

---

38. The traditional methodology in dealing with Qur'anic exegesis consisted of simply reading the commentary of the Qur'an, in particular the simple commentary called "Tafsir al-Jalāleyn". There were no substantial comments on the variety of contemporary issues.
39. Sheikh Maxamad Garyare was demoted and transferred to the Appellate Court in 1973 to serve as a judge.
40. Labaatan Jirow was a maximum security prison about 60 kilometres north of Baidoa. See the description of the prison by Dr. Maxamad Baaruud Cali. "Remembering the unsung and forgotten heroes of Labaatan Jirow," available from http://www.somalia watch.org/archive/000409631.htm (accessed on 25 June, 2010).

considered him their supreme educator. What follows is the testimony of Professor Yuusuf Axmad Nuur who frequented Sheikh Maxamad Macallin's Islamic circle during his high school time:

> I started attending Sheikh Maxamad Macallin Qur'anic study circle in September or October, 1970. The Sheikh revolutionized Qur'anic exegesis in the Somali language. I attended the study circle during all four years of high school. The Sheikh taught me almost everything I know about the Qur'an or about Islam for that matter. If it were not for that fateful evening when I prayed after sunset prayer (*Magrib*) in Sheikh Cabdulqaadir Mosque at the suggestion of a friend of mine who knew about the study circle and who thought that I would like to listen to the Sheikh, I don't know how my life would have turned out. For sure it would have been completely different from what it is today. Arguably, the Sheikh influenced, directly or indirectly, every Somali who is part of the Islamic awakening which had its beginnings in the late 1960s.[41]

Besides many former politicians and bureaucrats of the ousted civilian regime, the circle attracted mostly high school students and those opposed to the socialist programs. A dissident Islamic organization called Ahal was instrumental in mobilizing these students in order to recruit them as members. The following section will examine this historical development.

Ahl al-Islam (The Family of Islam) "Ahal"

The historical roots of Ahal go back to a youth group of the Qaadiriyah Sufi order that expressed their anger at the society's condition in the 1960s. They could be considered a neo-Sufi group with an inclination to reform traditional Sufi orders that

---

41. Yuusuf Axmad Nuur, interviewed by the author, January 12, 2010, Nairobi, Kenya.

directly addressed social and political concerns. What provoked this youth group is not clear; however, it could be speculated that one of the factors may be to counter young Americans sent to Somalia as members of American Peace Corps who arrived in Somalia in 1961 as voluntary teachers. The 1960s was a decade when youth counter-culture emerged worldwide, and likewise in Somalia. The American Peace Corps introduced that counter-culture to Somali students in the schools and streets of Mogadishu. The Somali youth reacted in one of two ways to this culture. One was to mimic Western culture, while another was to create a defensive counter-culture. The Qaaderiyah youth was headed by Cabdikariin Xirsi supported by Cabdulqaadir Sheikh Maxamuud "Ganey" and Xasan Indhoceel and presented this defensive counterculture of the Somali youth and bacame known as Ahal.[42] To achieve their objectives, founder of Ahal were closely engaged in the Islamic awareness activities using innovative Sufi poems in the Somali language which proved very attractive for the youth. The group was seemingly related to the Jaberti Mosque in Mogadishu, and its members might have been disciples of Sheikh Ismaciil or Sheikh Maxamuud Ciise, the administrators of that Mosque.[43] Moreover, it seems that the group was spurred on by those who lobbied to make the Cusmaaniya script the official script for the Somali language.[44] There are two indications for this

---

42. Cabdikariin Xirsi is the brother of a famous tuberculosis medical doctor in Mogadishu, Dr. Yuusuf Xirsi, and Cabdulqaadir Sheikh Maxamuud was their close relative. Cabdikariin joined the Institute of the Saudi established Islamic Solidarity and was expelled from it because of his incompliance with its norms and policies. Maxamad Yuusuf interviewed by the author on February 29, 2010, Kuwait.
43. Axmad Cali Axmad interviewed by the author, December 28, 2009, Nairobi, Kenya.
44. The Cusmaaniya script was invented in 1918 by Cismaan Yuusuf Keenadiid and Xirsi Magan, a graduate of Columbia University who was the most active supporter of the

speculation. First, although most Sufi poems are in the Arabic language, the group was focusing on the Somalization of these poems, supported by the Cusmaaniya followers. Also, the secretary for the Cusmaaniya group, Cabdiraxman Axmad Nuur, became a prominent leader in the organization, second only to Cabdulqaadir Sheikh Maxamuud.

Beyond their emotional attachment to Islam, the group members were not well versed in Islam. Below are excerpts from a poem, demonstrating the style and content of their short rhythmic poetry. This part of the poem was chanted to voice their rejection of the national election held on March 26, 1969.

26 Maarsoo, waa la kala miirmayaa maanta [on 26 March! Will be the day of disjointing]
Murtad iyo munaafaq maanta [When] apostates and hypocrites
Midigta u casaane maanta will have red [ink] on their right hand[45]

Another part of the poem was repeatedly cited during their demonstrations: *"Wallāhi, Bilāhi, qad kafaru al-Qur'āna,"* which means, "I swear to Allah, they disbelieved the Qur'an."[46] This poem regarded those who voted in the March 26 elections as apostates and hypocrites, which was displayed as the lack of understanding of Islam and was a sign for extremist tendencies. The group demonstrated the first sign of Takfiir (the practice of declaring someone else unbeliever) in its early development, a belief that many of its followers come to adhere later. Sheikh

---

Cusmaaniya script. See Abdirahman Ahmed, *"Arabic Language and Script in Somalia: History, attitudes and prospects"* (PhD diss., Georgetown University, 1999), 136.

45. The red hand signifies the red ink used to identify persons who had voted in the election. This poem was related by Axmad Cali Axmad interviewed by the author on December 23, 2009, Nairobi, Kenya.
46. Axmad Rashid Xanafi interviewed by author on January 11, 2010, Ottawa, Canada.

Maxamad Garyare said he knew Cabdikariin and his group and described them as follows:

> I met Cabdikariin in 1966 and he was a very enthusiastic young man. I participated in the meeting of his group several times and delivered some lectures. At other times, Sheikh Cabdulqani was with me. We tried to improve their comprehension of Islam and they were very dedicated. The relation of Nahdah with them was very good. They held their own regular meetings and were highly organized.[47]

However, when Cabdulqaadir Sheikh Maxamuud assumed leadership of the group, he found the best opportunity to educate the group and mobilize new recruits through the Qur'anic commentary of Sheikh Maxamad Macallin that began in 1968. Within this Islamic circle, Ahalwas established and nurtured. Although there is no reliable source to authenticate the date of Ahal establishment, all indications suggest that it was established in 1969. None of those interviewed had seen any bye-laws of the organization or had heard of it, so, most likely, its bylaws were not committed into writing. When Cabdulqaadir Sheikh Maxamuud took over the organization, he provided strong leadership and transformed it into an organization mainly targeting high school students.[48] The ideological transformation of Ahal members occurred, while its

---

47. Sheikh Maxamad Garyare interviewed by the author on July 5, 2009, Toronto, Canada.
48. Cabdulqaadir Sheikh Maxamuud graduated from Italian schools and worked in ENE "Ente Nationale Electrica" (National Electrical Authority). His Islamic education was minimal and therefore, as many interviewees reported, was very sensitive to include in his organization persons who are older than him or better educated in Islam. See Al-Shahid. *Qadiyat al-Shahr: al-Irhāb fi al-Somāl., Wahmūn am Haqīqah?* Special report on terrorism in Somalia published on January 15, 2010, available from http://arabic.alshahid.net/monthly-issue/7789 (accessed on May 25, 2010).

leaders and members were studying Islam from the Qur'anic commentary by Sheikh Maxamad Macallin. Also, the Islamic library established by Nahdah was offering additional educational opportunities. With this transformation, the organization was heading in a new direction. The speed of transformation accelerated when after the military coup of 1969 all political and social organizations were banned and Socialism was adopted as official ideology in 1970, which further provoked Islamic sentiments. In all likelihood, Ahal went underground and furthered its work by increasing its leadership and recruitment.

The organization did not have an official name or formal bylaw. The name of Ahal was used as a code name between members of the organization when they meet in public. Members asked each other, according to Somali tradition, "Ahalka ka waran?" which means, "How is the family?" signifying their organization. Therefore, the objectives of Ahal are not written down anywhere; however, there is a speculation that they were not different from the objectives of similar Islamic organizations whose ultimate goal was to make the Qur'an, the basics for the constitution of the state and to establish an Islamic state in Somalia. The interim programs and strategies were probably founded on opposing Socialism and intensifying the Islamic Da'wa by targeting young generations. Naturally, continuing this process for years provided an atmosphere of social acceptance. However, in repressive regimes such as Somalia, the climate was right for alternative options. Ahal provided such an alternative and began to work toward realizing it. The intention was to encourage, or even make it obligatory for certain members of the organization to join the national armed forces, infiltrate national intelligence services, and prepare for overthrowing the regime. This plan had two components. The first was to carefully select and recruit officers of the armed forces who were sympathetic to Islam and who were opposed to the socialist ideology. The second component was to identify individuals from within Ahal and direct them to join the armed forces. The implementation of this plan started in 1974. Two witnesses were interviewed about this plan. The first said the following:

> I graduated from 15 May High School in Mogadishu in 1974. I was recruited in 1973 to be a member of Ahal. We normally met once every month after completing reading of the whole Qur'an in the houses of the prominent leaders. One day, our Amiir Cabulqaadir called me for special meeting and directed me to join the army. I never thought of joining the army, however, I complied. After joining the army, I was sent to the Soviet Union and was trained as an officer. I remember we were about ten members who joined the army in 1974 and in the following years the numbers increased drastically. Interestingly, however, when we returned from the military training abroad, the same person who directed us to join the army ordered us again to leave the army after being converted to Takfiir ideology which prohibits working in the institutions of the un-Islamic (Jaahiliya) governments.[49]

The other witness commented on the work of Ahal in high schools and on their activities and recruitment process:

> In the 1970s, it was very normal for high school students to frequent Islamic circles in the mosques. It was a growing trend that many brilliant students were attracted to. I was a student in the Hawl-Wadaag high school in Mogadishu and was fascinated with some very religious and brilliant students in our school. They used to

---

49. Yuusuf Axmad Nuur interviewed by the author on December 24, 2009, Nairobi, Kenya.

explain to us some verses from the 30 parts of the Qur'an during break times. They were also active in delivering short talks at the student gatherings. I remember one student named Axmad Nuur Carab who was very active. They were recommending students to join the Qur'anic commentary of Sheikh Maxamad Macallin. There, we met many enthusiastic students from other schools and I joined Ahal in 1975. Our leader was Cabdulqaadir Sheikh Maxamuud, called the Amiir, and executive members included Cusman Cabdulle Rooble, Xuseen Cali Xaaji and Cabdulqaadir Maxamad Cabdullahi. I was ordered to join the army in 1975; however, after ten days of petitions and convincing reasons, I was later relieved from that assignment.[50]

Both these testimonies demonstrate Ahal's focus on high school activities, recommending to these students to join the Qur'anic commentary of Sheikh Maxamad Macallin and to attend regular monthly meetings of the members, reading and memorizing of the Qur'an. They also confirmed the important role of the Islamic library founded by Nahdah and, finally, the militaristic tendency of the organization in 1974. Moreover, the two testimonies confirmed that there was a required procedure for taking an oath of allegiance to the organization that included shaking hands. They further related that women were allowed to become members of the organization and a women's wing was established during the early years. Some prominent female leaders included Marian Xaaji Cabdiraxman, Marian Yuusuf and Marian Diini. Both testimonies also conveyed that the first branch of Ahal was established in Beletweyne, the town became an early center of the Islamic awakening.[51] Early members of the Beletweyne branch of Ahal included Adan Xaaji Xuseen, Cabdiraxman Sheikh Cumar and his brother Cabdixakiim

---

50. Axmad Cali Axmad interviewed by the author on December 23, 2009, Nairobi, Kenya.
51. Xasan Xaaji Maxamuud interviewed by the author on April 10, 2010, Nairobi, Kenya.

Sheikh Cumar, Xasan Mahdi and others.[52] The brutal execution in 1975 of Islamic scholars as a result of the Family Law (see section below) confrontation resulted in an unprecedented reaction that converted many people to the Islamic cause. Many Islamic scholars and prominent activists were either imprisoned or fled the country in the state security campaign of 1976. This massive confrontation was a prelude to the preparation for the second phase of the military regime, during which the Socialist Revolutionary Party was established in 1976 as the leading ideological party of the country. During these years, the Islamic movement continued underground and was administered by younger and less educated members. Most of the known activists such as Cabdulqaadir Sheikh Maxamuud fled the country to Saudi Arabia because of the economic boom and educational opportunities they offered to the Somali students.

In Saudi Arabia, Cabdulqaadir Sheikh Maxamuud was welcomed by the members of Ahal, e.g., Yuusuf Foodcade and Cabdulqaadir Aw-Muse. Some women's group members were also present, e.g., Madina Macallin.[53] During this time, the home of Xuseen Cali Diirshe, located in the district of *Nadwa al-Yamaniyah* in Jeddah, became the new headquarters for Ahal. Gradually, most members in Saudi Arabia were admitted to Saudi universities by 1977. For example, Cabdulqaadir Sheikh Maxamuud joined Um al-Qura University in 1978, from which he graduated four years later. Cabdulqaadir traveled to Egyptin 1979 and many believed he met with the leaders of Takfiir Jamaacain Egypt. Many interviewees believe that he was

---

52. Ibid.
53. Axmad Rashiid Xanafi interviewed by the author on January 10, 2010, Ottawa, Canada.

converted to Takfiir ideology in Saudi Arabia in early 1977 and traveled to Egypt to meet Egyptian leaders and to preach his new ideology toAhal members in Cairo.[54] Upon his return, the new Takfiir organization was founded and the ideological and organizational division of Somali Islamists became a reality. There are various speculative reasons why Cabdulqaadir converted to Takfiir. Among these are that he had lost his leadership role of Ahal when students contacted other great scholars from the Islamic world and some of them became more educated than him.[55] Nonetheless, the seed of Takfiir was implanted in the early year of Ahal and its militancy tendency is clear from directing its members to join the army. Therefore, Ahal members were divided into followers of Takfiir and those who refused that ideology and founded a new organization called Jamaaca Islaamiyah. Jamaaca Islaamiyah was founded in 1979 and designated a new leader: Sheikh Maxamuud Ciise. It recruited students who graduated from the Saudi universities and became influenced by Salafism. As a result, it gradually drifted from being a proto-MB to being a neo-Salafia organization. Jamaaca Islaamiyah and Waxdah were unified in 1983 and formed Al-Itixaad Al-Islaami

---

54. Shukri Mustafa was the leader of Takfiir in Egypt who was accused of being responsible for murdering Egyptian Minister *Muḥammad al-Ḏahabi*. He was captured and executed in 1978.
55. Axmad Rashiid Xanafi interviewed by the author on January 12, 2010, Ottawa, Canada. Also, Axmad Cali Axmad interviewed by authoron December 23, 2009, Nairobi, Kenya.

Wahdat al-Shabab al-Islami *(The Union of Islamic Youth)*

Wahdat al-Shabab (Waxdah) has left a great legacy and an imprint on the Islamic awakening in northern Somalia and is considered one of the great movements that shaped Somalia's modern history.[56] Following patterns similar to other Islamic organizations, it pushed for underground activities during the military regime (1969-1991). The history of this organization is also mostly unrecorded, as far as we know, and to reconstruct it, four basic documents were consulted: the founding bye-laws of Waxdah and three letters sent to the civilian and military government authorities in 1969.[57] In addition to that, these written sources are complemented by oral sources. Waxdah was officially formed by 13 members in Hargeysa on June 6, 1969.[58] The name of the organization, number of its founding members,

---

56. Cabdirisaaq Caqli interviewed by the author on November 29, 2009, Hargeysa.
57. The first letter was sent to President Cabdirashiid Cali Sharmarke during his visit in Hargeysa before his assassination at Laascaanood on October 15, 1969. The second letter was addressed to the Revolutionary Military Council on November 8, 18 days after the coup. The third letter was sent to the Revolutionary Council in Hargeysa. These documents were received from Sheikh Cabdiraxman Xaashi, one of the founders of Waxdah, who currently resides in Djibouti. Another source for the documents was from Sheikh Cabdiraxman Koosaar, one of the early members of Waxdah, currently living in Hargeysa.
58. The date of establishment is recorded in the letter sent to the Military Governor of Hargeysa after the military takeover. It requested a continuation of its overt operations. The names of the founding members are: Sheikh Cumar Xuseen (Arabic language teacher, graduated from al-Azhar) currently residing in the UK; Cali Ibrahim Iidle (Arabic language teacher), deceased; Xuseen Baraawe (businessman); Maxamuud Xaaji Ducaale (was employee of the Ministry of Animal Husbandry), currently residing in the UK; Sheikh Cabduraxman Xaashi Dubad (working and living in Djibouti); Dr. Cumar Axmad Xaaji Xuseen (worked in the Saudi Arabian University and became president of Burco University); Cabdiraxman Cabdullahi; Saciid Nuur (teacher); Dr. Maxamuud Muuse (aw-saliid); Sheikh Cabdiraxman Yuusuf (ina-Xananside), resided in Canada. Cabduraxman Koosaar interviewed by the author on May 20, 2008, Hargeysa. Also, Ismaciil Cabdi Hurre interviewed by the author on July 27, 2009, Nairobi and confirmed by email, January 6, 2010.

number of the executive officers, and number of articles in the bylaws all resembled those of the first nationalist party which was established in Mogadishu in 1943 by 13 young men. But, contrary to the SYL, Waxdah emphasized Islamic identity as their ideological orientation. The initial thinking, tendencies, and activities of the organization were unofficially begun in 1967 without a legal status, according to Sheikh Cabdiraxman Xaashi Dubad, one of its founders.[59] Its creation was mainly provoked by internal and external political and social upheaval in the Muslim world and in Somalia. Its objectives, according to its bye-laws, were simply "to realize Islamic principles" and its constitution was based on "The Qur'an and the Sunna of the Prophet Mohamed, peace and blessings be upon him."[60] In particular, a number of interviewees on the history of Waxdah agreed that two factors stimulated the formation of the organization. These factors were (1) the increasing westernization and the presence of the American Peace Corps and (2) the social dislocation of people and conflict after the elections of 1969.

The roots of the Peace Corps can be traced to 1960 when then Senator John F. Kennedy challenged students at the University of Michigan to serve their country in the cause of peace by living and working in developing countries. From that inspired appeal grew an agency of the US Federal Government devoted to world peace and friendship.[61] Members of the Peace Corps arrived in Somalia in 1961 as voluntary teachers in

---

59. Sheikh Cabdiraxman Xaashi Dubad interviewed by the author on November 14, 2009, Djibouti.
60. See Articles 4 and 2 of the Waxdah bylaws.
61. See the background history of Peace Corps in the official website of the Peace Corps, available from http://www.peacecorps.gov/index.cfm?shell=learn (accessed on 25 June, 2010).

intermediate schools, carrying with them the American youth counter-culture of the 1960s.[62] This cultural movement had its origins in the United States and Britain and spread through large parts of the world during the 1960s and 1970s. It gained momentum during the Vietnam War and expressed itself in many ways, including through music, dress, and sexual freedom.[63] Some of these young students embraced the hippie ethos by preaching the power of love and the beauty of sex as a natural part of ordinary life.[64] Other Western cultural influences, besides the counter-culture of the Peace Corps were also rapidly spreading among students in the intermediate and secondary schools in Somalia. In this way, the Somali counterculture was expressed in dress, particularly women's dress, and growing prostitution, listening to Western music, an increase in the number of night clubs, smoking, and drinking alcohol. This frustrated adherents of the traditional conservative Somali culture. It provoked an ideology of resistance against this intrusive alien culture, a resistance that was expressed by

---

62. Aw Jāma 'Umar 'isse, *Al-Sarā'beyna al-Islām wa Nasrāniyah fi al-Sharqi Ifrīqiyah* (no publisher, 1999), 54.
63. Some of these youths became prominent personalities in the US. For example, Charles Banquet, Director of the Center for Intercultural and International Programs, Xavier University of Louisiana (Somalia 1965-67), Robert Laird, opinion page editor for the *NY Daily News*(Somalia 1962-63), Thomas Petri, US Representative for Wisconsin (Somalia 1966-67), and R. Barrie Walkley,former ambassador to Gabon and the Democratic Republic of Sao Tome and Principe (Somalia 1967-69). See this information from its official websites available from http://www.peacecorps.gov (accessed on January 19, 2009).
64. The hippie subculture was originally a youth movement in the US from the 1950s to the early 1960s. A person belonging to this culture opposed to and rejected many of the conventional standards and customs of society, especially in socio-political attitudes and lifestyles. Adherents created their own communities, listened to psychedelic rock, embraced the sexual revolution, and used drugs to explore alternative states of consciousness. See Sam Binkle, *Hippies 2002*, available from http://findarticles.com/p/articles/mi_g1epc/is_tov/ai_2419100587/(accessed on August 11, 2009).

Islamic slogans and counter activities. The search for an Islamic awakening was driven by inspiration from the MB literature.

The annoyance of the founders of Waxdah with the westernization was clearly expressed in the two letters mentioned earlier. One of the letters was handed to the President Cabdirashiid Cali Sharmaarke in October 1969 during his official visit to Hargeysa, and the other was sent to the Supreme Revolutionary Council on November 8, 1969. Both letters expressed the same concerns about social maladies and called for Islam to be made the ultimate legal reference and solution in countering the mounting westernization. The letters expressed three major concerns regarding westernization: sexual freedom, drinking alcohol, and Christianization. In their petition against sexual freedom, the members of this group expressed their shame and antipathy about growing open prostitution. Prostitution had become so prevalent that a brothel in Hargeysa was named "the Fucking Quarter" while a similar one in Mogadishu was called "Tumbuluq".[65] They demanded closing down public prostitution and assigning a special branch of the police to monitor such misconduct. They also expressed their frustration that alcohol was increasingly sold publicly under the state license and demanded its total prohibition. Regarding their fear of Christian missionary activities by foreigners, Waxdah demanded that the government closely monitor activities of the foreigners and Christian activism. The second letter sent to the Revolutionary Council titled "Our

---

65. The quarter of "Tumbuluq" in Mogadishu was destroyed by the Military regime in 1971 because of its location in the center of the city, being old wooden buildings and becoming water pool during rainy seasons. However, this undertaking was not meant to curb prostitutions since big hotels had night clubs and prostitution was exercised openly.

opinion on the forthcoming constitution" speculated that a new constitution would soon be developed. It repeated the same three major concerns and added another demand: banning "freedom of religion" which allowed Muslims to be converted to other religions.[66] It is not clear what prompted this demand as the Somali constitution already outlawed spreading other religions except Islam in Somalia in 1963. These four issues were clearly phrased in the Arabic language and Islamic terms, and Qur'anic verses and Prophetic traditions were used to support these views.

Considering social dislocation and conflict, the fissure in society was widening after the election of Cabdirashiid Cali Sharmaarke as president and the subsequent political developments. The policies implemented under the Prime Minister Maxamad Xaaji Ibrahim Cigaal, who was from the northern constituency, provoked anger. Prime Minister Cigaal's policies, which fragmented political parties and marginalized specific clans and personalities in the north, caused social dislocation and clan conflict. In Hargeysa alone, 17 political sub-clan parties competed for 6 parliamentary seats. Reacting to this disorder and anger, the founders of Waxdah were convinced that Islam was the only way to bring brotherhood and unity to the divided society. To deal with growing clan conflicts, the letters from Waxdah to the government demanded the application of the Shari'a law in cases of deliberate homicide instead of the customary law of clans, or Xeer, which envisioned only the payment of Diya (material compensation for a homicide). Shari'a introduced the concept of Qisaas, which

---

66. According to the Somali Constitution of 1961, missionary activities are prohibited in Somalia. See Article 29.

literally means retaliation. It envisioned the right of the heirs of a homicide to demand execution of the killer instead of seeking compensation.⁶⁷ Introducing themselves to the new military governor of Hargeysa in 1969, Waxdah stated the following in a letter sent to him:

> We are the Union of Islamic Youth; we initiated our Islamic movement early this year when the election rows were rattling Somalia and the clan system succeeded in dividing the one nation into sects and parties because opportunists, who call themselves politicians of the country, employed this clanism. And, therefore, we formed our organization [immediately] after the [national] election on June 6, 1969 in Hargeysa. Our movement is not a political [party], but is an Islamic organization.⁶⁸

One of the strengths of Waxdah was the development of an Islamic and Arabic system of educationsimilar to the one in southern Somalia. Thegrowing impact of the Egyptian cultural center in Hargeysa, the Arabic language schools, and the Radio,Voice of Arabs in Cairo were encouraging. Besides that, they were influenced by the general trend of Islamic awakening in other parts of the world after the execution of Sayid Qutub and the defeat of the Arab forces in the war with Israel in 1967.⁶⁹

---

67. See the Qur'anic verse, "O you who believe, equivalence is the law decreed for you when dealing with murder - the free for the free, the slave for the slave, and the female for the female. If one is pardoned by the victim's kin, an appreciative response is in order, and an equitable compensation shall be paid. This is alleviation from your Lord and mercy; anyone who transgresses beyond this incurs a painful retribution" (2:178).
68. Excerpts from the letter to the Governor of Hargeysa [no date], though most likely it was written in the last month of 1969. Waxdah considered itself an Islamic social organization, as is evident from the letter "Munadama Islamiyah."
69. Sheikh Ismaciil Cabdi Hurre interviewed by the author on July 27, 2009, Hargeysa. Sheikh Ismaciil joined Waxdah in 1971 and became one of its leaders in 1975. Also, Sheikh Cabdiraxman Xaashi Dubad interview by the author on November 14, 2009, Djibouti.

As in other places, a lot of Islamic literature produced abroad reached Hargeysa. The first letter sent by Waxdah to the civilian government demonstrates the importance that the new organization was attaching to non-state schools, most of which had an Arabic language curriculum. They demanded that the state should support these schools by improving their facilities and training their teachers. They also advocated more hours of Islamic studies for state schools and called for improved quality of Islamic teachers.[70] Furthermore, they demanded the establishment of Islamic institutes and Islamic universities in the country.[71] The second letter sent to the Revolutionary Council proves influence of Sayid Qutub's works in the thinking of the Waxdah. In this letter, they cited the concepts of *Ḥākimiyah* [all earthly sovereignty belongs to Allah alone] and *Jāhiliyah* [ignorance], which were part of the central discourse espoused by Sayid Qutub and eloquently articulated in his celebrated book *Ma'ālim fi al-Darīq* (The Milestones).[72]

According to the bye-laws, the organizational structure of Waxdah was hierarchical and consisted of 13 executive officers. These included the chairman and his deputy, the secretary-general and his deputy, the secretary of Islamic Call and Guidance, the secretary of Cultural Awareness, the secretary of Sport, the secretary of the Treasury and the inspector general.[73] The bye-laws clarified the duties, responsibilities, and eligibilities of all these offices. For example, the chairman had to "be knowledgeable about Islamic jurisprudence, be virtuous

---

70. See the letter sent to the Supreme Revolutionary Council in 1969.
71. Ibid.
72. The Milestones is Sayid Qutub's major work considered to be the manifesto for Islamic activists. See Sayid Qutub, *The Milestone*, available from http://majalla.org/books/2005/qutb-nilestone.pdf (accessed on June 24, 2010).
73. See Article 9 of the Waxdah bylaws.

and have a good manner" and all other office holders had to have the same qualities. The bye-laws affirm the process for electing the office holders, thereby illustrating the internal democracy of the organization. The term for office holders was five years, and the chairman, at his discretion, could dismiss any office holder after consulting with his executive officers, while he himself could be removed from office with a two-third majority vote of no confidence by the office holders. No details of the process of the removal from office are given. It seems that during this early stage, there were only members and executive office holders and that a consultative council did not exist. According to the bye-laws, membership was restricted to persons who "should be faithful, committed to Islam and comply with the Islamic obligations. He has to be devoid of aiming personal gains [in joining the organization], meaning to be sincere, and genuine in religious beliefs."[74] Members had to pay a monthly contribution of three shilling to the Treasury.[75] As a rule, members of Islamic organizations were sworn in by reciting a special text, an allegiance pledge or *"Bay'a"*. On becoming a member of Waxdah, a person had to say aloud, while shaking the hand of the leader, *"Āmannā bi Allāhi, wa kafarnā bi Dāqūt"*, which means, "Webelieve in Allah and reject the 'Tagut'."[76]

Waxdah rented its headquarters in the city center of Hargeysa in 1969 and initiated Islamic education programs.

---

74. See Article 8 of the Waxdah bylaws.
75. See Article 13 of the Waxdah bylaws (which was equivalent to $0.5 at the time).
76. "Tagut" means "false God" or tyranny. This oath is derived from the Qur'anic verse "Whoever disbelieves in 'taghut' and believes in Allah, then he has grasped the most trustworthy handhold which will never break" (2:256). Cabdiraxman Koosaar interviewed by the author on August 15, 2009, Hargeysa. It is noteworthy that this statement of *Bai'a* is invented by Waxdah and does not follow MB *bai'a* statements.

These programs included studies of the prophets' biography, Islamic jurisprudence, commentary of the Qur'an (Tafsir), and Arabic language courses. Since most of its founding members were teachers of Arab and Islamic subjects in the schools, they attracted students from these schools. Initially, all students were boys, with a girls' program starting later.[77] There was also a weekly radio program on "Islamic manners," produced by Sheikh Cabdiraxman Xaashi, and public lectures at the headquarters every Thursday night.[78] These programs presented by Waxdah were very successful and attracted many people. They also opened an English-language private school to attract more students and to generate funds to finance the expenses of the center.[79] The initial Waxdah program was pioneered by teachers of Arabic and Islamic studies as a form of modern Sufism.[80] Most of the founding members used to chew Qaad, a tropical evergreen plant whose leaves are used as a stimulant and widely used in northern Somalia. They also recited *Qaṣīdat al-Burda*, the ode of praise to the Prophet Maxamad, composed by the reputed Sufi poet *Imām al-Būsiri*.[81] The activities of Waxdah had continued without interruption even after the revolutionary regime decreed a new law on January 10, 1970 (Law No. 54 of national's security). This law

---

77. Sheikh Ismaciil Cabdi Hurre interviewed by the author on August 14, 2009, Hargeysa.
78. See the letter sent to the local Hargeysa authority requesting the renewal of these programs.
79. Cabdiraxman Koosaar interviewed by the authoron August 15, 2009, Hargeysa.
80. The organization rented a small location where older members used to chew *qat* and recite the *Burdah* and *Munaqab*. It seems that the combination of traditional ways and those of the Sufis were attractive to the young.
81. The poems' actual title *al-Kawākib ad-Durrīya fī Madḥ Khayr al-Barīya* ("Celestial Lights in Praise of the Best of Creation") is famous throughout the Muslim world. It is in praise of Prophet Mohammad who cured the poet of paralysis by appearing to him in a dream and wrapping him in a cloak or scarf.

warranted the death penalty for a person found guilty of exploiting religion to create national disunity. The impact of this law was so great that most state employees abandoned Waxdah.

The ideological transformation of Waxdah from a modern Sufism to proto-MB transpired in 1974 as a result of two important events. The first was the establishment of the MB library that contained many Islamic reference books and Islamic revivalist literature. This library was sent from Kuwait by *Sheikh 'Abdallah 'Aqīl* through Saciid Sheikh Maxamad, one of the founding members.[82] These books included the works of Hasan al-Banna, the founder of Egyptian Muslim Brotherhood, and books by *Sayid Qutub* and his brother *Mohamed Qutub*. There were also books by the Syrian scholar *Said Ḥawa*, Lebanese MB scholar *Fathi Yakun*, Pakistani Islamic thinkers, such as *Abu al-A'lā al-Mawdūdi*, and Indian scholar, *Abu al-Ḥasan al-Nadawi*. Members of Waxdah eagerly read these books, which greatly transformed their thinking. They became followers of the MB methodology in their way of understanding Islam. Members moved from general attachment to Islam to following a specific direction in Islamic activism.

The second factor in Waxdah's transformation that had a negative impact on the organization's activities was the establishment of the Public Relations Office (PRO) by the military regime in preparation for the formation of the Socialist Revolutionary Party in Somalia. The followers of the leftist

---

82. Saciid Sheikh Maxamad, living during this time in Kuwait, had shipped these books to Hargeysa in 1974. These books were presented to Waxdah by the Sheikh Mana al-Qadan with the compliments of Sheikh Maxamad Garyare who was his disciple, former member of Nahdah and the director of the Ministry of Justice and Islamic affairs. There were two shipments of books: one shipment went to Nahdah in Mogadishu and the other to Waxdah in Hargeysa.

ideology of the regime had been campaigning to eliminate all other ideological groups. Consequently, they spread hearsay about the alleged dangerousness of Waxdah, including that it engaged in anti-revolutionary activities and was anti-Islamic, which frightened many members. As a result of this, some experienced members were transferred to other regions or traveled overseas. This meant that the leadership of Waxdah fell into the hands of young students. They were more committed to Islamic activism and recruited like-minded peers.[83] In the 1970s, Waxdah began to spread to other northern regions where they opened chapters in the regional capitals of Burco and Borama[84] as well as a third chapter in Djibouti.[85] The women's program was instituted in the early 1970s; however, Waxdah began to recruit women as full members in 1975. The impact of the Islamic call was evident in the streets of Hargeysa, Burco, and Borama, and in particular in high schools and among female students where the veil and proper Islamic dress began to appear. This occurrence, which was parallel to the happenings in other parts of Somalia, alarmed the regime and a campaign against Islamic activism was launched in 1976.

As a result of the continued campaign to curb Islamic activism, Cabdulqaadir Xaaji Jaamac, the leader of Waxdah, was

---

83. The well-known leaders of Waxdah during this time were: Cabdulqaadir Xaaji Jaamac, Cabdiraxman Yuusuf Abokor, Maxamad Cabdi Daauud, Xasan Cabdisalaam and Muuse Axmad Jaamac. Cabdulqaadir Xaaji Jaamac was their Chairman. Ismaciil Cabdi Hurre interviewed by the author on August 14, 2009, Hargeysa.
84. Sheikh Xasan Cabdisalam worked as a national service teacher in 1977 in Burco and recruited the first members of the Burco chapter, such as Mustafa Xaaji Ismaciil, Cabdi-Xakim Maxamad Axmad and others. Ibid.
85. The first recruited members in Borama included Cabdullahi Mu'min and Mahdi Saciid and Cabdalla Nuux.

imprisoned in 1978.[86] Also, Xaaji Cumar Hilowle (Hadrawi) and many others suspected of belonging to Waxdahwere put behind bars. Sheikh Xasan Cabdisalaam was also detained and jailed in Burco. In the end, the military regime took over the Waxdah headquarters in Hargeysa and appointed Saciid Muuse as the administrator. However, most of the leaders of the Waxdah were in Mogadishu to complete their Halane training program in 1977.[87] Some of them returned after completing their training such as Sheikh Ismaciil Dheeg and Sheikh Xasan Cabdisalaam while others joined Somali National University. After the state took over the Waxdah center in Hargeysa, activities were relegated to mosques and the organization went underground. During these years, *Da'wa* was intensified and a number of Qur'anic schools were opened. Waxdah was gradually being transformed into an Islamic movement. Although it was based in the northern regions and recruited most of its members from there, it was not isolated from other Islamic activities in Somalia and the rest of the world. By 1983, Waxdah and Jamaaca Islaamiyah formed Itixaad al-Islaami as already mentioned; however, many members of Waxdah who abandoned or abstained from Itixaad began to reorganize themselves and continued Waxdah as independent proto-MB organization. By

---

86. From his prison, Sheikh Cabdulqaadir wrote a letter to Ismaciil Cabdi Hurre requesting him to tell him about a girl with the name "Nura" (the light), meaning the Da'wa. Ismaciil Cabdi Hurre interviewed by the author on August 14, 2009, Hargeysa.
87. The Halane training program comprised three months military training for high school graduates. Afterwards, they joined the university or were offered jobs in different departments of the government. These leaders were Maxamad Cabdi Daauud, Cabdulqaadir Yuusuf Abukar, Abdo Maxamuud, Maxamad Xaaji Cawad and Xasan Cabdisalam. Ismaciil Cabdi Hurre interviewed by the author on August 14, 2009, Hargeysa.

1990s, Waxdah were also divided by repeatedly attempting to unite with other Islamist organizations under various pretexts. It completely disappeared in 1999 when its former members joined different organizations or preferred independent Islamic work. Besides former incorporation with Itixaad, the organization of Tajamuc confined to the Somaliland Islamists was created and later it also was incorporated with Itixaad under the name of and Ictisaam- a neo-Salafia organization. Members who abstained to join Tajamuc joined Islah in 1999 completing the total disintegration of Waxdah.

It could be concluded at this point that all three organizations, Nahdah, Ahal, and Waxdah, established after 1967 as part of the growing Islamic trend in the Muslim world, were enthusiastically engaged in Islamic activism in line with the MB methodology. As indicated, they were dealing with the challenges of westernization, secularization, and Socialism by employing Islam as their resistance ideology. They coordinated their efforts and shared roles; for example Ahal and Waxdah focused on recruiting high school and university students in their respective geographical locations, south and north. Nahdah assumed the role of providing Islamic education and supplied Islamic literature. The relationship between these organizations and the military regime gradually developed into an open confrontation which had a lasting impact on the further political developments in Somalia. In the next section, we will examine how these relations evolved.

The Military Regime and the Islamic Awakening

When the military regime took power in Somalia in a bloodless coup on October 21, 1969, there was little sympathy for the corrupt civilian government and the people of Somalia, who were eager for regime change, celebrated joyously. During the civilian regime, democracy "had lapsed into commercialized anarchy and a new type of strong rule was urgently required if the country was to be rescued from the morass of poverty, insecurity and inefficiency into which it had sunk."[88] However, the new military regime was gradually shifting its policies toward socialist ideology and dictatorship. In that atmosphere, relations between the military regime and the Islamic awakening were developed in three stages. Initially, they were characterized mutual confidence, steadily regressed to mutual distrust and, ultimately, overt confrontation.

The First Period: Mutual Confidence

The period of mutual confidence was the early period of the regime when most Somali people welcomed the military coup, as they were dismayed by the ousted civilian regime. The military coup was seen as saving the Somali state from complete collapse.[89] The first symbol of the military coup was the Qur'an, the gun, an army helmet, and swearing hand, symbolizing its Islamic tendency. In the first years, the military regime undertook popular steps such as nationalizing many foreign enterprises, offering jobs to unemployed elites, focusing on merit in public employment, expelling the Peace Corps, and continuously vilifying colonialism and imperialism.[90]

---

88. I. M. Lewis, *A Modern History of Somalia: Nation and State in the Horn of Africa* (London: Longman, 1980), 206.
89. Abdurahman Abdullahi, "Perspectives on the State Collapse in Somalia." In *Somalia at the Crossroads: Challenges and Perspectives in Reconstituting a Failed State*, ed. Abdullahi A. Osman and Issaka K. Soure (London: Adonis & Abbey Publishers Ltd., 2007), 43.
90. In December 1969, the military regime "gave US Peace Corps Volunteers notice to leave the country in two weeks. Siyaad pointed out that these youths, through their

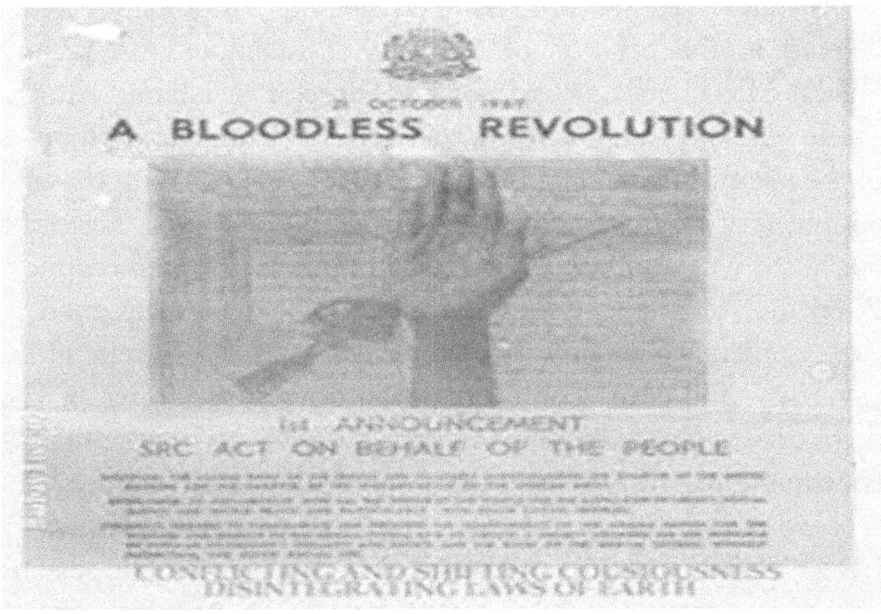

Figure 4. The symbol of the military coup of 1969

The regime also gained support by improving economic performance, expanding social services, and projecting a more sound governance culture. The regime articulated high respect for Islamic values, as was evident in a speech by the president a few months after seizing power:

> Our Islamic faith teaches us that its inherent values are perennial and continually evolving as people progress. These basic tenets of our religion cannot be interpreted in a static sense, but rather as a dynamic source of inspiration for continuous advancement.[91]

---

poor dress and their use of illicit drugs, were a threat to Somali value" see David Laitin and Said Samatar, *Somalia: Nation in Search of a State* (Boulder: Westview Press, 1987), 79.

91. See quotation in I.M. Lewis, *A History*, 219.

The new regime also assigned Sheikh Cabdulqani Sheikh Axmad to the position of Minister of Religious Affairs and Sheikh Maxamad Garyare became Director of Islamic Affairs. These scholars were the former leaders of Nahdah and pioneers of the Islamic awakening in Somalia. Nonetheless, with the first anniversary of the military coup, October 21, 1970, Scientific Socialism was adopted as the guiding ideology of the regime.[92] From that moment, the regime instituted policies designed to curb clanism vehemently and overtly – and the Islamic ethos covertly – and embarked on the road toward dictatorship. The dictatorial course of the regime became clearer with the enactment of repressive laws and the establishment of repressive institutions in 1970.[93] In particular, the law known as Law No. 54 on national security listed a number of serious crimes against the state as warranting death penalties or life imprisonment. Such crimes included "exploiting religion to create national disunity or to undermine and weaken the powers of the state."[94] The initial policy of the regime with

---

92. As narrated by Professor Maxamad Cali Tuuryare, a high-ranking delegation from the Soviet Union paid a visit to Mogadishu before the promulgation of Socialism in 1970. He and Colonel Yusuf Dheeg were assigned to accompany them. The mission aimed at discouraging the Somali military regime from adopting Socialism so early. However, President Maxamad Siyaad Barre had ignored their advice. The argument of the delegation was that the socio-economic environment in Somalia was not yet ripe for socialist transformation. Maxamuud Cali Tuuryare interviewed by the author on July 11, 2009, Nairobi, Kenya.
93. These laws are: Law No. 1 of January 10, 1970 on the power of arrest, Law No. 3 of January 10, 1970 on the creation of the national security court, Law No. 14 of February 15, 1970 on the creation of a national security service, Law No. 54 of September 10, 1970 on national security, Law No. 64 of October 10, 1970 on the promulgation of the right to habeas corpus, and Law No. 67 of November 1, 1970 on socialist defence. See Abdulaziz Ali Ibrahim "Xildhiban", *Taxanaha Taariikhda Somaaliya* (London: Xildhiban Publications, 2006), 105.
94. See Luigi Pastaloza, *The Somali Révolution* (Bari: Édition Afrique Asie Amérique Latine, 1973), 318.

respect to Islam was to emphasize its complementary relationship with Socialism regarding the notions of social justice.[95] In a speech in 1972, the President declared:

> Ours is the religion of the common man. It stands for equality and justice. Consequently, Socialism as applied to our particular condition cannot identify religion as the obstacle to the progress of the working class and therefore cannot negate it.[96]

Occasionally, Islam was used as an instrument for furthering socialist goals, as evidenced by the declaration, "Anyone opposing Socialism should at the same time be considered acting against the principles of Islam and against its very system of life."[97] After the first few years of Socialist rhetoric campaigns, the real nature of the dictatorial regime was unveiled and resistance, expressing itself in a variety of ways, began to mount. The first explicit form of opposition came during an internal rift within the ruling junta when two prominent generals of the Revolutionary Council (Generals Gabeyre and Aynaanshe) and a former Colonel (Colonel Dheel) were accused of organizing a counter-coup. These officers were accused, among others, of introducing "Islamic Socialism" and were publicly executed in July 1972.[98] Since the adoption of Socialism, former members of Nahdah speculated on the notion that the president was not a Socialist but a group of leftist activists who surrounded him were pushing him toward Socialism. To counter the influence of the leftists on the president and in an attempt to win him over, they organized a

---

95. I.M. Lewis, *A History*, 219.
96. See this quotation in Ahmed Samatar, *Socialist Somalia: Rhetoric and Reality* (London: Zed Press, 1988), 108.
97. See Pastaloza, 138.
98. Ibid., 150.

meeting with the president in April 1971. The delegation of five scholars included Sheikh Cabdulqani, Sheikh Garyare, Sheikh Maxamad Macallin, Sheikh Cali Xaaji Yuusuf, and another person.[99] This meeting was held one-and-a-half years after the military coup. Sheikh Maxamad Garyare narrates the event as follows:

> At the beginning of our meeting, the President opened his talk by teasing and, looking at Sheikh Maxamad Macallin, he said: 'you took from us all the people'; then, smiling, he glanced at me and said: 'Sheikh Garyare, you are Wahabi'. Sheikh Cabdulqani was not sitting with us because he was a minister; he just accompanied us to the office of the President. As we agreed, I opened the talks and expressed the aim of our meeting which focused on two issues: (1) to offer an Islamic position on the relations between the ruler (*al-ḥakim*) and ruled (*al-maḥkumin*); and (2) to express our concerns about growing leftist activities which were attempting to create conflict between Islam and the Revolutionary regime. We detailed these points from different perspectives and the President was listening attentively. One of the points we tried to emphasize was that the revolution and Islam were not conflicting and whoever tried to create such hostility was the enemy of the nation. We also explained explicitly how the group of leftists was trying to create such a rift between the people and the revolution. The President replied and I remember exactly some of his words: 'Jaalayaal (O comrades), the revolution now is one year and six months old. The enemies of the revolution are still looming. You have advised me, and I don't need advice because I am rightly guided (waa hanuunsanahay), so advise those who need your advice. Moreover, the persons whom you are talking against are the real patriots of this country'. Disappointed, we left the office of the President totally changed and convinced that our previous assessment about him was wrong. It was clear that the

---

99. The fifth person was a clan elder from the Hiiraan region but his name was not remembered by Sheikh Maxamad Garyare.

President and the leftists were on the same page.[100]

In the continuation of the confrontation with the leftists, the second major event occurred in 1972 when the Ministry of Religious Affairs was assigned to prepare the speech of the president on the birthday of the Prophet *Maḥamad*, celebrated every year at Maxfalka site in Mogadishu.[101] Sheikh Maxamad Garyare relates:

> I was assigned to write the President's speech and was later instructed to deliver it on behalf of the President. I was the Director of Religious Affairs of the Ministry of Religious Affairs. The speech was approved by the President and we had distributed it to all Muslim embassies. However, the speech contained clauses which said that Somali Socialism is "Islamic Socialism". The speech was widely reported in the local media which angered the leftists and lead socialist country embassies to protest. As a result, the President made another speech. This was the historic speech in which the president said: "our Socialism is not Islamic, is not African, it is Marxism-Leninism".[102]

The onerous task of the Islamic scholars to advise the president and challenge leftists within state institutions was over. The revolution was inexorably slipping toward Socialism where city streets, offices, and orientation centers were decorated with portraits of Marx, Engels, and Lenin alongside the picture of Maxamad Siyaad Barre. The initial symbol of the revolution that focused on the Qur'an was gone forever.

---

100. Sheikh Maxamad Garyare interviewed by the author on May, 2008, Toronto, Canada.
101. Maxfalka is a square in Mogadishu in the Shibis district where celebrations of the Prophet's birthday were annually held and government authorities participated in the event. The square was established by Shariif Caydaruus.
102. Sheikh Mohamed Garyare interviewed by the author by telephone on June12, 2009. Toronto, Canada.

The Second Period: Mistrust

The years 1972-74 could be considered the period of suspicion between the regime and the leaders of the Islamic awakening. After the execution of some military officers in 1972, the so-called "enemies of the socialist revolution and reactionary forces" were identified. These included wadaad xume (bad Sheikhs), signifying Islamic scholars who did not subscribe to Socialism and Marxist-Leninist ideology. In one of his speeches, the president reiterated:

> As far as Socialism is concerned, it is not a heavenly message like Islam but a mere system for regulating the relations between man and his utilization of the means of production in this world. ...However, the reactionaries wanted to create a rift between Socialism and Islam because Socialism is not in their interest.[103]

A story narrated by Sheikh Maxamad Garyare demonstrates the mounting mistrust between the regime and the leaders of the Islamic awakening. Sheikh Maxamad Garyare was demoted from the position of the director of Islamic Affairs in 1972 and was sent to the training camp of Halane, a military camp designated to indoctrinate civil servants with the ideology of Socialism. After finishing the training program, he was not assigned to any new position, due to a system known in Somalia as Buul, which means staying on without a specific job. During this period, Sheikh *Moḥamed Moḥamud al-Sawāf*, the adviser of Islamic Affairs to King Faisal of Saudi Arabia paid an official visit to Somalia carrying a letter from King Faysal to

---

103. See the quotation in I. M. Lewis, *A History*, 220.

President Siyad Barre.[104] Sheikh Garyare was assigned by the minister of foreign affairs, Cumar Carte Qaalib, to accompany him. The minister requested Sheikh Garyare to act as translator for the president. Relating this event, Sheikh Garyare said the following:

> In the meeting with the President, Sheikh *al-Sawāf* submitted a letter from King Faysal to the President, and then explained the content of the letter. Sheikh Sawaf read the letter and, in recollecting the main themes and some wording of the letter, he said: 'The letter started after the greeting: Islam is our common bond, and this is very important to all of us. You have announced that you have adopted the Marxist-Leninist ideology which is contrary to the Somali Muslim people's faith. The Prophet said: "A guide can never lie to his people".[105] Arab countries before you who adopted Socialism are reconsidering their position... I advise you, Mr. President, to turn away from adopting Socialism which corrupts the faith of the Somali people. We know that you are facing Ethiopia as the enemy of your country, if you wish weapons; the Kingdom will provide funds to purchase modern weapons from wherever you desire. And remember that the Soviets are not granting you weapons for free. Moreover, we guarantee you other assistance and investment packages and will encourage our friends to do the same. As you know, we are not a country seeking domination and we are doing all this to safeguard the faith and Islamic character of the Somali people. If we agree on these issues, we will visit you and kiss your head'. President Siyad replied briefly and spontaneously, and said: 'We are a free country and we accepted Socialism as our own choice. We

---

104. *Sheikh Moḥamūd Al-Sawāf* was the founder of the Iraq MB in the 1940s during his student years in Egypt; he met Hasan al-Banna, the founder of the MB in Egypt in 1928. See David Romano, *"An outline of Kurdish Islamist Groups in Iraq"*. Occasional paper issued by the Jamestown Foundation, September, 2007, available from http://www.ikhwanweb.com/uploads/lib/2C7GYEP2AMRGB65.pdf (accessed on April 12, 2010).

105. This is part of the Prophet's speech in the meeting with his kinspeople. See Safiur-Rahman Al-Mubarakpuri, *The Sealed Nectar: Biography of the Noble Prophet* (Riyadh: Darussalam Publishing, 2002), 99.

believe that with Socialism we can mobilize our people and rebuild our country. Somalia is a 100% Muslim country and does not need any preaching about Islam. We are not engaged in spreading propaganda against you and will not speak against you. If we can cooperate while we are on our socialist path, we welcome it. Otherwise, if you desire to cooperate in spreading Islam, many people in Africa needs our support and we can cooperate with that.' Discouraged by the answers of the President, *Sheikh al-Sawāf* left the country.[106]

However, the impact of that event did not subside. Sheikh Cabdulqani, the Minister of Religious Affairs, visited Sheikh Garyare in his home and told him that he had a meeting with the President. Sheikh Cabdulqani informed Sheikh Garyare that he will be imprisoned for anti-revolutionary activities. Sheikh Cabdulqani said as narrated by Sheikh Garyare:

> "I came here to warn you on that matter and I suggest that you try to meet the President and to face him directly instead of leaving him to believe rumors. If you are imprisoned in this way, I will resign and both of us will be meeting in prison". In this way, we agreed that I have to meet the President and the next night I was notified that I have an appointment with him. When I arrived at his office, he was playing tennis and many people were awaiting his audience. He told them that tonight he will only meet with Sheikh Maxamad Garyare and told the name of another person. I was received first and he began by saying, "Why do we not see you these days?" I said: "It is very difficult to come to your office." He said teasingly, while smiling: "My security guards know those who are not happy with us and do not allow them to enter our offices!"
>
> We were seated under a tree, and I said: "I have requested your audience and thanked Sheikh Cabdulaqani who arranged our meeting. I come here for two reasons: to greet you and to give you

---

106. Sheikh Maxamad Garyare interviewed by the author by telephone on June12, 2009. Toronto, Canada.

advice. I know you are very sensitive on security matters since you have taken power at gunpoint. And I am sure that you receive a lot of information and some of this information is not true. I advise you to validate this information." Finally, I briefly told him about my life, my educational background and the reasons I had returned to Somalia. The President said: "Jaalle (comrade), listen to me carefully, if the leaves of this tree under which we sit reverberates, we fire on it first and then we ask why. I tell you the truth, you are a treacherous man of this blessed revolution and we see you in that light. Be aware! You politicize Islam in your office; instead of improving relations between the people and the revolution you create enmity between them. You love the Arabs, and in particular Saudi Arabia and you always tell them about our misdeeds and never about the achievements of the revolution. These are your dark points. Moreover, the Sheikh who, after committing treason against his country Iraq, was expelled and employed by the king of Saudi Arabia, I believe what he said is what instilled in him". The President allowed me to answer and I said: "I do not understand what you mean by politicizing Islam, I proclaim Islam as I was taught. Regarding the love of Arabs, Mr. President, you are right. I love Arabs because they are our brothers, they are Muslims and most Somalis love them. In particular, I love the Saudis because I was educated there". And finally, I told him, "I swear you in the name of Allah; do you really believe that the man you have seen with his exceptional education and experience who is the adviser to the Saudi King, who came here with an official letter from him that I was behind all these things?" At the end of our discussion, the President changed his tone and said: 'Beware! We scrutinize information brought to us, and from the day you arrived in this country we have known everything about you. In reality, you have not many faults, your country needs you and you need your country, we are ready to offer you a better position, but Jaalle, demonstrate your loyalty".

Perhaps, the meeting between Sheikh Maxamad Garyare and the Somali President succeeded to diffuse temporarily the immediate confrontation between the regime and leaders of the Islamic awakening. Yet, it also indicated simmering mistrust and growing suspicion of the regime against these Islamic scholars—a trend that escalated into opens confrontation in the coming years.

The Third Period: Confrontation

The confrontation between the regime and Islamic awakening germinated in many fronts. It included what was termed "the Battle of *Ḥijāb*" (modest Muslim women's dress).[107] This battle was the result of the impact of the Islamic awakening on women and took place when *Ḥijāb* appeared in all walks of life. Wearing *Ḥijāb* was not common in Somalia, and only a few did so in the urbanized centers. Its appearance in the market, in the workplace, in the schools and universities was one of the remarkable successes for the Islamic awakening. It was in stark contrast to the unisex school uniform contradicting modest Islamic dress instituted by the military regime.[108] Moreover, to control Islamic activism, the regime regulated activities in mosques, unified Friday sermons, licensed Islamic *Da'wa*, and banned unauthorized Islamic education circles.[109] However, the breaking point in the relations was the adoption of the secular

---

107. See the Qur'an (33:59) "Those who harass believing men and believing women undeservedly, bear (on themselves) a calumny and a grievous sin. O Prophet! Enjoin your wives, your daughters, and the wives of true believers that they should cast their outer garments over their persons (when abroad). That is most convenient, that they may be distinguished and not be harassed".
108. 'Ali Sheikh Aḥmed Abūbakar, *Al-Somāl: Judūr al-Ma'sāt al-Rāhina* (Beirut: Dār Ibn al-Hazm, 1992), 95-105.
109. Ibid, 109-112.

Family Law. To exemplify this, a case study of the Family Law and its implications for the Somali state and Islamic awakening are provided below.

The Islamic Awakening and the Regime: A Case Study of the Family Law

The military regime promulgated the new Family Law on January 11, 1975. President Maxamad Siyaad Barre promulgated this controversial law in a publicly broadcasted speech at the stadium in Mogadishu, which offered "equality between men and women," including in matters of inheritance. The speech caught the public by surprise and caused frustration and fear. Nonetheless, public reaction was timid and cautious because of the overwhelming presence of the repressive security apparatus. However, five days later, on January 16, a few Islamic scholars found the courage to overtly criticize the law. These scholars condemned the law from the pulpit of the famous Cabdulqaadir Mosque in Mogadishu.[110] The location and timing selected for the protest were strategic. The Cabdulqaadir Mosque was the epicenter for the emerging Islamic movement where readings of Qur'anic commentary (*tafsīr*) based on Sayid Qutub's *In the Shade of the Qur'an* was regularly given by Sheikh Maxamad Macallin.[111] Moreover, the Friday prayer in this mosque was attended by many Islamic

---

110. The issue of the new secular family law was criticized in many mosques all over Somalia and about 10 mosques in Mogadishu alone. See ibid, 158.
111. Sheikh Maxamad completed his postgraduate studies at al-AzharUniversity and returned to Somalia in 1967. He was employed in the Ministry of Justice and Islamic Affairs. He is famous for his Qur'anic commentary during the 1970s in the Cabdulqaadir Mosque where most young Islamic activists of that time were educated. He was imprisoned for many years by the regime and died in Rome in 2000.

activists and individuals unhappy with the regime and its socialist ideology. At the same time, the mosque was under the watchful eye of the security apparatus of the regime that was suspicious of any signs of opposition under the guise of Islam. This resulted in the regime being able to quickly unleash its security apparatus and detain these scholars and hundreds of activists and sympathizers, although some were able to escape. Subsequently, on January 18 and 19, the National Security Court put on trial the first group of detained Islamic scholars and imposed death sentence on ten scholars, jailed six for 30 years, and jailed 17 others for 20 years.[112] In addition, hundreds detained from all regions were kept in prison without due process. The execution of the ten scholars took place hurriedly within three days of the court ruling.[113] On January 23, 1975, at the Police Academy in Mogadishu, the military regimeexecuted these ten scholars.[114]

The military regime's justification for adopting the new Family Law was founded on the president's claim that he was seeking to modernize the society and promote women's rights. He argued that socialist transformation would be deficient

---

112. The National Security Court was established by the Military Regime to deal with matters considered to be a threat to national security and its rulings were final. Its long-standing Chairman was Colonel Maxamuud Geelle Yuusuf. See Abubakar, *Judūr al-Ma'sāt*, 163.
113. Institutions that begged forgiveness from the President included al-Azhar and the Islamic university in Jeddah. Some individuals also appealed for leniency, including Ministers like Cusman Jaamac Kaluun and Cabdisalam Sheikh Xuseen and Islamic scholars such as Sheikh Aadan Sheikh Cabdullahi and others. Maxamad Haji Axmad, the former Deputy Minister of the regime interviewed by the author on July 5, 2009, Nairobi, Kenya. For the report on the refutation of the scholars' appeals for pardon, see Abubakar, *Judūr al-Ma'sāt*, 159.
114. The names of the 10 executed scholars are: Sheikh Axmad Sheikh Maxamad, Cali Xasan Warsame, Xasan Ciise Calbi, Sheikh Axmad Iimaan, Sheikh Muuse Yuusuf, Maxamad Siyaad Xirsi, Cali Jaamac Xirsi, Aadan Cali Xirsi, Suleimaan Jaamac Maxamad, and Yaasiin Cilmi Cawl. See Abubakar, *Judūr al-Ma'sāt*,136.

unless women were liberated, through revolutionary legal reform, from the shackles of culture and the traditional interpretation of religion. The regime was also claiming that the new Family Law was not contradicting Islam but that it simply offered a modernist interpretation.[115] Conversely, the focus of the Islamic scholars' counter-argument was that the new Family Law set the stage for increasing secularization of the society by engaging with its most sacred domain: the family. For them, the family was one of the areas that had detailed rules dictated by Islamic jurisprudence. Therefore, they considered the law a transgression of Shari'a and a refutation of the Qur'anic verses which was tantamount to explicit apostasy.[116] An intense mêlée between the Islamic scholars and the military regime broke out, centering on the role of Islam in the state and society. The issue of women's rights was merely the theater of confrontation between the two parties that were suspicious of each other because of the regime's orientation toward Socialism. The regime may have miscalculated the implications of the new Family Law, as many secular laws earlier enacted by the state

---

115. Islamic modernism departs from secularism in that it recognizes the importance of faith in public life. It also departs from Islamism in that it does accept most of the modern European institutions, social processes and values. Sometimes, its adherents stretch the meaning of the Qur'an and Sunna beyond their traditional limits. They draw conclusions and adopt laws that have no precedent in the Islamic Shari'a, and are considered anti-Islamic by the majority of scholars. Such phenomena are evident in the speech of the Present at the stadium in which he concluded: "I hope that those who are listening to me now on the radio will guide those who do not understand anything or those who are ignorant about these principles. And to those who did not understand anything about the meaning of the Glorious Qur'an and those who are demeaning Islam in their wrong understanding ...."(Translated from Arabic by the author). Abubakar, *Judūr al-Ma'sāt*, 126.
116. There are 10 verses in the *Qur'an* that deal with inheritance. These are 2:180, 2: 240, 4:7-9, 4:19, 4:33, and 5:16-18. See Abubakar, *Judūr al-Ma'sāt*, 126-132.

had not attracted any substantial reaction.[117] Also, conceivably, Islamic scholars were not expecting such harsh treatment for clearly and loudly stating their Islamic position.[118]

In Somalia, the traditional family law is based on Shafi'i jurisprudence, akin in some respects to the customary law known as Xeer, which varies from place to place. Indeed, Islamic jurisprudence has the capacity to absorb some elements of Xeer, as long as they do not go against the general principles of Islam. Moreover, it is permissible for the various Islamic schools to borrow rules from one another. These two sources, the viewpoints of the various jurisprudence schools and local customs, could have been used as a guide in the reformation of the Family Law. Following such roadmap, any new legislation could have been adopted as long as it did not contravene the explicit rules of the Qur'an and the authenticated Sunna of the Prophet. The new Family Law, under investigation here, however, directly contravenes the Qur'anic verses in some of its articles, and thus deviates from the accepted methodologies of Islamic Jurisprudence.[119]

After consolidating power in the first five years, by 1974, the military regime had realized a number of important achievements. For example, in July 1974, Somalia signed a friendship agreement with the Soviet Union during an official visit of the Soviet leader in Mogadishu. This agreement and

---

117. One example of these laws is the abolition of the *diya* payment system by the military regime in 1970.
118. The Islamic methodology in correcting wrongs is made up of three steps: correction by action, by tongue and by heart. Most Somalis opted to deny the secular Family Law in their hearts, while scholars had chosen the second option of expressing their views loudly by tongue.
119. Articles that contravene the *Qur'anic* verses, as analysed by Professor Cali Sheikh Axmad Abubakar, are: 4, 13, 31, 36, 158, 159, and 161. See Abubakar, *Judūr al-Ma'sāt*, 127-130.

subsequent establishment of a naval Soviet base in Berbera annoyed conservative regimes in the region and, in particular, Saudi Arabia, which perceived the agreement as a national security threat.[120] Somalia also joined the Arab League in February 14, 1974, securing important political and economic support from the Arab world, a first step toward pushing Somalia out from the Soviet block.[121] Moreover, the annual summit of the Organization of African Unity (OAU) was held in Mogadishu in 1974, with the Somali president becoming the chairman of the OAU and thereby boosting the image of the regime on the world stage.[122] The"Cultural Revolution" that was started in 1972 adopted the Latin script for the alphabet of the Somali language, finalizing debates on the appropriate script, Arabic or Latin, to the triumph of secular elites. The literacy campaign that began in July 1974 allowed more than 30,000 high school students and teachers, both male and female, to travel to rural areas to instruct the rural population in writing and reading in their own language.[123] On the other hand, Somalis strengthened their connection with the Arab world as Somali migrant's labor flocked to the Gulf States during the oil price boom of the 1970s. These migrant workers and students in the universities spread the new revivalist Islam that was gaining momentum in Somalia. This Islamic movement alarmed the regime, which was poised to implement Marxist ideology. Moreover, a new challenge to the regime emerged in neighboring Ethiopia, where the Marxist revolution had

---

120. Moḥamed Sharif Moḥamūd, "*Faslun fi al-'Alāqāt al-Somāliyah al-Sacūdiyah*", available from http://arabic.alshahid.net/columnists/analysis/8598 (accessed on April 21, 2010).
121. Ibid.
122. Lewis, *A History*, 227.
123. Ibid., 216.

triumphed on September 12, 1974. During this period, Ethiopia did not pose a military threat to Somalia having been weakened during the revolution. However, it was competing with the Somali regime in soliciting Socialist countries' patronage in the Horn of Africa. This competition pushed the Somali regime to undertake more programsand reforms geared towardsadopting Marxist programs.

The idea of the new Family Law took its inspiration when the United Nations adopted resolution 3010 on December 18, 1972, proclaiming 1975 as International Women's Year, calling on all member states to promote equality between men and women. In retrospect, the military regime offered new opportunities for Somali women to become more vocal and to participate in grassroots revolutionary programs. They became more visible in the public space, particularly in the Socialist Orientation Centers. They participated more actively in education programs and took up higher positions in the public service. There were women of high ranking among the officers in the army and the air force, and they took up positions as general managers, ambassadors, and directors-general. Moreover, the military regime issued a number of laws designed to promote women, such as ensuring equal salary for equal jobs and providing for paid maternity leave. Moreover, by abolishing the *Diya* payment system, the penalty for murdering a woman became the same as that for murdering a man.[124] Furthermore, the military regime had even established a women's mosque to show its commitment to the advancement of women in all aspects since they did not have their own

---

124. In the Somali traditional Xeer that accords to Islamic Jurisprudence, the diya of women is half that of men. However, there are emerging minority voices within Islamic jurisprudence that adhere to the equality of diya for all genders.

prayer spaces in the traditional mosques in Somalia.[125] It was in the context of the Socialist program of the military regime, which had matured and strengthened over the preceding five years and did not confine itself to Islamic boundaries, that the Family Law was introduced.

Establishment of the Family Law

The codification of the Family Law was initiated in 1972 by the Ministry of Justice and Religious Affairs, closely following the UN's proclamation on promoting gender equality. The available literature does not say much about the process of the codification; therefore, we must depend on an oral source. Nuurta Xaaji Xasan, a drafting commission member, related the history of the codification of the Family Law in an interview in Toronto, Canada, as follows:

> Sheikh Cabdulqani, the Minister of Justice and Religious Affairs in 1971-73, was attempting to introduce codified Islamic family law in light of the Egyptian Family Code. Perhaps that was the reaction of the Minister to the increased awareness of women's issues in the United Nations General Assembly. The Minister provided me with copies of Egyptian family law that comply with the Islamic law to share them with the Somali women employed in the different ministries and to solicit their support. During this time, many of these women were stationed in the Halane Military Training

---

125. This mosque was located near the Italian Club and NationalUniversity CityCenter in Mogadishu. Sheikh Aadan Sheikh Cabdullahi, a well-known scholar who delivered Qur'an commentary on Radio Mogadishu, used to run women's Islamic teaching circles in the mosque. Sheikh Ciise Sheikh Axmad interviewed by the author, July 20, 2009, Hargeysa.

Camp.[126] We selected a committee of five women and I was one of them.[127]

The selected group had been closely connected with the Italian Communist Party.[128] These women received ardent support and encouragement from Dr. Maxamad Aaden Sheikh, Dr. Maxamad Weyrah, and Dr. Cabdisalam Sheikh Xuseen – known leftists and cabinet members who were very close to the President. Later, the president appointed a seven-member commission in 1974 to draft the Family Law, directing them that it should be "progressive". The commission submitted the draft to the president in December 1974.[129] Following this, the Family Law was publicly proclaimed by the president. The president publicly announced, "As of today, Somali men and women are equal. They have the same equality, the same rights and the same share of whatever is inherited from their parents."[130] The president openly stated that the era of "one half, one third, one

---

126. Halane Camp is a military training school in Mogadishu that was used to train and inculcate civil servants of Socialist ideology.
127. Nuurta Xaaji Xasan interviewed by the author on October 15, 2007, Toronto, Canada. Nuurta was a member of the commission assigned to draft the Family Law and was a legal adviser to President Maxamad Siyaad Barre.
128. Italy reinstated its influence in Somalia after the establishment of the NationalUniversity, funded by an Italian cooperation program, by adopting the Italian language as the language of instruction and Italian lecturers as the main faculty members. Most of the younger generations of Somalia were educated there. The members of the committee were Italian-speaking women who had graduated from the NationalUniversity. See Poalo Tripodi, *The Colonial Legacy in Somalia: Rome and Mogadishu: from Colonial Administration to Operation Restore Hope* (London: Macmillan Press, 1999), 116-119.
129. The designated commission included Maxamad Sheikh Cusman (High Court), Cabdisalam Sheikh Xuseen (Minister of Justice), Maxamad Aadan Sheikh (Minister of Information) and four women, namely, Nuurta Xaaji Xasan, Marian Xaaji Cilmi, Faduma Cumar Xaashi and Raaqiya Xaaji Ducaale.
130. Maxamad Siyaad Barre,*My Country and My People: Selected Speeches of Jaalle Siyaad* (Ministry of Information and National Guidance, 1979), 3.

quarter" was gone forever.[131] Moreover, the president stressed that the new law would change the "unjust law of inheritance" ordained by the Qur'an that assigns different shares of the inherited wealth to the rightful heirs of men and women.[132] The Family Law consists of 173 articles and, according to Tahir Mahmood, "has the character of the dominant Shafi'i jurisprudence and adherence to the general principles of the Islamic law, however, on marriage, divorce and filiations, it had many commonalities with the amended Syrian Personal Code of 1975. On the issue of inheritance, the Somali Family Law had no equal in the Muslim world except Turkey."[133] Although the Law contained a number of articles that went against accepted Islamic Shari'a law, the most provocative ones were the articles on inheritance. They offered "equal rights for men and women under the rules of inheritance; a drastic curtailment of the list of heirs, and application of new rules for the division of the estate of a deceased person."[134]

As a general procedure, the regime mobilized public support for the new Family Law by organizing demonstrations, where state employees and students were forced to demonstrate and listen to Vice-President Xuseen Kulmiye Afrax's speech at the Unknown Soldier's Square near the old

---

131. See synopsis from the speech of the President at the stadium. Ali Sheikh Ahmed, *Judur al-Ma'sat*, 125.
132. The law was not passed in the Council of Ministers and it was a unilateral decision of the President. This is the testimony of the former minister Cabdullahi Cosoble Siyaad interviewed by the author on July 12, 2009, Nairobi, Kenya. Also, former Minister Jaamac Maxamad Qaalib interviewed by the author on December 26, 2009, Nairobi, Kenya. Moreover, the former Minister Cabdiqaasim Salaad (lately, the President of Somalia (2000-2004)) interviewed by author on November 13, 1999, Mogadishu, Somalia.
133. Mahmood Tahir, *Personal Law*, 225.
134. See Articles 158-169 of the Family Law. See Tahir, *Personal law*, 256.

parliament building in Mogadishu.¹³⁵ Even so, after five days, public anger was expressed in the Cabdulqaadir Mosque in Mogadishu. Sheikh Maxamad Garyare, who was present that Friday in the Cabdulqaadir Mosque, narrates the events as follows:

> After the Friday prayer in the famous Mosque of Cabdulqaadir, at about 1:00 pm, Sheikh Axmad Maxamad stood up and began to deliver his critical speech against the Family Law considering it "arrogant and a transgression of the borders of the Law of Allah that is unacceptable to the Somali Muslims." Successive speeches by other Islamic scholars continued until the afternoon prayer at about 3:30 pm where as many as nine other Islamic scholars criticized the Law. Most of the people [who had] prayed in the mosque also remained listening enthusiastically. Moreover, many people gathered in the surrounding areas of the mosque in a show of support for the scholars. However, the event was perceived by the regime as an anti-state protest and a threat to the revolution. After the afternoon prayer (*salat al-Asr*), security forces encircled the mosque from all sides, cut off the electricity to silence the scholars, and arrested hundreds of people in the mosque. There were no violent confrontations with the security forces inside the mosque and the people dispersed angrily.¹³⁶

Indeed, the protestation of the Islamic scholars was a spontaneous expression of anger and frustration. The Friday sermon was delivered by Sheikh Abdulaziz from Al-Azhar Mission in Somalia, who explained the "rights and fallacies" in

---

135. The Vice-President's speech at the state-sponsored demonstration is remembered for his use of the following expression: '*Yeere yerre yam, Yaxaas qaade Yam*' (Whoever speaks up will be eaten. The crocodile will take him and eat him). This expression is used in children's games and means that any attempt to confront the family will meet the strong hand of the revolution. Nurta Hagi Hassan interviewed by the author on October, 15, 2007, Toronto, Canada.
136. Sheikh Mohamed Garyare. Also, see Abubakar, *Judūr al-Ma'sāt*, 158.

Islam.[137] Analyses of the affiliations of these scholars demonstrate that most of these scholars belonged to the traditional jurists and Sufi orders. The initiator of the protest was Sheikh Axmad Sheikh Maxamad, a prominent jurist from the town of Ceynaba in northern Somalia, who came to Mogadishu at the invitation of Ismaciil Cali Abokor, a prominent member of the Revolutionary Council.[138] Other scholars came to the Cabdulqaadir Mosque for the Friday prayer. Sheikh Axmad considered the law "a transgression of Allah's law" and requested others to speak up in defense of Shari'a. Other scholars followed the same line in denouncing the Family Law. Most of these scholars were not part of the Islamic awakening that was then in its early development. Moreover, prominent scholars of the modern Islamic revival such as Sheikh Maxamad Macallin, Sheikh Maxamad Garyare, Sheikh Cabdulqani, and student activists belonging to Ahal were not among these scholars.[139] On Saturday, the second day, after the noon prayer, other scholars delivered supporting speeches, and the demonstration proceeded to the Municipality

---

137. Islamic scholars from al-Azhar University were engaged in Islamic activities in Somalia and taught in many schools. Sheikh Abdul-Aziz was ordered to leave Somalia within 24 hours after the incident. The first speaker after the prayer was Xaaji Cilmi known as "Xaaji Dhagax" who briefly expressed how the words of Sheikh Cabdul-Aziz were relevant to the Somali situation, most likely provoking the subsequent Islamic scholars' speeches. Sheikh Ciise Sheikh Axmad interviewed by the author, July 21, 2009, Hargeysa.
138. See Abūbakar, *Judūr al-Ma'sāt*, 165.
139. For example, Sheikh Maxamad Macallin did not attend Friday prayer in the mosque. He related to me in 1985 that "his student who was seemingly working with National Intelligence, Xasan Qamaan, did not allow him to go out of his house". According to this narration, the intelligence may have been aware the possibility of scholars angry response. On the other hand, Sheikh Maxamad Garyare prayed in the Mosque and he did not participate in delivering speeches. Moreover, none of the leaders of the student activists were evident there. All these facts indicate that the protest was not planned.

Headquarters where many others were imprisoned.[140] The military regime's use of such strong-arm tactics demonstrates that it perceived the peaceful protestation as a threat and a challenge to its authority and to Socialist ideology. Certainly, all forms of public protestation were prohibited according to Law No. 54 on the national security enacted in 1970.

The Family Law and Execution of the Scholars

There are three main perspectives to explain why the regime adopted the Family Law and executed the scholars. The first thesis claims that these actions were foreign-assistance-driven and denies any ideological motivation. It was simply a theatrical show of the regime's strength and a commitment to secular socialist ideology, competing with the new "Marxist Ethiopia" for assistance from socialist countries.[141] Indeed, Ethiopia had adopted Socialist programs and attracted substantial assistance from the Socialist block in competing with Somalia. Maxamad Siyaad Barre, who was playing the role of key friend to the Socialist block in the Horn of Africa, was losing that monopoly. Therefore, he aimed to prove that he was a "more committed socialist in the Horn of Africa who deserved to be considered as such and to be provided with generous support by the socialist countries."[142] The second thesis is

---

140. Sheikh Ciise Sheikh Axmad narrated that he personally participated in the demonstration and was only saved from imprisonment by his Egyptian teacher Ibrahim al-Dasuuqi who met him accidentally and recommended that I have to leave.
141. Marian Carriif Qaassim, a prolific writer and a politician interviewed by the author on November 12, 2007, Djibouti.
142. Cawad Axmad Casharo, a Member of Parliament and former director of the Ministry of Trade during the Siyaad Barre regime interviewed by the author on June, 30, 2009, Nairobi, Kenya.

founded on the dictatorial ambition of the Somali president. Some observers consider the Family Law event a purely pre-emptive strike on the emerging Islamic movement, perceived by the regime as one of the two "enemies of the Revolution," the other one being clanism. The earlier execution of Jeneral Maxamad Caynaanshe Guuleed and Jeneraal Salaad Gabeyre Kediye and Coloneel Cabdulqaadir Dheel Cabdulle in 1972 was considered a blow to the centers of clan power in Somalia. Thus, according to the regime's plan, it was the turn of the Islamists to be harshly suppressed in order to remove all potential obstacles thwarting revolutionary programs. The third thesis is that the motivation was ideological, assuming that the adoption of the Family Law and the crushing of Islamists was "part of the preparatory tasks to be accomplished before the formation of the Socialist Revolutionary Party in Somalia."[143] This party was established in 1976 as the second phase of the revolution to pioneer and vanguard for the Socialist transformation of the society. In conclusion, the adoption of the Family Law and the crushing of its opponents were intended to accomplish two objectives: recognition of the Somali regime by Socialist countries and the removal of potential local obstacles.

Impact of the Family Law on the Islamic Awakening

With the crackdown on Islamists after the Family Law proclamation, most leading scholars were either imprisoned or fled the country to Saudi Arabia. The Islamic awakening, hitherto united in its ideology and leadership, was fragmented and the ideology of extremism emerged strongly. This was

---

143. Cabduraxman Cabdulle Shuuke, former Minister of Education during the Siyaad Barre regime interviewed by the author on June 30, 2009, Nairobi, Kenya.

provoked by the harshness of the regime in dealing with Islamic scholars, the encouragement and support by the conservative Arab regimes of the Islamists, and their contact with the varieties of Islamic ideologies and activism that changed the Islamic landscape in Somalia. In August 1975, six months after the Family Law fiasco, 60 prominent and high-ranking officers were removed from their positions. Included in these were the leaders of the Islamic awakening: Sheikh Maxamad Garyare, Sheikh Maxamad Macallin, and Sheikh Cabduqani. Both Sheikh Maxamad Macallin and Sheikh Cabdulaqni were imprisoned, while Sheikh Maxamad Garyare fled the country via Kenya to Saudi Arabia.[144] In addition to those imprisoned some of the activists of the Islamic awakening fled to Saudi Arabia and Sudan and began to regroup there. Importantly, this occurred during the time of booming economies and Islamic revivalism throughout the Arab Muslim world. This economic well-being and education offered the emerging Islamic movement the impetus to reorganize themselves again. Among those who succeeded to flee was the leader of Ahal, Cabdulqaadir Sheikh Maxamuud. Also, students at Saudi universities who joined the MB in Sudan and Saudi Arabia were secretly working among new immigrants in Saudi Arabia, trying to recruit them into their underground organization. On the other hand, Ahal leader Cabdulqaadir was trying to regroup his members in Saudi Arabia. In spite of the different ideologies present in Saudi Arabia, he seemingly lost his leadership role, and a new period

---

144. Sheikh Garyare said: "I received the news of my arrest from Jeneral Axmad Jilacow who was high officer in National Security Service. Therefore, I have planned my escape route from Mogadishu via Kenya. I updated my passport and received Xajj Visa. At the 8:00 AM, I have moved from Mogadishu. The security service had arrived my home at 10:00 AM looking for me to arrest." Sheikh Garyare interviewed by the author, May 5, 2005, Toronto, Canada.

of searching for the reorganization of the Islamic awakening dawned.

On the other hand, the military regime was drifting further towards leftist ideology, established Somali Socialist Revolutionary Party (SSRP) in June, 1976 and embarked on militaristic course in which it was defeated in the war of 1977/78 with Ethiopia. As much the regime moved further towards socialist ideology and formed the vanguard ruling party as much it curtailed freedom and liberty and distanced itself from the nature of the society and its Islamic faith. The regime raised new slogan based on the loyalty to the socialist ideology and its military dictator Maxamad Siyaad Barre classifying its citizens into friends and enemies of the revolution. In this categorization, Islamic awakening was placed as one of the strategic threats to the socialist revolution. The emblem of the SSRP and its symbolism indicates the enormous departure of the military regime from the symbolism of its first paper that symbolized the Qur'an (see p.170). Following logo of SSRP represents the second stage of the military regime and its attempts to transform Somali people into socialist society, the dream that collided with the resilience of the society and the war with Ethiopia (1977/78).

Figure 5. The Emblem of Somali Socialist Revolutionary Party

This emblem demonstrates the map of "Great Somalia" that includes Somali Republic and other three parties such as Djibouti, Western Somalia in Ethiopia and NFD in Kenya. It also shows hoe and hammer, the symbols of peasants and workers, the proletarians exploited by the bourgeoisie class according to the Marxist theory. This symbol attests the total shift of the military regime towards Marxist ideology, an antithesis to the Islamic and traditional society and its early symbolism that included the Qur'an.

As a consequence of the migration of the Islamic activists to Gulf States because of the suppression of the regime after the adoption of the family law and forced secularization of the society was the bifurcation of the Islamic awakening when the Islah Movement announced itself publicly on July 11, 1978. This was three months after the retreat by the Somali army that was defeated in the war with Ethiopia.[145] Islah proclaimed representing an ideological continuation of the Nahdah and elected Sheikh Maxamad Garyare as its leader.[146] The second move toward the Islamist fragmentation was undertaken by Cabdulqaadir Xaaji Maxamuud, the former leader of Ahal since 1969. He professed Takfiir ideology in Saudi Arabia and later traveled to Egypt in 1979 to bolster his relations with the Egyptian Takfiir organization. Upon his return, he succeeded in convincing prominent leaders of Ahal to adopt his new ideology of Takfiir.[147] As a result, the Ahal organization ultimately ceased to exist. Other members of Ahal who were hesitant to join Al-Islah and the Takfiir established a new organization called Jamaaca Islaamiyah (The Islamic Congregation). This organization combined former Ahal members who considered themselves as belonging to the MB and many graduates from the Saudi universities who claimed adhering to Salafism. Gradually, however, the Salafia tendency gained the upper hand and the organization took on the character of a neo-Salafia movement. This organization evolved in 1983 to Itixaad when Waxdah and Jamaaca Islaamiyah were unified. Therefore, in the late 1970s and early 1980s, three organizations based on three different Islamic persuasions had appeared in Somalia: Islah, Takfiir and Itixaad.

---

145. The Somali government ordered its forces to retreat from Ethiopia on March 9, 1978, and the last significant Somali unit left Ethiopia on March 15, 1978, marking a disastrous end of the war.
146. Many of the former members of Nahdah were in prison and others were made aware of the reorganizing of the organization under a new name.
147. Xassan Xaaji Maxamuud interviewed by the author, April 10, 2010, Nairobi, Kenya.

Conclusion

The Islamic awakening was the culmination of the rising Islamic consciousness in Somalia and part of a wider awakening that was taking place in the Muslim world. It had gradually begun in the 1960s with the founding of the organizations Nahdah, Ahal, and Waxdah that were actively preaching the new ideas of the Islamic movement, in line with the MB's methodology.[148] Five factors played a pivotal role in strengthening the Islamic awakening in Somalia in the 1970s. The first factor is the role of Islamic scholars in spreading modern Islamic-movement concepts and ideas through public education programs and lectures. The second factor is the activities of student organizations of Ahal and Waxdah, especially their enthusiasm and outreach programs. The third factor is the influence of the MB literature brought to Somalia by Nahdah. The fourth factor is the encouragement by conservative Islamic countries such as Saudi Arabia. The fifth factor is the proclamation of the Socialist ideology and adoption of the secular Family law by the military regime, which ignited enormous Islamic sentiment.

Finally, even though the proto-MB institutions of the Islamic awakening were short-lived, their Islamic call and impact were significant and lasting. Nahdah operated for only three years, although its members remained prominent in the Islamic activism for a long period. Ahal ceased to exist in 1977 after about eight years of active work, and its members were divided

---

148. Sheikh Nuur Cali Colow (1918-1995) was a prominent scholar who relentlessly preached the ideas of Salafism in Somalia for more than 60 years (1935-1995). He graduated from the al-AzharUniversity in 1963 and returned to Somalia, establishing *Ihyā al-Sunna al-Muḥamadiyah* (the Revivification of the Sunna of Mohammedans) in 1967. He became Director of Religious Affairs in the Ministry of Justice and Religious Affairs. He was imprisoned twice from 1969-1970 and 1973-1976.

into different new Islamic organizations. Waxdah ceased to exist officially in 1983 when it was united with Jamaaca Islaamiyah and became part of Itixaad.[149] It is important, however, to characterize this period of the Islamic awakening as immature with an emotional attachment to the Islamic ideology. It was a period with very low organizational capacity, meager economic resources, and romantic approach to social and political realities. Next two chapters will focus on Islah Movement as a case study of the MB persuasion in Somalia.

---

149. This unification did not last long, and many members of Waxdah quit Itixaad and reorganized themselves. This group have made a great effort in working with SNM during the difficult period of the civil war. They have focused their work on the refugee camps and later influenced the Somaliland Constitution and flag. Ismaciil Cabdi Hurre interviewed by the author on August 14, 2009, Hargeysa, Somaliland.

CHAPTER FOUR

The Emergence of the Islah Movement in Somalia: The Formative Period (1978–1990)

On August 12, 2008, the Islah Movement publicly announced the result of its five-year term election, in which the *Majlis al-Shūra* (Consultative Council) elected its fourth chairman, demonstrating its firm commitment to the tradition of internal democracy even in these tumultuous times in Somalia.[1] Islah boasts continuous Islamic work since 1978 in clan-based society under the conditions of oppressive state, civil wars, and statelessness.[2] It represents the International MB network in Somalia, the loose coalition of national autonomies in many Muslim countries.[3] Thus, Islah derives its goals, objectives, and strategies from the ideology of the MB founded by *Ḥassan al-Banna* in Egypt in 1928. Moreover, it takes into consideration the specificity of the Somali society, its statelessness, and conflictual

---

1. The four chairmen of Islah are Sheikh Maxamad Garyare (1978–1990), Dr. Maxamad Cali Ibrahim (1990–1999), Dr. Cali Sheikh Axmad (1999–2008), and Dr. Cali Baasha Cumar Roraaye (2008–2018). The membership of Dr. Maxamad Cali Ibrahim was revoked after he joined the Islamic Courts Union in 2006. The communique on revoking his membership is available from http://www.Islah.org/arabic/bayaan21-6-06.htm (accessed June 7, 2010).
2. The result of the election was published in the official Islah website available from http://www.Islah.org/arabic/Dorashada%20muraaqikii%204%20Eexarakada%20Islaax.htm (accessed May, 1, 2010).
3. Islah joined the International MB in 1987. See Stig Jarle Hansen and Atle Mesoy, The *Muslim Brotherhood in the Wider Horn of Africa* (NIBR Report, 2009), 42. Also, Sheikh Mohamed Garyare interviewed by the author on March 12, 2010, Toronto, Canada. See also, Robert S. Leiken and Steven Brooke, "The Moderate Muslim Brotherhood," *Foreign Affairs* 86, no. 2, (March/April, 2007), 115.

circumstances.⁴ Accordingly, its programs and activities are locally driven and adaptable to the ever-changing situations of the different Somali regions. This chapter explores the historical development of the Islah Movement from 1978 to 1990. It examines this movement in three stages. The first stage is the early period of the introduction of the MB ideology to Somalia, its spread through local Arabic schools, and the provision of scholarships to Somali students in Arab countries. Moreover, this stage includes Somali students' contacts with the MB in Egypt, Sudan and Saudi Arabia. This stage also includes the early role of a few MB members in the period of the Islamic consciousness (Chapter Three) and period of the Islamic awakening (Chapter Four). The second stage explores the establishment of the Islah Movement, its nature, objectives, structure, and recruitment strategies. The third stage examines the programs of Islah and its activities from 1978 to 1990 as they interacted with the Somali socio-political realities during the dictatorial regime. It depicts challenges, limitations, achievements, and major activities before the collapse of the state.

Introducing the Muslim Brotherhood in Somalia (1953–1978)

The history of MB points out that the first chapter of MB outside of Egypt was established in Djibouti in 1933.⁵ The legacy of this chapter as reported by Sheikh Cabdiraxman Bashiir is

---

4. Ibrahim Dasuuqi Sheikh Maxamad interviewed by the author on May 28, 2010, Nairobi, Kenya.
5. See 'Abdallah Aqīl, *Min I'lām al-Da'wa wa al-Harakah al-Islāmiyah al-Mu'āsirah* (Dār al-Tawzi' wa al-Nashr al-Islāmyah, Qāhira: 2000), 380 quoted from *Jarīdat al-Ikhwān al-Muslimūn*, 24/6/1933.

identifiable to a certain point.⁶ They included Aḥmed al-Saqāf, the former Djibouti chief judge, Sa'īd Ba-Makhram, the former Imam of the Hamudi Mosque,⁷ Sheikh Cusmaan Waceys, an activist for the liberation movement of Djibouti, Sheikh Haaruun, the teacher of the nationalist Maxamuud Xarbi, and Sheikh Cafar.⁸ All these Islamic scholars were active and left lasting imprint in the history of Djibouti before its independence in 1977. However, there is no indication of extending their activities to other parts of the region such as Somalia. The Horn of African region inhabited by the Somali speaking people was not isolated from each other. The influx of MB outside of Egypt intensified since 1954 when the oppressive Nasserite regime of Egypt undertook brutal policy against them. Since then, many of its members fled Egypt and established chapters in other parts of the world.⁹ In particular, conservative Arab countries struggling against Arab nationalists led by Jamāl 'Abdi-Nāsser, welcomed MB immigrants and gave them residence and employment. In the Somali context, this period coincides with the UN trusteeship period administered by Italy in 1950s. It also covers the period

---

6. Sheikh Cabdiraxman Bashiir, the famous Djiboutian Islamic scholar, interviewed by the author on August 30, 2010, Djibouti.
7. Ba- Makhram died 1976 while giving Friday sermon in the mosque and was accused of belonging to MB by the French authorities. Sheikh Cabdiraxman Bashiir related that the newspaper Reveille reported this accusation (I could find the copy of the newspaper but was related that it is kept by the family member of sheikh Ba-Makhram).
8. He graduated from al-Azhar University and used to carry Sayid Qutub's book "in the shade of the Qur'an". He travelled to Eritrea in 1970s and never returned back.
9. The Muslim Brotherhood member, *Maḥmūd Abd al-Latīf* was accused of assassinating '*Abdi Nāsser* on 26 October, 1954. As result, more than 700 were accused of high treason, and finally six members of the MB were executed and thousands became political prisoners. See P.J. Vatikiotis, *Egypt from Mohamed Ali to Sadat* (London: Butler & Tanner Ltd., 1980), 384.

of the growing Islamic consciousness and the emergence of the Islamic awakening, examined in the previous two chapters. This period could be classified into three segments. The first is the introduction of the MB ideas in Somalia through Egyptian teachers and literature. These ideas were concomitant with the Somali nationalist movement for independence and the promotion of Islamic and Arabic culture against growing westernization, secularization, and Christianization. The consequence of the promotion of Arabic/Islamic education and scholarships provided to the Somalis resulted in some students meeting the MB members and embracing their ideology. The second segment begins with the return of the first Somali scholars who embraced the MB ideology and established Nahdah, which played a pioneering role in the Islamic awakening. The third segment begins when students, influenced by the Islamic awakening, traveled abroad and established direct contacts with the MB in Sudan, Egypt, and Saudi Arabia. These students later became the stamina for establishing an autonomous Somali MB organization- the Islah Movement.

The First Footstep of the MB in Somalia

Although "in the pre-independence Somalia, several of the founders of Somali Youth League (SYL), an organization that spearheaded the Somali struggle for independence, had personal connection with the [Muslim] Brotherhood," the MB entered Somalia in 1950s.[10] Egyptian Islamic scholar *Sheikh Moḥamūd Iid*, dispatched to Somalia among the al-Azhar

---

10. Stig Hansen and Atle Mesoy, The *Muslim Brotherhood*, 38.

Mission teachers in 1953, was the first known MB member to initiate activities in Somalia. Sheikh Mohamud attempted to create a network of disciples and friends among the Somali leaders in Mogadishu. As he related, he started a special instruction circle to form the MB chapter in 1954; however, he was suspected by the colonial authority and Egyptian intelligence and expelled from Somalia as *persona non grata* in 1955.[11] There is strong belief that some Egyptian teachers were also members of the MB or were influenced by their ideology. Some of these teachers were quietly injecting the idea of the MB among their students recommending extra-curriculum readings of books somewhat related to that ideology. For instance, Sheikh Cabdullahi Cali Xayle relates that he was a student in the Egyptian High School in Mogadishu when *Jamal 'Abdi-Nāsser* died in 1970. "Students were shocked, distressed and mourned, however, I remember how one of the teachers approached me and said: 'do not worry; *'Abdi-Nāsser* was very bad leader who killed many Muslims belonging to MB'.[12] Mr. Xayle joined the MB later and recalls that story, thinking his teacher may have been a member of the MB. Moreover, Xussein Sheikh Axmad Kadare testifies that in the 1950s, he was very sympathetic to the Arabic language and the Egyptians and developed intimate relations with them."One day," he said, "I

---

11. Sheikh Moḥamūd 'īd visited Somalia in July 1990 to participate in the symposium organized by the SomaliNationalUniversity. He was highly enthusiastic to meet some Islah members who were professors in the university and related his early attempts and challenges he faced during the 1950s. See Xassan Xaaji Maxamuud,*Tārikh al-Ḥaraka al-Islāmiyah:Durūf al-Nashi wa 'awāmil al-tadawur*" (unpublished draft).
12. Cabdullahi Cali Xayle is a former colonel, an Islamic scholar, and a member of the Islah Movement. See the communique of Islah on the Ethiopian Intervention on July 27, 2006, available from http://www.Islah.org/arabic/bayaan26-7-06.htm (accessed on May 5, 2010). Also, Cabdullahi Cali Xayle interviewed by the author on August 5, 2009, Hargeysa, Somaliland.

was invited to weekly Islamic education circle held in a house of one of the teachers. Participants were few selected members and it continued for few months."[13] He also believes that he was offered initial training to become a member of the MB.

Other interviewees believe that *Kamāl al-Addīn Sālaḥ*, the Egyptian Ambassador to the UN Consultative Council, might have been an MB member. They deduce their speculations in tracing his biography during his six-year tenure as Egyptian envoy to Palestine. During these years, he developed intimate relations with *Al-Ḥājji Amīn al-Ḥusseini*, the Grand Mufti of Jerusalem and the leader of the MB.[14] Hassan Xaaji Maxamuud, a Somali researcher, stipulates, "There is high probability of *Kamāl al-Addīn* being a member or at least influenced by the MB."[15] Furthermore, Sheikh Maxamad Garyare affirms the presence of the MB among the Egyptian teachers of the al-Azhar Mission in Somalia. He bases his testimony on his experiences of meeting Egyptian teachers working in Somalia while he was a student in Saudi Arabia in the 1960s, "They came for Hajj and participated in one of MB educational sessions. I remember the last name of one of them was *Al-Mahdi*."[16] Moreover, in 1967, Sheikh Garyare related that he met

---

13. *Kamal Addin Salah* was the Egyptian representative in UN Trusteeship Advisory Mission to Somalia. Xussein Sheikh Axmad "Kadare" interviewed by the author on July 11, 2009, Nairobi, Kenya.
14. *'Abdirahman al-Banna*, brother of *Ḥassan al-Banna* was sent to Palestine to establish the MB in 1935. See Azmul Fahimi Karauzaman, "The Emergence of Egyptian Muslim Brotherhood in Palestine: Causes, activities and formation of Identity," *Journal of Human Sciences* 44, no. 7, (January, 2010): 2.
15. Xassan Xaaji Maxamad interviewed by the author on April 30, 2010, Dubai, United Arab Emirates.
16. Note that Sheikh Maḥamed Al-Mahdi Maḥamūd was among six Islamic scholars from the al-Azhar Mission in 1953. Accordingly, two of the six al-Azhar expeditions to Somalia in 1953 were belonging to MB. See Hassan Makki. *Al-Siyāsāt al-Thaqāfiya fi al-Somāli al-Kabīr (1887-1986)* (Al-Markaz al-Islāmi li al-buhūth wa Nasri, 1990), 142.

a teacher of the al-Azhar mission while carrying one of Sayid Qutub's books, *The Milestones*. He said, "The teacher was gazing at the book and asked if I am aware of the writer of the book, and I replied affirmatively. Then, he stared at me with concern and said: 'Cling [persevere]; you are in the right course'."[17] All these testimonies demonstrate the likelihood of the presence of members of the MB among Egyptian teachers and their engagement in some form of Islamic activities.

Somalis on the Trail of the MB

With the increased cultural connections between Somalia and the Arab world in the 1950s and the growing Islamic consciousness, some Somali students in Egypt and Saudi Arabia joined the MB organization. The first known Somali member of the MB was Sheikh Cabdulqani Sheikh Axmad, who joined in 1956 while studying in the al-Azhar University, from which he graduated in 1957. The second person was Ambassador Cabdiraxman Faarax (Kabaweyne), who also graduated from al-Azhar University in the 1960s.[18] The third person was Sheikh Maxamad Garyare, who also joined the MB while studying at the Islamic University in Saudi Arabia in 1963. As Sheikh Garyare relates, *Sheikh Manna'al-Qaṭān* and Egyptian Professor *Maḥamad Sayid al-Wakīl* played crucial roles in his training and joining the MB.[19] Sheikh Cabdulqani returned to Somalia in 1957 and worked as a lecturer at the Somali University Institute, later joining the Ministry of Justice and Religious Affairs. These

---

17. Sheikh Maxamad Garyare interviewed by the author on February 10, 2010, Toronto, Canada.
18. Cabdiraxman Faarah "Kabaweyne" was one of the founding members of Nahdah and became its secretary general. See the bylaw of Nahdah.
19. Sheikh Mohamed Garyare interviewed by the author.

three members began their activities by establishing the Nahdah and promoting, guiding, and strengthening the Islamic awakening through lecturing and providing the MB literature. The MB team was very careful to recruit new members for a variety of unclassified reasons. Sheikh Maxamad Garyare did not provide a detailed explanation and simply replied: "Even though we did not focus on recruiting new members, we started our general Islamic activities in many ways and we propagated the idea of MB passionately."[20] When Nahdah was banned in1969, an Islamic awakening was gaining momentum and the ideology of the MB was penetrating strongly the younger generation. The confrontation between the regime and members of Nahdah led to many of the members being imprisoned. The conflict between Islamism and Socialism exacerbated and culminated in 1975 with the proclamation of the secular Family Law and the subsequent execution of Islamic scholars (see Chapter Four). During this period, young Somali Islamists were fleeing the country, seeking refuge, education, and employment in the rich Arab Gulf countries.

The Establishment of Somali MB Unit in Sudan

The third stage of establishing the Somali chapter of the MB occurred in Sudan. The MB had been active and public in Sudan since its formation in 1949. It emerged from Muslim student groups that began organizing in the universities during the 1940s, and educated elites remained its main support base. Somali students in Khartoum University were part of the MB student activism struggling against Communists. Somali students shared with the Sudanese Brotherhood in their

---

20. Ibid.

opposition to a similar Socialist military regime in Somalia. According to Dr. Maxamad Yusuf, in May 1973, five students at the Khartoum University who officially joined the MB in Sudan founded the first chapter of the Somali MB. Among this early group, three became founding members of the Islah Society.[21] The other two were Abdirizaq Sheikh Ciise and Burhaan Cali Kulane.[22]

Two of the founding members were Cali Sheikh Axmad and Maxamad Yusuf, who graduated in 1967 from the Institute of Islamic Solidarity funded by the World Islamic League. They were among the 10 top students offered scholarships to Saudi Arabia every year. However, the military regime nationalized all non-state schools and banned all scholarships to Arab countries and Europe in 1973.[23] The regime also restricted citizens' travel abroad by denying them travel documents. These two students were dedicated and committed to complete their higher education and decided to travel to Saudi Arabia via Ethiopia and Sudan without travel documents. Having experienced many risks and difficulties on their long journey to Sudan, they finally reached Khartoum and were welcomed by Axmad Rashiid Xanafi, the third founding member, who was a student in the University of Khartoum. Ahmed Rashid narrates this story as follows:

---

21. Members who participated in the foundation of Islah were Axmad-Rashid Xanafi, Cali Sheikh Axmad Abubakar, and Maxamad Yusuf Cabdiraxman.
22. Cadirisaq Cisse lived in Kuwait and worked for the Ministry of Religious Endowment and Islamic Affairs. Burhaan Cali Kulane migrated to Europe and came back to Kenya. He worked with his father in the transport business and died in 2000. Awale Kulane, the brother of Burhaan, interviewed by the author through email, Beijing, China, March 10, 2010. Also see Moḥamed Yusuf, "*Min dikriyāt al-Ḥarakah*", available from http://www.Islah.org/arabic/Tasiis1.htm (accessed on June 19, 2010).
23. Cali Sheikh Axmad interviewed by the author on June 5, 2009, Nairobi, Kenya.

When Cali Sheikh and Maxamad Yusuf arrived to Sudan, fortunately, they became my guests. Then, we contacted Sudanese MB, and after three months we were admitted in the organization. Subsequently, we started Islamic activities among Somali students and recruited other two members.[24] We pledged to establish MB Branch in Somalia under a tree at the university. When Cali Sheikh and Maxamad Yusuf were traveling to Saudi Arabia in 1973, I was assigned to take the responsibility in Sudan while they took the responsibility in Saudi Arabia. From 1974–76, I have succeeded to recruit other six persons and after graduating in 1976, I traveled also to Saudi Arabia to join my colleagues and seeking job opportunities.[25]

Cali Sheikh Axmad and Maxamad Yusuf received travel documents from the sympathetic Somali Ambassador in Khartoum and traveled to Saudi Arabia in September 1973 to join the Islamic University in Medina.[26] In 1973-1974, there was a severe drought in Somalia, and the local economy sharply deteriorated. However, "there was demand for labor in the Gulf, particularly Saudi Arabia as the oil boom took off. The lifting of certain restrictions by the Somali Government helped to facilitate migration."[27] Within this migrant labor force, Islamist students fleeing from state repressions also arrived in Saudi Arabia and started to join the Islamic universities. The Saudi government facilitated the admission of Somali students in its universities to confront the military Socialist regime and as part of its strategic policy to spread Salafism/Wahabism in

---

24. These two students were Burhaan Cali Kulane and Sheikh Cabdirisaq Cisse.
25. Axmad Rashiid Xanafi interviewed by the author on February 15, 2010, Ottawa, Canada.
26. They were not allowed to receive Somali travel documents being considered renegades and in opposition to the regime. General Holif, the Somali Ambassador in Khartoum, had close relations to these students.
27. UNDP, *UNDP Report on Somali Diaspora: Somalia's Missing Million: The Somali Diaspora and its role in Development*, (2009), 12.

Somalia. This policy was part of a general Saudi foreign policy under King Faysal, who allied with Islamist organizations, offered refuge for the oppressed activists, and provided thousands of scholarships to the Muslim communities around the world. In particular, Saudi Arabia was furious about the Somali military regime's execution of Islamic scholars in 1975, its Socialist ideology, and considerable Soviet presence in Somalia. It considered the Somali regime under Maxamad Siyad Barre as a threat to the Saudi national security. Subsequently, Saudi Arabia was poised to do whatever it takes through persuasion and pressure to eliminate the Soviet presence in Somalia.[28] One element of the Saudi pressure was to support all opposition groups, Islamists, as well other oppositions to the regime, through variety of means.

In this favorable environment and context, Cali Sheikh and Maxamad Yusuf joined the Islamic University in Medina and were welcomed by the MB chapter at the university. The MB activities at the university were very much public and tolerated by the Saudi establishment. During this period, Saudi Arabia was rebuilding its high education institutions and employed hundreds of professors from Arab countries, such as Egypt, Syria, Iraq, and Sudan. Many of these professors were renegade members of the MB, who coached and mentored MB student activities at the university. However, the task undertaken by the two Somali members of MB was tremendous, taking the responsibility of recruiting more members from the Somali community and students. Dr. Cali Sheikh Axmad, describing their major activities from 1973 to 1977, stated:

---

28. Moḥamed Sharīf, *"Faslūn fi al-'alāqāt al-Somāliyah al-Sacūdiyah"* available at: http://arabic.alshahid.net/columnists/analysis/8598 (accessed on April 21, 2010).

During these four years, besides graduating from the university and continuing post-graduate program, our work was focused on recruiting more Somalis to the MB. We succeeded to recruit about 10 new members and we held other 11 students in the pre-recruitment programs. It was a volatile period, which Salafia, Takfiir ideology and emerging clannish factions were competing [with] our efforts vehemently.[29]

However, when they tried to recruit these 11 members, they revealed their affiliation to the Ahal organization.[30] Even though they were convinced to join MB, these students prudently recommended to wait for the arrival of their leader, Cabdulqaadir Xaaji Maxamuud, whom they expected to join them. Cabdulqaadir fled the country in 1976 and arrived in Saudi Arabia. Nonetheless, after several meetings with Cali Sheikh Axmad and Maxamad Yusuf, he shut the door for further dialogue and, in all probability; had in mind a new plan for the future of Ahal organization.[31] This plan was made public later and aimed at transforming Ahal into Takfiir. In that way, the Somali MB group's vision for creating unified Islamic organizations affiliated with the MB was dashed.[32]

On the other hand, Sheikh Maxamad Garyare, who fled from the Somali regime, arrived in Saudi Arabia on January, 1,

---

29. Cali Sheikh Axmad Abubakar interviewed by the author on June 23, 2010, Nairobi, Kenya.
30. On October 15, 1975, at a meeting held in the Red Sea Hotel in Jeddah, attended by Xussein Cali Diirshe, Cabdiraxman Axmad Nuur, and Axmad Cusmaan Dheel from Ahal and Cali Sheikh Axmad, Maxamad Yusuf, and Axmad Rashiid Xanafi from the MB group, affiliations of the two groups were openly acknowledged. Ibid.
31. Axmad Rashiid Hanafi interviewed by the author.
32. Axmad Rashiid Xanafi, explaining the perspective of the founding members of Islah states, "When the three of us [Cali Sheikh, Maxamad Yusuf and Axmad Rashiid] affirming our pledge to establish MB in Sudan, our slogan was 'la ḥarakatāni fi al-Somāl,' which means 'there should be no two MB organizations in Somalia.'" Axmad Rashiid Xanafi interviewed by the author.

1976 and was very well received. His warm welcome was part of the Saudi policy to confront the repressive regime in Mogadishu and an expression of particular sympathy they held for Sheikh Maxamad Garyare, who was the first Somali graduate from the Islamic University in 1965. He was offered a respectable job in the *Dār al-Iftā* (Scientific Research and Religious Edicts), in the capacity of an "expert of the Islamic call in Africa."[33] Axmad Rashiid Xanafi, who graduated in 1976 from the Khartoum University, also got a job with Saudi Airlines in Riyadh. Therefore, by 1976, four of the founding fathers of Islah were well established in Saudi Arabia and began to explore the possibility of establishing the Somali MB organization. During this period, the early Ahal student organization was faltering since Cabdulqaadir Sheikh Maxamuud had reoriented to the ideology of Takfiir and was preparing to introduce it to his followers. On the other hand, some former members of Ahal, after joining Saudi universities, were attracted to the Salafia ideology, strongly promoted by the Saudi institutions. The general condition of the Somali Islamists in Saudi Arabia in the period of 1975-1978 could be characterized as living in the ideological ambivalence in which many of the students were driven mainly by opportunism.[34] With these ideological disorientations among Somali students, the MB members of Somali origin in Saudi Arabia were considering establishing the Somali MB organization.

---

33. Sheikh Maxamad Garyare interviewed by the author.
34. Many students were moving from one Islamic organization to another driven by opportunism, such as getting scholarships and jobs with Islamic institutions, which were highly rewarding during these early years.

The Establishment of Islah Islamic Society in 1978

It took 50 years from the time MB was established in Egypt in 1928 and 25 years since the first footstep of MB in Somalia to think of establishing Somali MB. The Somali MB by the name of the Islah Islamic Society was launched on July 11, 1978 in Riyadh, Saudi Arabia.[35] The founding members were Sheikh Maxamad Axmad Nuur (Garyare),[36] Cali Sheikh Axmad Abubakar,[37] Maxamad Yusuf Cabdiraxman,[38] Axmad Rashiid Sheikh Xanafi,[39] and Cabdallah Axmad Cabdallah.[40] In their founding meeting, the bye-law of the society was adopted and Sheikh Maxamad Garyare was elected to the position of the first chairman of Islah.[41] In 1978-1989, the organization was called the Islah Islamic Society and in 1989, it adopted the name The Islamic Movement in Somalia. The change of the name from Islah to the general name of Islamic Movement was intended to attract many Islamists and prominent personalities. However,

---

35. This date coincides with the Muslim Calendar, Sha'ban 6, 1398 H. See Xassan Xaaji Maxamuud, *Tāriikh al-Ḥarkah al-Islāmiyah* (unpublished manuscript).
36. Sheikh Maxamad Garyare (1935–), graduated from Al-Imām University, Saudi Arabia, in 1965 and returned to Somalia. He became director of the Islamic Affairs in the Ministry of Religious Affairs. He also became the first chairman of Islah (1978–1990).
37. Dr. Cali Sheikh Axmad (1951–), PhD from the Islamic University in 1984, Saudi Arabia. He became a professor in the KingSaudUniversity (1984–1994). He also became chairman of Islah (1999– 2008). Currently, he is the president of the MogadishuUniversity.
38. Dr. Mohamed Yusuf (1951–), PhD from the Islamic University, Saudi Arabia. Currently, works on the project of the Islamic Encyclopaedia, Kuwait.
39. Sheikh Axmed Rashiid Hanafi (1952–), MA in African Studies from OhioStateUniversity, lecturer at the MogadishuUniversity.
40. Cabadallah Axmad Cabdallah (1953–), graduated from the KhartoumUniversity in 1978 and lives in Washington, D.C.
41. Cali Sheikh Ahmed was elected initially to the position of the chairmanship, but relinquished, so that Sheikh Mohamed becomes the first functional chairman. See http://www.Islah.org/arabic/history.htm (accessed on May 22, 2010).

the abrupt collapse of the state aborted its major goals.[42] Although the organization continued to use the general name for years, its popular name remained Islah. The popular name of the organization took the catchy word of Islah, derived from the Qur'anic word *Al-Islah*, signifying that all its activities is founded on the profound meaning of that simple word.[43] This word carries various meanings, such as "reforming, betterment, reconciling and correcting."[44] Its logo, consisting of four elements, symbolizes this basic philosophy of the organization. It features the descending light illuminating an open book under which a handshake is depicted; this is surrounded by an oval frame of banana leafs joined at the bottom, with a ribbon on which *"inurīdu ila al-Islāh ma astada'atu"* is written. This means, "I decide naught save reform as far as I can able."[45]

Figure: 6. *Logo of Islah Movement*

The descending light signifies revelation that, by falling on an open book, transforms into the divine guidance of the

---

42. Cali Sheikh Axmad Abubakar interviewed by the author.
43. See the Qur'anic verse (11:88), which states "I decide naught save reform as far as I can able."
44. See the Glorious Qur'anic verse (11:88) and verses (49: 8–9).
45. See the Glorious Qur'anic verse (11:88).

Qur'an. This symbolism demonstrates that the ultimate reference of Islah is transcendental and universal. The handshake represents the strategy of Islah, based on peacefulness, dialogue, reconciliation, and cooperation. This notion may reflect Islah's attitude in the war-torn Somalia, which completely contravenes violent and extreme approaches in the name of primordial sentiment or those under the Islamic banner. Finally, the two oval-shaped banana leafs represent the theatre of Islah's operation, Somalia, known for its abundant banana plantations.[46] The cosmology of Islah's logo is "Peace, Qur'an, and Banana." It defied the famous Somali dictum *"Nabad iyo Caanno"* (Peace and Milk) or "the Gun, the Hand, the Helmet, and the Qur'an," which symbolized the first white paper of the 1969 military coup.[47] Besides the agreed-upon Islamic symbol of the Qur'an, the Islah logo snubbed two elements well attributed in the traditional Somali society: milk and weapons, the symbols of nomadism and war in the Somali context. Instead, Islah chose banana leaves and a handshake, the symbol of settlement and peacefulness.

Why was Islah established at this particular time in Saudi Arabia? Did the Saudi authority encourage its creation? These questions are relevant since the first chairman of Islah, Sheikh Maxamad Garyare, was a high-profile figure working for the Saudi Islamic Institution of *Dar Al-Iftā*. They are also more

---

46. Somalia was the largest exporter of bananas in Africa, with 12,000 hectares under cultivation and employing more than 120,000 people. However, it was affected by the civil war, and bananas ceased to be exported, though the potential remains. See E. Baars and A. Reidiger, *"Building the Banana Chain in Somalia: Support for Agricultural Marketing Service and Access to Markets (SAMSAM) experience"*, available fromhttp://www.new-ag.info/pdf/SAMSAM-report.pdf (accessed on May 18, 2010).
47. See the symbol of revolution issued on 21 October, 1969 in Cabdulaziz Cali Ibrahim "Xildhiban", *Taxanaha Taariikhda Somaaliya* (London: Xildhiban Publications, 2006), 40.

pertinent in the light that the second chairman of Islah (1990–1999), Dr. Maxamad Cali Ibrahim, expelled from the organization after leading the Islamic Union Court delegation to Khartoum in 2006, had criticized Islah for "precipitation." He bluntly stated that "there were a general agreement among all Somali Islamists to establish a unified Islamic organization, but leaders of Islah had precipitated."[48] Sheikh Maxamad Garyare was asked in what way Islah precipitated, and he offered the following comment on this issue:

> We have been evaluating the progress of our outreach activities to Ahal individuals since 1974 and we have finally come to the conclusion that any more postponement from our part will not yield any better result. Ahal students though were ardent in their Islamic commitment, had deficiency in the organizational culture. Most of them were self-educated and lacked basic Islamic knowledge and sufficient training. History confirmed our assumptions since most of the former Ahal members who claimed belonging to MB have followed Salafia theology and founded Itixaad.[49]

Moreover, he testifies that the timing of announcing Islah was the most appropriate. One must note that the Saudi authority, although was generally tolerant to the Islamic activities, was not behind and was not aware of the formation of Islah. Cali Sheikh Axmad concurred with Sheikh Maxamad

---

48. See Moḥamed 'Umar Aḥmed, "Ḥiwār Da'wa ma'a al-doktor Moḥamed 'Ali Ibrahim" available from http://www.somaliatoday.net/port/2010-01-04-21-22-23/349-2009-12-10-22-50-16.html (accessed on May 13, 2010). Dr. Mohamed Ali was expelled from the Islah Organization after leading a delegation of Islamic Union Court to Sudan, in which Islah rejected to participate. See the communiqué of Islah on that matter, available from http://www.Islah.org/arabic/bayaan21-6-06.htm (accessed on June 10, 2009).
49. Sheikh Maxamad Garyare interviewed by the author.

Garyare regarding the appropriateness of the timing and described the conditions under which Islah was formed:

> It was the era of the Cold War and strong confrontation with communist ideology in many Muslim countries. It was the era of economic boom in the Gulf States and building Saudi infrastructure in all sectors. It was the aftermath of 1973 war with Israel where Arab countries succeeded to regain some dignity and changed political equations in the Middle East. It was the time when many leaders of the Egyptian MB were released from the prison and Muslim student activism was very high in the universities. It was the golden decade of 1970s which MB organization was revived and reorganized. In the Somali context, it was three years after the execution of the Islamic scholars in 1975 and immediately after Somali regime's defeat in the war with Ethiopia in 1978. The aftermath of this defeat set off the emergence of oppositional organizations to dictatorial military regime. In this circumstance, Islah represented the Islamic opposition to the regime and Islamic political agenda in this particular historical juncture.[50]

Three main factors were considered in establishing Islah at this particular time. The first was the readiness of the local environment for an effective organization because of the accumulative effect of the Islamic consciousness and awakening since the 1950s. The impact of 25 years of continuous Islamic work; proliferation of Arabic schools; contact with the Muslim world; confrontation with westernization, secularization, and Christianization; and the battle for the Somali language script, all paved the way for the formation of the Islah Movement. Moreover, the formation of Nahdah, Ahal, and Waxdah, the prominence of the MB ideology, the confrontation with the military regime and its secularizing program that culminated

---

50. Cali Sheikh Axmad interviewed by the author.

the issue of the secular Family Law were highly provocative for the Islamic sentiment. This environment lacked an effective MB organization connected to the wider MB, carrying the vision of internationalism (*al-'Alamiyah*) and locality (*al-Maḥaliyah*), which Islah aimed to provide.

The second factor was the growing opposition to the military regime. This dissidence was in reaction to the accumulative social and political strain from the military regime's policies. In particular, the execution of Islamic scholars in 1975, the economic crisis, the establishment of the Socialist Revolutionary Party in 1976, and the defeat of the Somali army in the war with Ethiopia in 1977-78, all provoked multiple crises.[51] Moreover, the economic boom in the Gulf region had enabled thousands of Somali labor migrants to work and study in Saudi Arabia. Most of these Somalis thus received an improved awareness of Islam and supported the opposition to the Socialist regime. The Somali political situation of 1978 was very similar to the political situation of 1969, when one-party regime was established and political grievances were not addressed but rather exacerbated. The army that had saved the state from falling apart in 1969 was now fragmented, and its command structure lost its independence and professionalism, becoming an inseparable part of the ruling socialist party and

---

51. Relations between Somalia and the Soviet Union had deteriorated and Soviet experts were expelled from Somalia on November 13, 1977. This author was among the expelled Somali military officers from the USSR reciprocally. This point was also related by Tadesse who wrote that "the formation of radical Islamic movements in Somalia in 1978 was partially political reaction to an Ethiopian Military Victory." See Medhane Tadesse, *Al-Ittihad: Political Islam and Black Economy in Somalia: Religion, Clan, Money, and the Struggle for Supremacy over Somalia* (Addis Ababa: Meag Printing Enterprise, 2002), 20.

the regime.⁵² That is why the second attempted coup d'etat of April 9, 1978 was easily foiled, resulting in the execution of 18 army officers and the detention of hundreds more.⁵³ Some coup plot officers who succeeded in fleeing from Somalia began to form armed oppositions and received welcoming hand from Somalia's hostile neighbors, particularly Ethiopia.⁵⁴ The terrified regime adopted extreme security measures and indiscriminate incarcerations, and pitted "friendly clans" against "inimical clans" to the regime. Thus, the politics of clan polarization and factionalism had intensified in 1978 when the first armed faction was established.⁵⁵ Moreover, Islamic oppositions were growing and needed an effective organization that could mobilize the population against the regime by carrying an Islamic political agenda. Founders of Islah aimed at that particular objective, justifying the formation of their organization at this particular time.

The third factor was globally connected to the growing role of the worldwide Islamic movement in the 1970s. In particular, this growth had begun with the defeat of Arab nationalism in

---

52. The top command of National Army consisted of members of the Socialist Revolutionary Party, appointed because of their political allegiance rather than their military professionalism. This also brings in the clan factor, where certain clans were considered friendly to the regime and others inimical.
53. Most of these officers belonged to the Air Defence Third Brigade in Mogadishu. The author, though was not part of this coup, was suspected and detained for two weeks for being an officer attached to the Brigade for a short training assignment.
54. During this period, both Somalia and Ethiopia were supporting each other's armed oppositions. Somalia was supporting current leaders of Ethiopia and Eritrea, while the Ethiopian regime was supporting the Somali clan-based factions that toppled the Siyaad Barre regime; nevertheless, they failed to re-establish Somali nation-state.
55. The Somali Salvation Front (SSF) was the first opposition party founded in Nairobi in 1978. However, it was merged with other parties to form the Somali Salvation Democratic Front (SSDF) in 1981 in Eden. These three organizations were the SSF, the Somali Workers Party (SWP), and the Democratic Front for the Liberation of Somalia (DFLS).

the war with Israel in 1967 and the release of the MB members from the prisons in the 1970s. Moreover, the changing ideological orientation of Egypt during the reign of *Anwar al-Sādāt* compelled *Sādāt* to enlist the help of the MB against leftist opposition groups. He also needed the support of the vibrant religious groups during national mobilization for the war of 1973, where the strong Islamic slogan *"Allāh Akbar"* was used.This suitable environment enabled the MB to reorganize themselves worldwide, benefit from the Gulf economic boom, and recruit into its ranks a large number of student activists in Egyptian universities. Moreover, many Islamic books were published and widely distributed at that time. The 1970s was the golden decade of the MB and continued until *Sādāt* signed an agreement with Israel in 1979. On the other hand, when General Mohammad Zia-ul-Haq took over Pakistan in 1977, he initiated "a period [which had] witnessed the Islamization of laws, public policy, and popular culture, producing a unique case of systematic propagation of Islamism from above."[56] Zia's policies of Islamization sought to establish better relations with Arab states and cooperation with Islamic organizations. The two main Islamic organizations, the MB and *Jamāt-al-Islāmi* of Pakistan, were networked and expanded their activities and spheres of influence around the globe. However, the golden decade of Islamic moderation has been withering with the Soviet invasion of Afghanistan (1979) and the subsequent Jihaad, the triumph of Iranian Revolution (1979), the Iran-Iraq war, the capturing of the Grand Mosque in Mecca by Juhaiman (1979), and the assassination of *Sādāt* (1981). In the 1980s and

---

56. Vali Nasr, "Military Rule, Islamism and Democracy in Pakistan," *Middle East Journal* 58, no. 2 (2004): 95.

after, the entire Middle East region was boiling with armed conflict, with Islamic slogans being excessively employed.

The Nature of Islah

Islah is a moderate Islamic movement that operates in Somalia and within its Diaspora worldwide. It adopts a bottom-up reform process and pursues non-violent approaches. At the same time, inspired by the MB methodology, it has developed a special approach in dealing with stateless society in conflict.[57] Islah's moderate approach is derived from the methodological Islamic framework called *al-Wasadiyah* (moderation) in the Arabic language. Moderation means centrism or being middle of the road, center of the circle, balanced with no extremism. Moderation is a fundamental landmark of Islam. Sheikh *Yusuf Al-Qardāwi* states, "Islamic texts call upon Muslims to exercise moderation and to reject and oppose all kinds of extremism: *ghuluw* (excessiveness), *tanaṭu'* (trangressing; meticulous religiosity) and *tashdīd* (strictness; austerity)".[58] Moreover, *Ḥassan al-Banna* describes such moderation:

> Islam liberates the mind, urges contemplation of the universe, honors science and scientists, and welcomes all that is good and beneficial to mankind: 'Wisdom is the lost property of the believer. Wherever he finds it, he is more deserving to it.'[59]

---

57. This new approach was developed to deal with clan-based society in conflict. Details of this approach are presented in Chapter Six.
58. See the Qur'anic verse, "Thus have we made of you an Ummah justly balanced, that you might be witnesses over the nations and the Messenger a witness over yourselves" (2:143). Also, see Yusuf Al Qardawi, "*Islamic AwakeningbetweenRejection and Extremism*", available from http://web.youngmuslims.ca/online_library/books/iabrae/chapter_1.htm (accessed on June 19, 2010)
59. See Hassan al Banna, "Twenty Principles", available from http://web.youngmuslims.ca/online_library/books/tmott/index.htm#understanding (accessed on June 25, 2010)

Islah is not merely a conventional political party in the strict sense of the word, neither is it simply a typical religious social organization limiting its work to standard Islamic and social activities. It is a comprehensive movement that combines all aspects of social and political activism. Its multiple activities are guided by and derived from the comprehensive understanding of Islam articulated by *Ḥassan al-Banna*, "Islam is a comprehensive system which deals with all spheres of life. It is a country and homeland or a government and a nation… And finally, it is true belief and correct worship."[60] The various activities carried out within the spirit and Islamic morality include political activities, social programs, training and recruitment, the public propagation of Islam, civil society actions, etc. Islah pursues the main Islamic mission of the MB founded on raising the awareness of *"al-Ummah al-wāḥidah"* (one nation) among Muslim communities, clans, and ethnic groups to enable the reformation of secular states into Islamic states. Therefore, all its activities are rooted in the conception of Islam within the bounds laid by *Ḥassan al-Banna* in the treatise of *Risālah al-Ta'ālim* (The Message of Teachings), where "The Twenty Guiding Principles of Understanding Islam" are presented.[61] These twenty principles furnish fundamental guidelines and constitute the methodological framework for the common comprehension of Islam among the members of the MB. The twenty principles lumped together under the pillar of "understanding" are placed first among the ten basic pillars of the MB covenant on which pledges of allegiance (*Bai'a*) are offered. These ten pillars are: understanding, sincerity, action,

---

60. Ibid.
61. Ibid.

Jihād, sacrifice, obedience, perseverance, resoluteness, brotherhood, and trust.[62] Explaining these ten pillars is beyond our scope here, nevertheless, it should be understood that they constitute the common values and guiding principles of every member in the MB.

The Aims and Objectives of Islah

The main goal of Islah is to transform the Somali society and the state into a society and state that adopt Islam as its ultimate reference using evolutionary approach that offers enough consideration to the local and international environment.[63] The local environment includes cultural specificity, economic conditions, and the political state of affairs in Somalia. International environment consideration means to deal prudently with the globalized world and the international system, avoiding conflicts and promoting peace and cooperation. Islah developed 12 objectives in its bye-law that shed light on its orientation and course of actions. The first article emphasizes the centrality of the individual compliance to Islam as an agent for the Islamization of the society. Therefore, this article targets the way of transforming individuals through training and specialized programs.

> To instruct Muslim individual through comprehensive Islamic education in which spiritual, corporal, ideological, cultural, and political aspects complement each other. The right environment of collective and individual activism which helps the individual to

---

62. Ibid.
63. See Yusuf al-Qardawi, *Priorities of the Islamic Movement in the Coming Phase*, available from http://www.witness-pioneer.org/vil/Books/Q_Priorities/index.htm *(accessed on August 17, 2010)*

reach the higher level in these aspects should be provided until complete Muslim personality is shaped.[64]

Accordingly, the critical priority is the training of individuals to the level that enables them to undertake the mission of the Islamic propagation. Such individuals should "right up Islam in their heart, in order to right up in the society."[65] These individuals, in accordance with the program, should strive to establish harmonious relations compliant with Islamic principles in their homes and with their relatives, neighbors, and friends.

The second objective of Islah is articulated as follows: "To establish Islamic family, caring [for] its affairs and invigorating it to be the right foundation for the aspired Islamic society."[66] Presumably, this process gradually creates a number of families and communities that conform to the Islamic principles. Undertaking sustained Islamic work in all communities, districts, regions, and public spaces throughout years creates, according to this methodology, public opinion and communities that are more committed to Islam and supportive to the program of establishing an Islamic state. Following this logic, "Forming Islamic society and preparing the right Islamic basis" is the third objective. In this way, social Islamic values improve, individual piety increases, and community solidarity and charities grow. Via these long-term processes of social transformation through continuous Islamic education, the majority of the society is expected to accept Islamic principles and support a party with an Islamic agenda.

---

64. See the by-law of Islah, objective one.
65. The individuals should be dedicated enough to be able to claim the slogan.
66. See objective two of the bylaw of Islah.

The fourth objective is "To strive [to create] the Islamic state which practically implements Islamic Shari'a..." Of course, this long-term process of Islamization of the society does not work in a vacuum, and other ideologies compete. In particular, the post-colonial secular state blocked this peaceful means of societal transformation. The denial of freedom of association and ban on activism in Somalia during the era of the military regime bred extremism in the society, which also created obstacles for any peaceful transformation. In the Somali case, although after the collapse of the state, freedom was warranted, anarchy also prevailed and extremism exacerbated.

The fifth objective of Islah, which is distinctive from Arabic-speaking countries, is based on the promotion of learning the Arabic language in Somalia, without which Islamic propagation is defective. Somalia is a member of the Arab League; nevertheless, its people speak their own Somali language. Traditionally, Somali children study the Arabic alphabet in their early childhood as part of their Islamic education program. Therefore, most Somalis know the Arabic language to a certain extent and have memorized parts of the Qur'an. Islah focuses on the Arabic language as part of its drive for more Islamic education and to integrate the Somali society into the wider framework of Arab/Islamic societies. This objective is affirmed in the organization's bye-law that states:

> To spread Islamic call and Arabic language considering that it is the language of the Qur'an and the only means to the right comprehension of the Book [Qur'an], Sunna [of the Prophet] and Islamic heritage.

The next objectives (6, 7, and 8) focus on the social development issues. Two objectives are intended to promote material development in the society and social services such as education, health, and poverty eradication through encouraging charities and solidarities and to advocate for the compliance with the Islamic values.[67] The third objective, which is the most striking and pioneering among Islamic movements and traditional societies, is the issue of women's rights and development. This objective relates the issue of women as follows: "To care for the women and to revive [their] effective role in the society within Islamic framework." What does the Islamic framework mean? There are diverse interpretations of the role of women in the society, and their rights, particularly their rights to political participation, are widely controversial. However, the position of Islah is very clear in this point. Islah openly advocates the advancement of the rights of women and strongly supports their social and political participation in community affairs.[68] Moreover, Islah promotes women's education in all its social development programs. The effect of these policies was so resounding that Somali women now play important roles in politics and social life that were hitherto believed to be in the domain of men.[69]

Two other objectives (10, 11) are intended to address societal ailments such as clanism and sectarianism and to implant the value of freedom and consultation (Shura) or democratic culture in the society. These points are affirmed as follows:

---

67. See Objectives 6 and 7 of the Islah bylaw.
68. Abdurahman Abdullahi, "Penetrating Cultural Frontiers in Somalia: History of women's Political Participation during four Decades (1959–2000)," *African Renaissance* 4, no. 1 (2007): 34-54.
69. Ibid.

Article 7:10. To fight clanism, sectarianism and separatist tendencies, in order to melt artificial psychological barriers, and, to strive spreading the spirit of tolerance and brotherhood, intimacy, cooperation and solidarity among the people of the region.[70]

Article 7:11. To deepen the right meaning of the Islamic concept of *Shura* and to recognize freedom as a human value incarnated in Allah's dignification of the human being. For that [Islah] has to support general and individual freedom and human rights through establishment [relevant] political, economic and social institutions.[71]

Finally, the remaining two objectives (9, 12) are aimed to affirm the support for the right of people under colonial occupation to resistance (Jihad) and solidarity among Muslims to liberate Muslim countries under a colonial yoke. Moreover, Islah also vows to support the rights of Muslim minorities and the just cause of all oppressed people across the world.

The Organizational Structure of Islah

The structure of Islah has evolved through years; however, its current form was adopted in 1992.[72] It is based on autonomous zones akin to a federal system that enables Islah members dispersed in large geographical areas to operate effectively. The role of the center is confined to the coordination and preservation of organizational unity. Thus, the basic governing bodies of Islah consist of: (1) the chairman of Islah and his deputies; (2) *Majlis al-Shūra* (Consultative Council; CC) and *Mu'tamar al-Iqlimi* (Zonal Congress; ZC); (3) *Maktab al-Tanfidi* (Executive Bureaus; EB), *Martab al-Tanfidi al-Iqlimi* (Zonal

---

70. See Article 10 of the Islah bylaw.
71. See Article 11 of the Islah bylaw.
72. Cali Sheikh Axmad Abubakar interviewed by the author.

Executive Bureau; ZEB); and (4) Judiciary and disciplinary committees (Central and Zonal).[73]

The chairman of Islah chairs both the EB and the CC and is assisted by two independently elected vice-chairmen. The term of the chairman is limited to two five-year terms which offers room for leadership renewal. The eligibility conditions of the candidate are: to be at least 40 years old, a member of the CC, and an effective member in the organization for at least 10 years. He must have an experience of managing higher offices of the organization at least for three years and should not have been accused of any serious fault that called for disciplinary action.[74]

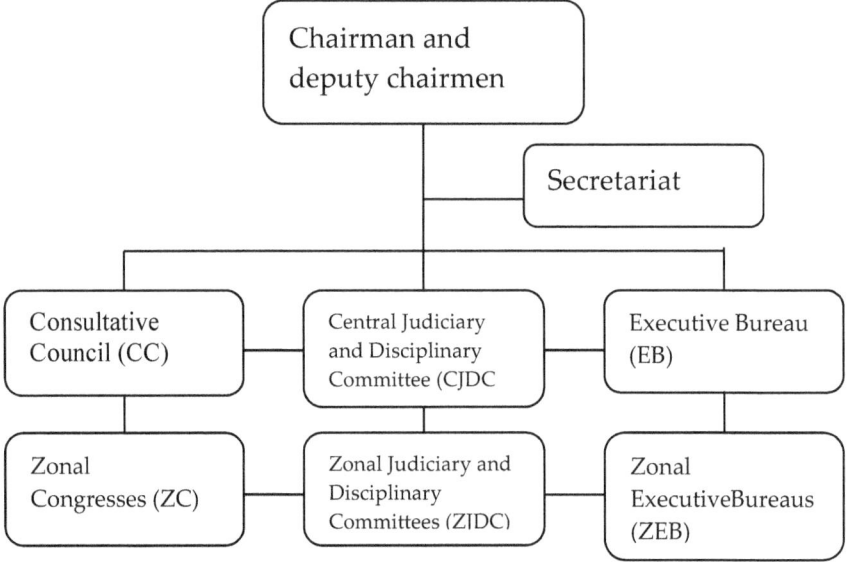

Figure 7. Organizational Structure of Islah

---

73. See Article 12 of the Islah bylaw. Also, see the organizational structure in Fig (2).
74. See Article 12 of the Islah bylaw.

The CC and ZC are two cameras of the Consultative Council that are elected consecutively. The effective members of the organization elect the ZCs in each Zone. Effective membership is acquired after three years of being full members and being promoted to such position in the process of the routine standard evaluations.[75] The ZCs numbers change from zone to zone and most likely are proportional to the number of their members.[76] The CC, consisting of 26 members, is elected from among members of the ZCs by the ZC members of each zone separately. The allocated number of CC members for each zone is mainly proportional representation of the members of the organization in each zone. Besides elected members of the CC, the National Chairman appoints two other members and the CC approves them. Five other members of CC are the founding fathers of Islah who hold permanent positions besides *ex-officio*. Therefore, there are total of 34 CC members. The CC is the highest authority in Islah, and its members have to offer the following pledge:

> I offer my pledge to Allah, the exalted and magnificent, to be the protector and truthful for the Islamic principles and pledge to safeguard the MB call committing [myself]to [abide]its laws and systems, implementing its decisions even if it differ from my personal opinion. Allah is the Disposer of my affairs.[77]

The third governing body is the EB and ZEB. The EB begins with the election of the Zonal chairman and his two deputies by the ZC from among the Zonal representatives of the CC.[78] Then,

---

75. Dr. Cali Baasha Cumar, the chairman of Islah, interviewed by the author on July 26, 2009, Hargeysa, Somaliland.
76. Ibid.
77. See the bylaw of Islah.
78. Dr. Cali Baasha Cumar interviewed by the author.

the elected Zonal chairman forms the ZEB, which the ZC has to approve. The chairman of Islah and two deputies are also elected by the CC. The new elected chairman takes the following oath:

> I offer my pledge to Allah, the exalted and magnificent, to uphold the Book of Allah and Sunna of His Prophet, to be the protector and truthful for the methodology of the MB and their constitution, executing their decisions of the CC and EB even if it differ from my personal opinion, striving to realize the exalted goals of the movement for the best of my ability, and give my pledge on that. Allah is the Disposer of my affairs.

After this procedure, the chairman forms the EB, which mostly consists of the CC members.[79] The EB consists of directors of the main departments and Zonal chairmen. The number of the EB members is flexible, and the chairman of Islah has the power to increase or decrease it as required. However, the main permanent departments are the department of Islamic propagation, the department of training and recruitment, the department of international relations and Diaspora chapters, the department of reconciliation and political activities, the department of finance, and Zonal chairmen. The national chairman also nominates these office holders, and each of them has to pass the vote of confidence by the CC. This procedure is waived from the Zonal chairmen who are directly elected by their ZCs.

The fourth component of the governing body of Islah is the judiciary and disciplinary committees (JDC), which include the Central Judiciary and Disciplinary Committee (CJDC) and the Zonal Judiciary and Disciplinary Committee (ZJDC). The CJDC

---

79. Ibid.

is similar to the Supreme and Constitutional Court. Its responsibility is to explain the constitution and bye-laws and to deal with the disciplinary actions of the CC and the EB. It comprises five high-ranking members who have legal qualifications. Similarly, the ZJDCs are responsible to carry out similar functions in their respective zones.

Membership and Recruitment

In principle, membership in the Islah Movement is gained only by invitation. In general, an individual should pass through three phases: identification phase, training and coaching phase, and recruitment phase.[80] The first process of searching for new members is done through general *Da'wa* programs. Islamic organizations are engaged in *Da'wa* in many public spaces, such as mosques, schools, and universities. Potential members are identified through Islamic activities in these places, through socialization and are targeted for future recruitment. Initially, the recruiters become acquainted with and befriend potential recruits through variety of means, such as relative networks, classmate connections, neighborhood relations, and so on. The best and easiest recruitment opportunity is to target relatives of members of the organization or their friends, since they are already familiar to the recruiters. Other individuals who have a high potential for recruitment are those belonging to the traditional religious families who had acquired Islamic knowledge and are more committed to Islam.

After proper identification, the second process is to place a person in a special training program, termed the *Usra maftūḥa*

---

80. Ibid.

(open circle), with other aspirants. In this program, the aspirants are offered the basics of Islamic knowledge and the principles of the Islamic movement. They are gradually convinced of the necessity to work within the organization and to be committed to the cause of Islam, according to the MB methodology. During this training program, their commitment and activities are continuously evaluated through practical activities, such as being given some *Da'wa* responsibilities and requesting to pay monthly financial contributions. Article 9 of the Islah Constitution delineates that a regular preparatory period of three years for the aspirants should pass before full membership can be acquired. Special exceptions may apply in some cases, and the program may be shortened or prolonged. The age of a person acquiring membership should not be less than 18 years.[81]

The third process to acquire full membership in Islah requires a set of rigorous bureaucratic procedures. After ascertaining that a person has fulfilled all requirements through the evaluation of the recruitment committees at the zonal or regional levels, the individual or a group of graduants are called to take the pledge of allegiance. New members recite the following text of the allegiance in the Arabic language after an Islah representative. The translated text of allegiance pledge as follows:

> I give my pledge to Allah, the Exalted and the Magnificent, to uphold the Book of Allah and the Sunna of the Prophet (SAW) and to uphold the principles of the MB and obey their leaders in hardship and easiness, unless I was ordered to commit sinful acts. In

---

81. Ibid.

that case, there is no obedience and Allah is the witness of what I declare.[82]

The ranks of membership develop along the following progression: *Nasīr* (aspirant), *Muntasib* (full member), *'Āmil* (effective member), and *Naqīb* (representative member). Each level of membership has its own training programs, responsibilities, and duties. A person is elevated from one level to another through the process of annual evaluation, measuring the individual's organizational commitment and his activities. The general basic measurement of the commitment is the attendance of the weekly training program, regular payment of the monthly contributions, and participation in the other designated activities. Membership is regulated in the Article 10 of the constitution, which states:

> Every member has to pay monthly financial contribution or yearly in accordance with the financial system of the region. In addition, members may contribute for the expenses of *Da'wa* through donations and Trust Fund and others. Moreover, the Da'wa has parts of the Zakat of the members as recorded in the financial regulation.[83]

The ranks in the organization are very important since they play a major role during election processes where certain ranks are qualified to elect and to be elected to certain positions in the organization.

Generally, Islah recruits young and educated segments of the society to its ranks during their last years of the high school or in the universities. These young generations are energetic and open, and because of their education, they grasp the

---

82. See the bylaw of Islah.
83. See the bylaw of Islah.

message of Islam easily and convey it to others.[84] This means that majority of its members is from young educated generations who through years become the intelligentsia of the society, growing in activism and internalizing organizational culture. Moreover, Islah began recruiting women to its ranks as equals to men in 1992, responding to the increased role played by women in the Somali society. This was in breach of the general policies of most MB organizations in the Arab world that were hesitant to recruit women to their ranks. The MB in Sudan was one of the pioneering organizations in recruiting women as full members.[85] It seems Deputy Chairman Sheikh Axmad Xassan al-Qutubi (1991–1995), who was educated in Sudan, transferred the Sudanese influence on women's role to Islah. Under the leadership of Sheikh Ahmed, the CC approved in 1992 the policy of recruiting women as equals to Islah. As a result, the first six women members joined Islah in 1992 in Mogadishu. Mustafa Abdullahi "Dheeg," who was assisting Sheikh Axmad Al-Qutubi in the women's recruitment, relates this event as follows:

> It was really a new beginning for our female activists who though worked with us in the Islamic activities, did not have the privilege to be recruited as equal members. However, after Sheikh Axmad al-Qutubi became deputy chairman, he promoted the role of women and the first six female members took the alliance oath and joined

---

84. History of Islam shows that the age of the Prophet Mohammad (PBH) was 40 years when he was sent as a messenger and all his early believers were younger than him, except his wife Khadija. Sheikh Axmad Xassan Al-Qutubi interviewed by the author on July 255, 2009, Hargeysa, Somaliland.
85. Ibid.

the organization in 1992. By the year 2000, women's membership in Islah reached about 10% in Mogadishu.[86]

In conclusion, it seems that compounded policies, such as careful screening of the recruitments, continuous training programs, and gradualism in acquiring leadership positions were the main reasons for the resilience of Islah in the torrent and tumultuous situations in Somalia. Moreover, it is noted that whenever these strict policies were overstepped, organizational vulnerability and internal troubles ensued.[87] Such internal problems occurred occasionally in the history of Islah but never in the higher leadership ranks.[88]

The Formative Period of Islah (1978–1990)

After grasping the nature of Islah, its objectives, structure, and membership processes, we will now turn to the way Islah interacted with its socio-political environment from 1978 to 1990. Islah began its activities inside Somalia during this country's difficult decade of the 1980s. The first decision after the official formation of Islah was whether to keep the organization underground or to make it public. Finally, the policy of being partially public and partially underground prevailed.[89] This policy meant announcing the formation of the organization and its chairman, while keeping the rest of the operations confidential. Accordingly, the public proclamation of

---

86. Mustafa Abdullahi "Dheeg" interviewed by the author on July 24, 2009, Hargeysa, Somaliland.
87. Ibid.
88. For instance all the founding members, three out of the four chairmen and eight out of nine of the vice-chairmen remain in the organization. Unfortunately, in the 2012 Sheikh Maxamd Garyare, the first chairman broke away from Islah.
89. Sheikh Mohamed Garyare interviewed by the author.

Islah was conducted during Hajj processions by distributing leaflets to Somali pilgrims. The leaflet was titled with the Qur'anic verse, *"Hāda Bayānun li al-Nāss"* (this is a proclamation for the people).[90] Islah was also publicized in 1981 in the Kuwaiti *al-Islāh Magazine*, where Sheikh Maxamad Garyare gave a lengthy interview explaining the nature of his organization, its policies, and opposition to the military regime in Somalia.[91] Moreover, Sheikh Maxamad also offered interviews to a Kuwaiti radio, explaining the Somali plight under the repressive rule of the military regime.[92]

Various Reactions to the Formation of Islah

The launching of Islah provoked strong reactions from various groups, such as secular opposition, various Islamic organizations, and the Somali government. Some of these reactions had significant consequences to Islamism in general and posed particular challenges to Islah.

Reaction of the Non-Islamist Opposition

The opposition to the regime had been simmering for a long period but lacked an appropriate avenue for expression. In

---

90. The verse titled is "This is a proclamation for the people, and a guidance and enlightenment for the righteous" (3:138). More than 10.000 leaflets were distributed during the Hajj. Axmad Rashiid Xanafi interviewed by the author on February 5, 2010, Ottawa, Canada.
91. In his interview, Sheikh Maxamad Garyare strongly criticized the military regime in the execution of the Islamic scholars and the adoption of socialist ideology. He requested Arab countries to assist Somali refugees through other means and to stop assisting them through the regime because that fund was diverted and used to oppress Somali people. See Sheikh Moḥamed Garyare. "Al-Masūl al-Awal 'an Jamā al-Islāḥ al-Islāmiyah fi al-Somāl yataḥadathu ila al-Mujtama,"*Majalat al-Islāḥ*, no. 524 (1981): 19-21.
92. Sheikh Maxamad Garyare interviewed by the author.

Somalia, the regime outlawed all dissidents and issued a law conferring death sentence to any organized opposition.[93] According to this law, in 1975, Islamic scholars were executed. The first attempt to form an opposition movement occurred in Kenya, where some former politicians who fled to Kenya and Saudi Arabia were attempting to create the first organization opposing the regime. For the organizers of the opposition, the escape of Sheikh Maxamad Garyare from the regime on November 18, 1975 and his established relations with the Saudi Kingdom were seen as an opportunity. Therefore, members of the opposition groups, namely Cusman Nuur Cali Qonof and Baashar Nuur Ileey, approached Sheikh Maxamad Garyare in early 1976 and requested him to join them. Sheikh Maxamad, who was obsessed with opposing the regime by any means, accepted their request wholeheartedly. Sheikh Mohamed explains that "this decision was not an Islah decision since it was not formed yet. It was personal judgment."[94] The organizing committee of the opposition was later enlarged to be more representative of the wider Somali audience and included 12 prominent personalities.[95] The opposition group developed strategic plan geared toward overthrowing the regime. Ostensibly, some foreign countries that were concerned with the regime's connection with the Soviets, including Saudi Arabia and Iran, supported the group.[96] However, the first internal conflict within the group arose when the discussion

---

93. Law No. 54 of September 10, 1970 on national security.
94. Sheikh Mohamed Garyare interviewed by the author.
95. The names of the group are: Cabdulqaadir dholo-dholo, Cali Kulane, Bashiir Nuur Iley, Xussein Abukar, Duqsi, Yusuf Dhuxul, Muse Islaan, Cabdi Gaawiide, Cusman Nuur Qonof, Xirsi Magan, and Maxamuud. Ibid.
96. The Iranian/Saudi connection was related by a source who requested for anonymity.

focused on the role of Islam in the future Somali state.[97] The group consisted of all shades of the ideological spectrum, such as secular socialists, traditionalists, liberals, and Islamists, and clearly, they disagreed on the role of Islam. Sheikh Maxamad says that "he was dismayed and suspicious of their efforts and his relations with some of the members have deteriorated sharply." Even so, suddenly, the plan was foiled because of a leak to the Somali intelligence, and members of the oppositions lost trust in each other.[98]

The failure in organizing the first opposition and behavior of the politicians offered good lessons and experience to Sheikh Maxamad Garyare. As a result, he was convinced that Somali non-Islamist oppositions lacked common ideology and national vision and they carried the virus of the clannish mentality and personal interests. Therefore, along with the other founders of Islah, he focused on Islamic work and pushed for the creation of effective Islamic opposition to the regime. On the other hand, some other members of the secular opposition "founded the Somali Democratic Action Front (SODAF) in Nairobi in 1976."[99] Sheikh Maxamad Garyare, who became the first leader of the Islah, was a well-known member of the opposition and a former friend, although he disagreed with them on their philosophy, strategy, and approaches. Despite these disagreements, many prominent individuals in the opposition had high regard for him and counted on his support.[100] This predisposition was

---

97. Sheikh Maxamad Garyare related that he told the group: "There are no differences between us and Siyaad Barre if we do not make Islam our ultimate reference. However, they were not ready for that."
98. Ibid.
99. See Ahmed Samatar, *Socialist Somalia: Rhetoric and Reality* (London: Zed Press, 1988), 139.
100. Sheikh Mohamed Garyare interviewed by the author.

indicated when Islah was invited to participate in the founding conference of the Somali Salvation Front (SSF) in 1979 in Addis Ababa.[101] Nonetheless, Islah vehemently refused to participate under the pretext that it does not accept Ethiopia as the base to oppose the Somali regime. Moreover, it believed the desired change had to come from within Somalia, opposing any military option coached by Ethiopia.[102] Despite all these differences, the non-Islamist opposition welcomed the formation of Islah, with the advantage of widening opposition against the regime. In that context, Islamic opposition and secular opposition movements, though differed in approaches, were contributing to weakening the power of the regime in many ways. On the other hand, even though Sheikh Maxamad Garyare, the chairman of Islah, had a personal rapprochement with the non-Islamist opposition, the method of armed struggle, clan-based organizations, and connections with Ethiopia had contravened Islah's method of reform. Because of that historical tie, Islah's relations with many leaders of the non-Islamist factions were not hostile, and both sides accepted their differences.

Reactions of the Islamist Groups

Former members of Ahal were highly distressed about the proclamation of Islah. Their first reaction emanated from Cabdulqaadir Sheikh Maxamuud, the former leader of Ahal, who haphazardly announced Takfiir ideology, hitherto circulated secretly. His primary objective was to restrain his members from joining Islah. Nonetheless, even though he succeeded in persuading most members of Ahal to follow the

---

101. Sheikh Mohamed Garyare and Ahmed Rashid interviewed by the author.
102. Ibid.

Takfiir line in the beginning, he gradually confronted stiff resistance.[103] Some members who repudiated the Takfiir ideology were mobilizing an ideological rebuttal using the same literature as the MB during their confrontation with similar phenomena in Egypt in the 1960s.[104] The anti-Takfiir group was also reorganizing remaining members of Ahal, including those who were confused with the surprising occurrences and undecidedly remained in the grey zone. However, the Takfiir group and remnants of Ahal perceived Islah as a potentially competitive organization with experienced leaders. Thus, former members of Ahal in Saudi Arabia, who refrained from the Takfiir ideology, discussed the way forward. Sheikh Cisse Sheikh Axmad, a former member of Ahal who was present in this meeting, testifies as follows:

> We have discussed how to react to the new situation where from one side Takfiir ideology is biting off and Islah was announced. There were two options to be discussed. The first option was to join Islah since it adheres to the MB ideology. The second option was to establish a new organization. Most members agreed to establish a new organization which supposedly unifies concepts of MB with Salafism. The new organization has to adopt Salafism in theology and MB organizational setting and training style. This program gives them hybrid system and more competitive advantage in recruiting students in the Saudi universities and attracts financial support from the Salafia institutions in the rich Gulf countries.[105]

---

103. Ibid.
104. The most important literature they used to confront the Takfiir ideology was Hassan al-Hudeibi's *Naḥnu du'ātun lā Qudāh* (Preachers, Not Judges), available from http://www.torathikhwan.com/savebook.aspx?id=7 (accessed on 24 June, 2010).
105. Sheikh Cisse Sheikh Axmad interviewed by the author on July 24, 2009, Hargeysa, Somaliland.

According to this line of thought, Jamaaca Islaamiyah was formed in 1979 to take the mantle of Ahal, adding the new component of the Salafia theology. The new leader of Jamaaca Islaamiyah aimed to unify all Islamic organizations, disregarding methodological differences (Ikhwan/Salafia). Subsequently, they approached Islah to carry out the unification project with them. Axmad Rashiid Xanafi, one of the founding members of Islah, relates that a delegation from Jamaaca Islaamiyah arrived in Riyadh in 1979 to meet with Islah. They proposed to dissolve both organizations and to create new organization that unifies all Somali Islamists.[106] Islah expressed uneasiness about such instantaneous merging and instead proposed the option of collaboration in the beginning and to explore its development further in the future.[107] There were many reasons for Islah's firm position as Sheikh Garyare relates such as previous unpleasant experiences with the Ahal members in Saudi Arabia. Moreover, Islah was not convinced with the possibility of uniting Somali Islamists for just being Somalis without giving consideration to their Islamic persuasion. Furthermore, combining MB methodology with Salafism Wahabism seemed tricky and unrealistic. The delegation of the Jamaaca Islaamiyah consisted of Cabdulaziz Faarax and Cabdullahi Abtidoon.[108] The impact of the failure of this negotiation for the future relations between Islamic

---

106. Their delegation composed of Cabdulaziz Faarah, Cabdullahi Abtidoon, and Cabdulqaadir Gerweyne, and Sheikh Cali Warsame was a member of Islah, but seemingly was convinced for the agenda of Jaamaaca Al-Islaamiyah. Axmad Rashiid Xanafi interviewed by the author.
107. Sheikh Mohamed Garyare interviewed by the author.
108. Research Center of the International Horn University in Hargeysa, Sheikh Ali Warsame interviewed by Sheikh Almis Haji Yahye, March 15, 2010, Burco, Somaliland.

movements was devastating. Islah was accused of rejecting the unity among Muslims enshrined by Islam and taking devious divisive course. Consequently, it lost some members including Sheikh Cali Warsame who later became the Chairman of Itixaad. Moreover, propaganda campaign was unleashed against Islah in all fronts which had poisoned the whole atmosphere of the Islamic work.[109] On the other hand, Islah also developed its counter-discourse and argumentations, which in due course also, exacerbated relations between Islamist organizations. After this occurrence, Jamaaca Islaamiyah undertook a dynamic program in the spirit of isolating and competing with Islah and reached out to other Islamist organizations. For that reason, it had contacted Waxdah, headed during this time by Sheikh Cali Warsame who joined it after quitting Islah in 1979. However, in a raw deal, Jamaaca Islaamiyah merged with Waxdah adopting the new name of Itixaad in 1983. However, this precipitate merging did not last long and succeeded only in dividing and weakening Waxdah.[110] Yet, this merging was a setback for Islah which was championing the MB ideology but failed to persuade Waxdah to join hands since 1979. As related by Maxamad Yusuf and confirmed by Sheikh Ismaciil Dheeg, the Islah delegation, consisting of Maxamad Yusuf and Cabdalla Axmad Cabdalla traveled to Hargeysa and succeeded in cutting a deal with Cabdulqaadir Xaaji Jaamac, the leader of Waxdah, based on which Waxdah would join Islah. However, this agreement did

---

109. Sheikh Mohamed Garyare interviewed by the author.
110. Waxdah was divided into two camps after merging with Jamaaca al-Islaamiyah in 1983. One camp remained in Itixaad and others began to reorganize themselves and restore former Waxdah, adhering to the MB ideology. Refer to ResearchCenter of the InternationalHornUniversity. Sheikh Ismaciil Cabdi Hurre "Dheeg," interviewed by Sheikh Almis Xaaji Yahya, March 20, 2010, Hargeysa, Somaliland.

not see the light, and Cabdulqaadir concealed it from the leadership of Waxdah.[111] Moreover, because of the fluidity of Islamists, Itixaad succeeded in persuading some members of Islah to join them such as Sheikh Cabdullahi Makki, and Sheikh Cabdullahi Cali Cumar.[112] The establishment of Itixaad in 1983 was encouraged and supported by the Sudanese Islamic Movement under the leadership of *Ḥassan al-Turābi*. In 1982, the Sudanese Islamic Movement broke from the International MB, and *Ḥassan al-Turābi* planned to establish a network of Islamist organizations linked to Sudan in Africa. Somalia was given priority in this plan, and the Sudanese Movement opened a special office in Mogadishu for that purpose under the guise of charity organization.The Sudanese envoy organized a number of meetings between different Islamist organizations, excluding Islah under the pretext that its connection with the International MB was problematic.

Other Islamic groups' reactions came into light when Sheikh Maxamad Macallin, the famous Qur'anic exegesis teacher for the Islamic awakening, came out of the prison in 1982. Both Islah and Jamaaca Islaamiyah made efforts to persuade Sheikh Maxamad Macallin to join their organization. At the same time, some former members of Ahal who stayed in the grey zone, confused by the competing groups of Islah, Takfiir, and Jamaaca Islaamiyah, had been organizing themselves and waiting for Sheikh Maxamad to take a different course. Sheikh Maxamad Macallin was a well-respected scholar and the main teacher of almost all Islamists, in particular, former Ahal members. However, during his prison term since 1976, a drastic change

---

111. Mohamed Yusuf interviewed by the author on March 16, 2010, Kuwait. Also, Ismael Dheeg interviewed by the author.
112. Xassan Xaaji Maxamuud interviewed by the author.

had occurred in the Islamist landscape in Somalia. For instance, many of his former students had joined Saudi universities and were converted to the Salafia doctrine. Being graduates of the Islamic universities, hundreds of them were sent to Somalia as Islamic preachers, sponsored by Saudi Islamic institutions.[113] These preachers were given the task of spreading the Salafi theology in Somalia and were routinely evaluated on their achievements. Moreover, a large amount of Islamic literature selected to spread Salafism was brought into Somalia, and a standard library consisting of hundreds of reference books was distributed freely to the individuals and libraries of the country. Furthermore, many Somalis were persuaded to join the Salafia movement through the provision of scholarships to Saudi universities and the promise of jobs after their graduation.[114] All the above-stated programs were used to promote Salafism in Somalia. In that context, some former students of Sheikh Maxamad, who were converted to the Salafia theology, debated with their former teacher and alleged that their former Sheikh belonged to the *Ash'arite* theology and the MB, which they considered devious from the right Salafi theology. Xassan Xaaji Maxamuud relates that, for instance, "Maxamad Cabdi Daahir, a former student of Sheikh Maxamad Macallin made a sermon in one of the mosques in Mogadishu and said: 'The prominent Islamic scholar in Somalia Sheikh Maxamad Macallin does not know the whereabouts of Allah,' citing controversial theological discourse between Ash'arites and Salafia theologies.[115]

---

113. Ibid.
114. Ḥassan Ḥāji Moḥamūd, "*Man al-Mas'ūl an al-Tadaruf fi al-Somāl?*" Available from http://www.somaliatoday.net/port/2010-01-04-21-40-35/2-2010-01-04-21-38-42/1216-2010-06-03-12-29-35.html (accessed on June 18, 2010)
115. Xassan Xaaji interviewed by the author.

Islah's attempt to persuade Sheikh Maxamad Macallin to join their organization also failed. Some interviewees speculate that Islah's local capacity to attract Sheikh Maxamad was insufficient and may be frustrating.[116] On the other hand, former members of Islah who had quit earlier were dissuading Sheikh Maxamad from joining Islah and were encouraging him to lead a new MB organization.[117] Islah's interest in Sheikh Maxamad was great and many attempts were made to organize a meeting between Sheikh Maxamad Macallin and Sheikh Maxamad Garyare in Saudi Arabia to strengthen Islah's engagement with Sheikh Maxamad. However, Islah's plan to gain Sheikh Maxamad Macallin did not happen as expected, leaving behind the severe consequences of divided adherents of the MB.[118]

Moreover, Salafia debates with Sheikh Maxamad created a strong reaction of protecting Sheikh Maxamad from the Itixaad and many of his rebellious former students. Initially, Sheikh Maxamad attempted to advise his students to stay outside of these organizations. However, when many of his former students who were either members of Islah or Jamaaca Islaamiyah quit their organizations and established a new organization named *al-Ikhwan al-Muslim*, he accepted to be their guide and mentor.[119] Therefore, although the followers of Sheikh Maxamad were adhering to the general ideology of the

---

116. The local leader of Islah was Sheikh Nuur Baaruud. Sheikh Maxamad Macallin, the spiritual teacher of the Islamic awakening, was not comfortable to give his allegiance to Sheikh Nuur Baruud as some interviewees argued. They entertained that he might have done so with Sheikh Maxamad Garyare, the former boss and friend with similar credentials. For instance, Xassan Xaaji Maxamuud adheres to such argument.
117. Cumar Iman Abubakar, *Tajrubat al-Maḥakim al-Islāmiyah fi al-Somāl: al-Taḥadiyāt wa al-Injazāt* (Al-Qāhira: Dār al-fikr al-'Arabi, 2008), 66.
118. Xassan Xaaji Maxamuud interviewed by the author.
119. Among those former members of Islah were Sheikh Yusuf Cali Caynte, Sheikh Maxamad Rashaad, Maxamad Cawl, and others.Ibid.

MB, they constituted local organization competing with Islah in Somalia. The new local organization of MB persuasion claimed that Sheikh Maxamad Macallin Xassan was the founder and guide *"murshid"* of MB in Somalia seeing Islah as illegitimate and unauthentic.[120] Therefore, Islah met strong opposition from all Islamist organizations, which posed great challenges to its outreach programs and its activities. The project of isolating Islah was supported by the Sudan Islamic Movement, which was competing with the international MB in the Horn of Africa and was coaching all other Somalia Islamist movements. The following table indicates the developments of the various Islamist organizations in Somalia from 1950 to 1990 and their persuasions.

Name of the organization	Date	Nature	First leader	Remarks
Al-Rābidah al-Islāmiyah	1950	MB/Arabism	Sharif Maxamud Cabdiraxman	Disbanded in 1969
Munadamah al-Nahdah al-Islāmiyah (Nahdah)	1967	Proto-MB	Sheikh Cabdulqani Sheikh Axmad	disbanded in 1969
Ahl al-Islām (Ahal)	1969	Proto-MB	Cabdulqaadir Sheikh Maxamuud	Divided (Takfiir, Jamaaca Islaamiyah) in 1969
Waḥdah al-Shabāb al-Islāmi (Waxdah)	1969	Proto-MB	Prominent leader Cabdulqaadir Xaaji Jaamac	United with Jamaaca Islaamiyah in 1983 and founded Itixaad. Some of Waxdah members revived the organization in 1986.
Jamā'at al-Islāḥ al-Islāmiyah (Islah)	1978	International MB	Sheikh Maxamad Garyare	Continues functioning
Al-Jamā'at al-	1979	MB/Salafia	Sheikh Maxamuud	Transformed into

---

120. See Afyare Abdi Elmi, Understanding the Somalia Conflagration: Identity, Political Islam and Peace building (London: Pluto Press, 2010), 57.

Islāmiyah(Jamaaca Islaamiyah)		(combined)	Ciise	Itixaad in uniting Waxdah in 1983.
Al-Itiḥād al-Islāmi (Itixaad)	1983	Neo-Salafia	Sheikh Cali Warsame	Divided into many groups after 1992.
Al-Ikhwān "Aala-Sheikh"	1983	Local MB	Sheikh Maxamad Macallin	Transformed into Tajamu'al-Islām in 2001.

Table 4. The Islamist Organizations in Somalia (1950–1990)

By 1990, there were four Islamist organizations: Itixaad, Islah, Waxdah and Ikhwan. Indeed, the Islamic awakening and its institutions were inclined to the MB methodology though lacked much of the organizational expertise until 1980. However, in the 1980s, Itixaad became the strongest Islamist organization in Somalia, and the Salafia ideology took prominence. The other three organizations adhering to the MB methodology were fragmented and competing each other because of many local and external factors.

The Reaction of the Somali Government

The military regime of Maxamad Siyaad Barre was weakening after its defeat in the war with Ethiopia in 1978 and the emergence of the armed Somali opposition movements. Distancing itself from the Soviets and seeking improved relations with the conservative Arab countries and the USA, the regime's iron fist was softened to a certain extend. Moreover, many migrant laborers had been working in the rich and oil booming Gulf States, which provided economic liberation and cultural influences.[121] The regime was facing opposition from its old friends, such as southern Yemen and Libya, which were supporting the Ethiopian regime and the Somali armed opposition groups in Ethiopia.[122] Therefore, in the early years of 1980s, the regime attempted to make rapprochement with Islah through numerous messages and envoys sent by the regime to improve relations without making any tangible concessions. However, the Islah leadership perceived these messages as tactical maneuvering aimed to abort mounting Islamic awakening.[123] While the regime was focusing on confronting secular armed clannish opposition groups, it discovered the threat of the Islamist movements was beyond proportion. In particular, the regime accused Islah of links with armed opposition groups and of being connected to the international MB, identifying it as the major Islamist threat of the regime. In addition, Islah were accused of influencing negatively regime's relations with the conservative Arab states.

However, perhaps the "hostility between Barre and its first leader" [of Islah] Sheikh Maxamad Garyare and its earlier involvement "as political and high regime–critical organization" had caused exceptional hostility of the regime to Islah.[124] By 1985, the regime had developed a strategy to obliterate Islah by

---

121. Somali labour migration to the rich Gulf countries was huge. It was estimated that "approximately more than 250,000 Somalis were migrated to the Arab peninsula." See David Laitin and Said Samatar,*Somalia: Nation in Search of a State* (Boulder: Westview Press, 1987), 145.
122. Ibid.
123. Some of these messengers included Xassan Xaashi Fiqi, Cali Xaaji Yusuf, Cabdiraxman Cabdi Xussein (Guulwade), and Maxamad Xaaji Yusuf. Sheikh Maxamad Garyare interviewed by the author.
124. See Hansen and Mesoy, The *Muslim Brotherhood*, 40.

eliminating its founding members living in Saudi Arabia.[125] The basic assumption of this strategy was "to expel founding members of Islah from Saudi Arabia, return them to Somalia in order to put them on trial under the legislation that gives them death sentence."[126] The Somali Ambassador in Kenya during that period and some Somali Islamic scholars in Kenya were assigned to implement this strategy.[127] These scholars signed a letter accusing the founders of Islah of "belonging to MB, disdaining Salafism and some of them to be part of the opposition factions in Ethiopia and some of them being Nasserite stooges and being threat for the security of Saudi Arabia."[128] This letter was widely circulated to the Islamic institutions in Saudi Arabia, such as *Dār al-Iftā, Rābidah al-'Ālam al-Islāmi,* and others. Subsequently, Sheikh Maxamad Garyare was summoned by *Sheikh Abdulazīz Inb al-Bāzz*, chairman of *Dār al-Iftā*, and was questioned about the issue. Sheikh Mohamed, who was hesitant to testify on this issue because of his respect for his Sheikh, stated the following:

> I have great respect for *Sheikh Inb al-Bāzz*, he was my former teacher. In reaction to the letter signed by Islamic scholars, he asked me about the letter and the accusations such as hating Salafism, belonging to MB since it was signed by six supposedly trustworthy Somali scholars. I simply replied that, I come here seeking the protection of Saudi Arabia from the oppressive regime of Somalia, and the regime is behind all these accusations. On the other hand,

---

125. All founding members were living in Saudi Arabia, either working or studying in the Saudi universities.
126. Cali Sheikh Axmad interviewed by the author.
127. Sheikh Maxamad Garyare abstained to tell their names. However, other sources told me that their leader was Sheikh Xassan Cabdiraxman living in Kenya.
128. Axmed Rashiid Xanafi and Sheikh Maxamad Garyare interviewed by the author.

you know what I stand for since 1960 and asked what is wrong being a member of MB! In this frosty mood, he opted for silence.[129]

Seemingly, Sheikh *Inb al-Bāzz* believed the contents of the letter and temporarily suspended Sheikh Maxamad Garyare from the job. However, with the mounting pressure on him, he was compelled to reverse his decision and Sheikh Maxamad returned to his job. Being cornered by the regime and its allied Somali Islamic scholars, the Islah founders explored possible ways to defend themselves from the looming threat. They decided to write a letter to the Saudi authorities explaining the conspiracy of the regime against them. This letter was submitted to the Saudis through the networks of colleagues who were upset by the developing scenario. In the end, Islah won the case and the attempted deportation of its leaders was blocked.[130] Nonetheless, after many years of continuing the work with strained relations and unwelcoming mood, Sheikh Maxamad Garyare voluntarily quit the job at *Dār al-Iftā* in 1985. The freedom of movement gained after quitting the job offered him flexibility and an opportunity to focus on rebuilding Islah inside Somalia and in the Diaspora and strengthening Islah's international networking through active participation in the international Islamic conferences and linking with other organizations.

Moreover, the Somali government, in cooperation with the Egyptian security, was focusing on countering emerging Islamist movements, with a special focus on Islah. Accordingly, Somali intelligence personnel dealing with Islamist movements were trained in Egypt and were provided expertise on

---

129. Sheikh Maxamad Garyare interviewed by the author.
130. Ibid.

countering the MB. Xassan Xaaji Maxamuud, a member of Islah detained by the Somali National Intelligence Service in 1985, was accused of belonging to the MB. He was carrying a pocket-size Qur'anic book, the only evidence shown in his interrogation. He related, "During my interrogation by the head of the section, the officer was suddenly summoned and left his office with open files. I succeeded to glance one of the files and have seen the list of all names of the prominent members belonging Islah."[131] Moreover, he said that whenever Islah initiated any program in one of the mosques, it was discovered immediately and the program was disbanded. During the early 1980s, it was difficult for Islah to establish successful public programs while the rival Itixaad was openly propagating in numerous centers in Mogadishu, and hundreds of people were gathering every night to listen to the Qur'anic exegesis and commentaries of the Prophet's biography in the major mosques in Mogadishu.[132] Based on this, Islah believes that it was targeted by the regime more than other organizations because of its linkage with the International MB.

Challenges, Limitations, Achievements, and Activities

The above four major areas will be explored and evaluated in tracing the performance of Islah during the military regime in Somalia.

Major Challenges

As has been examined earlier, Islah faced immense challenges from the rival Islamist organizations, non-Islamist opposition

---

131. Xassan Xaaji Maxamad interviewed by the author.
132. Ibid.

groups, and the Somali government. Nonetheless, the main objective challenge was emanating from the incongruity of the nature of the MB, as voluntary and hierarchical modern organization that demands high loyalty and individual activism, and the traditional society founded on loose primordial attachments and Sufi sheikh-disciple relations. This challenge was that the MB programs and the organization's literature are highly intellectual and written in the Arabic language, whereas most Somalis are not Arabic speakers. Education in the Arabic language was sidelined by the military regime after the adoption of the Somali language as the main language of education in 1972. Grasping the essence and ideology of the MB was founded on extensive reading of the basic sources of Islam, the Qur'an, and the Sunna, which requires extensive knowledge of the Arabic language. These were some pedagogical and cultural challenges that set hurdles to the grasping of the core message of the MB and adopting its organizational style. As a result, many individuals who joined Islah in the early years quit after a while because of the difficulty of compliance with the requirements of the organization, which were distinct from the cultural traits of the society.[133] Furthermore, early efforts of Islah to recruit prominent Islamic scholars, former friends of Sheikh Maxamad Garyare, and members of Nahdah, such as Sheikh Ibrahim Suuley, Sheikh Cali Xaaji Yusuf, Maxamad Xaaji Yusuf, and Sheikh Sharif Sharafow, did not bear significant accomplishment.[134] Recruiting such prominent scholars was not inline with the general policy of MB recruitment policy, which

---

133. Xassan Xaaji Maxamuud interviewed by the author.
134. On early recruitment to Islah see Mohamed Yusuf, "*MinḌikriyāt al- Ḥarakah*", available from http://www.Islah.org/arabic/Tasiis1.htm (accessed on June 24, 2010).

recommend avoiding the recruitment of notables and Public figures *"al-A'yān wa al-kubarā"* in the society.[135] The rationale behind that policy is that they have already shaped their world view and are difficult to reform. As expected, these prominent Islamic scholars could not accommodate themselves in the modern organizations in which institutional culture is strong and educated enthusiastic youth are its moving engine. Therefore, their organizational loyalty was ephemeral and their membership came to an end. However, within these complicated circumstances, the Islah leadership firmly adhered to the MB ideology and its organizational setting in the traditional society, despite complex organizational challenges.

Major Limitations

The major limitation of Islah during the military regime was the absence of the founding fathers and its top leaders from Somalia. Additionally, this limitation was augmented by the early leadership weakness inside Somalia. For example, Sheikh Maxamad Garyare, the first chairman of Islah, being a prominent political activist who fled from the military regime, could not travel to Somalia. What is more, his reputation and the regime's obsessive fear of the MB had complicated Islamic activities of Islah in Somalia.[136] In this intricate environment, Islah developed a plan of action based on sending various expeditions of students to Somalia during the summer break from the universities. For instance, Maxamad Yusuf and Cabdallah Axmad Cabdallah were sent to Mogadishu and Hargeysa in 1979. However, Cabdallah Axmad Cabdallah was

---

135. Fathi Yakun, *madā ya'nī intimāi li al-Islām* (Bairut: Mu'asasat al-Risālah, 1977), 117.
136. Cali Sheikh Axmad interviewed by the author.

detained and imprisoned in Mogadishu. Moreover, Cali Sheikh Axmad was dispatched to Somalia in 1980 and was detained in Hargeysa. His second trip in 1982 was to Tanzania, Uganda, and Kenya, and he was detained in Mandera, Kenya.[137] His detention was related to the Somali intelligence's influence on their Kenyan counterparts, which was very active in the border areas. He was accused of belonging to the MB; however, with the intervention of Somali local leaders, he was finally released.[138] After 1982, the Islah leaders could not travel to Somalia and were dependent on sending other less qualified members to network organizational activities in Somalia.

Moreover, the weakness of leadership inside Somalia was another contributing factor to the difficulties encountered by Islah in the early formative years. The leader assigned to set up the organization inside Somalia was Sheikh Nuur Baaruud. Sheikh Nuur had physical and organizational limitations, as he was blind and was a traditional Islamic scholar without prior organizational skills. He was expected to lead the modern MB organization in highly security-sensitive circumstances. His critics narrate that his leadership style was dictatorial as he was obsessed with secrecy. His extreme obsession with security concerns diminished the role of the members of the CC and the EB.[139] Moreover, these critics believe that this leadership style handicapped the development and the growth of the organization during the first seven years.[140] Indeed, the security precautions did not help much since Sheikh Nuur Baaruud was

---

137. Ibid.
138. Ibid.
139. Ḥassan Ḥāji Muhamūd, "*Tārikh al-Ḥaraka al-Islāmiyah al-Somāliyah: Duruf al-Nashi wa'awāmil al-tadawur*" (Unpublished manuscript).
140. Ibid.

imprisoned among other Islamist activists in 1986. Narrating about their detention, Sheikh Cabdirisaq said:

> In 1985, the government launched a campaign against Islamic activism and nine sheikhs were given death sentence in 1986. Included in these scholars two belonged to Islah,[141] three to Itixaad[142] and four for the non-affiliated Salafia working for Saudi institutions as preachers.[143]

These Islamist scholars were accused of engaging in subversive activities against the state, which was punishable by death. Moreover, they were accused of distorting religious doctrines of Islam and working for a foreign country. Nevertheless, they were pardoned and released in 1989 because of the intervention of Saudi Arabia, which was providing large economic assistance to Somalia. It seems that the Saudi/Somali relations have improved after the expulsion of the Soviets from Somalia in 1977 and Somalia's forging an alliance with conservative Arab countries and the West.

Responding to his critics, Sheikh Nuur Baaruud testified and described the situation as follows:

---

141. Four members of the Islah movement were imprisoned, and two of them received death sentence. These four members were Sheikh Nuur Baaruud (death sentence), Sheikh Maxamuud Faarah Hassan (death sentence), Sheikh Abdirisaq Xussein Cisse (15 years) and Sheikh Maxamad Habarwa (5 years).
142. Members of Itixaad were: Xassan Dahir Aweys (death sentence), Cabdullahi Cali Xaashi (released), Cabdulaziz Faarah Maxamad (death sentence), and Maxamad Sheikh Cusman Sidow (death sentence).
143. Four scholars who were given death sentence are: Sheikh Xaashi Colhaye, Sheikh Yusuf Macallin Cabdi, Sheikh Shaafici Maxamad Axmad and Sheikh Aweys Maxamad Ibrahim. Nevertheless, they were pardoned and released in 1989 because of the intervention of Saudi Arabia, which was providing huge economic assistance to Somalia. Six of the imprisoned scholars were working for *Dār al-Iftā* as Islamic preachers. Sheikh Cabdirisaq Xussein Cisse interviewed by the author on April 3, 2010, Bossaso, Puntland.

My responsibility was to make sure the welfare and security of the members of Islah who were working underground in very difficult conditions. This had necessitated me to undertake extreme security precautions. At times, I felt that founding members outside Somalia were pressuring me to do more, unconscious enough to the tough conditions we were working in. I still believe the way I run the organization during these formative period to be right irrespective of the critics.[144]

Early Islamic activities of Islah started in Mogadishu in 1980. Sheikh Cabdirisaq Xussein Cisse, one of the early preachers in Mogadishu, narrates how they initiated *Da'wa* programs. He said:

We have started the first public *Da'wa* program in 1980 in Xaaji Muse Boqor Mosque in the Waaberi district of Mogadishu, where three of us: Sheikh Nuur Baaruud, Sheikh Maxamad Sheikh Faarax, and myself propagated Islam publicly. This mosque was also the center of recruitment for Islah. The second center was established in 1981 in the Madina district, where Sheikh Cisse Sheikh Axmad, Sheikh Muhyiddin Cumar Jimcaale, and Sheikh Cabdullahi Azhari were very active. Moreover, in 1982, the first Islamic school was opened in Madiina, and Mustafa Abdullahi became its principal. Even with the excessive security precautions, Islah was gradually strengthening its activities.[145]

The alleged internal leadership weakness was being alleviated since 1986 because of the gradual relaxation of the regime's security grip with the appointment of a reform-minded new leader with administrative experience. After the short interim leadership of Sheikh Maxamad Sheikh Rashiid, a

---

144. Sheikh Nuur Baruud, as related by Xassan Xaaji, interviewed by the author, May 15, 2010, Nairobi, Kenya
145. Sheikh Cabdirisaq Xussein Cisse interviewed by the author on April 3, 2010, Bossaso, Puntland.

former pilot in the Somali air forces Cali Maxamad Ibrahim (Dayaar) was appointed as the deputy chairman of Islah in 1987. The change of leadership brought new activism and high organizational discipline. During this period, new members were recruited from different sectors, in particular from officers' ranks and the educated elite. Moreover, during this period, Dr. Ibrahim Dasuuqi returned to Somalia after completing medical training in Italy and the US and joined Islah en route to Somalia via Saudi Arabia. Upon his return, he started delivering groundbreaking lectures that combined science and Islam. His popular lectures attracted mostly university students and the educated elite. As a result, many members of the educated elite and university students joined Islah in 1987–1990.[146] Moreover, the new policy of openness and expanded consultations created an effective working team of scholars such as Sheikh Maxamad Sheikh Rashiid, Cali Maxamad Ibrahim (Dayaar), Sheikh Cisse Sheikh Axmad, Dr. Ibrahim Dasuuqi, Sheikh Xassan Maxamad (Okiyaallo), and others. In 1989, Sheikh Nuur Baaruud and Sheikh Maxamuud Faarax were released from prison by presidential pardon. Moreover, Sheikh Axmad Xassan al-Qutubi also returned Somalia. Sheikh Axmad al-Qutubi combined traditional Islamic and modern education. He completed his post-graduate studies in Sudan and worked for many years in Yemen. Thus, he acquired extensive experience in the Islamic work in Sudan and Yemen, and after joining Islah's Somalia team in Mogadishu, he became one of the organization's prominent scholars and preachers. His sermons

---

146. The first group recruited were former colleagues of Dr. Ibrahim Dasuuqi, like Dr. Cali Baasha Cumar, the current chairman of Islah, Dr. Maxamuud Zaahid, Engineer Abdulwahab and Engineer Ibrahim. Ibrahim Dasuuqi interviewed by the author on May 28, 2010, Nairobi, Kenya.

are remembered for his strong criticism of Salafism and his confrontational approach. He was considered a student of *Moḥamed al-Ghazāli* and *Yusuf al-Qardāwi* in Somalia in their critique of Salafist *Da'wa* approach.[147] With the return of these new educated scholars and the emergence of the new leader of the Islah with military background who was known for his team-building qualities, Islah became more vibrant and competent inside Somalia by 1990.

Major achievements

Most of interviewees agree that the major achievements of Islah in 1978–1990 were setting working MB organization under the repressive regime and safeguarding it from the tumultuous Islamic and political commotions of the late 1990s. Another achievement was qualifying to join the International MB networks. Having earlier examined challenges of setting Islahinside Somalia, here we will only examine the process of Islah's membership in the International MB. Islah's full membership in the MB, as an equal partner with all other organizations from the Arab/Islamic world, was considered a major achievement. It offered recognition and a platform to link to each other, exchange ideas, discuss strategic issues, adopt common policies, and share information. Article 49 of the International MB regulates all requirements and conditions of the membership in this international organization.[148] The three main conditions are that the joining organization must have a

---

147. These two scholars are famous for their bold critique of Salafism as it was projected by the Wahabis in Saudi Arabia and copied by Itixaad in Somalia.
148. See the bylaw of the International Muslim Brotherhood, available from http://www.ikhwanonline.com/Article.asp?ArtID=58497&SecID=211 (accessed on June 20, 2010)

bylaw compliant of with general MB vision, objectives, and methodology to be approved by the EB of the International MB. The second condition is to adopt *Manhaj al-Tarbiyah* (training curriculum) of the MB and to implement its training programs. The third condition is to have prominence and activities in its country. This means that the organization must experience and have a track record of compliance with MB ideology. "Islah society went through the best process of joining MB."[149] It started from individual memberships in the MB in different countries and at different times. Then, Islah was formed with the knowledge and coaching of the International MB while gradually growing, and it was evaluated and qualified for membership after 11 years. As a result, it acquired full membership in the International MB in the CC meeting held in Nuremberg, Germany, in 1987. Sheikh Garyare describes the process of acquiring membership and its advantages to Islah as follows:

> We applied for membership in the International MB in 1980. We met with its Deputy Guide Mustafa Mashhur in Kuwait in 1984 to push for the approval of the application of our membership.[150] Moreover, we have visited Cairo and met with the MB leaders in 1986.[151] Finally, a committee was appointed to evaluate our programs, activities, and progress towards membership requirement. The final report was submitted to the International MB Executive Bureau in 1987 held in Nuremberg.[152] I also submitted my report to the

---

149. Sheikh Mohamed Garyare interviewed by the author.
150. The delegation of Islah consisted of Dr. Maxamad Yusuf and Sheikh Maxamad Garyare. Ibid.
151. The Islah delegation consisted of Sheikh Maxamad Garyare, Sheikh Axmad Rashiid Xanafi, and Sheikh Maxamad Sheikh Rashiid. Ibid.
152. The delegation designated to evaluate Islah included *Sheikh Abdalla 'Aqil and Sheikh Mana Al-Qatan*, the two scholars who had been coaching Islah for years. Ibid.

Executive Bureau; and finally, MB in Somalia in the name of Islah Society was granted full membership.[153]

Islah's membership in the International MB offered a great moral boost to its members everywhere as it became the only legitimate MB recognized as such by other similar organizations worldwide. It was the first organization that acquired such membership in the sub-Saharan Africa after Sudan.[154] Islah benefited from its International MB membership in many ways besides realizing its general vision of the Islamic unity. Operationally, it networked with many experienced organizations around the world and learned from their activism and experiences. Moreover, Islah immensely enlarged its recruitment opportunities since many Somalis who joined the MB in the Diaspora had to join Islah as their home country organization. Furthermore, Islah acquired access to the international Islamic platform, where it explained the Somali debacle and through which, it reached out to charity organizations run by the MB or their sympathizers to seek assistance to the Somalis under the repressive military regime.

Major activities

Besides the initial focus on the internal construction of the organization through intensive recruitment and international connections, Islah interacted with the main events that took place in Somalia. These include the humanitarian assistance in the debacle of 1988 in northern Somalia and activities prior to

---

153. Ibid.
154. Ibid. Also, see Hansen and Mesoy, *The Muslin Brotherhood*, 42.

the collapse of the state, such as issuing the Islamic Manifesto and attempting to form a unified Islamic Front.

Humanitarian assistance in northern Somalia

One of the major milestones on the road to the collapse of the state in 1991 was the conflict in northern Somalia. As a consequence of the defeat of the Somali regime in 1978, armed opposition groups emerged. One of such faction was the Somali National Movement (SNM) formed in the United Kingdom in 1981. This movement expanded its activities in the 1980s in northern regions of Somalia, and the military regime used its draconian iron fist to suppress the group. On April 4, 1988, Somalia and Ethiopia signed a joint agreement, which included "ending subversive activities."[155] The SNM, which developed an effective guerrilla army and strategy, "overrun the main cities like Hargeysa and Burco in Northern Somalia during 1988–9."[156] When the SNM launched a major offensive in the northern Somalia in May 1988, the regime responded ruthlessly and indiscriminately. This caused the considerable loss of lives and properties and more than 500,000 civilians of the urban population fleeing to Ethiopia as refugees.[157] During this difficult time, Islah undertook three steps. First, it issued a communiqué denouncing the "barbaric actions of the regime against civilian population"and calling for international and

---

155. Hussein Adam, "Historical Notes on Islamic movement" (paper prepared for the International Somali Studies Association conference in Djibouti, December 2007), 12.
156. Ibid.
157. There is no precise number of the refugees, but UNHCR registered 381,369 Somali refugees in Ethiopia in 1990. However, many of the displaced went to many directions, including living with relatives, to migrate abroad, and to Djibouti. Mark Bradbury. *Becoming Somaliland* (London: Progresso, 2008), 73.

Islamic organizations to provide humanitarian assistance to the refugees and displaced population.[158] Second, it directed its members in the military not participate in this savage war. Subsequently, Axmad Xassan, an Islah air force pilot, refused to throw bombs on Hargeysa and landed the military Jet plane on the coast of Djibouti putting his live in danger.[159] Third, Islah formed a committee to mobilize humanitarian relief assistance to the refugee camps located near the Somali/Ethiopian border areas. The Islah CC decided this undertaking, aiming to take active action in mobilizing humanitarian assistance to the people in Somali refugee camps. Dr. Maxamad Yusuf, one of the founders of Islah who was working in Kuwait, was given the responsibility to carry out the operation. As he related, the Islah committee contacted major charity organizations in Kuwait and other Gulf countries, raised their awareness about the debacle in northern Somalia, and mobilized emergency assistance. Moreover, another committee consisting of prominent personalities from the northern community in Kuwait was organized to receive such assistance on behalf of the people. Another committee, consisting of Islah members and members of Waxdah, was organized in northern Somalia to take the responsibility of distributing the aid to the refugee camps in Ethiopia. Dr. Maxamad Yusuf related this event as follows:

> When the disastrous event occurred in the northern Somalia in 1988, Islah took the initiative of mobilizing assistance to the people in the refugee camps inside Ethiopia. I was assigned to lead the operation and we have contacted many charities in Kuwait to mobilize

---

158. The Islah Movement, Communiqué no. (1) On the Military Regime's attack of Northern towns, June 28, 1988.
159. Axmad Hassan interviewed by the author on July 16, 2002, Mogadishu, Somalia.

humanitarian assistance.¹⁶⁰ I have worked closely with Brother Cabdulqaadir Xaashi from the Northern Somalia.¹⁶¹ Our operation was very confidential and we have trusted few individuals like Sheikh Maxamad Xirsi, Cali Maxamad Faarax, Maxamad Axmad Maxamuud and Ibraahim Sheikh Axmad Cali. The amount of assistance received was about half a million dollars. Some members of Islah and members of Waxdah were distributing this assistance in the refugee camps; in particular, Xaaji Abshir Axmad was highly instrumental.¹⁶²

The impact of this assistance was great, and Haji Abshir, a member of Waxdah who actively participated in the distribution of humanitarian efforts relates it as follows:

> It was a very difficult period in the refugee camps and people were suffering. Waxdah established Da'wa program among the people and we were trying to mobilize humanitarian assistance from abroad. One of the major assistance was received from Kuwait in the form of cash money since in-kind assistance was impossible to reach there. Somali regime blockaded the border area and guerilla wars continued. We used to receive this assistance through trusted individuals since any allegation of belonging to SNM guerilla bore immediate danger of lives. I wastold later that this assistance was sent by Islah and in particular, Dr. Maxamad Yusuf was the main figure coordinating this program.¹⁶³

The positive contribution of Islah and its interaction with Waxdah during this crisis have created an environment of rapprochement, the fruits of which have produced closer relations and cooperation.

---

160. The three Kuwait institutions that provided this assistance were *Abu-badar, Bait al-Zakāt, and al-Hay'a al-Kheyriyah*. Maxamad Yusuf interviewed by the author.
161. Cabdulqaadir Xaashi is a well-known figure in Hargeysa. He is the owner of the famous Hotel Maasoor in Hargeysa.
162. Maxamad Yusuf interviewed by the author.
163. Xaaji Abshir interviewed by the author on April 15, 2009, Hargeysa, Somaliland.

Islah and its Reaction to the Collapsing Regime

The project of Islamist Manifesto. By 1989, the regime was further provoking Islamic sentiments. One of the major events in this regard took place on July, 14, 1989 when prominent Islamic scholars were detained after the assassination of the Bishop Salvatore Colombo, the Vatican representative in Somalia. This event occurred after the Friday prayer when demonstrations were organized from the mosques in protest against the detention of leading Islamic scholars; however, the Red Berets of the regime (special presidential guards) fired on the demonstrators. It was officially reported that 30 people were killed and 70 injured.[164] On the second day, on July 15, the regime summarily detained and executed 47 people suspected to be members of the SNM because of their clan affiliation.[165] In 1990, the situation in Somalia deteriorated further, and thewar between the armed opposition groups and the government was intensifying. There were many attempts to save Somalia from collapsing. One of these efforts was issuing the second Manifesto in October 1990. This Manifesto was released in response to the deteriorating situation in Somalia and as a reaction to the first Manifesto signed by the 114 prominent Somali elders on May 15, 1990. Organizers of the first Manifesto expressed "that they no longer remain passive spectators nor ignore the duties and responsibilities that we owe to our people

---

164. See Mohamed Mukhtar, *Historical Dictionary of Somalia* (African Historical Dictionary Series, 87. Lanham, MD: Scarecrow Press, 2003), 128.
165. For example, Engineer Isse who was in pre-recruitment process was very active in initiating demonstrations at Sheikh Cali Sufi Mosque. Ibrahim Dasuuqi interviewed by the author.

and the country, both Somali and Islamic point of view."[166] This Manifesto was addressing the intensification of the war between armed opposition factions and the government forces. It dealt with the growing concerns of the worsening security conditions, violation of human rights, corruption and mismanagement, and economic failure. Moreover, this Manifesto proposed holding a national reconciliation conference and nominated a committee for that purpose consisting of 13 members, including former president and speaker of the parliament, prominent Islamic scholars, former politicians, and traditional elders.[167] The reaction of the government to the Manifesto Group was ruthless and brutal; it detained most of its signatories.[168] This Manifesto was an expression of the nationalist voice, even though some Islamic scholars were on the list of the signatories. Other personalities like Sheikh Cabdirashiid Sheikh Cali Suufi declined to sign in the pretext that it was short of the demands for the application of Shari'a.[169]

---

166. Abdulaziz Ali Ibrahim "Xildhiban," "The Manifesto," *Taxanaha Taariikhda Soomaliya*, 101-107.
167. Among these personalities were: Aadan Cabdulle Cusman, former president; Sheikh Mukhtaar Maxamad, former speaker of the parliament; Xaaji Muse Boqor, former minister; Dr. Ismaciil Jumcaale Cosoble, former minister; Dr. Maxamad Raajis, former MP; Maxamad Abshir Muse, former chief of the police; Dr. Maxamuud Sheikh Axmad, chief of the high court; Suldan Duulane Rafle, prominent elder; Cali Shido Cabdi, former deputy chairman of SYL; Garaad Cabdulqani Graad Jaamac, prominent elder; Jirde Xussein Ducaalle, businessman; Sheikh Ibrahim Suuley, Islamic scholar; and Sheikh Sharif Sharafow, Islamic scholar. Ibid.
168. The signatories were 114 persons, including the former President Aden Abdulle Osman, former speaker of the Parliament, Sheikh Mukhrar, business leaders, Islamic scholars, intellectuals, and others. See "Xildhiban," 101-112. The Islah movement issued a communiqué denouncing the government for the detention of these prominent personalities. See The Islah Movement. Communiqué No (4) issued on the detention of the Manifesto Group, June 12, 1990.
169. See The Islah Movement. Communiqué No (5) on Islamist Manifesto "Sawt al-Xaq", October 1, 1990. Also see Abdirahman Hussein Samatar,*Sanawāt al-'ijāf al-ūlā fi al-Somāl* (Madbat Hamar, 2000), 27-27.

Consequently, many Islamic groups were dismayed by the rationalization of the organizers of the first Manifesto, who claimed that if they put the demand for the application of Shari'a, they would jeopardize the assistance of the Western countries. Thus, the issue of demanding application of Shari'a has polarized peaceful opposition to the regime into non-Islamists and Islamists; the latter considered the first Manifesto as only representing a non-Islamist viewpoint. Retrospectively, this rift should have been avoided through dialogue and setting short term common agenda limited only to safeguard the collapsing state.

In reaction to the above-stated reluctance of the organizers of the first Manifesto to accommodate the demand of the Islamist organizations and personalities, Islah undertook a plan to prepare the second Islamic Manifesto. It was intended to mobilize Islamist organizations in taking common position against the growing danger of the civil war. This Manifesto was a comprehensive document describing the regime's policies undertaken to curb Islam and the consequences of these policies. It demonstrated 11 points, which the regime used to tear down the Islamic principles and values. The harshest among them, according to the Manifesto, was adopting and spreading Socialism in the Muslim society.[170] Moreover, the second Manifesto accused the regime of curbing Islamic activism while promoting Christian missionary activities, allowing the latter to operate freely and enabling them to convert many Somalis to their religion. This Manifesto also related the dictatorial nature of regime and emphasized the deterioration of the political and economic conditions, as well as

---

170. Ibid.

educational and security sectors of the state. After these detailed descriptions of the awful conditions in the country were elaborated from an Islamic point of view, the Islamic Manifesto, called *Sawt al-Haq* (the voice of rightness), made a number of demands. These demands were: (1) abstaining from the referendum on the new constitution prepared by the regime that was not Shari'a compliant; (2) Demanding the resignation of the president and the government, (3) ceasing the ongoing fighting, (4) holding a reconciliation conference, (5) adopting a new Islamic-compliant constitution, and (6) holding free and fair elections. This Manifesto was prepared by the Islah committee consisting of four members and was signed by about 120 Islamic scholars and supporters of the Islamic agenda.[171] It was widely distributed in public places and government offices. Interestingly, other Islamist organizations such as Itixaad and Ikhwan did not participate in signing this Manifesto demonstrating that cooperation was also missing in the Islamist camps.[172] The reaction of the government to the Manifesto was quiet since former signatories of the first Manifesto were released from detention due to strong international pressure. Nevertheless, this Manifesto was an indication of the growing political activities of Islah before the collapse of the state and its aim of raising Islamic political voice in this critical historical juncture.

---

171. The Islah committee assigned to draft the Islamist Manifesto included Dr. Ibrahim Dasuuqi, engineer Cisse, Sheikh Axmad Xassan Al-Qutubi, and Dr. Cali Baasha Cumar, current chairman of Islah. Dr. Ibrahim Dasuuqi interviewed by the author on May 28, 2010, Nairobi, Kenya.
172. See Islamic Manifesto.

The Venture of the Islamist Front

The year 1990 is considered the golden year of Islah, and its growing political role and activities were evident attracting more membership.[173] After issuing the Islamic Manifesto in October 1990, Islah was encouraged to work toward establishing an Islamist Front, where most Islamist organizations would speak with one voice. This plan was presented in November 1990 in a meeting organized in the house of Adan Barando.[174] During this time, armed factions were closing on the regime. The Islah participants submitted their proposal, in which they alerted the Islamist organizations to the fact that the regime was falling apart and the non-Islamist armed factions were taking over. Islah proposed to the Islamist organizations to unify their efforts and come up with a unified program of saving the country. Specifically, Islah criticized the regime and armed factions and proposed to establish an "Islamist front." The proposal received an overwhelming support, and a committee consisting of 12 persons was formed to prepare the common Islamist agenda.[175] Seven secretaries from all the

---

173. Members of Islah in Mogadishu were estimated at about 60 in 1986, and by 1991 they were about 300. However, there were many members in the Diaspora and in other regions of Somalia. See The Islah Movement, *Comprehensive Internal Report*. This report was submitted to the leadership in Saudi Arabia, July, 13, 1991

174. The Adan Barando meeting was organized by some individuals belonging to Itixaad who initiated reconciliation between their two clans with the tacit support of the government. Ibrahim Dasuuqi interviewed by the author.

175. Four members were independent: Sharif Cabdinur Sheikh Aadan (chairman of the committee), Sheikh Cabdirashiid Sheikh Cali Suufi, Sheikh Ibrahim Muse, and Engineer Maxamad Cali Daahir. Moreover, from Majmac: Sheikh Maxamad Macallin and Sheikh Ibrahim Suuley. From Tabliq: Sharif Sharafow. From Islah: Dr. Ibrahim Dasuuqi Sheikh Mohamed. From Itixaad: Sheikh Cali Warsame, Cabdullahi Cali Xaashi, Cisse Soofe and Sheikh Maxamad Xaaji Yusuf. See The Islah Movement, *Comprehensive Internal Report*.

Islamist organizations were also appointed.[176] After in-depth situational analysis and laying out the Islamic foundations and justifications, the final document proposed an Islamic solution. The proposal was identical with the Islamist Manifesto based on the necessity of overthrowing of the regime, forming a transitional Islamic government, convening a general reconciliation conference, and preparing Islamic constitutions. This program seems ambitious and having high political ceiling beyond available capacity for the Islamic organizations.

However, discussions on the final versions of the communiqués were long, and some members withdrew from the meeting defending the regime, while others were highly supportive to the armed factions.[177] The clan factor among Islamists had shown its teeth, and immense challenges were faced from the collapsing regime and the armed factions in taking a unified position. However, while these Islamic scholars were discussing trivial matters and could not agree on any substantive common action, the first gunfire of the civil war was heard in Mogadishu. At that historical moment, Engineer Cisse from the Islah, disgusted with the Islamic scholars' indecisiveness, said, "This gun fire had responded to all of you," and the meeting of the Islamists was disbanded forever.[178] The concept of creating a unified Islamist Front dissipated indicating the immaturity of the Islamic organizations in Somalia during this period.

---

176. Three members were from Itixaad (Maxamad Daahir Aweys, Xussein Cabdulle (Codweyn) and Cabdulwaxid Xaashi). Three other members were from Islah (Engineer Cisse Maxamuud Cali, Sheikh Cisse Sheikh Axmed, and Dr. Ibrahim Dasuuqi).
177. The Islah Movement, *Comprehensive Internal Report*.
178. Ibid.

Major Events	Date	Remarks
The arrival of Sheikh Moḥamūd 'Īd in Mogadishu	1953	Sheikh Moḥamūd 'Īd was among al-Azhar Islamic scholars dispatched to Somalia in 1953. He was expelled from Somalia due to his Islamic activities in 1955.
The membership of Sheikh Cabdulqani Sheikh Axmad in MB in Egypt	1957	Sheikh Cabdulqani returned to Somalia, taught in the Somali University Institute, and became a member of the Supreme Court and a Minister in 1970s.
Founding of Munadamat al-Nahdah al-Islāmiyah in Mogadishu	1967	The three members of the MB in Somalia along with others founded this organization. These are Sheikh Cabdulqani, the chairman, Sheikh Maxamad Garyare, the deputy chairman, and Sheikh Cabdiraxman Kabaweyne, the secretary general.
Somali students joined the MB in Sudan	1973	Three of the founding members of Islah joined the MB in Sudan. These are Cali Sheikh Axmad, Maxamad Yusuf Cabdiraxman, and Axmad Rashiid Xanafi.
The establishment of the Islah Society in Saudi Arabia	1978	Five members who have been members of the MB established Islah after the defeat of the Somali army in the war with Ethiopia in 1978.
Islah joins International MB	1987	After 11 year of operation, Islah was granted membership after meeting the requirements in a meeting held in Nuremberg, Germany.
Issuing Islamist Manifesto (*Sawt al-Haq*)	October, 1990	This Manifesto aimed to unify Islamist organizations and to propose an Islamic solution to the Somali conflict. It was signed by 120 scholars.
The Project of an Islamist Front	November 1990	Islah proposed to all Islamist organizations and prominent Islamic scholars to create a unified Islamist Front to deal with the worsening situation in Somalia. However, the project did not take off and the war began in Mogadishu while Islamists debating on the proposal without reaching any agreement

Table 5. The Chronicle of Muslim Brotherhood in Somalia (1954–1990)

Conclusion

Even though the ideas of the MB, to which Islah belongs, reached Somalia in the 1953, the establishment of an effective MB organization took a long process of gestation and faced many challenges. The early institutions of the Islamic awakening such as Nahdah, Waxdah, and Ahal succeeded in propagating the ideas of the MB and confronting the secular Socialist military regime. Nevertheless, these organizations were disbanded, fragmented, and radicalized because of the inherent organizational weakness in the traditional societies. The first step of establishing an effective MB organization began in Sudan when the first group of Islah founders joined the MB's student activists. Since then, Somali MB members gradually acquired experiences of the MB and recruited many students. Efforts to establish a unified Islamic organization under the auspices of the MB were unsuccessful. Therefore, the founding members of Islah took a decision to form the Islah Society in 1978.

The reaction to the establishment of Islah was severe from the Islamist organizations and the government, though less problematic with the non-Islamist factions. Many former Ahal members did not acknowledge Islah as the representative of the MB in Somalia and established a competing organization, Jamaaca Islaamiyah. This organization absorbed many students in the Saudi universities, influenced by the Salafia ideology, and united with Waxdah establishing Itixaad in 1983. Another organization, called Ikhwan, was established after the release of Sheikh Maxamad Macallin from prison in 1982; it became another challenge for Islah. As evident, many leading individuals of the Islamist movements were quitting one organization and joining another, and as a result, these members blocked cooperation between these organizations. Moreover, the disagreement between the Sudanese Islamist Movement and the Egyptian-led International MB was another factor that contributed to the competition and conflict between the Somali Islamist organizations.

The Somali government's intelligence service, trained in Egypt, was focused on fighting the MB. They believed that the biggest Islamist threat was emanating from Islah. The regime's strategy to uproot Islah from Saudi Arabia was foiled; however, its repressive measures were frightening and containing Islah's activities in Somalia. The reaction of the armed factions to the establishment of Islah was positive as this organization was considered one more voice of opposition contributing to the toppling of the regime. Their relations and connections with Islah were mostly friendly, and they even tried to invite Islah to the conferences and absorb it within their ranks. Nevertheless, Islah kept its independent role and friendly relations with these factions.

The major limitations of Islah until 1990 were the absence of the founding leaders, a weakness of leadership obsessed with security in the first seven years, and strong competition from other Islamist organizations. The main achievements were adhering to its ideology in a volatile and turbulent society and gaining membership to the International MB. Moreover, major public activities were the issuance of the Islamist Manifesto, the procurement of humanitarian assistance in the northern debacle, and the attempt to form an Islamist Front.

In the final remarks, the formative period of Islah was hard and demanding. The early organizational weaknesses were evident, but throughout time, Islah was improving and sharpening its programs. Its relations with other Islamist organizations were strained, and the regime focused on its eradication. "Islah does not have tumultuous history" and "it is best to understand the development of Islah as one of slow evolution."[179] This tendency of evolution will be examined in the next chapter, which looks at Islah's role during the first 10 years of the civil war (1991-2000).

---

179. Andre Le Sage, *Somalia and the war on terrorism: Political Islamic movements and US counter terrorism efforts* (DPhil Thesis, Cambridge University/Jesus College, 2005), 160.

CHAPTER FIVE

The Islah Movement in the War-Torn Somalia: *(1991-2000)*

By the end of 1990, the situation in Somalia was gloomy and the military regime that had ruled since 1969 was weakened so much that it was preoccupied only with its survival.[1] In contrast, clan-based armed factions were gaining popularity and capturing more territories. For instance, the United Somali Congress (USC), a Hawiye-based faction, was widening its grip from the central regions toward Mogadishu. The Somali Patriotic Movement (SPM), an Ogaaden-based faction, was pushing its frontier from the southern regions of Baay and Bakool. Moreover, the Somali National Movement (SNM), an Isaaq-based faction, was preparing for a final assault on northern regions. Other factions such as Somali Democratic Movement (SDM) and SSDF were also organizing themselves with fewer forces. Reduced in size and power, the popular uprising led by the USC easily overwhelmed the regime after four weeks of fighting that was sparked on December 30, 1990.[2] People in Mogadishu were not anticipating a disastrous

---

1. Terrence Lyons and Ahmed Samatar, *Somalia: State Collapse, Multilateral Intervention, and Strategies of Political Reconstruction* (Brooking Occupational Papers, 1995), 20. Also, Mohamed Sahnoun, *Somalia: the Missed Opportunities* (United State Institute of Peace, 1994), 6-7.
2. Al-Ḥarakah al-Islāmiyah fi al-Somāl (Islah): Taqrīrun Shāmil (Comprehensive Internal Report submitted to the Leadership in Saudi Arabia, July, 13, 1991), 9. Also, Roland Marchal, "The Islamic dynamics in the Somali civil war: before and after September 11" in *Islamism and Its Enemies in the Horn of Africa*, edited by Alex de Waal (Indiana: India University Press, 2004), 122.

scenario, and their expectations remained high for a new era without the dictator Maxamad Siyaad Barre in power. However, these hopes dissipated with the outbreak of a devastating civil war.

This chapter explores the history of the Islah Movement during the civil war (1991–2000) and is divided into three sections. The first section sets the stage and provides a brief background on Somalia after the collapse of the state (1991–2000), its political development, security risks, international intervention, and implications. It also explores the Islah Movement in 1991–1992, including its survival strategy, policies, and interactions. Moreover, the activities and policies of the Islah leadership conference in 1992 in Djibouti are examined. The second section explores the political strategy, theoretical challenges, and reconciliation programs of the Islah Movement. It examines the theory and model of political participation in absence of the state. Moreover, the Somali Reconciliation Council (SRC) is examined here as a case study and the role of Islah in the Djibouti Reconciliation Conference of 2000 is analyzed. The third section investigates the social development strategy of Islah with a special focus on education. The concept of developing what is termed "popular educational revolution" and its implications are explained. At the end of the chapter, the Mogadishu University and Tadamun Social Society are projected as a case study and samples of developmental programs in war-torn Somalia.

Islah in the early years of the State Collapse (1991-1992)

In retrospect, although Islah became more active in 1990, its agenda to mobilize Islamic organizations and prominent Islamic scholars into an Islamic coalition was aborted.[3] The civil war broke out while Islamic groups were still debating a feasible common action. Evidently failing to agree on anything, each organization responded to the situation in its own way. How did Islah respond to the collapse of the state and flaring civil war? This section examines that account and provides background and context under which Islah operated.

Somalia: Sliding into Civil War (1991–1992)

On January 26, 1991, President Maxamad Siyaad Barre fled the "Villa Somalia" presidential palace for southern Somali regions. The conflict between the regime and the armed factions rapidly transformed into warfare between the two clan families: Hawiye and Darood.[4] Moreover, the capital city was engulfed in utter mayhem in which marauding and unbridled militias were engaged in plundering, looting, destroying, and killing. The situation vividly recalls a classical Khaldunite description of the behavior of nomads and their dominance of urban centers. In his "prolegomena", Ibn Khaldun explains that "the Arabs [nomads] need stones to set them up as supports for their

---

3. See Islah, Comprehensive Internal Report, 10.
4. Although attempts were conducted earlier within the government and USC played clan affinity card in the conflict, total transformation of the conflict into Hawiye-Darood occurred in April 1991 when allied forces comprising all Darood attempted to recapture Mogadishu. These forces advanced to the outskirts of Mogadishu, and USC was caught in panic and mayhem, and launched a counter offensive to throw them out. See Terrence and Samatar, 22.

cooking pots. So, they take them from buildings which they tear down to get the stones, and use them for that purpose. Wood, too, is needed by them for props for their tents and for use as tent poles for their dwellings".⁵ The USC political and military leadership lost control of its militia who were vying for prominence and capturing strategic locations such as the seaport, airport, and "Villa Somalia." In this anarchy, all state property such as industrial complexes, historical monuments, national documents, administrative offices, as well as social service sites such as schools, universities, and hospitals were gradually destroyed and looted. Moreover, private property such as houses, businesses, land, farms, and livestock were also captured and plundered. Nothing was spared from destruction. It was a perfect example of the Khaldunite description, "it is their nature to plunder whatever other people possess... They recognize no limits in taking the possessions of other people".⁶ Likewise, comparable behavior of pillaging and preying on the peaceful civilian population were witnessed from the SSDF, SPM and SNF militia in their push and pull fighting with USC forces. Xassan Cali Mire, a Somali veteran scholar describes these occurrences succinctly as though "all the pent-up frustrations of three decades of postcolonial independence exploded into the ugly rise of fratricide, which has made the barbaric killing of innocent members of other kin communities a worthy goal."⁷

---

5. Ibn-khaldun, *Muqaddimah: an Introduction to History*. Translated from the Arabic by Franz Rosenthal, (2nd ed.) (London: Routledge & Kegan Paul, 1967), 303.
6. Ibid.
7. Hassan Ali Mire, "On providing for the future" in edited Ahmed Samatar,*The Somali Challenge: From Catastrophe to Renewal?*(London: Lunne Rienner, 1994), 22.

Within two days, on January 28, a provisional government was announced, and Cali Mahdi Maxamad was designated as the interim president. This undertaking was considered a precipitated decision of the civilian USC in Mogadishu "Manifesto Group" preempting Mustaxiil accord between SNM, SPM and USC-General Caydiid faction. Conversely, the reaction of the Mustaxiil stakeholders was swift in rebuffing the new government.[8] In addition, General Caydiid considered the interim government a betrayal of the USC goals and a return of the former regime through the back door. Therefore, the previously divided USC further polarized into two antagonistic armed camps that formed along clan lines: the Cali Mahdi camp and the General Caydiid camp.[9] Moreover, the SPM and SSDF formed a coalition of Darood, allied with Maxamad Siyaad Barre's supporters in Gedo and Kismaayo. Contesting the USC, they mobilized military forces in Kismaayo and Gedo and assaulted Mogadishu on April 9, 1991.[10] The situation in northern Somalia was developing into a separation of the North from the South. Even though the separatist tendency was previously strong, the public in the North was enraged by the USC's unilateral decision to form a government in Mogadishu. Consequently, the public forced political leaders to immediately

---

8. The three armed factions SNM, SPM, and the USC-Aidid wing were bound by the Mustaxiil agreement in June 1990 to form an alliance. Moreover, this agreement was consolidated in October 1990 and rejected any negotiated settlement with the regime. However, the civilian USC in Mogadishu were furious with General Caydiid and the possible return of military rule in Somalia. It seems that divided USC and Mustaxiil agreement with one its faction may cause the precipitate formation of the interim government.
9. The two contesting leaders Cali Mahdi and Caydiid belonged to two Hawiye sub-clans: Mudulood and Madar-kicis, respectively, and clan mobilization was used for the power struggle.
10. See Lyons and Samatar, *Somalia: State Collapse,* 22.

break from Somalia. As a result, the SNM unilaterally revoked the act of Union of 1960 and declared the independent state of Somaliland on May 17, 1991.[11]

In Mogadishu, the appointment of the interim government triggered a bitter feud between rival Hawiye clan factions and power contenders, and all efforts to reconcile them despondently failed. Djibouti President Xassan Guuleed undertook the first initiative for reconciling Somali factions in Djibouti in June 1991 and July 15, 1991.[12] However, neither conference produced significant development toward peace and national reconciliation. Consequently, in September 1991, when all efforts for peaceful political agreement were exhausted, severe fighting broke out between the two USC factions in Mogadishu.[13] This fighting continued for about 100 days, destroyed the whole city and shattered its population. It was reported that this fighting caused more than 20,000–30,000 deaths and caused starvation in large parts of the country.[14] The humanitarian relief food could not reach starving people, as it was hijacked by warlords and their militia who exchanged most of it for weapons. By the end of 1991, the fighting had divided Mogadishu with a green line between the two USC factions. The

---

11. In the Grand Conference of Northern Peoples "Shirweynaha Beelaha Waqooyiga" held in Burco in May 1991, secession of Somaliland was pushed unplanned. The SNM leadership was negotiating for a new model of governance with the USC-Aidid faction in Mogadishu. Mark Bradbury writes: *"secession was not in the agenda of the SNM central committee"* in the Burco Conference. See Mark Bradbury, *Becoming Somaliland* (London: Progresso, 2008), 80. See also, John Drysdale, *Whatever Happened to Somalia?* (HAAN Publishing, London: 1994), 25.
12. See Sahnoun, *The missed opportunities*, 10.
13. General Caydiid declared a military coup and a toppling of the Cali Mahdi government. See Hussein Abdi Osman, *"Malaf al-Sarā' beyna 'Ali Mahdi wa 'Aidīd"* (unpublished paper submitted to the Horn of African Center for Studies, Mogadishu, 1993).
14. See Sahnoun, *The missed opportunities*, 11.

United Nations (UN) mediated a cease-fire agreement in March 1992 which reduced the magnitude of the conflict to some extent.

The war between the Somali National Front (SNF) and the USC faction of General Maxamad Faarax Caydiid for control of the southern coast and hinterland brought devastation to the grain-producing region between the rivers of Shabeelle and Jubba, spreading famine throughout southern Somalia. All attempts to distribute relief food were undermined by systematic looting by militias. The epicenter of famine, the town of Baidoa that had exchanged hands between various militias many times, became the theater for the conflict, and a massive number of deaths occurred in the Baay and Bakool regions. It was estimated that more than 300,000 died and more than a million people suffered severely in 1991 and 1992.[15]

The collapse of the Somali state coincided with the Gulf War, which started in January 1991, in which the UN and large coalition forces led by the US were mobilized to remove the regime of Saddam Hussein from Kuwait. Therefore, the attention of the world was deflected from the Somali crisis until January 1992 when Boutros Ghali, who was "more interested and engaged in Somalia"[16], took the office of the UN Secretary General. Immediately, the UN became involved, and the international concern about the Somali debacle was growing and gaining the support of the US administration. As a result, US forces landed in Mogadishu in December 1992, leading a

---

15. The total cost of lives was never fully tallied. Lewis provides a statistic of 300,000, see Lewis, *A History*, 265. See also Rutherford, Kenneth: *Humanitarianism under fire: The US Intervention in Somali* (Kumerian Press, 2008), 38. See also Ahmed Samatar, "Introduction and overview" in The Somali Challenge, 3.
16. See Rutherford, *Humanitarianism*, 20.

coalition of willing nations in accordance with UN Resolution 794, adopted on December 3, 1992. The aim of the intervention was to help create a secure environment for humanitarian efforts in Somalia. Thus, "Operation Restore Hope," consisting of a multinational force of more than 37,000 troops from 22 nations (24,000 troops from US and 13,000 from other countries), was dispatched to Somalia.[17] Among the providers of these forces were Arab and Muslim countries such as Pakistan, Malaysia, Saudi Arabia, United Arab Emirates, Egypt, and Morocco.[18] However, the mission was aborted on October 3–4, 1993 when a fight erupted between peacekeepers and the General Caydiid militia, which resulted in the death of 24 Pakistanis, 19 US soldiers, and 500–1,000 Somalis.[19] For that reason, the UN withdrew from Somalia on March 3, 1995 "in a state of violence and anarchy."[20]

Notwithstanding that the UN mission in Somalia was criticized on many aspects, the ramifications for Somalia was

---

17. Ibid.
18. The presence of forces from Arabic/Islamic countries provided some solace to the Somalis and belittled the suspicions of being new Western crusaders benefiting from the crisis. Moreover, the presence of Islamic forces attracted Islamic charities, which were very supportive of the Islamist agenda in Somalia. Roland Marchal considers that *"to a large extent, when southern Somalia witnessed the departure of the last UN contingents, the balance of power in favour of Islamic groups was positive"*. See Roland Marchal, "Islamic Political Dynamics in the Somali Civil War: Before and After September 11." In *Islamism and its Enemies in the Horn of Africa*, edited by Alex De Waal (Indiana University Press, 2006), 114-146,131.
19. The number of Somali deaths was highly controversial. For instance, Rutherford reported 500 deaths and 700 wounded. See Rutherford, *Humanitarianism*, 160. Other sources provide 500–1000. See Luke Glanville, "Somalia Reconsidered: An Examination of the Norm of Humanitarian Intervention", *Journal of Humanitarian Assistance*, available from http://www.jha.ac/articles/a178.pdf (accessed on June 19, 2010), 11.
20. The World Bank, "Conflict in Somalia, drivers and dynamics, 2005", available from http://siteresources.worldbank.org/INTSOMALIA/Resources/conflictinsomalia.pdf (accessed on June 31, 2010)

overall positive. The UN mission stopped famine, weakened the warlords, promoted civil society, and encouraged entrepreneurs and business ventures.[21] Moreover, many educated Somalis retuned home during this peaceful period, and some of them established social service programs and business ventures. In the aftermath of the United Nations Operation in Somalia (UNOSOM), the United Somali Congress/Somali National Alliance (USC/SNA) of General Caydiid disintegrated rapidly, and his clan-based coalition was severely damaged. Thus, in August 1996, General Caydiid died from gunshot wounds inflicted during a fight with a sub-clan faction led by Cusman Cali Caato.[22] The death of General Caydiid further weakened Mogadishu warlords who were ushering in a new era of civil society prominence. The promotion by the UNOSOM of the civil society produced new dynamics in Somalia and particularly in Mogadishu. The networked civil society organizations were engaged in numerous social service programs and undertook many local reconciliation initiatives.[23] Schools were reopened and many students frequented these schools and newly established universities.[24] Many of the displaced people returned to Mogadishu after the bloodshed was over. Mass media began to break the monopoly of the

---

21. This author was a Somali living in Diaspora who went back to Somalia during the UNOSOM period to work in the humanitarian field.
22. Cusman Cali Caato belonged to same sub-clan as General Caydiid and was his right-hand man during the peak of the civil war. However, he broke from him in 1995. As a result, fighting between the two men sparked, and Caydiid was wounded and died in August 1996.
23. Abdurahman Abdullahi, "Non-State Actors in the Failed State of Somalia: Survey of The Civil Society Organizations in Somalia during the Civil War," *Darsāt Ifriqiyah 31*, 2004, 57-87. Also, see NOVIBSomalia, *Mapping Somali Civil Society,* Nairobi: Kenya, 200 3, available fromhttp://www.somalicivilsociety.org/strength/phase1_Mapping%20som alicivilsociety.asp (accessed on November 10, 2009).
24. Abdullahi, *Non-State Actors*, 71–83.

warlords, and new commercial radio stations were opened, local newspapers thrived, and electronic media began to flourish.[25] These media outlets raised the awareness of the population and supported civic transformation of the society. Moreover, business figures, the former warlord financiers, broke from them to create business ventures with individuals from other clans. Through this process trans-clan business ventures were created which necessitated coping with the growing business competition. As a result, business groups created their own trans-clan security apparatus. In particular, communication sector and money transfer companies, which required vast networking to all cities, mobilized share-holding businesses that included members of different clans.[26] Moreover, local security arrangements were initiated by establishing clan-based Islamic courts, which improved security in the respected area to a certain extent.[27] Gradually, Mogadishu was taking a new shape and regaining some resemblance of its glorious days when many people from all over Somalia were creating businesses and resettling.

---

25. See Jamal Abdi Ismail, "Somalia: Research findings and Conclusions" (African Media Development Initiative) available from http://www.radiopeaceafrica.org/assets/texts/pdf/SOM_AMDI_Report_pp4%201.pdf (accessed on June 30, 2010). Also, see Abdelkarim
A. Hassan, "Somali Media, Ethics, Truth and Integrity", February 25, 2010, available from http://www.wardheernews.com/Articles_10/Feb/25_Somali%20Media_abdel.pdf (accessed on June 30, 2010).
26. See Ken Menkhaus, "Remittance companies and money transfers in Somalia, 2001", available from www.Somali.jna.org (accessed on June 31, 2010).
27. Shari'a Courts were established in North Mogadishu in 1994 and spread to other regions. It was supported by the business community and the clans. See Andre Le Sage, "Prospects of Al-Itihad and Islamist Radicalism in Somalia." *Review of African Political economy*, volume 27, number 89, 2001, 472, available from http://www.emro.who.int/somalia/som-AlItihadBrief.pdf (accessed on June 31, 2010).

The culmination of these developments was a change in national reconciliation and the growing role of the civil society. As a result, the National Reconciliation Conference driven by the civil society was held in Djibouti in 2000, after 10 years of failing warlord-driven conferences.[28] Indeed, this was a complete shift in the paradigm of reconciliation, driven by the warlords since 1991.

Islah in the Early Years of the Civil War (1991–1992)

The first day of the civil war in Mogadishu coincided with the failed attempt of Islah to create a common Islamist position among all Islamist organizations and prominent personalities.[29] These meetings were a litmus test for the Islamist groups' impartiality with respect to the clan-based factions supported by Ethiopia and clan-cloaked oppressive regime. The option of forming an Islamist coalition could have provided an exit strategy from the political and ideological deadlock. However, Islamist groups were "inefficiently developed to pose any meaningful challenge to political clanism," which was escalating violently.[30] Seemingly, Islah was pushing the agenda for an Islamist Front since February 1990 when it changed its name from the Islah Society to the Islamic Movement in Somalia (*al-Xaraka al-Islāmiyah fi al-Somāl*).[31] In so doing, it was aware of its limited capacity to act alone and was searching for a common Islamist agenda. Hansen puts the case as follows:

---

28. Abdurahman Abdullahi, "Penetrating Cultural Frontiers in Somalia: History of women's political participation during four decades (1959–2000)."*African Renaissance*. 4:1 (2007), 34–54.
29. See Islah, Comprehensive Internal Report, 9.
30. Abdurahman Abdullahi "Tribalism, Nationalism and Islam: Crisis of the Political Loyalties in Somalia" (MA thesis, Islamic Institute, McGill University, 1992), 112
31. Cali Sheikh Axmad interviewed by the author.

By 1989, the Islax [Islah] leaders understood that the end of the Barre regime was approaching but they also understood their organization's weaknesses and saw that it lacked membership. Al Islax [Islah] saw the weakness of the Siyad Barre regime as an opportunity to reverse the secularization trend of Somalia, but knew that it had little chance to do so by itself. So it looked for help to another organization, the Al Ittihad Al Islamiyah [Itixaad]. The two organizations had their differences: Al Ittihad was closer to Turabi's Sudan and had a strong Wahhabi-Salafist element. Several former members of Al Islax [Islah], such as the Al Ittihad leader Sheik Ali Warsame, had left Islax to join Ittihad, which led to some hostility between the two but also to better connections as former members stayed in touch with their friends in Islax.[32]

During this time, Islah was in a leadership transition because it had lost its founding father, *al-Murāqib al-'ām* (general guide), Sheikh Maxamad Garyare, who immigrated to Canada in 1990. Sheikh Garyare relinquished the chairmanship position, and the leadership vacuum was not easily replenished. Sheikh Maxamad Garyare explained the reason for this hasty migration from Saudi Arabia:

> I lived in Saudi Arabia as political asylum and after so many years and with my children grown up, I decided to look for other opportunities. Because of the family pressure and the necessity of my personal security, I found that it was the right time to migrate to Canada. However, I was confident that Islah was matured and there were many prominent leaders to take the responsibility.[33]

---

32. Note here the spelling of Islah (Islax). See, Stig Jarle Hansen and Atle Mesoy, The *Muslim Brotherhood in the Wider Horn of Africa* (NIBR Report, 2009), 45.
33. Sheikh Maxamad Garyare interviewed by the author on July 23, 2010, Hargeysa, Somaliland.

During 1990, all founding members of Islah were in the Diaspora. Sheikh Axmad Rashiid Xanafi and Cabdulla Axmad Cabdalla were in Canada and the USA, respectively. Dr. Maxamad Yusuf was working in Kuwait, and Dr. Cali Sheikh Axmad was a lecturer at King Sa'ud University in Saudi Arabia. However, prudently, they decided to empower the Central Committee (CC) members inside Somalia to make the choice of a new leader. Surprisingly, the CC members in Somalia elected Maxamad Cali Ibrahim, a PhD student in Saudi Arabia. Apparently, they failed to grasp the importance of moving the leadership to Somalia during the tumultuous period.[34] In this manner, Islah maintained the culture of an absent leader and designated management of the organization inside Somalia to the deputy chairman. Thus, there was the new turbulent decade of the 1990s with the same leadership disadvantage of the 1980s, but this time, by Islah's free choice.[35] However, "some improvements were made in the governance such as adopting a culture of collective leadership and expanding CC." There was a growing influence of modern elites educated in secular institutions such as physicians, engineers and military personnel.[36]

---

34. Ḥassan Ḥāji Maxamud, "Tārikh al-Ḥaraka al-Islāmiyah: Duruf al-Nashi wa awamil al-tadawur" (unpublished manuscript, 2009), 18.
35. Xassan Xaaji argues that "if the absence of Sheikh Maxamad Garyare from Somalia was considered justifiable because of the security concerns from the oppressive regime, there was no obvious justification for electing a student to a top leadership position during this period". Xassan Xaaji Maxamuud interviewed by the author on July 21, 2010, Hargeysa, Somaliland.
36. Sheikh Axmad Xassan Al-Qutubi interviewed by the author on April 10, 2010, Hargeysa, Somaliland.

The Reaction of Islah to the Civil War

Most Somalis were not anticipating a dramatic collapse of the state and a transformation of the conflict into clan-lines. Similarly, Islah did not develop a comprehensive emergency plan for a civil war except a plan for saving its members.[37] Therefore, the actual reaction to the civil war began on the second day, December 31, 1990, when the Mogadishu leaders of Islah held an extraordinary emergency meeting in the al-Aqsa school. The civil war erupted in the northern part of the city on Sunday, December 30, 1990, and skirmishes continued between the USC militia and government forces. The first decision in this meeting was to evacuate Islah members and their families from the affected area to more peaceful southern quarters of the city to be hosted by other members.[38] At the same time, Islah moved its center of operations to the Cusman Ibn-Caffan Mosque in the Madiina district, located in the southern part of the city.[39] Furthermore, as part of ongoing efforts to stop the fighting, on January 4, 1991, Sheikh Axmad Xassan al-Qutubi made a highly emotional sermon at the al-Salam Mosque during the Friday congressional prayer, and a petition for stopping the war was suggested and immediately prepared.[40] The petition included a call for the immediate resignation of the president and the

---

37. In a side talk between Itixaad and Islah at the Aden Barando meetings, they agreed to prepare a common plan based on encouraging their members to migrate from Mogadishu to peaceful areas. Also, they warned their members not to get involved in the civil war. However, those initial discussions did bear any results. See Comprehensive Report. Also, Dr. Ibrahim Dasuuqi interviewed by the author on May 22, 2010, Nairobi, Kenya.
38. Ibid., 10
39. Ibid.
40. Ibid. Also, Sheikh Axmad Xassan Al-Qutubi interviewed by the author on July 21, 2010, Hargeysa, Somaliland.

government, cessation of the war, the establishment of a transitional government, a national reconciliation conference, and a general election. The points raised in the petition were identical with the position of Islah. In a demonstration led by Sheikh Axmad al-Qutubi, the petition was handed over to the interim Prime Minister Maxamad Xawaadle Madar. Regrettably, "the peaceful demonstration was disturbed by a car accident resulting in 12 deaths and numerous injuries."[41]

Moreover, the Islah leadership in Saudi Arabia continuously issued communiqués to clarify Islah's position on the developing situation, suggesting some solutions and appealing for humanitarian assistance. The first of such communiqué was released at the beginning of the civil war in Mogadishu in which Islah called for concerted efforts to topple the regime, to organize a national conference, and respond to the human suffering.[42] The communiqué also suggested an initial agenda for the proposed national conference. This agenda included restoration of the rule of law, releasing all political prisoners, preparing an Islamic compliant constitution, adopting a multi-party system, granting freedom of the press, and conducting a free election.[43] Apparently, in this communiqué, Islah also called for a new democratic Somalia in which the constitution would not contravene with the general Islamic principles. Based on this position, Islah prepared comprehensive program guidelines intended to be submitted at the proposed reconciliation conference to be held in Mogadishu on February

---

41. Ibid., Sheikh Axmad related that one of the Islah members died in this accident. His name was Axmad Maxamad Hussein (Xanqi). See also, Islah Comprehensive Internal Report, 11.
42. See Al-Ḥarakah al-Islāmiyah fi al-Somāl (Islah): Bayān (communique) no.7, issued on 5/01/1991.
43. Ibid.

28, 1991. However, the conference was boycotted by all armed factions.[44] The major activities of Islah since the collapse of the state on April 28, 1991 were to emphasize Islah's firm adherence to a policy of neutrality toward warring factions, continued efforts to create a common Islamist front, and to aggressively seek humanitarian assistance desperately needed by Islah members and the masses. Neutrality was emphasized even more when the civil war transformed entirely into a clan conflict. In April 1991, allied forces, comprised of Siyaad Barre supporters from his Darood clan-family, advanced to the outskirts of Mogadishu to recapture the capital. Nonetheless, the USC, represented by Hawiye, was caught in a panic and launched a counter offensive that thwarted these forces. This encounter further complicated clan sensitivity; innocent people were indiscriminately killed and property was seized by both sides because of their clan affiliations.

Islah was frustrated by the lack of receptiveness from Itixaad and "the idea that the two large Islamist organizations could better withstand the coming storm together" was not being considered.[45] In fact, the turning point in the relations between the two organizations occurred when Itixaad took sides in the conflict between the USC and SSDF/SPM near Kismaayo.[46] This war destroyed the last hope for any Islamist coalition. Dr. Ibrahim Dasuuqi considers this war "the beginning of successive adventures of Itixaad who threw Islamist agenda in

---

44. See Al-Ḥarakah al-Islāmiyah fi al-Somāl (Islah): Program for National Reconciliation issued on February 25, 1991.
45. Al-Ḥarakah al-Islāmiyah fi al-Somāl (Islah).*Al-Ḥalah al-Rāhina* (The Current state of Affairs in Somalia), April 27, 1991.Also, see Stig Jarle Hansen and Atle Mesoy, The *Muslim Brotherhood*, 45.
46. See Islah, Comprehensive Internal Report, 23.

the clannish conflict."⁴⁷ He further articulates that "Islah was compelled to distance itself from all warring factions including Itixaad."⁴⁸ A report produced by Islah in June 1991 characterizes the war as "clannish and unnecessary war which eventually is not a Jihad for the sake of Allah."⁴⁹ This report ostensibly demonstrates the reaction of Islah to Itixaad's partaking in the civil war called by the latter the "Islamic Jihad." Summing the main themes of these communiqués and reports from December 1990 to July 1991, Islah supported toppling the regime, in principle, with the reservation of a possible development into a clan conflict. Therefore, Islah consistently warned against mounting clan polarization and alerted its members to abstain from becoming involved. After the collapse of the state, Islah maintained distance from the fighting factions and retained a neutral position with an emphasis on reconciliation. This position was completely different from the other Islamist groups. For example, Itixaad was drifting toward militancy and was busy establishing training camps, while the *Majma al-Ulama* were working closely with the USC in Mogadishu. Moreover, Waxdah was fully cooperating with the SNM in northern Somalia.

Evidently, the Islah position during the civil war was not based only on the decision of the field leaders in Mogadishu; during 1990, the CC made a decision to abstain from the brewing war between the regime and the armed factions.⁵⁰ This decision was derived from the Islamic position of how to act during *"Fitna"* (tribulation) wars. From the Islamic point of

---

47. Dr. Ibrahim Dasuuqi interviewed by the author.
48. Ibid.
49. See Islah, Comprehensive Internal Report, 23.
50. Dr. Cali Sheikh Axmad interviewed by the author, June 24, 2010.

view as interpreted by Islah, the fight between the Muslim Somalis belonged to a type of war termed *"Hurub al-Fitna"* in Islam. As a result, Islah held fast to the Prophetic Hadith, "Verily Fitan [tribulations] shall take place. Fitan wherein the one setting is better than one walking and the one walking is better than the one hastening forth...."[51] In view of that, Islah made every effort, by maintaining internal cohesion and supporting displaced and overseas members, to protect its members from falling into the tribulation wars. Moreover, Islah lobbied Arabic/Islamic charities in the rich Gulf countries for providing humanitarian assistance to the needy people of Somalia. Dr. Cali Sheikh, former chairman of Islah, describes this period, "We did every effort possible to seek humanitarian assistance for our brothers inside Somalia and their family which was our priority. We also activated Islah Charity to mobilize resources for the people of Somalia."[52] As a result, Islah adopted its triple slogan in the first year of the civil war: *"al-Igātha, Islāḥdat al-Bayn, al-Da'wat wa al-Irshād"* (humanitarian assistance, reconciling warring parties, and intensification of the Islamic *Da'wa*).[53]

The Impact of the Civil War on Islah

After losing its first chairman to immigration in 1990, Islah also lost its deputy chairman in the first week of the civil war. Colonel Cali Maxamad Ibrahim, nicknamed Ali Dayaar, was

---

51. Al-Maktab al-Siyasi.*Al-Ḥaraka al-Islāmiyah wa al-'Amal al-Siyāsi* (Mogadishu: Markaz al-Qani al-Ifriqi li Darsāṭ al-Insāniyah, 1996), 9–10. See the long Hadith in Sheikh Muhammad Islam'il Muqadam, *Ba'ira al-fitan (the Way out of Tribulation)* translated by Fahia Yahya (Alexandria: Dar Al-Tawhid, 2009), 39.
52. Dr. Ali Sheikh interviewed by the author.
53. Al-Maktab al-Siyasi.*Al- Ḥaraka al-Islāmiyah*.

killed in the government's shelling of the civilian quarters in Mogadishu.[54] Moreover, Islah's chief political officer, engineer Cisse, was also killed in November 1991 while supporting the displaced people from Mogadishu. Dr. Cali Baasha, the current chairman of Islah, relates the story of the killing of engineer Cisse as follows:

> When the civil war began, I was injured and was evacuated to the town of Bula-burte about 180 Km from Mogadishu at the road connecting the capital with the central and northern regions. It was Engineer Cisse's hometown and I resided his house. Bandits used to loot traveling people in the anarchic period. One day, these bandits looted 10 vehicles carrying about 120 persons. Engineer Cisse mobilized the elders and succeeded to feed the people and to return their looted vehicles and other properties. However, looters sucked the fuel out of the vehicles. In order to get fuel, he traveled to Mogadishu. After securing the resources, he was injured while crossing the road near Gurguurte Hotel. He died at Madina Hospital within days.[55]

To fill the leadership vacuum, Sheikh Axmad Xassan Al-Qutubi was elected to the deputy chairmanship in January 1991. The situation under which Sheikh Axmad took office was volatile and worsened day by day in southern Somalia where the politics of guns and bullets, clan solidarity, organized robberies, and the humiliation of weaker clans was mounting. The transformation of war to clan-lines between Hawiye and Darood complicated Islah's operation as a non-clan institution. Darood Islah members in Mogadishu became a target in looming revenge killings by Hawiye clan militia. In these

---

54. See Al-Ḥarakah al-Islāmiyah fi al-Somāl (Islah): Bayān (Communique) no.8 on the killing of its deputy Chairman on January 8, 1991.
55. Dr. Ali Baasha Cumar interviewed through email by the author on June 20, 2010.

circumstances, the Islah leadership decided to evacuate 50 members and their families to their original home villages and towns. Some of the evacuees included prominent leaders such as Sheikh Nuur Baaruud, Sheikh Maxamud Faarax, and Sheikh Cisse Sheikh Axmad.[56] Moreover, the war had caused a huge displacement of Islah members, and the leadership, side-by-side with the rest of the population. The process of regrouping the people was difficult, as most did not know each other due to the underground nature of the organization.[57] The scope of the displacement was vast and covered almost all villages and localities in Somalia and neighboring countries such as Kenya, Ethiopia, and Djibouti. Migration to Europe, USA, and Canada intensified.

How did Islah cope with this situation during these difficult days? As related by Dr. Ibrahim Dasuuqi and Mustafa Cabdullahi, the Islah organizational network had been seriously disrupted.[58] The reason was that the Islah organization was based on a clandestine cellular structure, in which only members of each cell (5–7), called *"Usra"* in the MB literature, meaning "family," knew each other. In this system, leaders of a number of cells constitute the upper cell and know the others up to the highest hierarchy of the leadership. This cellular organizational structure was necessary to work under the repressive regime. Therefore, with the massive displacement of people during the early days of the war, many members were cut off from their

---

56. Dr. Ibrahim Dasuuqi and Cabdullahi Cali Xayle were assigned to accompany them until they crossed the border. They used a lorry belonging to one of the Islah members, Sheikh Maxamad Dhaqane who lived in Beletweyne. Dr. Cali Baasha Cumar interviewed by the author.
57. Mustafa Cabdullahi interviewed by the author on July 26, 2009, Hargeysa, Somaliland.
58. Ibid.

cells. Some of them died unreported in the war. To cope with these conditions, Islah leaders developed a new innovative method. The concept was based on establishing a general meeting place "Barta Kulanka" where members could spread the word to whomever they knew. As a result, all members were invited to attend a permanent open meeting held every week. The meeting was held in the al-Aqsa School near Sheikh Sufi Mosque, and people used to sit under a big tree named *"Al-Shajara al-Mubāraka"* (the blessed tree).[59] The objectives during this period were to raise the awareness of the members about current affairs, to conduct training and teaching programs on relevant Islamic topics, to recruit new members, and to debate current affairs. Dr. Ibrahim Dasuuqi characterizes the debates and discussion that took place there as follows:

> It was an exercise of open and participatory democracy in a period of war and clan division. It was the epitome of brotherhood and pristine era. Moreover, under that tree, charities sent from the leaders in Saudi Arabia were evenly distributed to all members. Also, Islah Charity was activated and began as voluntary medical unit. I initiated to offer free medical service until it was developed into comprehensive Charity in 1993.[60] Those who died or were injured were reported and those who intend to travel passed there to farewell their brothers. Islah members in Mogadishu drastically increased from about 100 persons due to huge displacement to about 600 in the period between Februarys/November, 1991. Indeed, this was a "golden period of Islah" with all its challenges.[61]

---

59. The school was one of the five schools in Mogadishu administered by Islah, and its principle was Maxamad Faarah Buuh. Dr. Cali Baasha Cumar interviewed by the author through email on June 29, 2010.
60. The Islah Charity was founded in the last years of the military regime, however, the decision to activate it was taken in the congregational meeting in al-Aqsa school and Cabdulqaadir Maxamad Kutub was assigned as its director. Dr. Dasuuqi was interviewed by the author.
61. Ibid.

Later in 1993, after conflict settled, the excessive recruitment during this period was criticized and some members termed it *"taḥta al-Shajara"* (under the tree), having a pejorative connotation of a lack of commitment because of easy recruitment. Mustafa Cabdullahi, one of the leaders of that time, responded to such criticisms as follows:

> The open meeting in al-Aqsa school was necessary for regrouping and continuing Islah activities. It was important to minimize the damage of Islah from the civil war. However, later, two schools developed within Islah regarding recruitment. Those who believed to ease recruitment processes claiming they are following Hassan Al-Banna during early freedom yeas of MB. The other school belonged to later period of oppression where MB became underground and recruitment was tightened. Members belonged that the later schools used to criticize harshly the process of recruitment that was taking place in Mogadishu.[62]

The displacement of Islah members was an opportunity for Islamic activism to flourish and spread to remote areas to hitherto unthinkable locations. Moreover, Islah encouraged students to travel abroad for higher education, particularly to Sudan.[63] Many students traveled through Ethiopia to reach Sudan and attended universities there. The displaced members in refugee camps, particularly in Kenya, were reorganized and began rigorous activities. In the Diaspora, migrant members of Islah were actively reaching out and spreading the message of Islam.These members were reorganized and were connected with the International MB affiliates in Europe, Canada, and the

---

62. Ibid.
63. Ibid.

United States of America. Many more students were joining universities in Pakistan, India, and Yemen.

Other dominant activities during this period were to be distinguished from Itixaad (*al-Tamayuz*). This was important for Islah because the public could not distinguish between Islah and Itixaad and termed all Islamists Ikhwan to differentiate them from traditional Islamic scholars. Nevertheless, when the dream of establishing an Islamist coalition dissipated with the militaristic Itixaad approach in April 1991, Islah began to overtly criticize Itixaad.[64] Both movements, disagreed on many issues, such as issuing the Islamist Manifesto, which Itixaad refused to sign; yet, they had many common positions during the early civil war period. The relationship between the two organizations was mended to a certain extent during the Aden Brando meetings when they developed a common plan for saving members of the two organizations from becoming involved in the war.[65] However, the entire rapprochement was frustrated when Itixaad drifted toward militancy and participated in the Kismaayo war on April 14, 1991. Apparently, Itixaad's hawks of the former Army officers, infiltrated by unknown members of Al-Qaida, steered Itixaad toward Salafia/Jihadism.[66] Moreover, the strong assistance from the Jihadist sympathizers in the Gulf countries in the form of relief assistance contributed to pushing Itixaad toward militancy.[67]

---

64. Somali masses and external observers could not distinguish Islah from Itixaad during this time. For them, they all belonged to Ikhwan, a general term used to signify modern Islamic movements. The term Ikhwan was used by media reporters, and this annoyed Islah, which considered Itixaad to belong to Salafia.
65. Aadan Barando is the name of the house owner where the meeting of the Islamic organizations were initiated.
66. See Cabdi Shakuur Mire, *Koboca Islaamiyiinta*.
67. Indeed, Abdurahman al-Qaidy, an alleged al-Qaida operative who was regional director of the Saudi International Islamic Relief Organisation (IIRO) was implicated

Itixaad's new militant direction compelled Islah to distance itself from any connections with Itixaad and to adopt a policy of distinction. This policy was based on educating the public on the difference between the MB represented by Islah and the Salafia School represented by Itixaad.

Another development of Islamic activism was the establishment of *Majma'al-'Ulamā* (The Congress of Islamic Scholars; hereafter Majmac) on February 2, 1991 in a meeting at the Kaah Hotel in Mogadishu. The concept of Majmac was introduced during this meeting by famous Islamic scholars, including Sheikh Maxamad Macallin, Sharif Sharafow, Sheikh Ibrahim Suuley and Cali Xaaji Yusuf.[68] Their aim was to create a Supreme Islamic Council that would play the role of an umbrella organization for Islamic personalities and groups. The idea developed after these scholars met with Interim President Cali Mahdi Maxamad, who offered them a courteous reception. The interim president requested that they take the responsibility of implementing Shari'a in the country.[69] He also assured them that he was ready to work with them and to listen to their directions and advice. These scholars, who were imprisoned and humiliated by military regime, seemed satisfied with the president and believed his request wholeheartedly. Sharif

---

in the provision of huge assistance to Itixaad disguised as humanitarian relief assistance. However, after the defeat of Itixaad in the Araare battle near Kismaayo in 1991 masterminded by Somali al-Qaida operatives, Al-Qaida infiltration in Itixaad was growing. It is alleged that representatives of Usama bin Ladin living in Sudan were regularly training, equipping and providing technical know-how to the Itixaad in Somalia. See International Crisis Group, *Somalia's Islamists* (Africa Report N°100 - 12 December 2005), 6, available from http://www.crisisgroup.org/~/media/Files/africa/ho rn-of-africa/somalia/Somalias%20Islamists.ashx.Also, see Cabdi Shakuur Mire, *Koboca Islaamiyiinta.*

68. See Islah, Comprehensive Internal Report, 13.
69. Ibid.

Sharafow, in particular, was highly enthusiastic and considered their meeting with the president a golden opportunity for the application of Shari'a. Euphorically, while speaking to the audience, he uttered famous MB slogan: "Allah is our goal, The Messenger is our example, The Qur'an is our constitution, Jihad is our way, and martyrdom is our desire."[70] Moreover, Sheikh Maxamad Macallin told the audience that he was requested by the president to organize the participation of the Islamic scholars in restoring governance to the country. As a result, he said: "This meeting is intended to form an umbrella organization and to unify all efforts of Islamic workers."[71]

Nonetheless, Islah was disappointed with the limited goal of the meeting and attempted to widen the agenda. The head of the Islah delegation, Dr. Ibrahim Dasuuqi, explained the emerging clan conflict in the country and the great responsibility that was placed on the shoulders of the Islamic scholars. After that, he proposed to form an independent Islamist Front, prepare an Islamic Constitution, and participate in the reconciliation conference to be held in Mogadishu one month later, instead of creating a Supreme Islamic Council that would collaborate with the interim USC regime.[72] Moreover, he warned against losing neutrality and supporting one side in the Somali conflict. Evidently, Dasuuqi's speech at the Kaah Hotel outlined the Islah program during this period based on "neutrality, Islamic constitution, and Islamist coalition party."[73] Dr. Dasuuqi describes this meeting as follows:

---

70. Ibid.
71. Ibid.
72. Ibid.
73. Dr. Dasuuqi interviewed by the author.

It was open and haphazard organized meeting. Scholars were invited via Radio Mogadishu. Many famous personalities who were the instrument of the collapsed regime to fight against Islamist organizations were present. Moreover, staunch supporters of USC were also there. Besides that, some opportunistic elements showed their face. We tried our best to reform the meeting, to change its agenda, and finally to put in its supreme council reasonable scholars. However, we finally convinced that we were entrapped in the USC show case and so, we decided to withdraw from it.

In that sense, Islah considered the Majmac as an instrument of the new interim government intended to last only 28 days after which the reconciliation conference would be held in Mogadishu. As a result, Islah withdrew from the Majmac and accused it of being a biased clan-based organization and an instrument of the USC provincial government.[74] Meanwhile, Islah was accused by the supporters of the Majmac of breaking Muslim unity and dividing concerted efforts in the crucial period of Somali history.[75] In the footsteps of Islah, Itixaad also withdrew from the Majmac, entertaining similar accusations to those of Islah.[76] Nevertheless, as the French scholar Roland Marchal narrated, the "success and influence [of *Majma Al-Ulama*] were short-lived and it played no major role in the country or in the capital city afterwards."[77] Majmac is remembered initiating the first Islamic court in 1991 which was initially supported by Cali Mahdi Maxamad. As Professor Afyare reports, "according to the leaders and soldiers who

---

74. See Islah, Comprehensive Internal Report, 19.
75. Ibid.
76. Ibid.
77. Roland Marchal, "Islamic Political Dynamics in the Somali Civil War" In *Islamism and its Enemies in the Horn of Africa*, edited by Alex De Waal (Indiana University Press, 2006), 114-146, 125.

worked for the first Islamic court, those in the power at the time [Cali Mahdi and Caydiid], undermined and then destroyed the efforts to create the lasting court."[78] Evidently, Islamist groups and organizations were very much fragmented like the armed factions. Although differences in Islamic ideology played a major role, clan attachments also played undeniable roles. Occasionally, beneath ideological facades, clanism and opportunism were not entirely absent. Evidently, the relationship among Islamist organizations of Islah, Majmac, and Itixaad deteriorated sharply in 1991 because of the different visions, interactions with the civil war and agendas.

The Rebirth of Islah: The Djibouti Conference of 1992

After the collapse of the state, communications between Somalia and the world were disrupted, and, as a result, it was very hard for the executive of Islah in Saudi Arabia to communicate with the field leaders in Mogadishu. However, "expanded consultation and collective leadership had played a major role in harmonizing Islah's decisions and policies."[79] This does not mean, however, that occasional disputes did not evolve into critical issues. To ease tension and enhance teamwork, the leadership in Saudi Arabia sent Cabdulaziz Xaaji Axmad, a member of the Executive Bureau, to connect the two leaderships.[80] Upon his arrival, he conveyed the message to the field leaders that six new members were included in the CC.[81]

---

78. Afyare Abdi Elmi, *Understanding the Somalia Conflagration: Identity, Political Islam and Peace building* (London: Pluto Press, 2010), 63.
79. Sheikh Axmad Xassan al-Qutubi interviewed by the author.
80. Dr. Dasuuqi interviewed by the author.
81. The new members of CC were Dr. Ibrahim Dasuuqi, Dr. Cali Baasha Cumar, Engineer Cabdiwahab, Colonel Cabdullahi Cali Xayle, and Mustafa Cabdullahi. These were the

The inclusion of these professional members in the CC ushered in a new era of diversified leadership in Islah. They were medical doctors, engineers, and army officers. Besides that, Cabdulaziz Xaaji Axmad pressured for unification with one of the Islamist groups.[82] Cabdulaziz, who was exceptionally enthusiastic about the project of uniting with other Islamist organizations, persuaded the majority of the leaders in Mogadishu to accept the unification project with a splinter group from Itixaad called *Ansar-Al-Sunna*.[83] However, the project was short-lived and failed during the 100-day war in Mogadishu before it could be carried out.[84] Moreover, another incident resulted in extreme pressure of Maxamad Cali Ibrahim, the chairman of Islah, to form the unified Islamist coalition with Itixaad, Waxdah, and Majmac, sponsored by Sudan in 1992.[85] This meeting was held while Itixaad waged war with SSDF in Puntland, supported by *Usāma bin Lāddin* who was residing during this period in Sudan. Moreover, Sudan had major concerns about the US intervention in Somalia.[86] The Islah delegation was pressured by its leaders, Islamist groups, and the Islamic movement of Sudan to sign a Memorandum of Understanding that lay the framework for creating a network of Islamic organizations. All Somali Islamist organizations, namely, Itixaad, Waxdah, and Majmac, were very enthusiastic about the agreement; however, Islah delegation remained skeptical and believed that the project would serve short-term

---

backbone of the Islah leadership in Mogadishu. Dr. Dasuuqi interviewed by the author.
82. Ibid.
83. Dr. Ibrahim Dasuuqi interviewed by the author.
84. Ibid.
85. Abdishakur Mire, *Koboca Islamiyiinta*.
86. Ibid.

Sudanese Movement interest and Itixaad objectives at war in Puntland.[87] When this project failed, Islah was accused by other parties of having derailed the deal. During this period, some top leaders of Islah in Saudi Arabia communicated the leaders in Somalia pushing them towards militancy.[88] These personal preferences had created confusion and rift among the top leaders of Islah before the conference in Djibouti in 1992. Subsequently, most of the field leaders in Mogadishu boycotted the conference as a sign of protestation. The conference was, nevertheless, successful, and many leaders from the Diaspora participated besides the CC, and part of the conference was moved to Mogadishu to resolve internal organizational discord.[89]

By 1992, Islah was isolated from the clan-based factions and Islamist organizations that were engaged in one way or another in the conflict. Islah's position of neutrality and peaceful settlement was a minority voice during this period. Finally, the conference of 1992 was considered a new milestone in Islah's work; in this conference, differences were resolved, activities were evaluated, and new strategies were developed. These strategies responded to two main questions: How Islah should we reorganized in the new socio-political atmosphere? And, what will be the socio-political strategy for the coming years? The issue of organizational development has been discussed in Chapter Five. The following two sections will address Islah's

---

87. Dr. Ibrahim Dasuuqi interviewed by the author on April 5, 2010, Nairobi, Kenya.
88. Furthermore, when Itixaad opted for militancy and opened training, Maxamad Cali Ibrahim, in a break from Islah's adopted policy, sent a letter to Mogadishu leaders encouraging them to open such camps, while Cabduaziz Xaaji sent a similar letter to Cabdullahi Cali Xayle. Cabdullahi Cali Xayle and Ibrahim Dasuuqi interviewed by the author.
89. Cali Sheikh Axmad interviewed by the author.

social and political strategies and the way they were implemented during the period of 1992–2000.

The Political Strategy and Programs (1992–2000)

The Islah Movement proclaimed its political philosophy from its inception, expressing its objective of reforming the Somali society in accordance with moderate Islamic methodology derived from the MB based on "democratic/constitutional Approach".[90] During its formative period (1978–1990), political space was entirely blocked, a poisonous political atmosphere of the dictatorial regime was brewing, and armed clan-based organizations were wrangling and wrestling. Moreover, all Islamist organizations including Islah were in their infancy and played no concrete roles in the political scuffling. Furthermore, with the collapse of the state and subsequent civil war, there was no room for peaceful political activism. Itixaad opted for taking up arms to compete with armed clans for power, whereas Islah continued its peaceful reform approach in the tumultuous environment. From here arises a question of how Islah contemplated political participation when society was divided into clans and was dominated by armed factions. What would be the entry point for such political participation? This section examines how Islah developed its political prominence by 2000. The study begins by examining a theoretical

---

90. Abdurahman Abdullahi, "Islah Movement in Somalia: Islamic Moderation in the war-torn Somalia" (paper presented at the Second Nordic Horn of Africa Conference. Oslo: OsloUniversity, 2008), available from http://www.scribd.com/doc/1 4642683/The-Islah-Movement-Islamic-Moderation-in-Somalia (accessed on June 30, 2010). Also, See Hussein M. Adam, "Political Islam in Somali History" in Markus Hoehne and Virginia Luling (edited), *Milk and Peace, Drought and War: Somali Culture, Society and Politics* (London: Hurst & Company, 2010), 119-135, 131

framework under which Islah operated and the model developed for political engagement. Moreover, institutions of political participation and practical models are studied here. Finally, the outcome of Islah's political engagement that culminated in the Somali Reconciliation Conference in Djibouti in 2000 is explored.

Theory and Model of Political Participation

Organizations face enormous difficulties during a transition period, in particular when they reform from an underground cellular setting into an open organization. This process requires not only changes in attitudes and mindsets, but also a clear set of rules and policies besides competent leaders at the top of the organization who believe in reform. Socio-political realities in Somalia changed radically after the collapse of the state in 1991, shifting from the rule of a dictator to anarchic clan supremacy. Dealing with the clans was something new to the members of Islah. Their training programs were based on the normative Islamic thought and the MB method of reforming society ruled by a secular state. Studies of the local political dynamics were minimal, and Islah's comprehension of clans and clanism was very much influenced by the nationalist discourse.[91] Hansen observes, "The Brotherhood [Islah] showed outright contempt for clan-based politics, and strongly maintained that Islam

---

91. Somali nationalists glorified nationalism and rebuffed clan identities. Their approach was "don't pronounce its name, don't talk about it, and let us shame it as bad and evil." That was a simplistic approach of the Somali nationalists that could not be sustained over time. See Abdurahman Abdullahi, *"Can we surpass clan based organizations?"* available from http://www.scribd.com/doc/15420091/Can-we-surpass-clanbased-organizations (accessed on July 6, 2010).

transcended clans."⁹² As a result, clans were projected as the cancer of the nation and were abhorred and vilified from the Islamic point view.⁹³ This concept of clanism weakened relations between Islah members and their extended families and clans. Nonetheless, this concept departs from the moderate Islamic perspective based on judging actions of the people, not on their organizational setting. Indeed, societies can organize themselves as to what suits them, and there is no particular form of organization sanctioned by Islam. Certainly, Somali society was organized in the form of clans and sub-clans, and after the collapse of national institutions, clan organizations became the only available form for most people. This form of organization was the only one they knew and accepted before colonial powers introduced an alien form of organization. In such clan-based environment and poisonous political culture, how could a trans-clan ideological organization become involved in community affairs without making concessions in its ideology? Other than the organizational cultural barriers stated above, the issue was very complicated, as there are no historical precedents to draw lessons from, and the theory of social reform of the MB falls short in addressing that issue. In fact, the basic premise of the MB reform assumes the presence of a secular state, which, through a gradual process, is transformed into an Islamic state. This proposition was completely changed in Somalia where there was no state to change, and society was at war with itself.

---

92. Hansen and Mesoy, The *Muslim Brotherhood*, 40.
93. Islam refuses all forms of *'Asabiyah* and the Prophet says: *"Leave it. It is Rotten"*. In another Hadith, the Prophet says: *"He is not one us who calls for 'Asabiyah."* These 'Asabiyah includes all forms of solidities and is not necessarily always negative. The forbidden 'Asabiyah is what causes transgression of the rights of others.

Moreover, Islah had adopted a strategy of peaceful participation in politics in combination with social Islamic activities to achieve its projected reform. Isolation from political activism is against Islah's basic doctrine that clings to the concept that Islam is a religion and the state.[94] Thus, the model and strategy of political participation is what required a new way of thinking and wisdom from Islah. Accordingly, Islah considered three possible options to actively participate in politics.[95] The first option was to form a shared political party with other members of the society. This option was rejected because of its impracticality in a country where parties were non-existent and people were cut off from each other in warlord-dominated enclaves. The second option was to transform the movement into a political party, an option which shares the first option on the absence of suitable ambiance. Moreover, after examining the human resources available and considering the domestic, regional, and international atmosphere and challenges, Islah abstained from this venture too. The third option was to allow members of Islah to individually participate in the existing political entities. This concept removed restrictions from the interested members for political participation in their clans or any political groups. This model of political participation was flexible, doable, and appropriate for Somalia in the chaotic situation. However, adopting such model required attitudinal change and significant reform within the organization. As a result, a policy of political realism known as *"al-Ta'āmul ma'a al-Wāqi'"* (dealing with the reality) was embraced. It was a practical approach

---

94. For details on the relations between Islam and politics, see Yusuf al-Qardawi, *State in Islam* (Cairo: El-Falah Publishing and Distributions, 1998).
95. Al-Maktab al-Siyasi.*Al-Haraka al-Islamiyah*, 13.

guided by the objectives of the Islamic law *"Maqāsid al-Sharīah"*.[96]

The definition of "dealing with reality," according to Islah literature and interviews, could be summarized as follows.[97] It is to consider the existing socio-political realities and to push the clan-based organization toward the desired Islamic society and Islamic state. The core idea of this policy was to break with historical isolation promoted during the oppressive regime and clandestine operations and to open up to society at large. Its objectives included encouraging members of Islah to participate in the existing socio-political organizations and to become involved in all such groups. Syndromes of both isolation from the society and assimilation with the clan culture were discouraged. Instead, prudent and positive engagement was promoted. The aim of this policy was to take the Islamic activities to all areas, without reservations, and to transform Islah into a dynamic organization that changes its techniques with the changing conditions, time, and space. It is also meant to promote Islamic activism from its defensive position to more assertive one with innovative initiatives corresponding to the changing conditions. Moreover, the policy of "dealing with reality" rejects idealism and offers more weight to realism, differentiating the descriptive from the normative. This theory is one of the core principles of Islamic thought; nevertheless, it is less revived and developed. The difficulties of reforming organizational culture were evident once the policy was

---

96. According to the objectives of the Islamic law, *"al-waqiyah"* is considered in all aspects of Islamic Shari'a. Dr. Liban Hussein Isse, professor of Islamic Shari'a interviewed by the author on July 28, 2009, Hargeysa, Somaliland.
97. Al-Maktab al-Siyāsi.*Al- Ḥarakah al-Islāmiyah*, 26-27.

adopted in 1995 after five years of heated debates.[98] As a result, Islah individuals who were capable of political participation were allowed to do so. Adopting this policy enabled Islah to become more involved in politics and reconciliation processes. Accordingly, two programs were initiated to implement this policy effectively. In a collective manner, Islah became engaged in a reconciliation program conducted through the Somali Reconciliation Council (SRC), a new institution created for that purpose. Moreover, certain individuals joined political entities to influence the policies of their entities toward reconciliation and peace

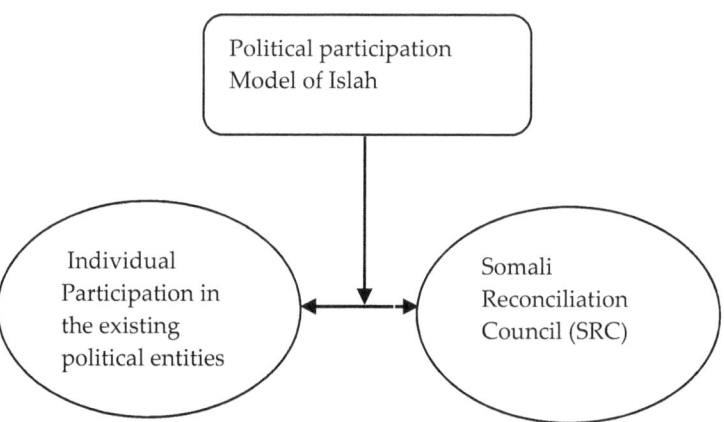

Figure 8. The Model of Political Participation (1994–2000)

---

98. The issue of how the movement should deal with the new realities in Somalia was first discussed in Toronto, Canada, after the fall of the regime in January 1991. See Abdurahman Abdullahi, "The Islah Movement: Islamic Moderation, available from http://www.scribd.com/doc/14642683/The-Islah-Movement-Islamic-Moderation-in-Somalia (accessed on July 8, 2010).

Reconciliation: The Entry Point for Political Participation

Although reconciliation between warring clans and factions, *"Islah dat al-bayn,"* was one of Islah's priority programs since the onset of the civil war, its approach was modified in 1992. While developing a political strategy, reconciliation was considered as the entry point for peaceful political participation. Moreover, it was considered to be the only peaceful way to recover the Somali state. Consequently, institutionalization of the reconciliation efforts was sought and initiated with the establishment of the Somali Reconciliation Council (SRC) in 1994.[99] The main objectives under the reconciliation strategy were "to cease the war through reconciliation process and sustain such reconciliation by utilizing local Islamic courts."[100] This meant that after initial reconciliation, communities should create local Islamic courts to maintain order and to provide arbitration services to conflicting parties.[101] To implement this objective, the SRC was founded by prominent Islah figures. The

---

99. "The believers are brothers; therefore, make reconciliation between your brothers, and fear Allah, that you may find Mercy" 49:10. "No good is there in much of their intimate discourse except in enjoining charity, righteousness, or reconciling between people..." 4:114. "Shall I inform you about a deed which is higher in degree than prayer, fasting, and charity? The Sahaba said: 'Yes, prophet of Allah.' He said: 'It is to end a dissension between people'" (i.e., to conciliate between them).
100. These early Islamic courts were not infiltrated to extremist groups and were simply local institutions for security and arbitration of disputes. The SRC trained its judges and provided office material for most of the courts See Moḥamed Aḥmed Sheikh 'Ali, "Itiḥād al-Maḥākim al-Islāmiyah: Al-Nash'a wa tadawur wa āfāq al-Mustaqbal (November 1, 2008), available from http://somaliatodaynet.com/news/index.php?option=com_content&task=view&id=88&Itemid=31 (accessed on July 3, 2010). Also, see Bryden, Matt. *"Profile of Somali Islamic Courts"*, October 24, 2006 (unpublished paper).
101. Mahasin El-Safi, "The attitude and Reaction of the Islamic Groups to US/UN Intervention in Somalia 1991-1995." In Jorg Tanze (ed.), *What are Somalia's development Perspective? Science between Resignation and Hope* (Das Arabische Bush: Proceedings of 6th SSIA Congress, Berlin 6-9 Dec. 1996, 2001).

role of the SRC was to provide logistical and organizational support and to raise awareness, utilizing traditional methods and Islamic principles. Moreover, the SRC played the role of the third neutral party necessary for the success of reconciliations, besides providing a neutral venue at the SRC centers, located in most southern regions. In particular, five main centers were very active in Mogadishu (two centers), Kismaayo, Beletweyne, and Baidoa.[102] Reconciliation committees were also active in all regions where chapters of Islah were functioning.

The main structure of SRC consisted of a Board of Trustees (BOT), an Executive Bureau, and regional chapters. The role of the BOT was to raise funds for the reconciliation and to oversee its activities.The types of reconciliation were divided into three complementary levels: grassroots, social, and political.[103] Grassroots reconciliation focused on ceasing conflicts between clans. Naturally, in the absence of state apparatus, any conflict within clan groups easily developed into clan fighting unless traditional conflict resolution was employed. However, "traditional elders and Islamic scholars were drastically weakened in the southern Somalia and their legitimacy was curtailed by the faction leaders."[104] Moreover, the conflicts became numerous with the proliferation of armies, and the scope of the conflicts widened with modern transportation and communications. Therefore, traditional leaders lacked both resources and organizational capacity to cope with the magnitude and frequency of these conflicts. Hence, the SRC

---

102. See Andre Le Sage, "Somalia and the War on Terrorism: Political Islamic Movements and US Counter-terrorism Efforts" (PhD diss., Jesus College, Cambridge University, 2004), 171.
103. Al-Maktab al-Siyāsi, Al- Ḥarakah al-Islāmiyah, 20.
104. Sheikh Axmad Abarone Amin, former director of SRC interviewed by the author on July 30, 2007. Mogadishu, Somalia.

intervened in support of these traditional leaders, empowering them was necessary to contain the conflict and to weaken the authority of the warlords. The provided resources enhanced the capacity of the traditional leaders for local reconciliation, improved their image, and increased their authority. The implications of this undertaking and Islah'sreturn in terms of the support for its ideology were impressive. This served as a practical learning process of social engagement and culture. Many members of Islah were involved in the reconciliation, and interacting with the traditional elders improved their network of friends and sympathizers. Sheikh Axmad Abarone, the executive Director of SRC who led Caravan of Reconciliation to Hiiraan region, says:

> Hiiraan region was devastated by wars between most of its clans. We have initiated regional approach for reconciliation and initiated comprehensive meeting in our SRC center in Mogadishu. We invited leaders of all eight major clan one by one and finally, held a common meeting of all clan elders and political leaders of Hiiraan clans. Finally, agreements were concluded to travel to Hiiraan and undertake comprehensive reconciliation. A Caravan of Peace carrying more than 100 persons left Mogadishu to Hiiraan and for about a month, we held reconciliation between all clans. All these clans became aware that Islah was peaceful, promotes reconciliation and does not engage in religious conflict with the traditional Sufi orders. The leaders of these clans remain friendly to Islah.

Moreover, Cabdullahi Cali Xayle, one of Islah leaders who led the Caravan of Reconciliation in the central region, says: "It was great experience to work with the traditional elders and learn their way of conflict resolution. Moreover, our relation with them became intimate and they will no longer confuse

Islah with Itixaad."[105] Moreover, some of these elders joined Islah, and some clans became sympathizers of Islah and encouraged their people to join. Furthermore, while working closely with the traditional elders and scholars in the peace building program, Islah distinguished itself further from Itixaad, which was engaged in the local wars. In the Somali society, customary law Xeer and Islamic Shari'a are used to manage conflicts between and among clans. Traditional agreements are based on codes designed to prevent conflict and avert an escalation of violent clashes.[106] The conflict resolution process is either mediated directly by the traditional elders of the two parties or by an accepted third party. SRC followed the traditional conflict resolution mechanism, which included the initial cessation of hostility "Colaad-joojin", disengagement of forces "Kala-rarid/ Kala-fogeyn", and a ceasefire "Xabbad-joojin".[107] Conflict prevention was rarely used; intervention began after conflicts flared, and clan elders from the confronting parties were mobilized to confer at the SRC centers. If these traditional elders failed to reach an agreement, the third accepted party intervened; the SRC always played the role of the third party.

The second level of reconciliation was called "social reconciliation." Its aim was to conduct workshops, seminars, and lectures. Social reconciliation targeted the intellectuals marginalized during the civil war, most of whom were unemployed and excluded by the warlords from playing any role in the communities. Noticeably, the uneducated warlords

---

105. Sheikh Axmad Abarone, former director of SRC, interviewed by the author on July 4, 2006, Mogadishu, Somalia.
106. Ibid.
107. Ibid.

and their militia chiefs abhorred the educated elite of their sub-clans and considered them potential competitors for political power. This group of intellectuals included university professors and teachers, government officials, and officers in the military, among others. Many of these intellectuals had no opportunity to meet and discuss social and political issues because of the clan divisions. Many of them were classmates, colleagues, and co-workers. There were no social and cultural activities, and everyone was living secluded in their clan ghettos.[108] The SRC targeted these intellectuals by organizing seminars, symposiums, workshops, and lectures. The reconciliation centers played the role of a social club that these intellectuals frequented and where they organized programs. Some services were provided by the libraries of the centers, such as tea service and reading materials. Of course, most of the materials in the centers were Islamic literature and, in particular, that propagating the MB ideology. For example, according to Abukar Sheikh Nuur, "there were books of Hasan al-Banna, Sayid Qutub, Yusuf al-Qardawi, Fathi Yakum, and many others. Moreover, audio and video facilities were provided to allow the people to listen to hundreds of lectures in the Somali language produced by Islah scholars."[109] The impact of social reconciliation was great and lasting. Abukar Sheikh Nuur Jumcaale, one of SRC directors says: "I remember the first workshop we held in northern Mogadishu where we invited intellectuals from the southern part of the city controlled by General Caydiid. Old friends from armed forces and professors had met for the first time in four years and tears were shed from

---

108. Abukar Sheikh Nuur Jimcaale, former Executive Director of the Somali reconciliation Council (SRC) interviewed by the author on July 15, 2009, Djibouti.
109. Ibid.

many of them to see each other alive."[110] Hundreds of these intellectuals became part of the SRC, and some of them participated in the reconciliation activities between the clans. Moreover, many of them were influenced by the work of Islah and later joined this organization. As some of these intellectuals became the backbone of the emerging civil society,[111] social reconciliation was very successful in mobilizing educated Somalis and connecting them with Islah as sympathizers or members. As reports demonstrate, from 1994–1996, the SRC conducted 78 local reconciliations in 11 regions, in which 2,710 individuals participated. Moreover, during these three years, 132 lectures and 20 seminars and workshops were conducted.[112]

Reforming Political Wing of the Clans

The third level of reconciliation was political reconciliation. The slogan of this program was *"Man Yuslih al-qaba'il yuslih al-Somal"* (whoever reforms clans reforms Somalia).[113] This means that Somalis constitute clans and if the leadership of the clans is reformed, the whole society would be reformed. It is based on a practical bottom-up process. Prior to initiating national reconciliations, local reconciliations had to be bolstered. To achieve that objective, some individuals of Islah joined their clan-based factions, and others became prominent clan elders. For example, four Islah members were in the executive of the United Somali Congress-Somali Salvation Alliance (USC/SSA)

---

110. Ibid.
111. Ibid.
112. Al-Maktab al-Siyāsi, *Al- Ḥarakah al-Islāmiyah*, 22.
113. Ibid., 26.

and were pushing hard for peace and reconciliation.[114] As an example, Maxamad Axmad Beerey, became the secretary of education for the USC/SSA and played a great role in Islah's educational programs in the area under Cali Mahdi's control. Maxamad Beerey says: "I learned great deal in joining USC/SSA and serving my community and my organization in very delicate balance."[115] In fact, political reconciliation was the last part of the program and was initiated after acquiring some experience in understanding and dealing with clan culture. Its concept was derived from the practical application of the policy of "dealing with the reality." In demystifying clans and eliminating clan-phobia, Islah studied the internal political dynamics of the clans, their factions, and ways in which clans were transformed after the civil war. Of course, in the traditional system, clan elders and Islamic scholars dominated socio-political authority, and only recently have economic factors started playing a role in the urban centers.[116] However, after the civil war, two new power centers within the clans emerged, namely the warlords and heads of the armed militia. Therefore, pentagonal power centers were observed in most of the armed clans. The social, economic, military, spiritual, and political groups in these power centers had a specific role to play within the clan. For instance, the social wing was represented by the clan elders, whereas the spiritual wing was represented by traditional Islamic scholars. The economic wing included business people and the Diaspora community, which provided financial contributions for defending the clan and

---

114. Maxamad Axmad Beerey, former secretary of education of the USC/SSA, interviewed by the author in August 3, 2009. Hargeysa, Somaliland.
115. Ibid.
116. Ibid.

advancing its political agenda. Finally, the most villainous wing was the armed militia responsible for waging various forms of war. The clan faction leader or the warlords were the top leaders and represented their clans in the political arena. When these clan-based factions created a form of administration in their area of influence, Islah members could participate in such administrations and seek service portfolios in education, health, or reconciliation. Islah members were banned from any activities that could engage them in war and conflict. The remaining wings were the traditional centers of power of every clan, representing peace and reconciliation. Islah worked with these wings comfortably.

Reconciliation from Below: Shifting Paradigm

The Somali reconciliation was warlord-driven for 10 years (1991–2000) in a top-down process. These armed factions failed to reach any real peace and restore the state. They have been characterized as "a forgery of reality and a deceptive invention of the failed elites. ... It was observed that, wherever factions were weakened or dissolved, local administration generally emerged."[117] This was the case in Somaliland and Puntland, which succeeded in establishing local administrations after disbanding their armed factions, the SNM and SSDF, respectively. Other than an early conference that was held in Djibouti in 1991, four conferences were considered serious. The first conference in which all faction leaders participated was held in Addis Ababa in March 1993 under the UN sponsorship

---

117. Abdurahman Abdullahi, "Tribalism and Islam: The Basics of Somaliness." In *Variations on the Theme of Somaliness*, edited by Muddle Suzanne Liluis (Turku, Finland: Centre of Continuing Education, Abo University, 2001), 236.

and funded by the Peace and Life Institute of Sweden.[118] The other three major conferences were held in Kenya (1994), Ethiopia (1996), and Egypt (1997). Participation in all these conferences was mainly limited to the warring political factions based exclusively on clan affiliations. Critics of these conferences argued that the reasons for their continual failure were the policy of subversion and sabotage that existed between vying regional actors and the absence of civil society.[119] Nevertheless, after the continuous failure of these conferences, the image of the factions was tarnished to a great extent, and any possibility of reconciliation was significantly curtailed. Moreover, they lost the support of local people and regional sponsors. On the other hand, modern civil society in Somalia emerged in response to the conditions of the state collapse in 1991. It was also stimulated by the worldwide tendency in the late 1990s toward democratization, which started after the end of the Cold War. Moreover, the most significant threshold for modern civil society occurred during the US-led multilateral military intervention in Somalia in 1992 and the subsequent influx of hundreds of international NGOs.[120] These NGOs required local partners to reach out to distant locations and to facilitate access to local populations, given the precarious security situation at that time. In addition, UN agencies also needed these partners to implement small-scale development

---

118. At the conclusion of this conference, it was agreed that at the next conference, the participants would be representatives of the 18 regions of Somalia, each region sending four delegates, including one woman. However, the next conference failed, and women never participated.
119. Abdullahi, "Tribalism and Islam", 237.
120. On the emergence of the local NGOs, refer to Abdurahman Rage, "Somali NGOs: A Product of Crisis," in *Mending Rips in the Sky*, eds. Adam Hussein & Richard Ford (Asmara: Red Sea Press, 1997).

projects. Hence, thousands of Somali NGOs mushroomed throughout the country, many of them as implementing partners. Most of these transient organizations were disbanded with the departure of the international forces and the international NGOs from Somalia in 1995. However, some dedicated local NGOs remained in the area of humanitarian operations, with their focus being primarily on education, health, peace advocacy, human rights, and professional networking. These NGOs depended mainly on locally-generated funds and advanced their organizational capacities by networking. Many of such NGOs were established by Islah members, in particular in the field of education and youth development. Therefore, coordinated efforts of the traditional civil society were mobilized under the auspices of the SRC, and modern civil society served to further weaken warlords and prepare Somalia for innovative reconciliation driven by civil society. Indeed, Islah contributed much to the transformations that were taking place in all sectors of Mogadishu, which had created new dynamics beyond warlord domination.

The new socio-political dynamics in Mogadishu encouraged the Djibouti government to initiate a new reconciliation attempt driven by the civil society, a paradigm shift after 10 years of failed processes. This initiative was a remarkable milestone for political realism as the conference departed from the warlord-driven process, the concept of a "building block," and radical nationalist perspective.[121] Consequently, the hitherto underesti-

---

121. For further information on Building Block, see UN OCHA Integrated Regional Information Network for Central and Eastern Africa (IRIN-CEA), "Somalia, are building blocks the solution?" July 17, 1999. Radical nationalist perspective rejects any form of power sharing on the basis of clans called "Traditional Democracy". See Abdullahi, Abdurahman. "Women and Traditional Democracy in Somalia: Winning Strategies for Political Ascendancy."*African Renaissance*.4: 3 & 4 (2007).

mated factors of political division such as clans, minorities, religion, and women were accounted for, recognized, and addressed within the power sharing arrangements.[122] Djibouti President Ismail Omar Guelleh, in his capacity as the chairperson of the Intergovernmental Authority on Development (IGAD), articulated in his speech at UN headquarters on September 22, 1999 that any Somali reconciliation conference should be driven by Somali civil society. The Djibouti initiative coincided with the immense mobilization efforts in Mogadishu, which was pioneered by Islah. Many intellectuals, clan elders, Islamic scholars, and civil society organizations combined efforts to make a difference in Mogadishu. Similarly, Islah made a breaking-point decision in 1998 to work aggressively to recover the Somali state in an innovative way.[123] As a result, a delegation was sent to Puntland and Somaliland to explore such an idea with the leaders of these two administrations.[124] Also, "Mogadishu Reconciliation" was initiated in 1999 before the proclamation of the Djibouti conference. Islah was the backbone of this reconciliation conference that continued for about 10 months and participants were from all spectrums of people in Mogadishu. Subsequently, Mogadishu was prepared for a reconciliation driven by civil society. Islah mobilized itself for aggressive participation in the

---

122. For more information on the women's participation in the conference refer to Abdurahman Abdullahi, "Penetrating Cultural Frontiers in Somalia: History of women's Political Participation during Four Decades (1959-2000)."*African Renaissance*. 4:1 (2007): 34 54, available from http://www.scribd.com/doc/15418552/Penetrating-Cultural-Frontiers-in-Somalia-History-of-Womens-Political-Participation-in-four-Decades-19592000 (accessed on July 4, 2010).
123. Abdurahman Abdullahi, "Islah Movement in Somalia: Islamic Moderation in the War-torn Somalia" (paper presented at the Second Nordic Horn of Africa Conference, Oslo University, 2008), 21.
124. Ibid.

Djibouti conference and reached out to the Djibouti Reconciliation Commission as early in December 1999. A delegation from Islah visited Djibouti in December 1999 and had the opportunity to meet with President Ismael Omar Guelleh and exchanged ideas on the best way to conduct this conference.[125] The subsequent Somali Peace Conference was held in Djibouti in two phases. Phase one was inaugurated in March 2000 with the intention of mobilizing ideas and garnering support for the conference from a variety of Somali groups. The second phase was launched on May 2, 2000, and more than 2,500 Somalis participated.[126] The most difficult issue to be resolved was the criteria for acceptable participation in the conference. There were no political parties to share power, and all Somalis were divided into clans, which had no statistical data that could be considered in approaching power sharing. Therefore, after tedious discussions and consultations concerning all available options, the option of a clan-based representation ultimately prevailed. Although Islah supported a non-clan approach developed by Cabdulqadir Aadan Cabdulle, this approach was turned down by most of the participants who opted for clan-based power sharing formula.

The formula for political power sharing was based on the criterion of 4.5 quotas comprising four equal quotas for the major clan families: Dir, Darood, Hawiye, and Digil and Mirifle, and half of the quota for the remaining clans. This formula was based on an accepted temporary agreement until general

---

125. Dr. Ibrahim Dasuuqi interviewed by the author.
126. Official delegates numbered 810, consisting of four clan delegations of 180, each including 20 women, and 90 minority clan alliance representatives, including 10 women. Among the 810 delegates, women gained 90 delegate places, or about 9% of the delegates. In addition, more than 1,500 observers were allowed to attend the conference.

elections were held and "one person one vote" system replaces clan quota system. Until then, it is very difficult to come up with acceptable and legitimate participatory system. The same system was used in Somaliland and Puntland, and, lately, Somaliland political participation transformed its clan-based system into political party system.[127] Women lobbied for separate clan status because the clans did not include them among their official delegates. Thus, women gained separate clan status with the strong support of the Djibouti President Guelleh, civil society groups and Islah movement.[128] As a result, they were able to participate in all aspects of the conference as the sixth clan. The quota system adopted by the conference allocated 44 seats to each of the four major clans; 24 seats to the alliance clans, and 25 seats to women. In addition, 20 seats were designated for selected individuals as an adjustment and reconciliation gesture. Islah members actively participated in this process and established an operation center in Djibouti. They considered that their major achievements would be: (1) participating in restoring national Somali state, (2) adopting National Charter compliant with the Islamic principles, (3) and gaining respectable number in the national assembly. Islamization of the constitution was a life-long project of Islah. The new charter was regarded as the most Islamized Constitution in the history of Somalia. It included two important provisions. Article 2.2 states, "Islam shall be the

---

127. Somaliland started its institution by clan power sharing; however, it was transformed into a political party system. The law permitted only three parties. Recently, free and fair elections were conducted in Somaliland. A presidential election was held on June 26, 2010.
128. Abdurahman Abdullahi, "Penetrating Cultural Frontiers in Somalia: History of Women's Political Participation during Four Decades (1959-2000)." *African Renaissance* 4, no. 1 (2007): 34-54.

religion of the state and no other religion or ideas contrary to Islam may be propagated in its territory."[129] Article 4.4 affirms that "The Islamic Shari'a shall be the basic source for national legislation. Any law contradicting Islamic Shari'a shall be void and null."

Besides gaining Islamization of the Constitution, members of Islah became members of the parliament and cabinet ministers. Benefiting from their policy of "dealing with the reality," they were selected by their clans. Thus, Islah received 24 seats in the parliament out of 245, which is about 10%. For instance, Dr. Ibrahim Dasuuqi, a prominent medical doctor and Islamic scholar, became an MP. Moreover, Dr. Ali Baasha, a medical doctor and current chairman of Islah, also became an MP. Nonetheless, Islah was dismayed with the government in the first few months because of its internal conflicts and lack of progress. Whatever caused the inaction of the interim government, such as backlash from the 9/11 or Ethiopian opposition, there was no doubt that the regime created in Djibouti failed to meet the high expectations of the Somali people. Nonetheless, the legacy of this conference in creating a new model for traditional democracy remains in history as the best reconciliation ever performed for Somalia. Islah actively participated in this conference and became politically prominent. One of the ramifications of the conference was: "The Djibouti conference caused Islax [Islah] to emerge on the political radar of Ethiopia and the United States."[130] Probably, Islah was given more weight because it was assumed that most of the prominent political and business personalities from

---

129. See the Article 29 of the Somali Constitution of 1960.
130. Hansen and Mosley, *The Muslim Brotherhood*, 53.

Mogadishu belonged to Islah. For instance, the idea was entertained that the elected President Cabdiqasim Salad was an Islah member, a claim both the president and Islah repudiate. Other observers characterized the conference, and exaggerated it, as a showcase for Islah. Matt Bryden wrote, "In early 2000, the Djibouti government's Arta conference became a showcase for al-Islah, which threw its political andfinancial backing behind the peace process and the Transitional National Government that ultimately emerged."[131] Therefore, the role of Islah alarmed Addis Ababa, which considered Islah an extremist organization affiliated with Itixaad. These concerns were expressed by Matt Bryden, who wrote, "Where Al-Islah played a key role and managed to secure itself a significant share of seats in the Transitional National Assembly (TNA) was viewed by Addis Ababa with some alarm."[132] Discussing the consequences of the Djibouti Reconciliation Conference for Islah is beyond the scope of this work; however, there is no doubt that the political profile of this organization improved substantially and subsequently exaggerated with its negative ramifications. This consequence is witnessed in the subsequent conference in Kenya in 2004 where Islah and authentic civil society groups were targeted and excluded from the conference by the organizers dominated by Ethiopia.

---

131. Matt Bryden. "No Quick Fixes: Coming to Terms with Terrorism, Islam, and Statelessness in Somalia." *Journal of Conflict Studies*, Vol. 22, No. 2 (Fall 2003), 39.

132. Ibid; 47.

The Social Strategy and Programs (1992-2000)

With the collapse of the state, almost all national institutions were ruined. The society reverted to a pre-state period in which clan affiliation was the only organization available. There was no central authority to administer justice or provide electricity and water, basic education, or primary health care. In particular, Mogadishu, an urban metropolis, became a ghetto for various sub-clans under the warlords.[133] In 1991–92, some international organizations and UN agencies provided limited services in the form of primary health care and relief assistance programs. The warlords cared less about essential services and frustrated humanitarian efforts by extorting and looting major part of the assistance. Thus, providing social services was left to the community networks, charity-minded individuals, and organizations. The strong Somali culture of social solidarity networks through relatives and religious communities was in place and saved many lives. Besides, voluntarism, which is part of modern Islamic activism, was revived to a certain extent. In that context, prior to the 1992 conference, Islah was already managing five schools in Mogadishu and initiated a provision for free medical services.[134] The social development strategy or "civil society option strategy", to borrow from Professor Hussein Adam "Tanzani", adopted in the 1992 conference was ambitious and offered priority to education.[135] The major

---

133. After the collapse of the state, USC militia divided the city into sub-clan quarters in which every sub-clan militia dominated specific districts and levied an unregulated tax called *"Legio"*.
134. Dr. Ibrahim Dasuuqi interviewed by the author.
135. See Hussein M Adam. "Political Islam in Somali History." In *Milk and Peace, Drought and War: Somali Culture, Society and Politics* edited by Markus Hoehne and Virginia

assertion of the strategy was not counting only on the potential capacity of Islah but envisioned the possibility of mobilizing the entire society to address the education issue seriously and in an innovative way. Andre Le Sage writes, "The promotion of education is one key area of al Islah activity."[136] Dr. Cali Sheikh says, "Islah's role in this venture was propagating the idea and setting the role model."[137] Providing modern education was seen as an indispensable means for the Islamization program as well for promoting peace and reconciliation in the society. Education aimed to nurture a new generation more committed to the values of Islam, peace, and national vision.[138] The question was how Islah should approach this strategic option and raise the necessary financial resources. This section traces the educational initiative of Islah and provides some examples of institutional models.

Educational Initiative of Islah

This initiative derived its inspiration from the MB founder Hassan Al-Banna who stated, "Islam liberates the mind, urges contemplation of the universe, honors science and scientists."[139] Accordingly, education was considered the central component "for forming human 'cadres' and Islamic vanguards bringing up the aspired generation of victory, whose members will

---

Luling (London: Hurst&Company, 2010), 119-135, 130. Also, Al-Maktab al-Siyasi.*Al-Haraka al-Islamiyah*, 11.
136. Andre Le Sage, *Somalia and the War on Terrorism*, 170.
137. Dr. Cali Sheikh Axmad interviewed by the author.
138. See Student's Prospectus (2007–2008): *Ten years of achievement (1997–2007)* (MogadishuUniversity, 2007), 1.
139. See Hassan al-Banna, *The Message of Teaching: article 18*, available from http://web.youngmuslims.ca/online_library/books/tmott/index.htm (accessed on July 6, 2010).

understand and believe in Islam in full, including knowledge, work, call and struggle."¹⁴⁰ This concept of education repudiates the delineation of human actions into secular and religious spheres. Instead, it emphasizes the concept of comprehensive religion, which addresses the metaphysical world as well as the temporal world. This concept is well articulated in the mission statement of the Mogadishu University, established by Islah, which seeks "to integrate social and Islamic values, scientific knowledge and technical skills required for sustainable development of Somalia."¹⁴¹ Based on that concept, "the purpose of Islamic education is not to cram the pupil's head with facts but to prepare them for a life of purity and sincerity. This total commitment to character-building based on the ideals of Islamic ethics is the highest goal of Islamic education."¹⁴² It is a holistic educational system that promotes spiritual enrichment and critical thinking.

Accordingly, one of Islah's objectives is "to strive in providing social services like education and health care."¹⁴³ It also developed the concept of "Bottom-up Educational Revolution" (BER), which derives its inspiration from the traditional Somali education system. This system showed considerable resilience, as it was based on faith and it was deemed necessary to educate children about their religion so that they could exercise Islamic rituals and duties. This

---

140. Yusuf al-Qardawi, *The Priorities of the Islamic Movement in the Coming Phase*, available from http://www.witness-pioneer.org/vil/Books/Q_Priorities/index.htm (accessed on June, 23, 2010).
141. See Student Prospectus, Mission statement of MU.
142. S. N. Al-Attas, *Aims and Objectives of Islamic Education* (London: Hodder and Stoughton, 1979), 104.
143. See the objectives of Islah, available from http://www.Islah.org/arabic/goals_objectives.htm (accessed on July 4, 2010).

education system was completely funded by the community. Therefore, the BER concept is founded to mobilize the entire society to consider the provision and funding of modern education similar to those of the traditional education.[144]

How did Islah ignite BER? Three elements were applied to mobilize BER: "raising awareness, setting a role model and generating competition."[145] In setting the role model, Islah members in all regions were encouraged to form non-governmental organizations (NGOs) and to open schools on a voluntary basis. Most of these schools began small at the perimeters of the mosques, and some were upgraded Qur'anic schools. Opening schools was a responsibility of the Islah chapters and part of their voluntary Islamic call. Many small schools started through this process and grew with community and Diaspora support. Some of these schools were large and played a pioneering role in Mogadishu. For instance, the school of *Mujama Um al-Qura*, initially supported by the Muslim World League and administered by Islah members, was the first of its kind in Mogadishu opened in 1993. The student population of the school exceeded 3,000 at all levels by 1995. Since the collapse of the state in 1991, the first 20 students from this school received high school certificates in 1995.[146]

Moreover, traditional and modern forms of education were integrated in an innovative way. Two ways of the integration were sought: admitting students to the Qur'anic schools and sending those from the informal Islamic circles to modern schools after admission tests and evaluations. This was easier

---

144. Dr. Ali Sheikh interviewed by the author.
145. Ibid.
146. Arabow Ibrahim, the principal of the school of *Mujama Um Al-Qura*, interviewed by the author on May 18, 2006, Mogadishu, Somalia.

for such students, as the instruction language of the modern schools was Arabic, and traditional education focuses on learning the Arabic language. In this way, many of these students began their education at intermediate levels or higher levels. However, the modern education curriculum had to include strong Islamic education and introduce practical Islamic components into the schools such as prayer places, safeguarding Islamic values and manners in all activities. Moreover, all types of schools openly benefited from community-funded education. In all ways, it served to promote the educational initiative of Islah by combining secular and religious education into a new hybrid system that had complementary features. It also served to advance the idea that all segments of the society should participate in education.

The second approach that ignited BER was to generate competition from other Islamist organizations, non-Islamists, and Western donors. In particular, Itixaad, which was entangled in armed conflicts from 1991 to 1997, thought that Islah's advancement in the field of education was winning the hearts and minds of the society. Thus, in the spirit of competition, Itixaad established many educational institutions. Besides that, competition was making major strides in all regions where education became the new field of clan prestige. As a result, all Somali communities were competing with each other to construct schools and raise funds for education. Also, Diaspora communities contributed to the education projects immensely by providing financial and technical resources. Moreover, competition was ignited between Arabic and English curriculum schools and between Arab-phones and Anglophones. In other words, competition was created between Islamists and non-Islamists. Anglophone schools were encouraged and supported by some Western donors in competition with the Arab-phone ones supported by Islamic charities.[147]

The role of Islamic charities and education in Arabic language alarmed many Western circles, in particular after 9/11. Islamic charities "were accused of being a financial channel for terrorist groups, propagating extremist ideology, recruiting Islamic militants, and providing a safe haven for terrorists."[148] Obviously, educational programs administered by the Islamist organizations attracted less support from Western donors who were promoting Western ideals of secularism. Moreover, Islah was aware of the lack of sustainability of Arab/Islamic donations based mostly on emotionalism, as most donors were interested in specific programs such as building mosques, helping orphans, and relief assistance.[149] Therefore, the strategy of Islah, since its inception in 1992, was founded on self-reliance. Two local sources of funding were activated to establish sustainable education programs: voluntarism of Islah members and community participation.

The voluntarism component was granted by the Islah members everywhere, but how could communities be motivated to participate in self-reliance educational programs? The Somali society enjoyed free education from the basics up to the

---

147. See Andre Le Sage and Ken Menkhaus. "The Rise of Islamic Charities in Somalia: An Assessment of Impact and Agendas" (paper presented to the 45th Annual International Studies Association Convention Montreal, March 17-20, 2004), available from http://www.allacademic.com//meta/p_mla_apa_research_citation/0/7/3/2/1/pages73214/p73214-1.php (accessed on July 6, 2010).
148. Ibid., 2.
149. Most of the charity givers in the Muslim world knew only traditional means of providing donations such as building mosques, assisting orphanages, digging small wells and so on. Shuayb Cabdulatif Bashiir, the executive director of ZamZam Foundation interviewed by the author in July 2009, 2010.

university level during 30 years of Somali state. Therefore, people were not psychologically prepared to pay for the education of their children in the modern schools, although they regularly paid for traditional education. Other than that, unemployed teachers were not prepared for privatization of education. Members of Islah held successive meetings with teachers and community leaders. Nonetheless, verbal motivation alone without showing the case as a model did not help much. Islah schools began to charge monthly fees of $1 dollar per student in 1993. This system of charging fees attracted teachers and schools who considered it a source of employment. Gradually, the fee was increased to $5–10 for all levels, and teacher salaries rose to $100–150 per month.[150] The system was self-sustaining and expandable, and hundreds of teachers found employment. Schools opened in every corner, and the education sector became the biggest employer.[151] In that respect, BER had succeeded, and Somali communities were educating their children. Of course, there were great challenges in the form of the absence of a regulatory body, curriculum standardization and certification, and gaining recognition from other countries so that students could attend universities abroad.

To address these challenges, Islah mobilized institutions and schools to create a national educational network.[152] According to Roland Marchal, "The main Islamic NGO at that time (and still today), al-Islah [Islah], contacted other schools that shared its orientation and set-up some kind of coordination

---
150. The self financing schools reached more than 25%. See Le Sage and Menkhaus, 13.
151. Mogadishu University estimates that more than 50% of its students work in the education sector as part-time teachers. Ibrahim Maxamad Mursal, director of administration, interviewed by the author on May 22, 2009, Mogadishu, Somalia.
152. See Le Sage, *Somalia and the War on Terrorism*, 170.

mechanism."[153] As a result, Formal Primary Education Networks (FPENS) were established in September 1998 by 14 local and international NGOs that conferred in Mogadishu, and the number grew to 32 charity members by 2002.[154] Founders of this network were Islah's social institutions and other Arab-phone institutions and schools. FPENS played the role of the Ministry of Education in the stateless Somalia. Its mission demonstrated a clear Islamic orientation. Its aims were "to revive destroyed basic education in Somalia with the community initiatives through participatory approach and community ownership concepts. This education shall be internationally competitive, community value-oriented and comprehensive."[155] By 2000, FPENS was administering 140 schools with a student population of 50,000, mostly from southern Somalia. This number grew to 100,000 by 2004.[156] Moreover, a unified high school certificate was issued, which was recognized everywhere in the world. Sudan was the first country to recognize FPEN's certificate, and other countries followed suit. This recognition was acquired when the president of the Mogadishu University met with the former

---

153. Roland Marchal, A Survey of Mogadishu Economy, 2002, 100 (research commissioned by European Commission, Somali Unit, Nairobi), available from http://www.delken.e c.europa.eu/en/publications/Mogadishu%20Economic%20Survey-Final%20Report.pdf (accessed on July 6, 2010).
154. Andre Le Sage and Ken Menkhaus, "The Rise of Islamic Charities in Somalia: An Assessment of Impact and Agendas" (Paper presented to the 45th Annual International Studies Association Convention, Montreal, 17–20 March, 2004), 18. For a good description of FPENS also see Saggiomo, *from charity to Governance. Islamic NGOs and Education in Somalia*.Manuscript from the author (to be published on Open Area Studies Journal, Bentham Publishers, in early 2011).
155. Abdullahi, *Non-State Actors*, 81.
156. Abdullahi, *Non-State Actors*, 81.
157. See Inter-peace and Center for Research and Dialogue (CRD). *A dialogue for Peace*, 2006, available from http://www.interpeace.org/pdfs/Publications_%28Pdf%29/ Current_Reports/A_Force_for_Change.pdf (accessed on July 5, 2010).

Minister of Culture of Sudan *Abdul-Basid Abdul-Majid* who became instrumental to the Sudanese positive decision on this matter.[157] Indeed, Sudan and Syria were the only two Arab countries who opened their educational institutions for Somali students during the civil war without restrictions. Somali students were treated as equals to the citizens of these two countries in the field of education. Besides FPENS, a new English-curriculum educational network emerged and competed with FPENS. This network was called Schools Association for Formal Education (SAFE). It was established in 1998 and provided an English and Somali language curriculum "with 234 teachers and employees to an estimated 15,000 students in 30 schools."[158] Moreover, there were hundreds of independent schools supported by the communities or international NGOs. The end-product of all this competition was a bottom-up educational revolution that took place in every corner of Somalia.

Higher education became a priority by 1995 with the success of establishing educational programs with community support. The problem was to absorb high school graduates to further their education and nurture new educated human resources for the country. The focus of Islah since 1995 was geared toward establishing a higher education program considered by the community to be in the domain of the state. It was unimaginable, from the public's point of view, to contemplate opening a university with non-state actors. However, with the dedication and commitment of Islah, Mogadishu University was established in 1996, the first of its kind in southern Somalia

---

158. Cali Sheikh Axmed Abubakar interviewed by the author.
159. Le Sage and Menkhaus, *Islamic Charities*, 31.

after the civil war. It generated various levels of competition in the field of higher education. Subsequently, every region opened a university.[159] The Mogadishu University was the biggest in terms of student enrolment, campuses, teaching staff, and international recognition.[160] Although the education quality may not have been satisfactory, the Somali people had established self-reliant programs in the field of education. The president of the Mogadishu University, the former chairman of Islah, said: "The vision of Islah is to continue playing the role model and to be the premier in the field of education. Let the competition continue and we push the horizon further. In this way, revolution in field of education is taking off."[161] Some examples of the educational institutions well-known for their leading role in this field are presented below.

Samples of Institutions Founded by Islah

Various organizations were established by Islah members in all Somali regions; some of these were charities, while others were social organizations such as youth and women development organizations. Some of these organizations were small and regional, while others were national and prominent in the country. Hansen writes that Islah's charities "in general are fairly successful and fairly moderate."[162] He adds that these charities "are efficient, and its policies of pacifism almost unique in a Somali setting."[163] Below, we will depict two

---

160. See 14 universities in Somalia and their ranks, available from http://www.4icu.org/so/ (accessed on July 5, 2010).
161. See Universities in Somalia: by 2010 University Web Ranking, available from http://www.4icu.org/so/ (accessed on July 5, 2010).
162. Dr Cali Sheikh interviewed by the author.
163. Hansen and Mesoy, *the Muslim Brotherhood*, 57.
164. Ibid., 58.

selected model samples of the successful institutions, namely, the Mogadishu University and the Tadamun Social Society (TASS).

Mogadishu University (MU)

The idea of establishing MU emerged along with reviving basic education through the community's initiatives. The initial idea was discussed in 1993 when a number of professors from the former Somali National University and intellectuals belonging to Islah congregated in Mogadishu. They explored the possibility of establishing continuing education program and to revive one faculty from Somali National University, in particular in Islamic and Arabic studies.[164] However, the initiative did not succeed at the time because of security challenges.[165] The idea was revived in 1995, and this time the National Institution for Private Education (NIPE) was established to promote community-based education and to further develop the idea of establishing a university by the year 2000. A committee under NIPE, which was formed to study the proposal, approved the creation of MU in 1996. The dream came true when MU was inaugurated on September 22, 2007.[166] The opening of MU "was a defining moment for the recreation of a nation defiant to despair," says Ali Sheikh, the president of the University.[167] The first MU campus was located in the former Maxamuud Axmad Cali Secondary School; however, the university constructed its own large campus in Mogadishu with

---

165. For more details on the historical development of MogadishuUniversity, see, Abdurahman Abdullahi, *Non-State Actors*, 72-79.
166. The University center was looted by militias, see Ibid.
167. See the official website http://www.mogadishuuniversity.com/. Also, Student's Prospectus (2007-2008), 5.
168. Ali Sheikh Ahmed interviewed by the author.

the assistance of the Islamic Development Bank in Saudi Arabia and other donors. It also constructed another campus in Bossaso in 2009. Nevertheless, the road to establishing MU was not easy. Several times, MU was looted and destroyed by the militias; however, it survived against all odds.

MU is the largest university in the war-torn Somalia with many faculties and multiple specializations.[168] It enjoys international recognition and is a member of a number of regional and international organizations.[169] It ranked among the top 100 universities in Africa.[170] It has two campuses in Mogadishu and Bossaso and runs post-graduate programs in collaboration with Sudanese and Malaysian universities.[171] During the past 15 years, about 15,000 students were enrolled and about 5,000 students have graduated in different specializations.[172] MU places a special emphasis on the education of women and has adopted affirmative action to increase their enrolment. Under a special program called "Young Women Leadership Scholarship (YWLS)", hundreds of female students received scholarships, which increased their enrolment from 9% in 1997 to 35% by the 2009–2010 academic years.[173]

---

169. Abdinoor Abdullahi, *Constructing Education in the Stateless Society: The Case of Somalia* (PhD thesis submitted to the University of Ohio, 2007), 80.
170. The university is a member of the Federation of Islamic World Universities (FIWU), Association of Arab Universities (AAU), Islamic Universities League, and Association of African Universities (AAU). It had also established bilateral links with AalborgUniversity in Denmark, KansasUniversity in the USA, and many others. See Student's Prospectus (2007–2008), 32.
171. See 2010 University Ranking: Top 100 Universities and Colleges in Africa, available from http://www.4icu.org/topAfrica/ (accessed on July 5, 2010).
172. The post-graduate program is conducted in collaboration with OmdurmanUniversity in Sudan and Open University of Malaysia. See student's prospectus (2007–2008), 26.
173. See unpublished statistical report of MU in the academic year 2012–2013.
174. Ibid.

Finally, MU operates in the epicenter of the Somali conflict and is considered one of the success stories in Somalia during the civil war. It was characterized as a "beacon of hope."[174] Without doubt, argues Le Sage, "the success of Mogadishu University has brought a significant degree of attention and prestige to the [Islah] movement – both from within Somalia and internationally."[175] Finally, Marian Warsame, a Somali medical doctor from the Diaspora who visited the university in 2002, wrote in the visitor's book: "This is a group will, a group of Somalis who have vision, ambition and dedication."[176] Besides providing educational opportunities to thousands of Somalis, MU also promotes Islamic moderation in line with Islah's moderate view of Islam. There are four general university requirement courses to familiarize all students with Islam and its contemporary development. These are Islamic Civilization, Contemporary Islamic Issues, Islamic Education, and Islam and State. These four subjects inform all students about Islam, at the same time aiming to diminish all forms of extremism in abundance in Somalia.

Tadamun Social Society (TASS)

Based on the concept of providing services to the society, TASS was established in 1992 by Islah members who escaped civil war in Mogadishu and retuned to their original home in Puntland. Upon establishing this development institution, they distinguished themselves from Itixaad which was a formidable

---

175. See Abdulatif Dahir, "Varsity strives as beacon of a hope amid chaos", available from http://www.upiu.com/articles/varsity-strives-as-a-beacon-of-hope-amid-chaos (accessed on July 5, 2010).
176. Le Sage, *Somalia and the War on Terrorism*, 171.
177. A note of Marian Warsame (MD, PhD), visitor's book at MU on July 28, 2002.

force to reckon with in Bossaso by 1992.[177] TASS was registered with the local SSDF authority and initiated development programs, while Itixaad was engaged in a war with SSDF. According to its profile, TASS is "a non-governmental, non-profit and non-political organization that was established in 1992 by national intellectuals who felt the importance and need in the region of such an NGO."[178] Its vision is to participate in the building of the Somali society by improving livelihood and restoring the dignity and rights of the Somali people. Its mission is to work toward promoting peace and stability, social development through education, as well as health, water, and disaster preparedness. TASS's main areas of intervention are education, health, water, youth, and women. It cooperates with a number of UN agencies such as UNFPA, UNICEF, and ILO. It also partners with the International Islamic Development Bank (IDB), Novib Oxfam, and Mercy-USA. Through donors, TASS carries out projects with an annual budget of $1.5 million –$3 million, while 30% of these funds are raised by the Somali community through schools run by TASS.[179] TASS has offices in the main Puntland towns of Bossaso, Garoowe, and Gaalkacyo as well as projects in other regions. Their budget and scope of operations is unparalleled in Puntland.

The major activities of TASS are in the field of education. It runs 22 community schools in five regions, one large technical college of veterinary medicine in Galkayo and Ajyaal institutes in Garowe and Bosaso and PANCARE institute for teacher

---

178. Abdishakur Mire, *Koboca Islamiyiinta* (unpublished manuscript, 2010).
179. See the official website of TASS available from http://www.tadamun.org/ (accessed on July 3, 2010).
180. Ibid.

training in Puntland main towns.[180] TASS also promotes women's education and supports five schools in Bossaso through direct sponsorship to 400 female students as well as hires female teachers. Similarly, TASS has trained female school-dropouts in crucial trades such as tailoring, handcrafts, hygiene, first-aid, and cookery. In the healthcare field, TASS focuses on tuberculosis, which is endemic to Somalia; TASS claims to have cured about 2,014 individuals since 1996.[181] In the field of water management, TASS has drilled 56 hand-dug wells and a number of boreholes. In the field of Islamic work, it runs a number of Qur'anic schools and mosques. TASS is a model of "Al Islah's ability to provide these services on a private basis, using funds donated by activists and private sector business models, and with minimal foreign assistance, is a strong demonstration of the potential success of their platform for change."[182]

Conclusion

In the turbulent time since the collapse of the Somali state in 1991, the entire society drifted into extremism and was polarized into clans. Clan-based armed factions could not agree on any peaceful political settlement. The formation of an interim government was the beginning of successive fighting between various factions, including within the USC. In the northern part, SNM proclaimed a separate state in May 1991. An unprecedented humanitarian effort in response to the

---

181. TASS Anunal Report, 2014.
182. Ibid.
183. Andre Le Sage, "Somalia and the War on Terrorism: Political Islamic Movements and US Counter-terrorism Efforts" (PhD diss., Jesus College, Cambridge University, 2004), 182.

disaster in southern Somalia aroused the international community, and UN forces were dispatched to Somalia in 1992. Without a doubt, the presence of the UN forces saved lives, weakened warlords, and promoted civil society and the business sector. Nevertheless, these forces were evacuated in 1995 without leaving behind any form of functioning governance.

During this difficult time, Islah adhered to its principles of peaceful reform in a violence-appealing atmosphere. Islah promoted an anti-war and pro-reconciliation platform in 1991–1992. Yet, its attempts to establish a common Islamist Front with other Islamic organizations failed. Therefore, acting alone, Islah developed a new organizational style and remodeled its recruitment process. Moreover, it offered special care to its members through solidarity and charity networks and extended that service to the public. As a result, new branches were established in all regions and in the Diaspora. During its first conference in July 1992, some misunderstandings were resolved regarding safeguarding the internal unity of Islah. The rebirth of Islah brought a new political and social strategy and a decentralized form of organization.

The political strategy of Islah adopted an innovative model of political participation that was flexible, doable, and appropriate in a chaotic situation. Accordingly, a policy of political realism was embraced. The aim of the policy was to consider Islamic activities without restrictions and transform them into a dynamic process that changed with shifting conditions, time, and space. This policy alleviated the clanphobia among the members of Islah and emboldened them to participate in the social affairs of the communities. Two complementing programs were initiated for political participation. A collective program was conducted through the SRC and individual efforts of the members who joined existing political entities. The mobilization efforts of Islah within traditional and modern civil society in 1995–1999 culminated in the Reconciliation Conference held in Djibouti in 2000. Islah's role was prominent, and it had succeeded in effectively restoring the national Somali state and the Islamization of the charter, and had 10% of the deputies in the National Assembly.

The social strategy of Islah formulated at the 1992 conference was to mobilize the entire society in a "Bottom-up Educational Revolution," inspired by the sustainable traditional system of education regarding ownership and financing. Three combined approaches were used for this venture: raising awareness, setting a role model, and generating competition. However, the sustainability of these programs depended on the success of the self-reliance and prioritization of education within communities. Fierce competition that took place between various groups, and demand for education grew extensively, which further expanded the education sector. This sector became the biggest employer in Somalia. Islah-established institutions advanced the horizon of competition further. The Mogadishu University, the largest higher educational institution in Somalia, and TASS in Puntland are the examples of such successful institutions.

CHAPTER SIX

Conclusion and the Aftermath of 9/11

Conclusion of the Research

History is a subjective process of recreating past occurrences and is also a matter of perspective depending on some theoretical assumptions. Thus, modern Somali scholarship is dominated by the schools of modernization and dependency theories, both of which offer perspectives that are rooted to the secular Western philosophies. These two perspectives view Islam from the margins of history and through Orientalist and secularist discourses and security perspectives. This dissertation aims to reconstruct the history of the Islamic movement and its evolution in the period (1950-2000). The perspective employed departs from these two perspectives and adopts a post-colonial framework. Post-colonialism is a useful means of confronting the residual effects of colonialism on cultures of the colonized people and provides space for multiple voices. It allows revisiting formerly constructed history of Islam and narrating its modern development from the local viewpoint. Besides post-colonialism, this dissertation is informed by two other theoretical discourses. The first theory is the Khaldunite theory of Asabiyah founded on the premise that tribal societies can establish functional states only by making use of some "religious coloring", thereby giving a distinctive character to and exerting an influence on the society. "Coloring" is a general term that may be interpreted in different ways, but here we mean by seeking legitimacy through making ultimate reference to Islam. Thus, this dissertation argues that it is very difficult to recover the collapsed Somali state without addressing the hitherto conflicting Somali equation of clan, Islam, and the state in a new social contract. This social contract should provide comprehensive reconciliation between all the components of tradition and modernity. The second discourse in this dissertation is the road map of social movement theory applied to the Islamist movement as part of the similar global social phenomenon in terms of the mechanism of activism and collective actions. It traces the multiple crisis factors introduced by the Western modernity during colonialism and in the post-colonial state, which provoked various Islamic responses in different historical contexts. These include the responses that grew radical whenever radical policies were applied in the form of external armed intervention or radicalized secularism. In particular, the theory of social movement is utilized in keeping the orientation of the historical reconstruction and analysis of the Islah movement through difficult decades of social and political turbulence in Somalia.

Islam, according to the successive Somali constitutions, is the religion of the state and society. Its introduction to Somalia is argued to have taken place in the early years of the Muslim migration to Abyssinia. However, historians agree that Islam was practiced in Somalia and reached its different parts peacefully through trade and migration in the first century of the Muslim calendar (700-800 AD) registering mass conversion between eleventh and thirteenth centuries AD. Nonetheless, in the eighteenth century with improved systems of Islamic education, increased settlement and urbanization, and revitalization of the Sufi orders, Islam was revived strongly.

Two major centers of Islamic learning have developed: the Banaadir coastal cities and the Harrar areas in western parts of Somali people's territory.[1] From these centers, Islamic education and Sufi orders were being revived, reorganized, and spread throughout Somalia. The impact of the Sufi orders in Somalia is enormous; their emergence diluted the rigid clan divisions and proved the irrelevance of clan affiliations in the Sufi leadership. In their countering the colonial regime, both militancy and moderation were used as they suited the conditions in the northern and southern parts. The result of their concerted efforts is that Somalia remains a mainstream Sunni territory with a unified Shafi'i school of jurisprudence. The modern development of the Islamic consciousness should be seen as historical evolution that includes a range of responses to the challenges from specific tensions – colonial incursion and its harsh policies. It was also concurrent with the growing nationalism in the second half of the twentieth century. Both of these ideologies – Islam and nationalism – constitute identities that shaped the modern history of Somalia overtaking the traditional system that was gradually declining. Within this system, a new form of Islamic movement emerged in successive stages.

Modern development of moderate Islamism in Somalia began with the rising Islamic consciousness in the 1950s being a product of both Nasserism with its Arab nationalism project

---

1. I use the term "Somali people's territory" as non-political term disregarding various names given by different countries and groups. This geographical area is inhabited by the Somalis, and was annexed by Ethiopia in the 19th century. It is had been given many names such as Ogaden (by colonial powers and Ogaden clan members), Western Somalia (official name used by Somali government), and, currently, after the establishment of the Ethiopian Federation, it is given by Ethiopia the name of the Somali State of Ethiopia.

and the opposing Egyptian MB ideology. Nasserism offered Arabic-language-based education and Islamic culture, which strengthened Somali capacity to counter Western acculturation in the 1950s and 1960s and implanted the early Islamic consciousness. Somalia, being a geopolitically strategic backyard of the Egyptian Nile River and Suez Canal waterways, received special Egyptian consideration, reciprocated with Somali irredentism that needed to secure Egyptian support against Ethiopia. However, within Nasser's rigorous Arabization agenda, the MB has quietly introduced its ideology and Islamic activism by 1953. Moreover, moderate Islamism is also a reaction to the Christianization and Westernization of elite culture that became evident in the 1950s. It is not against modernity, broadening its definition from exclusively denoting Western European culture to cosmopolitan and acknowledging "multiple modernities," a post-colonial perspective.[2] Concerted activities of the Christian missionaries such as the Mennonite Mission, Sudan Interior Mission, and Roman Catholic Mission led to immense Islamic agitation and provoked various responses. The early reaction was pioneered in the 1950s by the organization of the Islamic League founded by Shariif Maxamuud Cabdiraxman in southern Somalia and *Hizbu Allah* of Sayid Axmad Sheikh Muse in northern Somalia. These organizations promoted Arabic and Islamic studies and invigorated Somali connections with the Arab world, in particular, Egypt.

---

2. See Gerard Delanty. "Modernity."*Blackwell Encyclopaedia of Sociology*, edited by George Ritzer. 11 vols (Malden, Mass.: Blackwell Publishing, 2007). See also, Shmuel Noah Eisenstadt. *Comparative Civilizations and Multiple Modernities*, 2 vols (Leiden and Boston: Brill, 2003).

The role of Islam in the state after the independence in 1960 remained much the same since the Somali nation-state inherited colonial system of laws and administration even though the new Somali constitution accepted Islam as the state religion. In practical application, however, Islam was not adopted as the ultimate reference for the state and played a peripheral role in the modern Somali state similar to that in other post-colonial Muslim nation-states. This means that despite the societal Islamic practice, the post-colonial state has been quasi-secular (cilmaani Uyaal), in the post-independence era and secular (cilmaani) during the military regime. The dissimilarity between the two periods is that Somali Constitution of 1960 indicated that the state was not secular; however, the way of life continued the secular trends prevalent during the colonial era. On the other hand, the ideology of Socialism adopted during the military regime that negated Islamic values qualifies the military regime as secular regime. After the independence, the secular trend of the state was challenged by the Islamist organization of Nahdah in 1967, which continued early Islamic scholars' efforts with more robust organization, wider activities, higher capacity, and closer attachment to the MB ideology. Moreover, besides mounting secularism and Christianization, American Peace Corps with their counter-cultural activities of the 1960s irritated many young Somalis. Some of the young generation mimicked Western cultures whilst others created defensive counter-culture organizations such as Waxdah in the north and Ahal in south in the late 1960s. The culmination of these defensive efforts produced the phenomenon known as "Islamic awakening" whereby young generation became more committed to the religious values and engaged in various Islamic activities.

With the growth of the Islamic awakening to counter Christianization, Westernization, and secularism by the mid-1960s, the harmonious Somali society in which religious and secular leaders collaborated, tradition and modernity coexisted, and tolerance and dialogue that were exercised began to falter and fall apart. The seed of the new societal conflict implanted since the early colonial rule was bearing its sour fruits after long process of gestation in reshaping the society. As a result, traditional leaders were integrated into the colonial system and Islamic scholars were contained and marginalized. Thus, the resurgence of new Islamic elites in the 1960s was a revival of early Islamic resistance to the Western culture with new peaceful approach and modalities. Following the footsteps of similar movements in the Arab world, in particular in Egypt, Somali Islamists established the organization of Nahdah in 1967. It came out to the limelight after the defeat of Arab armies in the 1967 war with Israel. This humiliating defeat set off a wave of soul-searching among Arabs and Muslims and demanded new ideology to take the place of the defeated Arab nationalism. Hence, the suppressed MB ideology took extraordinary prominence and received massive followers among Arab masses. The defeat also changed Egyptian political landscape inimical to MB after the death of *'Abdi Nāsser* in 1970 and the reign of *Anwar al-Sadat*. President Sadat pioneered a new and more liberal period and released long-imprisoned MB members. As a result, the decade of the 1970s became a golden decade of Islamic moderation and revivification of the peaceful MB methodology of the Islamic call. Islamism in Somalia also was boosted and intensified because of the indirect influence of the Egyptian MB and generous literature published during the economic boom in the Gulf States. Likewise, the military takeover in Somalia in 1969, adoption of Socialist ideology, and secularization programs provoked Islamic awakening already in motion in the 1960s. The major milestone of Islamist reaction in Somalia was the adoption of the secular Family Law in 1975 and the subsequent execution of 10 Islamic scholars. This occurrence was a defining moment in the history of Somalia in creating severe fracture in the societal fabric and heralding the clash of the military regime with the embryonic Islamist movement. The ramifications of this tragic event were far-reaching in terms of the fragmentation and radicalization of the budding Islamist movements. Moreover, the shock of the defeat of the Somali army in the war with Ethiopia in 1978 became another factor that instigated soul-searching. Likewise, the defeat of the Arab forces in 1967 war with Israel, the aftermath of the defeat in the war with Ethiopia in 1978, Somalia crossed the threshold to new hard phase of its history. From there, internal upheaval commenced and armed opposition movements and Islamist organizations were rallying for public support.

In the local context, Islamic moderation was gradually challenged after the military coup of 1969. The implication of harsh military regime's policies of curbing moderate Islamic activism and imprisoning prominent Islamic scholars in 1975 led to the underground Islamist movement run by young generations cut off from the proper guidance of Islamic scholars. Hence, misunderstanding and misinterpretation of Islam occurred, and young Islamic activists were vulnerable to embracing looming Takfiir ideology. On the other hand, many students who fled the country after 1975 were welcomed in Saudi Arabia and given admission in the Saudi universities where they received Salafia indoctrination. Within a couple of years, hundreds of the graduates from these universities were offered well-paid jobs as Islamic preachers and were sent back to Somalia carrying with them ample Islamic literature. This literature was aiming to implant Salafism and Hanbali jurisprudence creating Islamic conflict with the traditional Islam based on Ash'ariyah theology, Shafi'i jurisprudence, and Sufism. Salafia preachers called for what is termed the "Salafia theology" and considered Ash'ariyah and Sufism dangerous heresies. Moreover, new Islamic centers and mosques were built to serve as the staging sites for spreading Salafism. With its economic well-being, higher education opportunities, better and bigger mosques, and job opportunities, the Salafia movement attracted a large following in the 1980s. Moreover, connecting to the ideologies in the Muslim world, the extremist Takfiir ideology was introduced in Somalia and found a welcoming environment in the initial period. The reason was that, besides weak Islamic education among young Islamic activists, the higher echelon of leadership of Ahal such as Cabdulqaadir Sheikh Maxamuud and other prominent leaders embraced Takfiir ideology and induced young members of Ahal to follow suit. The Somali Islamic awakening could be characterized during the 1970s as immature with an emotional attachment to the Islamic ideology, very low organizational capacity, meager economic resources, and romantic approach to social and political realities.

In the global context, by the end of the 1970s, Islamic moderation was challenged with the triumph of the Iranian Revolution, which gave new hope for the possibility of establishing Islamic order through revolutions. This trend also was strengthened by the reign of General Ziau-al-Haq in Pakistan in 1979, which came to power through military coup initiating rigorous Islamization programs. The success in establishing Islamic order by means of revolution or military coup compared with little progress made by the peaceful and gradual means had attracted many Islamists. Moreover, two other events in the 1970s and early 1980s were highly instigative for the radicalization of Islamism. First was the Soviet invasion of Afghanistan and the beginning of the global Islamic Jihad against Communist expansion. The Jihad of Afghanistan was greatly encouraged and supported by the conservative Arab countries, the Western countries, and Islamist movements. However, its impact in planting the seed of extremism and violence became unprecedented. From there, the idea of Al-Qaida was developed, nurtured, and spread to the entire world. Secondly, the other important radicalization factor of the Islamic response was the signing of a peace treaty with Israel by the late president of Egypt *Anwar al-Sādāt* in 1981. This unpopular treaty traumatized Muslim masses and divided Arab countries, eventually causing the assassination of *Sādāt* by militant Egyptian Islamist group. All above-stated occurrences had ushered in a new era of the upsurge of extremism in the Muslim world in the 1980s.

Within these local and global contexts of rising Islamic banners, revolutionary ideologies, Islamist armed groups, and extremism, the Islah Movement was founded on July 11, 1978, 50 years from the time the MB was established in Egypt in 1928. It was germinating 25 years since the first footstep of MB in Somalia in 1953. The timing was appropriate, being immediately after the Somali defeat in the war with Ethiopia in 1978, and the organization proclaimed itself a peaceful Islamic opposition to the regime in contrast to the growing armed oppositions. Nonetheless, Islah was challenged by the military regime, growing Salafism, and competing Egyptian and Sudanese Islamist movements since 1982. The military regime undertook a ruthless agenda of destroying the Islah base in Saudi Arabia, where the founders of this movement worked and studied. It also offered special attention to its activities inside the country in partnership with the Egyptian intelligence which trained and coached its counterpart in Somalia. Nonetheless, albeit the regime's efforts curtailed Islah's local activities, they failed to eliminate its base in Saudi Arabia and its activities in the Diaspora. Moreover, the Salafia movement initiated as successor organization of Ahal, renamed itself as Jamaaca Islaamiyah and transformed into Itixaad in 1983. The creation of Itixaad was encouraged by the Sudanese Islamist Movement and its prolific leader *Ḥassan al-Turābi* who deserted the International MB led by Egyptian MB in 1982. Dr. Hassan al-Turabi undertook a plan of creating an African Islamic movement attached to Sudan rivalling Egyptian MB. Somalia was given priority in *Turban*'s agenda, and after numerous failed attempts to create a unified Islamist organization from all shades of ideologies, Islah was singled out to be isolated because of its linkage with the International MB. Moreover, moderate local MB organizations such as Ikhwan and Waxdah were weakened by either unifying with Itixaad or frustrating their potential unification with Islah to bolster Islamic moderation. No doubt, the *Turābi* factor played destructive role in weakening Islamic moderation and promoting armed extremism in the name of Islam, in particular when *Usāma bin*

Lāddin lived in Sudan. It could be argued that while Ethiopia was encouraging, hosting, and fragmenting Somali non-Islamist armed oppositions, *Turābi* was following the same strategy with the Islamist organizations. Radicalization of clans, represented by numerous armed factions such as SSDF, SNM, USC, and SPM, and radicalization of Islamism, represented mainly by Itixaad, were the general features in Somalia since the 1980s.

The formative period of Islah from 1978 to 1990 was hard and demanding. The early organizational weaknesses were evident, but throughout time, Islah was improving its organizational capacity and sharpening its strategy and programs. Its main achievements in the first decade were adhering to its methodology of Islamic moderation in a volatile and turbulent society and gaining membership in the International MB in 1987. Moreover, major public activities were the issuance of the Islamist Manifesto in 1990, the procurement of humanitarian assistance in the northern debacle in 1988, and the attempt to form a united Islamist Front. The latter project failed because of the continued fragmentation of the Islamist organizations and weakness in copping with the upsurge of extreme clanism. After the collapse of the state in 1991, Islah undertook a strategic policy of abstaining from the roving civil wars, raising the awareness among the population and its members of the calamity, focusing on humanitarian assistance and developmental programs, and sustaining its peaceful reform programs in a very difficult terrain of conflict and fighting.

During the difficult decade of the civil war in the 1990s, Islah adhered to its principles of peaceful reform in a violence-appealing atmosphere and promoted an anti-war and pro-reconciliation platform. Acting alone after the failure to establish an Islamist front, Islah developed a new organizational style and remodeled its recruitment process. Moreover, it offered special care to its members through solidarity and charity networks and extended that service to the public. As a result, new branches were established in all regions and in the Diaspora. Islah's first conference after the civil war of 1992 is considered to be its second rebirth that brought a new political and social strategy and a decentralized form of organization.

The socio-political strategy of Islah in 1992-2000 was flexible, doable, and appropriate in the chaotic and segmented societal conditions. The political component oozes from reviving the policy of "political realism" aimed to carry out Islamic activities more assertively and transforming this policy into a dynamic process changeable with the shifting conditions, time, and space. The policy of "political realism" alleviated habitual clan-phobia prevalent among members of Islah through years of underground activities and emboldened them to participate in social and political affairs of the society. Islah programs of institutionalized reconciliation, participation in the community activities and civil society work offered them experience that was tapped during the first National Reconciliation Conference in Djibouti driven by the civil society in 2000. The prominent role of Islah in the Djibouti Peace process achieved primary strategic objective that is Islamization of the National Charter and offered respectable political participation of 10% of deputies in the National Assembly. In its social strategy, the "Bottom-up Educational Revolution," inspired by the sustainability of the traditional system of education in view of the fact that it is owned by the community was emulated and reproduced. The three approaches used by Islah to promote grassroots education initiative was raising awareness, setting a role model, and generating competition among all groups. Because of societal cultural insights, educational initiative triggered fierce competition between various groups, and Islah-established institutions advanced the horizon of that competition further. Mogadishu University, the largest higher educational institution in Somalia, stands as the symbol of this venture whilst Tadamun Charity ranks at the top of the non-state actors in Puntland.

Finally, despite the first half of the 1990s was very difficult in terms of the voracity of the civil war; the second half presents a different picture. In the first part of the decade, Islah laid its organizational and strategic foundation of the social reform programs and political participation modalities. Nonetheless, the practical implementation of these programs occurred in the second half of the decade. The landslide change of the decade happened with the international intervention of 1992-95, which promoted economic recovery, emergence of civil society networks, and weakening of the ruthless warlords. The end product of the accumulative effect of this decade was the weakening of all forms of extremism—in the name of Islam and clan, promotion of moderation, and establishment of some administrations such as Somaliland and Puntland. Moreover, the experience of establishing administrations in Somaliland in 1991 and Puntland in 1998 encouraged a paradigm shift of Somali reconciliation from warlord-driven to civil society-driven. In 1999, the time was ripe for a new round of Somali reconciliation held in Djibouti in 2000, which was highly successful in restoring Somali ownership, adopting comprehensive national Charter that integrated all Somali equations—Islam, clan, and the state and to recover the national Somali state. The role of Islah in the reconciliation conference was prominent and complementary to the leadership and organizational skills of the Djibouti authority.

Finally, Islah's peaceful credentials in tumultuous period of Somalia are credited to its approach of Islamic moderation, internal democracy, level of education of its members, and its culture of collective leadership. Following table illustrate the four chairmen of Islah elected in the last 33 years and their qualifications.

Name of the Islah leaders (1978-2010)	Term in the office	Qualifications and current status
Sheikh Maxamad Nuur Garyare	1978-1989	BA in Islamic Studies in 1965, Islamic University of Medina, Saudi Arabia. He was director of Islamic affairs, Ministry of Islamic affairs (1969-1973). Currently lives in Toronto, Canada.
Dr. Maxamad Cali Ibrahim	1989-1999	PhD in Hadith Science in 1994, Islamic University of Medina, Saudi Arabia, expelled from Islah in 2006 after joining Union of Islamic Courts defying non-violence Islah policy.
Professor Cali Sheikh Axmad Abubakar	1999-2008	PhD in Islamic Studies in 1984, Islamic University of Medina, Saudi Arabia. Currently, he is the President of Mogadishu University.
Dr. Cali Basha Cumar	2008-2018	Medical Doctor in 1976 specialized in ophthalmology and lectured in the Medical Faculty of Somali National University, former member of the Somali Parliament (2000-2008)

Table 6. The four chairmen of Islah and their qualifications

Somalia in the Aftermath of 9/11 Terrorist Attack

In the aftermath of 9/11 and the Bush administration's proclamation of the Global War on Terrorism, Somalia was listed among the states that are potential havens for terrorism. Moreover, the United States included Al-Barakaat Group Co. (a Somali company), the *Al-Ḥaramain* charity (a Saudi charity operating in Somalia), and the Itixaad Islamist Movement on its list of suspected terrorist organizations.³ The first victim of the Global War on Terrorism was the Transitional National Government (TNG) claimed to have in its ranks many Islamists. Moreover, the TNG, in which Islah invested a great amount of effort, became dysfunctional because of many factors, including low capacity of leadership and the opposition of the warlords supported by Ethiopia. Furthermore, the aftermath of the 9/11 attacks and the agenda of the Global of War on Terrorism assisted Ethiopia for a new round of reconciliation conference that would empower the warlords. In this situation, even though the TNG was falling apart and was not resisting enough to the Ethiopian/warlord agenda, Islah, along with other civil society groups, were adamantly poised to defend the

---

3. "On 23 September 2001, less than two weeks after the 9/11 terrorism attacks in the U.S., President George W. Bush signed Executive Order 13224, which blocked the assets of 27 organisations and individuals linked to terrorism. Tenth on the list was a little-known Somali organisation, *al-Itihaad al-Islaami* (AIAI)". See, International Crisis Group, *Somalia's Islamists* (Africa Report N°100 – 12 December 2005), available from http://www.crisisgroup.org/~/media/Files/africa/hornfafrica/somalia/Somalias%20Isla mists.ashx. Also, see Abdurahman Abdullahi, "Recovering the SomaliState: the Islamic Factor." In *Somalia: Diaspora and State Reconstitution in the Horn of Africa*, edited by A. Osman Farah, Mammo Mushie, and Joakim Gundel (London: Adonis & Abby Publishers Ltd, 2007), 196-221, 196. However, on August 27, 2002, US removed from its list of designated terrorist list. See Terrorist Financing Staff Monograph, Al-Barakaat Case Study: *The Somali Community and alBarakaat, available from http://www.91 1commission.gov/staff_statements/911_TerrFin_Ch5.pdf (accessed on August 25, 2010)*, 85.

achievements of the Djibouti Peace process. Apparently, the political gambit was for the advantage of warlord domination and the Ethiopian agenda. As a result, the IGAD-sponsored Eldoret/Mbagathi peace process discriminated against and excluded Islamist organizations and prominent Somali civil society figures. Wrapping up, the exclusive warlord-dominated conference was concluded with the formation of the Transitional Federal Institutions and outright triumph of the Ethiopian agenda. Nevertheless, the warlord triumph proved short-lived with the internal conflicts of the assembly members and government, lack of governance capacity, and rampant corruption that paralyzed the recovery process of the state institutions.

Moreover, USA counter-terrorism covert operations offered financial and political support to the former warlords who established "The Alliance for the Restoration of Peace and Counter-Terrorism".[4] This alliance was aiming to uproot Mogadishu-based Islamists; notably the Union of Islamic Courts (UIC) in February 2006. However, this undertaking provoked an unprecedented upsurge of Islamic rage in Mogadishu under the UIC leadership, and the US-backed warlord program was aborted and dissipated. Thus, the political environment of Somalia changed dramatically with the outright victory of the UIC over the warlords and their uncontested power in Mogadishu and the surrounding regions. Nevertheless, the jubilation of the UIC was also short with the impasse of the peaceful dialogue in Sudan and escalation into a total war participated by the Ethiopian military with tacit US support.

---

4. The alliance consisted of 8 Mogadishu based warlords. See "Somali warlords hold 'secret anti-terrorism' talks with US agents: witnesses", *Agence France Presse*, February 28, 2006.

The UIC was defeated within a short time at the end of 2006, and a new round of resistance against Ethiopia began with various forces of different agendas.

Islamic moderation and peaceful reform of Islah expressed by its approach and performance had been strongly challenged again with the triumph of the UIC in Mogadishu. All Islamist organizations and many clan-based forces in Mogadishu except Islah and the Sufi orders had joined hands and participated in this venture. It had also been supported by the most Somalis in the Diaspora influenced by the skilful use of the media outlets by the UIC supporters. Nonetheless, Islah, being an organization with a track record of peaceful Islamic work, had publicly turned down to join the armed groups's project. On the other hand, the UIC clever use of Islamic, nationalistic, and clan mobilization tactics had attracted great popular support, and Islah was temporarily isolated and looked at as unfaithful to its Islamic and nationalistic agenda. Moreover, some members of Islah, departing from the policy and the program of their organization, were fascinated by the impressive success of the UIC and joined it. This situation pressured Islah leadership to take strong public action in distinguishing themselves from the UIC and to expel from Islah's ranks all persons who joined the UIC, including its former chairman Dr. Maxamad Cali Ibrahim.[5] This undertaking caused Islah high security risk to its members and institutions, and as a result, its activities were restricted, festivities banned, and some of its prominent members were

---

5. See Islah Communiqué on 21/6/2006 of the expulsion of Dr. Mohamed Ali Ibrahim from Islah, available from http://www.Islah.org/arabic/bayaan21-6-06.htm (accessed on August 14, 2010).

assassinated or displaced.[6] During this difficult period, Islah continued its program of reconciliation and tried to broker peace between the UIC and the government; nevertheless, this effort failed miserably by the rejection of the UIC.[7] Thus, Islah with its insightful understanding of the situation, personalities involved in the UIC, and looming extremist ideologies, adamantly and consistently distanced itself from their venture.

After the defeat of the UIC, oppositions gathered in Asmara, the capital city of Eritrea, and Alliance for the Re-liberation of Somalia (ARS) was formed in September 2007. Islah also refused to be part of ARS and while continuing condemning Ethiopian intervention and Transitional Federal Government policies.[8] It persistently remained firm in its policy of supporting Transitional Federal Institutions (TFIs) considered to be necessary for the existence of the Somali state. In maintaining this delicate balance of refusing to seek foreign power assistance to gain political power and objecting to all forms of violence among Somalis, which both the Transitional Federal government and the oppositions of ARS were exercising, Islah remained true to its principles of moderation. Moreover, it also encouraged reconciliation between the TFG and ARS held in Djibouti in 2009, which finally produced new TFIs that combine former TFG and ARS. However, the precipitate reconciliation process sponsored by the United Nations proved ineffective,

---

6. See Islah Communiqué on 17/8/2006 on the banning Islah festivities organized to commemorate its 28th anniversary, available from http://www.Islah.org/arabic/bayaan %2017-8-2006.htm (accessed on August 14, 2010).
7. See Islah Communiqué on 22/7/2006 on the formation of reconciliation committee between the UIC and the TFG, available from http://www.Islah.org/arabic/bayaan22-7-06.htm (accessed on August 14, 2010).
8. See Islah Communiqué on 26/7/2006 on the Ethiopian Intervention in Somalia, available from http://www.Islah.org/arabic/bayaan26-7-06.htm (accessed on August 14, 2010).

and TFIs remain dysfunctional under the protection of African forces (AMISOM). On the other hand, Al-Shabab, an extremist group ideologically affiliated with Al-Qaida, is in control in most regions of southern Somalia and extends its terrorist attacks to Uganda, Kenya, Djibouti, threatening other African countries that are contributing troops to Somalia security mission.

In the final remarks, since its inception in 1978, Islah had passed through four historical periods where its existence was endangered or its peaceful programs were in jeopardy; yet, all of these attempts had failed. The first period was in 1983 when the government of Somalia devised a plan to uproot Islah leadership from Saudi Arabia. The basic strategy was to convince the Saudi authority that Islah poses danger for its national security and the leaders of this movement should be extradited to Somalia. Undoubtedly, the aim was to be able to apply the national security law warranting them death penalty. The second period was when Ḥasan al-Turābi, the leader of the Sudanese Islamist movement, attempted to unify all Islamist organizations with different ideologies in 1992. If this strategy had succeeded, Islah would have either been divided or become part of Islamist militancy in Somalia.[9] Indeed, the tendency of rapprochement with the armed Itixaad and drifting toward militarism had some minority support within Islah leadership.[10] The third period was after 9/11 when Ethiopia attempted to put all Islamist organizations including Islah under the umbrella of

---

9. A similar process happened to Waxdah, which after uniting with Jamaaca Islaamiyah and forming Itixaad, was divided and weakened.
10. Some leaders during this period, in particular the chairman of Islah Dr. Maxamad Cali Ibrahim, his financial officer Cabdulcaziz Xaaji Axmad, and Sheikh Nuur Baaruud, were very supportive of establishing training camps and cooperating with Itixaad. Xassan Xaaji Maxamuud, interviewed by the author.

Itixaad listed among the terrorist organizations.[11] Finally, the most dangerous moment for Islah was during the UIC uprising in Mogadishu, which Islah snubbed to participate in. Subsequently, Islah was depicted through propaganda machine of the UIC as having pro-government, pro-Ethiopian, and anti-Islamic agenda. This situation deteriorated drastically when some former Islah leaders joined the UIC, led UIC delegation and were expelled from the organization.[12] During this difficult time, Islah was in the bottleneck, caught between Somali Islamist extremists and Ethiopian strategic venture in Somalia. Nonetheless, through all these dangerous historical moments, Islah has survived with its peaceful method intact and its organization sustaining and developing.

Wrapping up, the phenomenon of extremism in the name of Islam in Somalia is part and parcel of the worldwide project undertaken by al-Qaida and its associates. Somalia is simply an extension of that global movement, which depends on the global sponsors for the leadership, inspiration, guidance, and resources. Weakening extremism in Somalia depends on the success in the other fronts such as Afghanistan, Yemen, and Iraq. Indeed, extremism will not be solved by military might alone and requires concerted efforts of the countries in the region and a combined strategy that includes promoting Islamic moderation, raising awareness of the population, establishing

---

11. See Medhane Tadesse, *Al-Ittihad: Political Islam and Black Economy in Somalia: Religion, Clan, Money, and the Struggle for Supremacy over Somalia* (Addis Ababa: Meag Printing Enterprise, 2002).
12. Former leaders of Islah such as Maxamad Cali Ibrahim, Cabdulcaziz Xaaji Axmad, and Sheikh Nuur Baaruud, who joined the UIC and were expelled from Islah, were the same persons who attempted in 1991 and 1992 to make Islah deviate from its peaceful program by proposing joining hands with Itixaad and opening training camps which was rejected by Shura council of Islah.

responsible state institutions, providing educational opportunities and jobs for the young generations, promoting democratic system of governance, and minimizing provocative policies such as foreign military interventions. In these efforts, Islah's vision of Islamic moderation, inclusive approach to politics, educational programs, and its long-standing track record in these spheres is great asset for Somalia's future recovery and civic transformation. On the other hand, de-radicalization of the entire society living in anarchy and statelessness for more than two decades and the establishment of functioning state institutions in Somalia is a great challenge. Yet, it is possible to overcome with new approaches, resources, and dedication. This will further be possible if lessons are learned from previous reconciliations in the past two decades, which were excluding one group or another, and from reconciliation tailored toward power sharing model that produced low capacity leaders failing to attract public support and sufficient international assistance. Moreover, to recover Somali state, a pan-clan national civic movement is required that surpasses clan based organizations that invigorates the concepts of citizenship and democratic governance on the one side and accommodates Islam and clan system in a new social contract on the other. Only and only through that national movement with multiple persuasions and organizations united in the strategic goals of restoring Somali state and tolerant to each other, capable and qualified leadership emerges. This kind of qualified leadership will bring Somalia back to the family of nations as responsible state participating in the global peace and development.

Bibliography

Abdelwahid, Mustafa. *The Rise of the Islamic Movement in Sudan (1945-1989)*. UK: Edwin Millen Press, 2008.

Abdi, Sheik Abdi. *Divine Madness: Mohammed Abdulle Hassan (1856-1920)*. London, UK: Zed Books Ltd., 1993.

Abdinoor, Abdullahi. "Constructing Education in the Stateless Society: The Case of Somalia."PhD diss., University of Ohio, 2007.

Abdirahman, Mohamed Yusuf. *"Min ḍikriyāt al-Ḥarakah."* http://www.Islah.org/arabic/Tasiis1.htm.Islah official Web site (accessed on June 19, 2010).

Abdi-Samad, Asha."Brief Review of Somali caste systems: Statement of the Committee on the elimination of Racial discrimination," August, 2002.Available from http://www.m adhibaan.org/faq/somalia brief 2002.pdf (accessed on August 18, 2010).

Abdullahi, Abdurahman. "Tribalism, Nationalism and Islam: The crisis of the political Loyalties in Somalia."MA thesis, Islamic Institute, McGill University, 1992.

Abdullahi, Abdurahman. "Tribalism and Islam: The Basics of Somaliness." In *Variations on the Theme of Somaliness*, edited by Muddle Suzanne Lilius. Turku, Finland: Centre of Continuing Education, Abo University, 2001: 227-240.

Abdullahi, Abdurahman. "Non-State Actors in the Failed State of Somalia: Survey of the Civil Society Organizations in Somalia during the Civil War".*Darasaat Ifriqiyayyah* 31 (2004): 57-87.

Abdullahi, Abdurahman and Ibrahim Farah. "Reconciling the State and Society in Somalia: Reordering Islamic Work and Clan System." A paper presented at International Somali Studies Association Conference, Ohio State University, 2007.

Abdullahi, Abdurahman. "Perspectives on the State Collapse in Somalia. In *Somalia at the Crossroads: Challenges and Perspectives in Reconstituting a Failed State,* edited by Abdullahi A. Osman and Issaka K. Soure. London: Adonis & Abby Publishers Ltd., 2007: 40-57.

Abdullahi, Abdurahman. "Recovering the Somali State: the Islamic Factor." In *Somalia: Diaspora and State Reconstitution in the Horn of Africa,* edited by A. Osman Farah, Mamo Mushie, and Joakim Gundel. London: Adonis & Abby Publishers Ltd, 2007: 196-221.

Abdullahi, Abdurahman. "Women and Traditional Democracy in Somalia: Winning Strategies for Political Ascendancy."
*African Renaissance*4, no. 3&4 (2007): 23–32.

Abdullahi, Abdurahman. "Penetrating Cultural Frontiers in Somalia: History of Women's Political Participation during Four Decades (1959-2000)." *African Renaissance* 4, no. 1 (2007): 34-54.

Abdullahi, Abdurahman. "Islah Movement in Somalia: Islamic Moderation in the War-torn Somalia". A paper presented at the Second Nordic Horn of Africa Conference, Oslo University, 2008.

Abdullahi, Abdurahman. "Women, Islamists and the Military Regime in Somalia: The new family Law and its Implications." in Markus Hoehne and Virginia Luling (ed.) *Milk and Peace, Drought and War: Somali Culture, Society and Politics.* London: Hurst&Company, 2010, 137-160.

Abdullahi, Abdurahman. "Can We Surpass Clan-Based Organizations?" http://www.scribd.com/doc/15420091/Can-we-surpass-clanbased-organizations (accessed on July 6, 2010).

Abdullahi, Sayid Omar Moallim. "Somali Egyptian Relations." MA thesis, Institute of Islamic and Arabic Studies in Cairo, 2006.

Abdul-Majid, Najmi.*Eden (1839-1967)*. Eden: Markaz Ubadi li darsat wa Nashr, 2007.

Abdulqadir, Abdishakur. *"Lamḥatun 'an al-saḥwa al-Islāmiyah fi al-Somāl"*. AlJazeera Online. http://www.aljazeeraonline.net /index.php?t=9&id=31

Abubakar, Ali Sheikh Ahmed. *Al-Da'wa al-Islāmiyah al-Mu'āsira fi al-Qarni al-Ifrīqi*. Riyadh, Saudi Arabia: Umayya Publishing House, 1985.

Abubakar, Omar Iman. *Tajrubah al-Mahākim al-Islāmiyah fi al-Somāl: al-Taḥadiyāt wa al-Injāzāt*. Al-Qāhira: Dār al-Fikr al-'Arabi, 2008.

Abubakar, 'Ali Sheikh. *Al-Somāl: Judūr al-Ma'sāt al-Rāhina*. Beirut: Dār Ibn al-Ḥazm, 1992.

Abu Isway, Mustafa. "Salafism from theological discourse to political Activism." Available from http://www.passia.org/m eetings/rsunit/Salafism.pdf(accessed on November 8, 2010).

Abyan, Ibrahim Mohamud and Ahmed Gure Ali.*Non-formal Education in Somalia*. A document produced by the United Nations Education and Cultural Organization at a meeting of experts on alternative approaches to school education at the primary level, held in Addis Ababa, 6-10 October, 1975.

Adam, Hussein M. "Islam and politics in Somalia."*Journal of Islamic Studies* 6 (1995): 189-221.

Adam, Hussein M. "Historical Notes on Somali Islamism." A Paper prepared for the International Somali Studies Association conference in Djibouti, December 2007.

Adam, Hussein M. "Political Islam in Somali History." In *Milk and Peace, Drought and War: Somali Culture, Society and Politics* edited by Markus Hoehne and Virginia Luling. London: Hurst&Company, 2010: 119-135.

Adam, Fawzia Yusuf Xaaji. *Geedi Nololeedkii Yusuf Xaaji Aadan (1914-2005): Taariikhdiisii Halgan ee Waxbarashada, Siyaasadda, Dhaqanka, iyo Suugaanta.* London: African Publishing, 2007.

Ahmed, Ali Jumale. *Daybreak is Near: Literature, Clans, and the Nation-state in Somalia.* Lawrenceville, NJ: Red Sea Press, 1997.

Ahmed, Ali Jimale (edited). *The Invention of Somalia.* Lawrenceville, NJ: The Red Sea Press: 1995.

Aḥmed, Moḥamed 'Umar. "*Hiwār da'wi ma'a al-doktor Mohamed 'Ali Ibrahim.*" Available from http://www.somaliatoday.net/port/2010-01-04-21-22-23/349-2009-12-10-22-50-16.html (accessed on May 13, 2010).

Al-Attas, S. N. *Aims and Objectives of Islamic Education.* London: Hodder and Stroughton, 1979.

Al-'Eli, Sheikh 'Abdiraḥman ibn Sheikh 'Umar. *Jalāl al-'Eyneyn fi Manāqib al-Shaykheyn. Al-Sheikh al-waliyi Sheikh Aweys al-Qaderiyi wa Sheikh al-kāmil Sheikh 'Abdiraḥman al-Zayli'i.* (no date).

Al-'Eli, 'Abdiraḥman ibn Sheikh 'Umar. *Jawhar al-Nafisfi Khawās al-Sheikh Aweys.* Kenya: Sidik Mubarak&Sons, (no date).

Al-Banna, Ḥassan.*Risālah Al'Aqīdah.*Available from http://web.youngmuslims.ca/online_library/books/the_creed/index.htm#salaf_khalaf (accessed on June 20, 2010).

Al-Banna, Ḥassan.*The Message of Teachings.*Available from web.youngmuslims.ca/online_library/books/tmott/index.htm#understanding (accessed on June 20, 2010).

Al-Ḥarakah al-Islāmiyah fi al-Somāl (Islah).*Al-Ḥalah al-Rāhina* (The Current state of Affairs in Somalia), April 27, 1991.

Al-Ḥarakah al-Islāmiyah fi al-Somāl (Islah): *Al-Nidām al-Asāsi*(The Constitution of Islah).

Al-Ḥarakah al-Islāmiyah fi al-Somāl (Islah): Bayān (communique) no.7, issued on 5/01/1991.

Al-Ḥarakah al-Islāmiyah fi al-Somāl (Islah): Bayān (Communique) no.8 on the killing of its deputy Chairman on January 8, 1991.

Al-Ḥarakah al-Islāmiyah fi al-Somāl (Islah): Bayān (Communique) No. 2 on the Reason of Public Uprising, July 15, 1989.

Al-Ḥarakah al-Islāmiyah fi al-Somāl (Islah): Bayān (Communique) No. 4 issued on the detention of the Manifesto Group, June 12, 1990.

Al-Ḥarakah al-Islāmiyah fi al-Somāl (Islah): Bayān (Communique) No. 5 on Islamic Manifesto "Sawt al-Xaq", October 1, 1990.

Al-Ḥarakah al-Islāmiyah fi al-Somāl (Islah): Bayān (Communique) No. 6 on Islah position regarding the civil war, December 6, 1990.

Al-Ḥarakah al-Islāmiyah fi al-Somāl (Islah): Bayān (Communiqué) No.1 on the military regime's Attack of Northern towns, June 28, 1988.

Al-Ḥarakah al-Islāmiyah fi al-Somāl (Islah): Bayān (Communique) on Mohamed Ali Ibrahim. June 21, 2006. Available: http://www.Islah.org/arabic/bayaan21-6-06.htm (accessed on June 10, 2009).

Al-Ḥarakah al-Islāmiyah fi al-Somāl (Islah): Program for National Reconciliation issued on February 25, 1991.

Al-Ḥarakah al-Islāmiyah fi al-Somāl (Islah): Taqrīrun Shāmil (Comprehensive Internal Report) submitted to the Leadership in Saudi Arabia, July, 13, 1991.

Al-Hudeibi, Ḥassan.*Naḥnu du'ātun lā Qudāh (Preachers, Not Judges)*. Available from http://www.torathikhwan.com/saveb ook.aspx?id= 7 (accessed on June 24, 2010).

'Ali, Mohamed Aḥmed Sheikh. *"Itiḥād al-Maḥākim al-Islāmiyah: Al-Nash'a wa Tadawur wa Afāq al-Mustaqbal"*.Available from http://somaliatodaynet.com/news/index.php?option=com_co ntent&task=view&id=88&Itemid=31 (accessed on July 22, 2010).

Ali, Mohamed Baarod. *"Remembering the unsung and forgotten hero's of Labaatan Jirow"*. Available from http://www.somalia watch.org/archive/000409631.htm (accessed on June 25, 2010).

Ali, Salah Mohamed. *Hudur and History of Southern Somalia*. Place: Nahda Book Publisher, 2005.

Al-Maktab al-Siyāsi.*Al-Ḥaraka al-Islāmiyah wa al-'Amal al-Siyāsi*. Mogadishu: Markaz al-Qarni al-Ifrīqi li Darsāt al-Insāniyah, 1996.

Al-Mubarakpuri, Safiu al-Rahman.*The Sealed Nectar: Biography of the Noble Prophet*. Riyadh: Darussalam Publishing, 2002.

Al-Muḥami, Mohamed 'Ali Luqmān. *Rāid al-Nahdah al-fikriyah wa al-adabiyah al-hadīthah fi al-Yaman*. Collected works (Nov.6 1898-Mrach 22, 1966).Yemen, (no publisher) 2005.

Al-Muḥami, Mohamed 'Ali Luqmān. *Rijālun wa shu'ūnun wa dikriyātun*. Yemen, (no publisher) 2009.

Al-Najjār, 'Abduraḥmān.*Al-Islām fi Al-Somāl*. Al-Qāhira: Madba'at Al-Ahrām Al-Tijāriyah, 1973.

Al-Naqīra, Moḥamed 'Abdallah. *Intishār al-Islām fi sharq Ifrīqiyah wa munāhadat al-Garbi Lahu.* Riyad: Dār al-Marīkh, 1982.

Alpers, Edward. "Mogadishu in nineteenth century: A regional Perspective." *Journal of African History* 24, no. 4 (1983): 441-459.

Alpers, Edward. "The Somali community at Eden in the Nineteenth Century."*North Eastern Studies* 8, no. 2-3 (1986): 143-168.

Al-Qardawi, Yusuf.*Al-Ḥalal wa al-Ḥaram fi al-Islām.* International Islamic Federation of Student Organizations, 1989.

Al-Qardawi, Yusuf.*Islamic AwakeningbetweenRejection and Extremism.* Available fromhttp://web.youngmuslims.ca/onlin e_library/books/iabrae/chapter_1.htm (accessed on June 19, 2010).

Al-Qardawi, Yusuf.*MuhammadAl-Gazāli kamā 'Araftuhu: Riḥlat Nisf Qarn.* Beirūt: Dār Al-Shurūq, 2000.

Al-Qardawi, Yusuf.*State in Islam.* Cairo: El-Falah Publishing and Distributions, 1998.

Al-Qardawi, Yusuf.*The Priorities of the Islamic Movement in the Coming Phase.*Available from http://www.witnesspioneer.org /vil/Books/Q_Priorities/index.htm(accessed on June 23, 2010).

Al-Sālim, Ḥamdi al-Sayid.*Al-Somāl qadīman waḥadithan.* Al-Qāhira: Dār al-qawmiyah li dabā 'at wa nashr, 1965.

Alshāhid.*Qadiyat al-Shahr: al-Irhāb fi al-Somāl, Wahmun amḤaqīqah?* Special report on terrorism in Somalia published on January 15, 2010. Available from http://arabic.alshahid.ne t/monthly-issue/7789 (accessed on May 25, 2010).

Amin, Maxamad Husein. *Taariikhda Bangiyada Somaaliyeed.* Sharjah: UAE, Amazon Printing Press, 2004.

Aqīl, 'Abdallah. *Min I'lām al-Da'wa wa al-Harakah al-Islāmiyah al-Mu'āsirah*. Dār al-Tawzi' wa al-Nashr al-Islāmyah, Qāhira: 2000.

Assowe, Mohamed Omar. "Understanding the Emergence of Al-Shabab in Somalia". MA thesis submitted to the US Army Command and General Staff College, Fort Leavenworth, Kansas, 2011-02.

Baali, Fuad. *Society, State, And Urbanism: Ibn Khaldun's Sociological Thought*. New York: State University of New York Press, 1988.

Baars, E., and A. Reidiger. "Building the Bana Chain in Somalia: Support for Agricultural Marketing Service and Access to Markets (SAMSAM) experience." Available from http://www.new-ag.info/pdf/SAMSAM-report.pdf (aaccessed on June 19, 2010).

Bahau Addīn, Aḥmed. *Mu'āmaratun fi Ifrīqiyah*. Al-Qāhira: Dār Ihyā al-kutub al-'Arabiyah, 1956.

Barnes, Cedric, and Harun Hassan. "The Rise and fall of Mogadishu's Islamic Courts." Chatham House Briefing Paper, April, 2007. (AFP BP 07/02).

Barre, Mohamed Siyaad. *My Country and my People: Selected Speeches of Jaalle Siyaad*. Ministry of Information and National Guidance, 1979.

Bassey, Magnus O. *Western Education and Political Domination in Africa: A Study in Critical and Dialogical Pedagogy*. Westport, Conn.: Bergin & Garvey, 1999.

"Biography of Sheikh Abdulqani." The official Islah website. Available from http://www.Islah.org/arabic/Sh%20Abdulqani.htm (accessed on June 20, 2010).

Bradbury, Mark. *Becoming Somaliland*. London: Progresso, 2008.

Bryden, Matt. "No Quick Fixes: Coming to Terms with Terrorism, Islam, and Statelessness in Somalia."*Journal of Conflict Studies* 22, no. 2 (Fall 2003), 24-56.

Bryden, Matt. "Profile of Somali Islamic Courts." October 24, 2006. Unpublished paper.

Burton, Richard. *First Footsteps in East Africa.*BiblioBazaar, 2009.

Cabdullahi, Maxamad Xaaji "Ingiriis". *Taariikh Nololeedkii Sheikh Maxamed Macallin (the Biography of Sheikh Mohamed Moallim).*Available from http://www.himilo.com/?pid=content&aid=4 (accessed on December 17, 2009).

Caqli, Abdirisaq. *Sheikh Madar:Asaasaha Hargeysa.* (A Somali-language book on Sheikh Madar). No date or publisher.

Caroselli, Francesco. *Ferro e fuoco in Somalia: Venti Anni di Lotte Contro Mullah e Dervisc.* Roma: Sindicato Italiano Arti Grafiche, 1931.

Cassanelli, Lee. *The Shaping of Somali Society: Reconstructing the History of a Pastoral People, 1600-1900.* Philadelphia: University of Philadelphia Press, 1982.

Cassanelli, Lee and Farah Sheikh Abdulqadir."Somali education in transition."*Bildhaan: An International Journal of Somali Studies*7 (2007), 91-125.

*Catholic Church in Somalia.*Available from http://www.catholic-hierarchy.org/diocese/dmgds.html (accessed on October 30, 2010).

Chinua, Achebe. *Things Fall Apart.* London: Heinemann, 1958.

Clarke, Walter and Gosende, Robert. "Somalia: Can a Collapsed State Reconstitute itself"? In Robert I. Rotberg (ed.), *State Failure and State Weakness in a Time of Terror.* Washington: Brooking Institution Press, 2000, 129-158.

Contini, Paolo. *The Somali Republic: An Experiment in Legal Integration*. London: Frank Cass & Company, 1969.

Christianity in Somalia. Available from http://www.museumstuff.com/learn/topics/Christianity_in_Somalia (accessed on October 30, 2010).

Dahir, Abdulatif. "Varsity strives as beacon of a hope amid chaos". Available fromhttp://www.upiu.com/articles/varsity-strives-as-a-beacon-of-hope-amid-chaos (accessed on July 5, 2010).

Dastūr Munadamah al-Nahdah al-Islāmiyah (The Constitution of Organization of Islamic Renaissance), 1967.

Dawisha, Adeed. *Arab Nationalism in the Twentieth Century: From Triumph to Despair*. Place: Princeton Press, 2003.

Delanty Gerard. "Modernity."*Blackwell Encyclopaedia of Sociology*, edited by George Ritzer. 11 vols. Malden, Mass.: Blackwell Publishing, 2007.

Dexter, Lewis. *Elite and Specialized Interviewing*. Evanston: Northwestern University Press, 1970.

Drysdale, John. *The Somali Dispute*. New York: Praeger Publishers, 1982.

Drysdale, John. *Whatever Happened to Somalia?* London: HAAN Publishing, 1994

Ehret, Christopher. "The Eastern Horn of Africa, 1000 BC to 1400 AD: The historical Roots."In *The Invention of Somalia*, edited by Ahmed Jumale. Lawrenceville: The Red Sea Press, 1995, 249-58.

Elby, Omar.*A Whisper in a Dry Land: A Biography of Merlin Grove, Martyr for Muslims in Somalia*. Place: Herald Press, 1968.

Elby, Omar.*Fifty Years, Fifty Stories: The Mennonite Mission in Somalia, 1953-2003*. Place: Herald Press. 2003.

Elechi Amadi. *The Great Bonds*. London: Heinemann, 1969.

Elmi, Afyare Abdi. *Understanding the Somalia Conflagration: Identity, Political Islam and Peace building*. London: Pluto Press, 2010.

El-Safi, Mahasin."The attitude and Reaction of the Islamic Groups to US/UN Intervention in Somalia 1991-1995." In Jorg Tanze (ed.). *What are Somalia's development Perspective? Science between Resignation and Hope*. Proceedings of 6th SSIA Congress, Berlin 6-9 Dec. 1996. Das Arabische Bush, 2001

Eno, Mohamed. "Inclusive But Unequal: The Enigma Of The 14th SNRC And The Four Point Five (4.5) Factor." In *Somalia at the Crossroads: Challenges and Perspectives on Reconstituting a Failed State*, edited by Osman Abdullahi and Issaka Souare. Place: Adonis &Abby Publishers Ltd., 2007

Esteban, Demian. "Religion and State in Ibn Khaldun's Muqaddimah."MA thesis, Islamic Institute, McGill University, 2004.

Fakhry, Majid. *A History of Islamic Philosophy*. New York: Columbia University Press, 1983.

Farah, Ibrahim. "Foreign Policy and Conflict in Somalia, 1960-1990." PhD diss., University of Nairobi, 2009.

Fulbrock, Marry. *Historical Theory*. New York: Routledge, 2002.

Garraghan, Gilbert J. *A Guide to Historical Method*. New York: Fordham University Press, 1946.

Glanville, Luke. "Somalia Reconsidered: An Examination of the Norm of Humanitarian Intervention." *Journal of Humanitarian Assistance*. Available from http://www.jha.ac/articles/a178.pdf (accessed on June 19, 2010).

Goldziher, Ignaz. *Muslim Studies*, Vol.1, London: George Allen & Unwin Ltd., 1910.

Gottschalk, Louis. *Understanding History: A Primer of Historical Method*. New York: University of Chicago Press, 1963.

Haddad, Yvonne."Mohamed Abdu: Pioneer of Islamic Reform."*In* 'Alī Rāhnamā (ed.). *Pioneers of Islamic Revival*. Palgrave Macmillan, 1994.

Haji, Aweys Osman and Haji, Abdiwahid Osman.*Clan, sub-clan and regional representation 1960-1990: Statistical Data and findings*. Washington Dc., 1998.

Hansen, Stig, and Mesoy, Atle. The *Muslim Brotherhood in the Wider Horn of Africa*.NIBR Report, 2009.

Hasan, Noohaidi. *Laskar Jihad: Islam, Militancy, and the quest for identity in post new Order Indonesia*.SEAP Publications, 2006.

Ḥāshi, Ibrahim.*Al-Somāl bi Luqat al-Qur'ān*.Mogadishu, 1962.

Hassan, Abdelkarim A. "Somali Media, Ethics, Truth and Integrity". February 25, 2010. Available from http://www.wardheernews.com/Articles_10/Feb/25_Somali%20Media_abdel.pdf (accessed on June 30, 2010)

Hassan, Sheikh Mohamed Moallim. Interviewed by Mohamud Sheikh Dalmar in 1994. BBC, August 21, 2009. Available from http://www.bbc.co.uk/somali/news/story/2009/08/090821_falanqeynta21082009.shtml (accessed on December 17, 2009).

Healy, Sally. "Reflections on the Somali State: What went wrong and why it might not matter." In Markus Hoehne and Virginia Luling (ed.) *Milk and Peace, Drought and War: Somali Culture, Society and Politics*. London: Hurst&Company, 2010, 367- 384.

Hersi, Ali."The Arab Factor in Somali Society: the Origins and Development of Arab Enterprise and Cultural Influence in the Somali Peninsula." PhD Thesis, University of California, Los Angeles, 1977.

Hess, Robert. *Italian colonialism in Somalia*.Chicago: University of Chicago Press, 1966, 63.

Hull, Cecilia, and Emma Svensson.*The African Union Mission in Somalia (AMISOM): Exemplifying Africa Union Peace keeping Challenges.* Stockholm: Swedish Defense Research Agency, 2008.

Ibn-Khaldun. *Muqaddimah: An Introduction to History.* Transl. by Franz Rosenthal, (2nd ed.). London: Routledge & Kegan Paul, 1967.

Ibn-Taymiyah, Taqi al-Addīn Aḥmad.*Sharḥ Al-'Aqīdah Al-Wāsiṭiyah.* Translated and commented by Muhammad Khalil Harras. Riyadh: Dar-Us –Salam Publications, 1996.

Ibrahim, Cabdulaziz Cali "Xildhiban". *Taxanaha Taariikhda Somaaliya.* London: Xildhiban Publications, 2006.

Ibrahim, Sheikh 'Ali Ḥaji. *Al-Murshid fī mā Marra fi al-Ma'ārif al-Somaliyah fi al-Iqlīm al-Shimāli min al-Ma'ārik al-'Ilmiyah wa al-Munādarat al-Dīniyah.*Mogadishu, (no publisher).

International Crisis Group. *Somalia: Countering Terrorism in a Failed State.* Africa Report No. 45 (May 2002).

International Crisis Group. *Somalia's Islamists.* Africa Report No. 100 (December 12, 2005).

International Crisis Group.*Understanding Islamism.* Middle East/North Africa Report No. 37/2 (March 2005).

Inter-peace and Puntland Development Research Center (PDRC).*A Dialogue for Peace: Peace making at the cross Roads.* Inter-peace publications, 2006.

Ismael, Jamal Abdi. "Somalia: Research findings and Conclusions. African Media Development Initiative. Availab le from http://downloads.bbc.co.uk/worldservice/trust/pdf/ AMDI/somalia/amdi_somalia_full_report.pdf. (Accessed on August 15, 2010)

Issa-Selwe, Abdisalam. "The failure of Daraawiish state: The clash between Somali clanship and state system." A Paper presented at the 5th International Congress of Somali Studies, December 1993. Available from http://www.somaliawatch.or g/archivemar03/040629602.htm. (Accessed on August, 2010)

Isse, Aw Jama Omar.*Al-Sarā' bayna Al-Islām wa al-Nasrāniyah fi Sharqi Ifrīqiyah.* (No Publisher),1999.

Isse, Aw Jama Omar.*Safaḥāt min Tārikh al-'allāma al-Ḥāji 'Ali 'Abdiraḥman Faqigh (1797-1852).* Sana: Markaz Ibādi li dabāt wa nashri, 2009.

Jābiri, Moḥammad 'Ābidi.*Fifr Ibn-Khaldūn: Al-'Asabiyah wa Dawlah.* Dār al-Nashr al-Magribiyah, n. d.

Jardine, Douglas L. *The Mad Mullah of Somaliland.* London: Jenkins, 1923. New York: Negro Universities Press, 1969.

Jhazbhay, Iqbal. "Islam and Stability in Somaliland and Geopolitics of War on Terror."*Journal of Muslim Minority Affairs* 28, no. 2 (2008): 173-205.

Jumale, Ahmed. *The Invention of Somalia.* Lawrenceville: The Red Sea Press, 1995.

Jumale, Mohamed Ahmed "Castro". "Dawr 'Ulamā Junūb al-Somāl fi al-Da'wa al-Islāmiyah (1889-1941)."PhD diss., University of Om Durman, Khartoum, 2007.

Karauzaman, Azmul Fahimi. "The Emergence of Egyptian Muslim Brotherhood in Palestine: Causes, activities and formation of Identity," *Journal of Human Sciences* 44, no. 7, (2010), 1-21.

Kassam, Karim-Aly."The clash of Civilization": The selling of Fear. Available from https://dspace.ucalgary.ca/bitstream/18 80/44170/1/Islam.pdf (accessed on February 14, 2011).

Keddie, Nikki. "Sayyid Jamal al-Din "Al-Afqhani."*In* 'Alī Rāhnamā (ed.). *Pioneers of Islamic Revival.*Palgrave Macmillan, 1994.

Keynan, Hassan. "Male Roles and Making of Somali Tragedy: Reflections on Gender, Masculinity and Violence in Somali Society." In *Variations on the Theme of Somaliness,* edited by Muddle Suzanne Liluis. Turku, Finland: Centre of Continuing Education, Abo University, 2001, 241-249.

Kramer, Martin. "Coming to Terms: Fundamentalists or Islamists?" *Middle East Quarterly* (Spring 2003), 65- 77.

Kuperus,Tracy. "Frameworks of State Society Relations."Availa ble from http://www.acdis.uiuc.edu/Research/S&Ps/1994-Su/S&P_VIII 4/state_society_relations.html (accessed on February 14, 2011).

Kusow, Abdi (ed.). *Putting the Cart before the Horse: Contested Nationalism and the Crisis of the Nation-State in Somalia.*Lawrenceville: The Red Sea Press, 2004.

Laitin, David D., and Said Samatar. *Somalia: Nation in Search of a State.* Boulder: Westview Press, 1987.

Lefebvre, Jeffrey A. "The United States, Ethiopia and the 1963 Somali-Soviet Arms Deal: Containment and the Balance of Power Dilemma in the Horn of Africa." *Journal of Modern African Studies* 36 (1998): 611-643.

Lefebvre, Jeffrey. "The US Military in Somalia: A hidden Agenda?" *Middle Eastern Policy*, l: 2 (1993).

Leiken, Robert S., and Steven Brooke."The Moderate Muslim Brotherhood."*Foreign Affairs* 86, no. 2, March/April 2007, 107-121.

Le Sage, Andre and Ken Menkhaus. "The Rise of Islamic Charities in Somalia: An Assessment of Impact and Agendas." A Paper presented to the 45th Annual International Studies Association Convention, Montreal, 17–20 March, 2004.

Le Sage, Andre. "Prospects of Al-Itihad and Islamist Radicalism in Somalia."*Review of African Political Economy* 27, no. 89, 2001, 472-477.

Le Sage, Andre. "Somalia and the War on Terrorism: Political Islamic Movements and US Counter-terrorism Efforts."PhD diss., Jesus College, Cambridge University, 2004.

Lewis, I. M. *Saints and Somalis: Popular Islam in a Clan-based Society.* Lawrenceville, N.J.: Red Sea Press, 1998.

Lewis, I.M. *Blood and Bone: The Call of Kinship in Somali Society.* Lawrenceville, Nj: Red Sea Pres, 1994.

Lewis, I. M. "The Somali Conquest of Horn of Africa", *The Journal of African History* 1, no. 2 (1960), 223.

Lewis, I. M. *A Modern History of Somalia: Nation and State in the Horn of Africa.* London: Longman, 1980.

Lia, Brynjar. *The Society of the Muslim Brothers in Egypt: The Rise of an Islamic Mass Movement.* Reading, UK: Garnet, 1998.

Luling, Virginia. *Somali Sultanate: The Geledi City-State over 150 Years.* London: Haan Publications, 2002.

Lyons, Terrence, and Ahmed I. Samatar.*Somalia: State Collapse, Multilateral Intervention, and Strategies for Political Reconstruction.* Place: Brooking Occasional Papers, 1995.

Lyons, Terrence. "Crises on Multiple Levels: Somalia and the Horn of Africa" in Ahmed Samatar (ed.), *The Somali Challenge: From Catastrophe to Renewal?.*Lynne Rienner Publishers, 1994.

Madison, Megan. "Islamism sui Gereris: Probing the West's Construction of the Islamic Threat." A Paper submitted to the College of Literature, Science and the Arts, University of Michigan, 2009.

Magnus, Nurell. "Islamist Networks in Somalia." FOI Somalia Papers: Report 2, Swedish Defense Research Academy, 2008.

Māḥ, Aḥmed Barkhat. *Wathāiq 'an al-Somāl wa al-Ḥabasha wa Eriteriya*. Al-Qāhira: Shirkat al-Dhawbagi li Dabā 'ah wa Nashr, 1985.

Maimbo, Samuel Muzele (ed.). "Remittance and Economic Development in Somalia." *Somalia Development Papers: Conflict Prevention and Reconstruction*. Paper no.38, November 2006.

Makki, Hassan. *Al-Siyāsāt al-Thaqāfiya fi al-Somāli al-Kabīr (1887-1986)*. Al-Markaz al-Islāmi li al-Buhūth wa al-Nashri, 1990.

Mansur, Abdalla Omar, "Contrary to a Nation: the Cancer of the Somali State." In *The Invention of Somalia*, edited by Ahmed Jumale. Lawrenceville: The Red Sea Press,1995, 107-116.

Mantzikos, Ioannis. "US Foreign Policy towards Ethiopia and Somalia (1974-1980)." Available from http://www.unc.edu/depts/diplomat/item/2010/0103/comm/mantzikos_policy.html (accessed on November 15, 2010).

Martin, Bradford G.*Muslim Brotherhoods in Nineteenth-Century Africa*.Cambridge University Press, 2003.

Martin, Bradford G. "Shaykh Uways bin Muhammad al-Barawi, a Traditional Somali Sufi." In *Manifestations of Sainthood in Islam*, edited by G. M. Smith and Carl Ernst. Istanbul: ISIS, 1993, 225-37.

Martin, Bradford. G. "Sheikh Zayla'i and the Nineteenth-century Somali Qaderiya."In *the Shadows of Conquest.Islam in Colonial Northeast Africa*, edited by Said Samatar. Trenton, NJ: The Red Sea Press, 1992.

Marchal, Roland. "Islamic Political Dynamics in the Somali Civil War: Before and After September 11." In *Islamism and its Enemies in the Horn of Africa*, edited by Alex De Waal. Place: Indiana University Press, 2006, 114-146.

Marchal, Roland."A Survey of Mogadishu Economy." A research commissioned by European Commission, Somali Unit, Nairobi. 2002.

Maxamad Ibrahim Maxamad "Liiq-liiqato". *Taariikhda Somaaliya: Dalkii Filka Weynaa ee Punt*. Mogadishu: Mogadishu Press, 2000.

Mausalli, Ahmad. "Wahhabism, Salafism, and Islamism: Who is The Enemy?" Available from http://conflictsforum.org/2009/wahhabism-salafism-and-islamism-who-is-the-enemy (accessed on November 8, 2010).

Mayall, James. "Self determination and the OAU."In I.M. Lewis (ed.) *Nationalism and Self determination in the Horn of Africa*. London: Ithaca, 1983.

Medani, Khalid."Globalization, Informal Markets and Collective Action: The Development of Islamic and Ethnic Politics in Egypt, Sudan and Somalia." PhD Thesis submitted to the University of California, Berkeley, 2003.

Menkhaus, Ken. "Remittance Companies and Money Transfers In Somalia, 2001." Available from www.Somali.jna.org (accessed on June 31, 2010).

Menkhaus, Ken."US Foreign Assistance Somalia: Phoenix from the Ashes?" *Middle Eastern Policy*, 1:5 (1997).

Miller, Helen. *The Hardest Place: The Biography of Warren and Dorothy Modricher.* Place: Guardian Books, 1982.

Ministry of Planning and Statistics, Puntland State of Somalia."Puntland Facts and Figures." 2003.

Mire, Abdi Shakur.*Koboca Islaamiyiinta Somalia.*Unpublished manuscript.

Mire, Hassan Ali. "On Providing for the Futute," In *The Somali Challenge: From Catastrophe to Renewal?* edited byAhmed Samatar. London: Lunne Rienner, 1994.

Mitchell,Richard. *TheSocietyoftheMuslimBrothers.*London: Oxford University Press, 1969.

Mogadishu University Annual Report for the Academic Year (2009/2010), Unpublished.

Mohamed, Hamdi. "MultipleChallenges, Multiple Struggles: A History of Women's Activism in Canada." Ph.D. diss., University of Ottawa, 2003.

Mohamed Nuh, Mohamed. "History in the Horn of Africa, 1000 BC to 1500 AD." PhD Thesis, University of California, Los Angeles, 1985.

Mohamed, Mohamed. "US Strategic Interest in Somalia: From Cold War Era to War in Terror".MA thesis, State University at Baffalo, USA, 2009.

Mohamed, Osman. *The Road to Zero: Somalia's Self-Destruction.* Place: Haan Associates, 1992.

Moḥamed, Sharīf Moḥamūd. "Faslun fi al-'Alāqāt al-Somāliayah al-Saūdiyah, 2010." Available from http://arabic.alshahid.net/columnists/8598 (accessed on February 6, 2010).

Mohamoud, Abdullah. *State Collapse and Post-Conflict Development in Africa: The Case of Somalia (1960-2001).* Indiana: Purdue University Press, 2006.

Moḥamūd, Ḥassan Ḥāji."*Man al-Mas'ul 'an al-Tadaruf fi al-Somāl?*" Available from http://www.somaliatoday.net/port/2 010-01-04-21-40-35/2-2010-01-04-21-38-42/1216-2010-06-03-12-29-35.html (accessed on June 18, 2010).

Moḥamūd, Ḥassan Ḥāji."Tārīkh al-Ḥarakah al-Islāmiyah al-Somāliyah: Durūf al-Nashi wa'Awāmil al-tadawur."Unpublished manuscript, 2009.

Moḥamūd, Ḥassan Ḥāji."Al-Somāl: al-Ḥawiyah wa al-Intimā". Unpublished manuscript.

Moḥamūd, Moḥamed Sharīf. "'Abdirizāq Ḥāji Hussein, Rais wasarā al-Somāl (1964-1967)." 2009. Available from http://arabic.alshahid.net/columnists/6110 (accessed on April 21, 2010).

Moḥamūd, Moḥamed Sharīf. "Al-Ra'īs Ādan 'Abdulle 'Usman – Awal Ra'īs li al-Jamhūriyah al-Somāliyah." 2009. Available from http://arabic.alshahid.net/columnists/1458 (accessed on June 6, 2010).

Moḥamūd, Moḥamed Sharīf. "Tarjumah li Sharīf Moḥamūd 'Abdiraḥman, Ra'īs al-Rābidah al-Islāmiyah." 2009. Available from http://arabic.alshahid.net/columnists/650 (accessed on April 21, 2010).

MU Visitor's Book."A Note of Marian Warsame (MD, PhD)." July 28, 2002.

Mukhtar, Mohamed Haji. "Islam in Somali History: Fact and Fiction." In *The Invention of Somalia*.edited by Ali Jumale Ahmed. Lawrenceville: The Red Sea Press, 1995.

Mukhtar, Mohamed. *Historical Dictionary of Somalia*.African Historical Dictionary Series, 87. Lanham, MD: Scarecrow Press, 2003.

Nasr, Vali. "Military Rule, Islamism and Democracy in Pakistan." *The Middle East Journal* 58, no. 2 (2004), 195.

Nincic, Donna. "The State Failure and Re-Emergence of Maritime Piracy." A Paper presented at 49th annual convention of International Studies Association, California Maritime Academy, California State University, San Francisco, California, March 26-29, 2008.

Noor, Abdirahman Ahmed. "Arabic Language and Script in Somalia: History, attitudes and prospects." PhD diss., Georgetown University, 1999.

NOVIB-Somalia."Mapping Somali Civil Society."Nairobi, Kenya: 2003. Available fromhttp://www.somalicivilsociety.org/strength/phase1_Mapping%20somalicivilsociety.asp (accessed on November 10, 2009).

Nurell, Magnus. "Islamist Networks in Somalia." FOI Somalia Papers: Report 2 (Swedish Defence Research Academy, 2008).

Omar, Mohamed Osman. *The Road to Zero: Somalia's Self Destruction*. Place: HAAN Associates, 1992.

Omar, Mohamed Osman. *The Scramble in the Horn of Africa: History of Somalia (1827-1977)*. Mogadishu: Somali Publications, 2001.

Osman, Abdulahi. "The Role of Egypt, Ethiopia, the Blue Nile in the Failure of the Somali Conflict Resolutions: A Zero-Sum Game." Paper presented at the annual meeting of the International Studies Association, Hilton Hawaiian Village, Honolulu, Hawaii, March 2005.

Osman, Abdullahi A. "The Somali Internal War and the Role of Inequality, Economic Decline and Access to Weapons." In *Somalia at the Crossroads: Challenges and Perspectives in*

Reconstituting a Failed State, edited by Abdullahi A. Osman and Issaka K. Soure. London: Adonis & Abby Publishers Ltd., 2007, 83-108.

Osman Hagi, Aweys and Osman Hagi, Abdiwahid. *Clan, Subclan and Regional Representation in the Somali Government Organization 1960-1990: Statistical Data and Findings.* Washington, DC, 1998.

Osman, Hussein Abdi. "Malaf al-Sarā' beyna 'Ali Mahdi wa 'Aidīd". Unpublished paper submitted to the Horn of African Center for Studies, Mogadishu, 1993.

Pankhurst, Sylvia. *Ex-Italian Somaliland.* London: Wattas & Co., 1951.

Pastaloza, Luigi. *The Somali Revolution.*Bari: Edition Afrique Asie Amerique Latine, 1973.

Pathlom, Christian P. *The Theory and Practices of African Politics.* New Jersey: Printice Hall Inc., 1976.

Puntland State of Somalia, Ministry of Planning and Statistics."*Puntland* Facts and Figures" (2003).

Puzo, Daniel William. "Mogadishu, Somalia: Geographic Aspects of its Evolution, Population, Functions and its Morphology." PhD diss., University of Los Angles, 1972.

Qasim, Maryan Arif. *Clan versus Nation.* Sharjah: UAE, 2002.

Qassim, Mohamed. "Aspects of Benadir Cultural History: the case of the Baravan Ulama."In *The Invention of Somalia,* edited by Jumale Ahmed. Lawrenceville: The Red Sea Press,1995, 107-116.

Qutub, Sayid. *The Milestone.* Available from http://majalla.org/books/2005/qutb-nilestone.pdf (accessed on June 24, 2010).

Rage, Abdurahman Osman. "Somali NGOs: A Product of Crisis." In *Mending Rips in the Sky*, edited by Adam Hussien and Richard Ford. Asmara: Red Sea Press, 1997.

Rees, Scott S. "Patricians of the Banadir: Islamic Learning, Commerce and Somali Urban Identity in the Nineteenth Century."PhD diss., University of Pennsylvania, 1996.

Reese, Scott S. *Urban Woes and Pious Remedies: Sufism in Nineteenth-Century Benaadir (Somalia)*. Place: Indiana University Press, 1999.

Report of FAO and World Bank."Somalia: Towards a Livestock Sector Strategy."Report no. o4/0011C-Som. April 20, 2004.

Rutherford, Kenneth. *Humanitarianism under Fire: The US Intervention in Somalia*. Place: Kumerian Press, 2008.

Saggiomo, Valeria. "From Charity to Governance.Islamic NGOs and Education in Somalia" Manuscript from the author, to be published in *Open Area Studies Journal, Bentham Publishers*, in early 2011.

Sahnoun, Mohamed. "Somalia: the Missed Opportunities." United State Institute of Peace, 1994.

Samatar, 'Abdiraḥman Hussein. *Sanawāt al-'ijāf fi al-Somāl*. Place: Madbat Hamar, 2000.

Samatar, Abdi. "Destruction of State and Society in Somalia: Beyond the Tribal Convention."*The Journal of the Modern African Studies* 30 (1992): 625-641.

Samatar, Ahmed. "Interview with Professor Said Sheikh Samatar." *Bildhan: An International Journal of Somali Studie*.6, 2006, 1-24.

Samatar, Ahmed. "Introduction and Overview." In *The Somali Challenge: From Catastrophe to Renewal?* London: Lunne Rienner, 1994, 3-19.

Samatar, Ahmed. *Socialist Somalia: Rhetoric and Reality*. London: Zed Press, 1988.

Samatar, Ahmed. "The Curse of Allah: Civic Disembowelment and the collapse of the State in Somalia" in Ahmed Samatar (ed.), *The Somali Challenge: From Catastrophe to Renewal?* Lynne Rienner Publishers, 1994.

Samatar, Said (ed.).*In the Shadows of Conquest.Islam in Colonial Northeast Africa.* Trenton, NJ: The Red Sea Press, 1992.

Samatar, Said. "Sheikh Uways Muhammad of Baraawe (1847-1909): Mystic and Reformer in East Africa."In *the Shadows of Conquest.Islam in Colonial Northeast Africa*, edited by Said S. Samatar. Trenton, NJ: The Red Sea Press, 1992, 48-74.

Samatar, Said. *Oral Poetry and Somali Nationalism: The Case of Sayid Mahammad Abdille Hasan.* Cambridge: Cambridge University Press, 1982.

Samatar, Said."Unhappy Masses and the Challenges of Political Islam in the Horn of Africa."Available form www.wardheernews.com/March_05/05 (accessed on February 14,2011).

Schwoebel, Mary Hope. "Nation-building in the land of Somalis."PhD diss., George Mason University, 2007.

Shank, Michael. "Understanding Political Islam in Somalia." *Contemporary Islam, Dynamics of Muslim Life* Journal No. 11562, March 2007.

Shay, Shaul.*Somalia between Jihad and Restoration*. London, New Brunswick: Transaction Press, 2008

Sheikh Mohamed Garyare. "Al-Masūl al-Awal an Jamā'a Al-Islāḥ al-Islāmiyah fi al-Somāl yataḥadathu ilā Al-Mujtama'."*Majalat al-Islāḥ*, no. 524 (1981): 19-12.

Sheikh Cumar, Sheikh Cusman Xidig. *Tarjumah Sayidī Aḥmad*. Unpublished manuscript.

Sheikh Moḥamad Islām'īl Muqadam. *Basā'ira al-fitan (the Way out of Tribulation)*.Transl. Fahia Yaḥya. Alexandria: Dār Al-Tawḥīd, 2009, 39.

Shmuel, Noah Eisenstadt. *Comparative Civilizations and Multiple Modernities*, 2 vols. Leiden and Boston: Brill, 2003.

Simons, Anna. *Networks of Dissolution: Somalia Undone*.Boulder, CO: Westview Press, 1995.

Somali Transitional Government.*Transitional National Charter adopted in Djibouti Reconciliation Conference*, 2000.

*Somalia: Somali Democratic Republic.*Available from http://www.hmnet.com/africa/somalia/somalia.html (accessed on October 28, 2010).

Somalia: Al Shabab Militia Destroys the Grave of Well Known Sheikh in Mogadishu. Available from http://www.raxanreeb.com/?p=42206 (accessed on June 18, 2010).

Somalia Votes to Implement Shari'a. Available from http://english.aljazeera.net/news/africa/2009/04/200941895049381692.html (accessed on October 2010)

Student's Prospectus (2007-2008). *Ten years of achievement (1997–2007)*. Mogadishu University, 2007.

Tadesse, Medhane. *Al-Ittihad: Political Islam and Black Economy in Somalia: Religion, Clan, Money, and the Struggle for Supremacy over Somalia*. Addis Ababa: Meag Printing Enterprise, 2002.

Tahir, Mahmood. *Personal Law in Islamic Countries*.New Delhi: Academy of Law and Religion, 1987.

Tareke, Gebru. "The Ethiopia Somalia War Revisited."*International Journal of African Historical Studies* 33, no. 3, 2000, 615-34.

The Constitution of Somali Republic, 1961.

The Constitution of the International Muslim Brotherhood.Available from http://www.ikhwanonline.com/Article.asp?ArtID=58497&SecID=211 (accessed on June 4, 2010).

The International Crisis Group Report."Understanding Islamism."Middle East/North Africa Report no. 37/2, March 2005.

The Islah Movement."Communique of Islah on the Ethiopian Intervention in Somalia." July 27, 2006. http://www.Islah.org/arabic/bayaan26-7-06.htm (accessed June 21, 2010).

The Organization of African Unity. "Resolutions adopted by the first ordinary session of the assembly of the heads of the state and government." Cairo, UAR, from 17 to 21 July, 1964.

"The Manifesto."In Abdulaziz Ali Ibrahim "Xildhiban", *Taxanaha Taariikhda Soomaliya*. London: Xildhiban Publications, 2006. 101-107.

Tibi, Bassam. *The Challenge of Fundamentalism: Political Islam and the New World Disorder*. Place: University of California Press, 2002.

Togane, Mohamud. "The Skin of A Dog."*Zymurgy Literary Review* 6, vol. III, no. 2 (1989), 95.

Touval, Saadia. "The Organization of African Unity and Borders."*International Organization* 21, no. 1 (1967): 102-127.

Touval, Saadia. Somali Nationalism: International Politics and the Drive for Unity in the Horn of Africa. Cambridge: Cambridge University Press, 1963.

Trimigham, Spencer. *Islam in Ethiopia*. Oxford: Oxford University Press, 1952.

Tripodi, Poalo. *The Colonial Legacy in Somalia: Rome and Mogadishu: from Colonial Administration to Operation Restore Hope*. London: Macmillan Press, 1999.

UN OCHA Integrated Regional Information Network for Central and Eastern Africa (IRIN-CEA). "Somalia, are building blocks the solution?" UN, July, 17 1999.

UNDP Report on Somali Diaspora. "Somalia's Missing Million: The Somali Diaspora and its Role in Development." UNDP, 2009, 12.

"Universities in Somalia: 2010 University Web Ranking." http://www.4icu.org/so/(accessed on July 5, 2010).

Vatikiotis, P. J. *The history of modern Egypt: from Muhammad Ali to Mubarak*. London: Weidenfeld and Nicolson, 1991.

Waxdah."A letter to President Abdirahsid."Hargeysa, 1969.

Wahadah."A letter to Regional Revolutionary Council."Hargeysa, 1969.

Waxdah."A letter to the Revolutionary Council."Mogadishu, 1969.

Waxdah."Al-Nidān al-Asāsi (The Constitution of NAHDAH)." 1969.

Wiktorowicz, Quintan (ed.). *Islamic Activism: A Social Theory Approach*. Bloomington & Indianapolis: Indiana University Press, 2004.

Woodward, Peter. *The Horn of Africa: State Politics and International Relations*. New York: Tauris Academic Studies, 1996.

World Bank.*Conflict in Somalia, Drivers and Dynamics*. 2005.

World Fact Book, available from https://www.cia.gov/library/publications/the-world-factbook/geos/so.html (accessed on October 28, 2010).

Yaḥyá, Jalal Yaḥya. *Al-'Alāqāt al-Misriyah al-Somāliyah (Egyptian-Somali Relations)*. Al-Iskandariyah: al-Maktabah al-Afrīqiyah, 1960.

Yohannes, Okbbazghi. *The United States and the Horn of Africa: An Analytical Study of Pattern and Process*. Place: Westview Press, 1997.

Yakun, Fathi. *Madā ya'nī intimāi li al-Islām.* Beirut: Mu'asasat al-Risālah, 1977.

Yūnus, Moḥamed Abdul-Mūmin. *Al-Somāl Wadanan wa Sha'ban.* Al-Qahira: Dar al-Nahda al-Arabiyah, 1962.

Yusuf, Sayid Mohamed. *Somaliland: Sooyaalka Somaliland ka hor 26 Juun 1960.* Hargeysa: Dariiqo Publisher, 2001.

Zaman, Muhammad Qasim.*The Ulama in Contemporary Islam: Custodians of Change.* Princeton, NJ: Princeton University Press, 2002.

Index

A

Abdi-Nāsser, Jamāl, 99, 236, 238
Abisaab, Rula, Vii
Abyssinia, 30, 376
Aden, 31, 48, 75, 82, 94, 109, 117, 299, 321, 330
Africaness, 15
Ahal, 27, 170, 171, 182, 185, 186, 187, 188, 189, 203, 225, 228, 231, 232, 245, 246, 250, 251, 273, 275, 277, 280, 305, 379, 382, 384
Ahmed, Abdirahman, X, 17, 30, 31, 36, 51, 91, 124, 125, 128, 132, 138, 140, 146, 167, 184, 207, 223, 242, 261, 268, 273, 308, 311, 314, 368, 398, 399, 405, 409, 411, 412, 415, 416, 417, 418, 419
Ajuran Dynasty, 86
Al-Ash'Ari, Abu Al-Hassan, 20
Al-Azhar University, 119, 174, 179, 240
Al-Ghazāli's Way, 20
Al-Islaax, 231, 248, 357
Al-Jeylaani, Sheikh Cabdulqaadir, 37
Al-Kawnayn, Sheikh Yuusuf, 32
Alliance For The Re-Liberation Of Somalia, 392
Alliance For The Restoration Of Peace And Counter-Terrorism, 390
Al-Qaida, 330, 331, 383, 393
Al-Shabab, 393, 403
American Peace Corps, 183, 192, 379
Arabness, 15
Arta Conference In Djibouti, 25
Ash'Ariyah Theology, 20
Asmara, 351, 392, 418

Association Of Helpers Of Religion, 170
Association Of Protectors Of Religion, 170
Axmad, Cali Sheikh, Vii, Viii, 57, 154, 177, 216, 240, 244, 245, 274, 290, 291, 299, 304, 334, 393, 394
Axmadiyah, 20, 26, 40, 41, 43, 50, 55, 56, 60, 64, 66, 67, 74, 95

B

Baarmaale, 52, 58
Baghdad, 44, 53, 69, 87
Bakht Al-Riḍāh Institute Of Education In Sudan, 95
Banaadir, 29, 40, 42, 43, 51, 54, 58, 63, 76, 87, 94, 95, 147, 377
Barre, Maxamad Siyaad, 136, 144, 222, 226, 331, 403
Basra, 60, 66
Beletweyne, 59, 107, 188, 327, 344
Berbera, 30, 31, 47, 48, 49, 50, 63, 65, 71, 74, 76, 79, 96, 108, 121, 219
Bottom-Up Educational Revolution, Xi, 360, 374, 386
British Broadcasting Corporation (BBC), 103
British Military Administration, Xi, 82, 84, 122
British Somaliland, 65, 76, 80, 82, 91, 95, 96, 107, 108, 109, 117, 122, 132, 139, 141, 144, 148, 149

C

Cabdulqaadir Mosque, 129, 178, 179, 180, 182, 215, 224, 225

Cabsiiye, Sheikh Maxamad, 66
Ceeldheer, 57, 58
Christian Missions, 131, 137
Christianization, 115, 116, 117, 194,
    237, 251, 378, 379, 380
Ciise, Sheikh Maxamuud, Viii, 65, 74,
    183, 190, 216, 221, 225, 226, 242, 280
Cold War, 15, 90, 92, 98, 103, 137, 146,
    156, 160, 162, 165, 251, 351, 414
Colombo, Bishop Salvatore, 298
Cultural Challenges, 286
Cultural Revolution, 219
Culumo, 39
Czechoslovakia,, 102, 145

D

d'Antonio, Mario, 151
Da'wa Programs, 176, 265, 290
Darawiish Movement In Somalia, 95
Dasuuqi, Ibrahim, Viii, 226, 235, 291,
    298, 301, 302, 303, 321, 323, 324,
    327, 328, 332, 334, 335, 336, 354,
    356, 358
Day Suufi, 52
Dayaar, Ali, 325
De Vecchi, Mario, 62
Diaspora, 75, 243, 255, 264, 284, 294,
    302, 316, 320, 329, 336, 349, 361,
    362, 370, 373, 384, 386, 389, 391,
    397, 422
Dikri, 37
Diya, 153, 195, 220
Djibouti Reconciliation Conference,
    309, 357, 420
Dulbahante, 63

E

Egypt, 15, 27, 31, 43, 44, 46, 49, 65, 87,
    94, 97, 98, 99, 100, 102, 105, 107,
    114, 115, 119, 120, 138, 145, 154,
    156, 160, 161, 162, 169, 178, 179,
    189, 190, 211, 231, 234, 235, 236,
    240, 244, 247, 254, 274, 284, 304,
    306, 315, 351, 378, 380, 383, 411,
    413, 416, 422
Eritrea, 76, 100, 236, 253, 392
Ethiopia, 15, 30, 39, 41, 43, 44, 55, 56,
    67, 75, 80, 85, 89, 90, 91, 100, 102,
    117, 121, 123, 146, 149, 161, 167,
    211, 219, 226, 229, 230, 231, 242,
    251, 252, 253, 273, 281, 283, 295,
    296, 304, 318, 327, 329, 351, 356,
    377, 378, 381, 384, 389, 391, 393,
    410, 412,416, 420, 421

F

Formal Primary Education Networks,
    365

G

Garoowe, 69, 371
Garyare, Sheikh Maxamad Axmad,
    Viii, 174, 179, 180, 208, 224, 225, 228
Ghali, Boutros, 314
Global War On Terrorism, 28, 389
Gordon College, 95
Grand Mosque In Mecca, 254
Great Somali League, Xi, 149
Greater Somalia, 16, 100, 103, 109, 163,
    167
Grove, Merlin, 123, 125, 129, 405
Gulf States, 219, 230, 251, 281, 381

H

Hadith, 35, 36, 325, 339, 388
Hanbali Jurisprudence, 382
Hargeysa, 32, 42, 45, 49, 56, 57, 58, 59,
    60, 62, 65, 66, 72, 74, 109, 110, 116,
    119, 120, 141, 169, 170, 178, 191,
    194, 195, 196, 198, 199, 200, 201,

202, 221, 225, 233, 238, 263, 268, 269, 274, 275, 276, 287, 295, 297, 319, 320, 321, 327, 341, 349, 404, 422, 423
Harrar, 30, 31, 32, 42, 43, 44, 46, 48, 49, 63, 86, 87, 95, 131, 132, 178, 377
Harrar,, 43, 44, 48, 49, 132, 178
Hiiraan, 40, 45, 59, 61, 208, 345

I

Ibrahim (Gurey), Imaam Axmad, 30
Indian Ocean, 31, 57, 59, 65, 70, 86, 90, 100
Institute Of Islamic Solidarity, 97, 242
Intergovernmental Authority On Development, 353
Iranian Revolution, 254, 382
Iran-Iraq War, 254
Isha Prayer, 181
Islaax Islamic Society, 27, 247
Islam And Somaliness, 89
Islamic Revivalist Movements, 154
Islamic Awakening, 137, 164, 171, 203, 215, 227
Islamic Development Bank, 369, 371
Islamic Institute, Vii, X, 17, 106, 108, 109, 112, 120, 139, 157, 318, 396, 406
Islamic Shari' A, 63
Islamic University In Medina, 161, 243, 244
Islamist Elites, 26, 153, 154, 156, 158, 163, 168
Islamist Politics, 18
Islamization Of The Somali Peninsula, 86
Italian Somaliland, 44, 80, 81, 107, 108, 144, 149, 417
Italian-Ethiopian War, 78, 147

J

Jam'Iyat Ihyā Al-Sunna, 170
Jamaaca, Xi, 39, 40, 45, 49, 50, 60, 61, 65, 67, 71, 190, 202, 231, 233, 275, 276, 277, 279, 280, 305, 393
Jamaaca Weyn, 45, 49
Jamaacooyin, 40, 45, 153
Jigjiga,, 43, 178
Jihaad, 254, 261
Jilidda Xer-Cilmiga, 35
Juba Valley, 122

K

Kenya, 15, 51, 52, 53, 57, 60, 76, 90, 93, 114, 116, 119, 136, 155, 167, 172, 174, 182, 183, 184, 187, 188, 190, 206, 216, 223, 226, 227, 228, 230, 231, 235, 239, 242, 245, 271, 283, 288, 290, 291, 301, 316, 321, 327, 329, 336, 351, 357, 399, 416
Khaldunite Theory Of Asabiyah, 375
Khartoum University, 241, 246
King Faysal, 210, 211, 244
Kismaayo, 91, 107, 122, 125, 141, 312, 323, 330, 331, 344
Kuwait, 167, 174, 177, 179, 183, 200, 242, 247, 277, 293, 296, 297, 314, 320

L

Laascaanood, 69, 191
Lafoole, 52, 62
Latinized Alphabet For Somali, 131
Liberal Somali Youth Party, Xi, 149
Lind, Wilbert, 124, 129

M

Mahdiyah Movement, 31, 44, 95
Marganiyah, 60
Marxism-Leninism, 209

Maxamad, Fatxuddiin Cali, Ix, 62, 68, 144, 279, 333
Maxamuud, Xasan Xaaji, Viii, 54, 57, 59, 66, 77, 172, 188, 202, 231, 238, 239, 245, 247, 273, 285, 393
Mcgill University, Canada, Vii, Viii, X, 17, 106, 139, 157, 318, 396, 406
Medani, Khālid Mustafa, Vii, 413
Menelik, 44
Mennonite Mission, 91, 104, 121, 124, 126, 127, 129, 131, 378, 405
Mercy-USA For Aid And Development, Ix
Middle East, 98, 251, 254, 255, 408, 410, 416, 421
Ministry Of Religious Affairs, 166, 177, 180, 209, 247
Mogadishu, Vii, 29, 31, 41, 42, 43, 44, 46, 51, 52, 53, 54, 58, 60, 61, 63, 76, 80, 83, 91, 94, 97, 98, 101, 102, 110, 112, 113, 123, 124, 125, 129, 133, 134, 135, 136, 141, 143, 144, 155, 160, 169, 170, 173, 177, 178, 181, 183, 187, 192, 194, 200, 202, 206, 209, 215, 218, 221, 222, 223, 224, 225, 228, 238, 246, 253, 268, 269, 277, 278, 285, 287, 290, 291, 296, 302, 303, 304, 308, 309, 310, 312, 313, 314, 316, 317, 318, 321, 322, 324, 325, 326, 328, 329, 331, 332, 333, 334, 335, 336, 344, 345, 346, 347, 352, 357, 358, 360, 361, 364, 365, 366, 368, 369, 370, 374, 387, 388, 390, 391, 394, 401, 402, 403, 407, 408, 413, 414, 416, 417, 420, 422
Mogadishu University, Vii, 60, 309, 360, 365, 366, 368, 370, 374, 387, 388, 414, 420
Munadamat Al-Nahdah Al-Islāmiyah, 27, 168, 171, 304

Muslim Brotherhood, Vi, Xi, 19, 21, 96, 98, 169, 170, 171, 174, 200, 234, 235, 236, 237, 239, 282, 292, 304, 319, 323, 339, 356, 367, 407, 409, 410, 421
Muslim Calendar, 29, 86, 247
Muslim World League, 161, 177, 361
Muslim-Christian Tensions, 137
Muslims Versus Christians, 85
Muxdaar, Sheikh Abiikar, 47, 51, 52, 95

N

Nahdah., Viii, 171, 172, 176, 177, 232, 240
Nakhtiin, 32
Nasserism, 377
Nasserite Ideology, 119, 135
National Institution For Private Education, 368
National Reconciliation Conference, 318, 386
National Security Court, 216
National United Front, 149
Native Betterment Committee, 82, 142
Nimow, 51, 52
Northern Frontier District, 76, 167

O

Of Mareegat, 57
Ogaaden, 308
Operation Restore Hope, 83, 102, 222, 315, 422
Organization For Islamic Renaissance, 27
Organization Of African Unity, 219, 421
Ottoman Empire, 31, 86

P

Patriotic Beneficiary Union, 82
People Of Islam, 27, 170
Primordiality, 90
Prophet Mawliid, 37
Puntland, 43, 69, 77, 289, 290, 335, 350, 353, 355, 370, 372, 374, 387, 408, 414, 417

Q

Qaadiriyah, 20, 26, 37, 38, 40, 41, 43, 44, 45, 46, 48, 50, 52, 53, 54, 55, 56, 63, 66, 67, 68, 71, 73, 78, 80, 94, 121, 159, 179, 180, 182
Qaadiriyah Order, 45
Qaaraan, 151
Qasaaid, 37, 54
Qisaas, 195
Qoryaweyne, 63, 66
Qulunqul, 41, 43, 45, 46, 53, 54, 66
Qur'anic Memorization, 138
Qur'anic Schools, 26, 34, 35, 58, 108, 110, 134, 140, 202, 361, 372

R

Red Sea, 17, 31, 44, 51, 73, 100, 152, 167, 245, 351, 399, 405, 409, 410, 411, 412, 413, 415, 417, 418, 419
Revivification Of The Prophet's Tradition, 170
Roman Catholic Church, Xi, 91, 121, 131

S

Saalixiyah, 40, 41, 42, 55, 60, 61, 62, 63, 66, 71, 74, 78, 80, 95, 122
Salafia Ideology, 246, 281, 305
Salafism, 19, 20, 162, 170, 171, 190, 231, 232, 243, 274, 275, 278, 283, 292, 382, 384, 398, 413
Samatar, Cabdi Ismaciil, Viii, 17, 38, 40, 41, 45, 47, 64, 72, 73, 74, 76, 80, 91, 108, 119, 121, 128, 140, 146, 154, 172, 205, 207, 272, 282, 299, 308, 310, 311, 312, 314, 418, 419
Samatar, Said, Viii, 17, 25, 29, 38, 40, 41, 43, 44, 45, 47, 64, 72, 73, 74, 76, 80, 91, 108, 114, 119, 121, 128, 136, 140, 146, 154, 172, 174, 176, 205, 207, 272, 282, 299, 308, 310, 311, 312, 314, 410, 411, 413, 414, 418, 419
Sanuusiyah, 60
Saudi Arabia, 27, 29, 43, 46, 51, 94, 97, 113, 119, 145, 154, 160, 162, 166, 177, 189, 210, 213, 219, 227, 231, 232, 235, 237, 239, 240, 242, 243, 244, 245, 247, 249, 252, 271, 274, 275, 279, 283, 289, 291, 292, 302, 304, 306, 308, 315, 319, 320, 322, 328, 334, 369, 382, 384, 388, 393, 398, 401
Saudi Islamic Institutions, 278
Scoula Disciplina Islamica, 106
Second World War, 26, 78, 83, 84, 85, 113, 122, 139, 140, 147
Secularization, 115, 116, 161, 162, 171, 203, 217, 230, 237, 251, 319, 381
Shafi'i, 20, 35, 87, 158, 218, 223, 377, 382
Shāfi'īyah School Of Jurisprudence, 20
Sharmarke, Cabdirashiid Cali, 136, 166, 168, 191
Sheikh College School, 65
Shirwac, Sheikh Madar Axmad, 45, 47
Shura, 260, 261, 394
Socialist Revolutionary Party, Vi, 189, 200, 227, 229, 230, 252, 253

Index

Somali Democratic Movement, 308
Somali Islamic Awakening, 168, 382
Somali Islamic League, 106, 113, 115
Somali National Alliance, Xii, 316
Somali National Front, 314
Somali National League, Xii, 84, 108, 120, 149
Somali National Union, 149
Somali National University, 143, 202, 368, 388
Somali Nationalism, 64, 79, 82, 85, 93, 97, 137, 168
Somali Old Boys Association, Xii, 82
Somali Patriotic Movement, 308
Somali Reconciliation Council, 309, 342
Somali Salvation Alliance, 348
Somali Salvation Front, 253, 273
Somali University Institute, 174, 240, 304
Somali Youth Club, 82
Somali-Ethiopian War, 126
Somalis Of Yemeni Origin, 95
Somalization Program, 143
Soviet Union, 92, 99, 100, 145, 155, 187, 206, 218, 252
Sudan Interior Mission, Xi, 91, 121, 124, 126, 131, 378
Suez Canal, 15, 31, 90, 100, 161, 378
Sunna, Xi, 36, 39, 192, 217, 218, 232, 259, 264, 266, 286, 335
Swedish Lutheran Overseas Church, 130, 131
Swedish Overseas Lutheran Church, 91, 122, 124

T

Tadamun Charity, 387
Tanganyika,, 78
Tanzania, 53, 288

Transitional Federal Institutions, 390, 392
Turgay, Uner, Vii

U

Ulama, 51, 55, 78, 324, 333, 417, 423
Um Al-Qura University, 189
UN Advisory Council, 101, 105, 118, 119
UNESCO, 134, 135, 142
Union Of Islamic Courts, 388, 390
Union Of Islamic Youth, 27, 170, 191, 196
United Nations Operation In Somalia, Xii, 316
United Somali Congress, Xii, 308, 316, 348
United Somali Party, 149
United States Of America, 330
University Of Michigan, 192, 412
Urabi Revolt, 114

V

Vietnam War, 193

W

Wadaado, 39
Wahaabiyah Penetration, 69
Wahdat Al-Shabāb Al-Islāmī, 27
Waxdah, Viii, 25, 27, 107, 170, 171, 190, 191, 192, 194, 195, 196, 197, 198, 200, 201, 203, 231, 232, 233, 251, 276, 280, 281, 296, 297, 305, 324, 335, 379, 384, 393, 422
Western Civilization, 23, 99
Westernization, 85, 89, 115, 116, 117, 120, 146, 161, 162, 192, 194, 203, 237, 251
World Islamic League, 159, 242

X

Xasan, Sayid Maxamad Cabdulle, Vii, 39, 72, 91, 121, 139, 154, 221, 222

Y

Yabarow, Sheikh Ibrahim, 50, 67

Yemen, 20, 43, 44, 55, 87, 94, 95, 96, 109, 282, 291, 330, 394, 401

Yeshaq, Emperor Negus, 30

Z

Zanzibar, 43, 65, 68, 70, 76

Zaylac, 30, 31, 76

www.ingramcontent.com/pod-product-compliance
Lightning Source LLC
Chambersburg PA
CBHW070058020526
44112CB00034B/1431